D0292424

East Main Street

East Main Street

Asian American Popular Culture

EDITED BY

Shilpa Davé, LeiLani Nishime, and Tasha G. Oren

FOREWORD BY

Robert G. Lee

New York University Press

NEW YORK AND LONDON

NEW YORK UNIVERSITY PRESS
New York and London
www.nyupress.org

Library of Congress Cataloging-in-Publication Data
East Main Street : Asian American popular culture / edited by Shilpa Davé,
LeiLani Nishime, and Tasha Oren; foreword by Robert G. Lee.
p. cm.
Includes bibliographical references and index.
ISBN 0–8147–1962–7 (cloth : alk. paper) —
ISBN 0–8147–1963–5 (pbk. : alk. paper)
1. Asian Americans—Intellectual life.   2. Asian American arts.
3. Popular culture—United States.   4. Asian Americans—Race identity.
5. United States—Race relations.   I. Davé, Shilpa.
II. Nishime, LeiLani.   III. Oren, Tasha G.
E184.A75E17   2005
305.895′073—dc22   2004022335

New York University Press books are printed on acid-free paper,
and their binding materials are chosen for strength and durability.

Manufactured in the United States of America

c 10 9 8 7 6 5 4 3 2 1
p 10 9 8 7 6 5 4 3 2

Contents

Acknowledgments

This project began as a discussion around a Madison kitchen table and developed across disciplines and Eastern, Central, and Pacific time zones. We thank our contributors for their participation, innovative work, and investment in a multidisciplinary approach to popular culture and Asian American studies. We are grateful to Eric Zinner, Emily Park, and everyone at NYU Press for their encouragement, work, and support of this project. The editors received institutional support from the University of Wisconsin–Milwaukee, Sonoma State University, Brandeis University, Cornell University, Wesleyan University, and the University of Wisconsin–Madison, and we thank our colleagues and friends there. Finally, we would like to thank our families, whose patience, support, and love is sustenance for our work.

Foreword

Robert G. Lee

In response to the following passage from a 1736 poem promoting the English settlement of South Carolina, Georgia asked its readers to imagine the American colony as a potential commercial rival to China and India.

> The frugal matron and blooming Maid;
> The expiring Insects curious Work resume
> And wind materials for the British Loom:
> Our web to these shall all the Beauties owe,
> Which Asia boasts and Eastern Pride can show;
> With skilful China's richest Damasks vie,
> And emulate the Chint's alluring Dye."[1]

While Georgia's experiment with sericulture soon foundered on the wrong species of mulberry tree, the verse nevertheless serves to remind us that Asia has been present in the American popular imagination from the onset of European settlement in the Americas.

Desire and revulsion are the dialectic that defines America's cultural engagement with Asia. Europeans discovered "America" in their search for a new path to the riches of the Indies and China and used its vast stores of silver to purchase the spices and manufactures of the "East." Americans have long imagined the markets of Asia to be the answer to periodic crises in the economy. If Asia was the object of commercial desire, Asians themselves were, however, the objects of social revulsion. As the racial Other marked as indelibly foreign, the Oriental subject has been central in the ongoing debate about what and who belongs in American culture.

America's contradictory fascination with Asia was reflected in the country's first museums. By the 1830s an emergent urban middle class in New York, Philadelphia, and Boston could visit China vicariously at P. T. Barnum's American Museum, the East India Maritime Society Museum, Dunn's Chinese Museum, or Peale's Chinese Museum where they could see Chinese artifacts, splendid luxury items of ivory, porcelain, and silk that had shaped American elite taste (and wealth) in the early Republic. At P. T. Barnum's American Museum they could even see real Chinese people in a diorama of a "Noble Chinese Family." Later at Barnum's and at other venues they saw Ah Fong Moy, a "Chinese Lady" who performed Chinese-ness in dioramas and tableaux or Chang and Eng, the celebrated "Siamese" twins who began a thirty-year career with Barnum and later toured internationally on their own. Throughout the nineteenth century, Chinese, Japanese, and Indian performers could be seen on the burlesque and vaudeville stage as magicians, singers, and dancers.

But looking at Asian things or even people as artifacts of the exotic was one thing, Asian settlers in America was quite another. From the mid-nineteenth century well into the twentieth century, the image of Asian im-migrants, first the Chinese, then the Japanese, and then the Filipino were marked in songbooks, minstrel shows, and plays as well as labor broad-sides and newspapers as an unalterably foreign threat to white American workers and the American way of life.

Even as it closed the door to Asian immigrants at the turn of the twentieth century, America conquered a formal colonial empire in the Pacific and pursued an informal empire in Asia whose markets American businessmen imagined to be a panacea for periodic crises of "overpro-duction." The captains of industry and trade built pavilions in the Chi-nese style in their formal gardens or constructed Japanese tea gardens where they staged elaborate Oriental-themed parties. Middle-class women also consumed the Orient, donning silk kimonos, sticking chop-sticks in their hair, and setting their dining tables with tableware etched with Japanese-themed designs.[2] Such was the popularity of the exotic Oriental motif that the nascent film industry made Sessue Hayakawa along with Rudolph Valentino among its first romantic stars.[3] At the same time, the Worlds Fairs in Chicago, St. Louis, and San Francisco laid out for thousands to see a great chain of being in which "Western" Civi-lization, that is to say European and North American culture, was at the undisputed apex while Asian and Pacific cultures were ranked among the lower orders.

After Japan's victory over Russia in 1905, in Europe, Britain, and the United States anxiety over the "Yellow Peril" became a nightmare.[4] Sax Rohmer's fictional Fu Manchu became the archetypal Oriental villain. Androgynously sexy, Western-educated, but Oriental in his cunning and cruelty, his mission was to engineer the downfall of Western civilization. Fu Manchu became the first Asian celebrity with name recognition in American culture. Only later would he be rivaled by a "good" Oriental figure, the rotund and fatherly Charlie Chan. The absolute Oriental Otherness of Fu Manchu and Charlie Chan was underscored on the silver screen where they were consistently played in Yellowface long after Blackface had left the commercial stage.

The bloody but brief Japanese challenge to Anglo-American hegemony in the Pacific resulted in the transformation of the Pacific into an American lake. Although China was "lost" to the American imperium, later to be joined by North Korea and Vietnam, the imperatives of the Cold War in Asia dictated a new set of policies and attitudes toward Asian immigration. Beginning in 1943 with the abrogation of the Chinese Exclusion Acts, legal barriers specifically aimed at Asian immigrants were gradually dismantled. A massive immigration of middle-class professionals from Asia in the late 1960s and 1970s fed a new image of the Asian immigrant as a model of assimilation into middle-class American mores and a conservative model for the behavior of African Americans, Latinos, and working-class whites on the margins of an economy in crisis.

A new Yellow Peril fear has emerged in reaction to the transformation of the postwar Fordist economy based on large-scale industrial production in favor of flexible accumulation and multinational finance capital, the dismantling of the New Deal social compact, and the rise of Asian capitalism. In contemporary narratives of American decline, such as *Year of the Dragon, Falling Down,* and *Rising Sun,* Asian Americans are once again identified as the Yellow Peril, as the agents of an Orientalized capitalism responsible for America's economic ruin.

The critique of these representations of Asians in American culture and the racialization of the Asian American as indelibly foreign has been a major task of Asian American studies. This impulse has been driven both by the need to expose the stereotypes and refute racist claims made about Asian Americans and the need to understand the historical moments in which Asian Americans made their own history. While Asian Americans have been active producers of American popular culture since Ah Fong Moy sat in dioramas for the American Museum, Chang and Eng drew crowds for P. T. Barnum, and Lee Tung Foo sang on the vaudeville stage or Sessue Hayakawa, or Anna May Wong lit up the silver screen, Asian American cultural producers (other than writers) have received little public visibility or critical attention.

The essays in this volume make a decisive turn toward foregrounding Asian Americans as agents in the production of popular culture. In an era of globalization, Asians and Asian Americans are becoming ubiquitous in American popular culture. In the past several decades the shift to flexible accumulation, the compression of time and space through changes in transportation and communications, mobility of capital and labor—all those economic phenomena that are collectively referred to as globalization—have resulted in massive immigration from Asia to North America. Globalization has also been accompanied by intensified transnational cultural practices and cultural hybridities in societies around the world. As Neil Lazarus has observed, these multicultural practices are the cultural logic of globalization.[5] In the 1990s, the Asian American presence became commonplace if not ubiquitous in American popular culture both as producers and consumers. With rapidly expanding market segmentation through cable and satellite, it is now possible to watch television programs in Hindi or Tamil, Cantonese or Mandarin even in such provincial outposts as Providence, Rhode Island. Service calls from your bank or telephone companies are most likely to come from Mumbai or Bangalore. Asian American newsreaders are common, though for many complicated reasons Asian American talking heads are not.

The essays in this collection take us across a wide range of cultural arenas, locales, and sites, to see the diverse ways in which Asian Americans produce, consume, and critique popular culture, reminding us that popular culture continues to be a contested terrain. Taken together these critical essays serve to warn us against a premature celebration of a multicultural utopia. They remind us that multiculturalism serves the state in its management of difference, obscuring the contradictions of contemporary globalization and the savage inequalities that it has generated.

NOTES

1. "Ode to Tomo Chachi," Warwick, England, 1739.

2. See Mari Yoshihara, *Embracing the East, White Women and American Orientalism* (New York: Oxford University Press, 2003).

3. See Robert Lee, *Orientals, Asian Americans in Popular Culture* (Philadelphia: Temple University Press, 1999).

4. See, for example, Jack London, "Yellow Peril," in *Revolution: And Other Essays* (New York: Macmillan, 1912); Homer Lea, *The Valor of Ignorance* (New York: Harper & Bros., 1909).

5. Neil Lazarus, "Charting Globalization," *Race and Class* (1998–99) 40:91–110.

Introduction

Shilpa Davé, LeiLani Nishime, and Tasha G. Oren

From henna tattoo kits available at your local mall to "faux Asian" fashions, house wares, and fusion cuisine; from the new visibility of Asian film, music, video games, and anime to current stylistic blending of hip hop, martial arts motifs, and "Japanese kitsch style," Asian influences have thoroughly saturated the U.S. cultural landscape to become part of the vernacular of popular culture. Paradoxically, this current visibility of global "Asianness" renders the cultural presence of Asian Americans in mainstream American culture conceptually problematic: simultaneously hypervisible and out of sight. In the midst of a boom in both Asian American population numbers and cultural productions, Asian Americans continue to occupy a precarious position in the popular American imagination, lodged in that hazy symbolic space that blends the seemingly opposite impulses of global proximity with the exotic. How do we address the Asian American presence within our hyperglobalized mainstream culture? How can we theorize Asian American popular culture while acknowledging its traditions, accounting for innovations and creative fusions while also maintaining its distinctions?

Born from political activism, cultural isolation, and historical erasure, Asian American studies has developed along two parallel streams that largely dominate contemporary work in the field. While one approach explores Asian American representations as "others" in mainstream U.S. media culture, another tradition focuses on Asian American-produced media, literature, and cultural practices within Asian American communities. This collection marks a turning point in Asian American studies by introducing readers to innovative contemporary work that challenges received definitions of the field by reconceptualizing the popular. Through a consideration of cross-cultural influences and global cultural trends, the essays here thrive at the interdisciplinary intersection of Asian American studies with media, literature, sociology, film, performance, and cultural studies. Together, they offer a new, inclusive approach that brings the maturing field of Asian American studies into productive dialogue with both new and well-established disciplines.

Traditional models for Asian American studies have been wary of acknowledging and readmitting the complexity of their own immigrant roots and the uncontrollable multiplicity of the populations the field purports to represent. Recent developments in global immigration flows, accelerated cross-cultural mixing, and local changes within Asian American cultural production outside and (increasingly) within mainstream popular culture have left these approaches ill-equipped to account for and theorize current popular culture. Concurrently, popular culture scholarship has lagged behind the general trend toward ethnic, economic, and geographical diversity in the study of Asian Americans. Popular culture studies often seems mired in an out-of-date vision of Asian America as solely Chinese or Japanese American, male, straight, and middle class. Further, contemporary developments in other fields such as media and cultural studies, as well as a new scholarly emphasis on globalization, have brought previously distinct fields of inquiry into a new proximity as scholars have begun considering Asian American cultural production and representation within the joint contexts of U.S. mainstream culture and global cultural trends.

Popular culture is an enduring interest in Asian American studies. Widely acknowledged as one of the first collections of Asian American literature, *The Big Aiiieeeee!* edited by Jeffery Paul Chan, Frank Chin, Lawson Fusao Inada, and Shawn Wong introduced and influenced Asian American theory for years to come and came out swinging against the image of the passive and eternally foreign Asian in America. Yet their anthology has also come under fire for neglecting non-Japanese and Chinese Asian Americans as well as its introduction's macho, heterosexist rhetoric. However, its emphasis on overturning stereotypes with examples of outspoken and resolutely American writers still echoes through contemporary criticism. Books such as Russell Leong's anthology *Moving the Image* (1991), Amy Ling and Shirley Lim's anthology *Reading the Literatures of Asian Americans* (1992), and King-Kok Cheug's *Articulate Silences* (1993) have continued to shed light on neglected work by Asian Americans. Even more recently, writers such as Lisa Lowe, David Eng, Peter Feng, Josephine Lee, and David Palumbo-Liu have begun to expand the boundaries of what constitutes Asian American cultural production.[1] Lowe and Palumbo-Liu cross generic boundaries to read city streets and academic cannons, while Eng, Feng, and Lee move to establish how Asian Americans revise and reorient queer theory, dramatic performance, and film theory. It is in the spirit of these authors that we began to collect the diverse voices of this anthology.

The other main strain of Asian American popular cultural scholarship focuses on representations of Asian Americans in popular society. Traditionally, the primary focus was on roles and representations in film and television. Studies include such well-known works as the documentary *Slaying the Dragon* (1991) and Darrell Hamamoto's *Monitored Peril: Asian Americans and Television* (1994). Just as gender studies began to move away from image-based analysis to explore representations of women in a more fluid context, Asian American cultural analysis has turned to a dynamic understanding of racial representations. In the past few years Robert Lee's *Orientals* (1999) has done much to historicize the depiction of Asians and broaden the scope of analysis to newspapers, popular songs, and other cultural discourses. In addition, Dorinne Kondo's *About Face* (1997) offers new directions in scholarship by emphasizing the interrelation between culture, race, and performance and the multifaceted nature of Asian American culture. These last two writers, like the authors collected here, focus on the uneven exchange between popular and Asian American culture.

Taken together, the essays in this volume engage not only with the broadening of the traditional definitions of "what counts" as Asian American studies but shift critical emphasis from the celebrated margins into the mainstream. They eschew the familiar representation-based models that emphasize victimization and alienation in favor of a multifaceted approach that highlights the intricacies and internal tensions in contemporary Asian Pacific American cultures. To this end, the volume facilitates an expansion of the field from film and video to the arena of global communications, the Internet, youth and immigrant subcultures, and alternative modes of culture that have yet to be fully addressed in any book-length collection.

The category "Asian American" has grown to encompass over fifteen different ethnic and national backgrounds from sixth-generation Chinese Americans to Hmong refugees to Pacific Islanders. The latest census figures estimate that over 12 million Asians and Asian Americans live in the United States. Hence the term Asian American is a group identity in flux, a fluid and changing identity that initially served as a political rallying point but now recognizes multiple histories and contexts and seeks to interrogate ethnic categorizations. This volume presents a broad vision of Asian America that includes often neglected groups such as South Asians, multiracial Asians, and teenagers. It also examines the contrary nature of established racial and ethnic categories so as to open up the discussion of what constitutes Asian American popular culture.

Far from presenting a comprehensive picture, we view this collection as only the beginning, a first step. Instead of attempting to account for each group, interest, and form of cultural practice, or seeking to present a self-contained "record" of Asian American popular culture today, we offer this collection as an introduction to new work and a call for more. Thus, we conceptualize Asian American cultural presence in a trans-Asian and dynamic context. Specifically we argue for the centrality of popular, mainstream culture in understanding the particular complexity of Asian American identity in a contemporary, increasingly global environment that often feels inflected with "Asianness."

Divided into three key thematic parts, the opening set of articles in the collection examines the transnational flows of culture inside and outside national and international boundaries, whereas the second section focuses on how political, social, and global economies influence and direct cultural history. The last section specifically addresses the marketing and consumer patterns of popular culture as a way to engage and challenge how we produce and understand racial identities. However, the essays also speak to each other across categories and their grouping into these particular sections is more suggestive than indicative. Other categorical groupings are just as likely—gathering the essays by genre or ethnicity, for example. The fluidity of themes, concerns, and foci further emphasizes the fundamental links the essays share, and as the editors of this volume we hope readers will explore these connections and devise their own pathways of conceptualizing and categorizing Asian American popular culture.

In sum, the collection presents Asian American media and popular studies as cultural studies, a collection of divergent approaches that considers the current constructions of culture as processes of symbolic and political significance.

Globalization and Local Identities

While few scholars and critics still maintain the trope of authenticity and cultural insularity, preferring models of dynamic and constant cultural exchange, fewer still would deny that contemporary forces known jointly as "globalization" have accelerated such exchanges to a near-frenzied pace. As Aihwa Ong has argued, global communication systems, media technologies, increased leisure and labor mobility, and the finely coordinated commercialization of transnational product and media flows have together facilitated the emergence of "global trends."[2] Indeed, theorists such as Lisa Lowe and David Palumbo-Liu have outlined the ways in which Asian American identity has been transformed by the increasingly porous boundaries between America and Asia. While concerns over Western imperialism (and Americanization, in particular) of mass culture continue to draw significant scholarly attention, fewer academic works have addressed the equally powerful phenomena of "counterflows" and the pervasive popularity of Asian accents and influences within popular culture, particularly in the United States.

The increased commercialization of Asian culture, dance, and music—particularly among the young and trendy—fuels new international formations and is the subject of Sunaina Maira's "Trance-Formations: Orientalism and Cosmopolitanism in Youth Culture." Maira delves into the influence of South Asian iconography on rave culture and its implications for traditional conceptions of both Orientalism and the opposition of the global and local. The process by which a local cultural product becomes a part of the global marketplace is also the subject of the following two essays by Kieu Linh Caroline Valverde and Jigna Desai. However, as both authors demonstrate, it has very different implications for immigrants, diasporic communities, and their relationship to a "homeland." Valverde's "Making Transnational Vietnamese Music: Sounds of Home and Resistance" documents the two-way influence of Vietnamese and *Viet-Kieu* music and the political implications of the movement of music between Vietnam and America. In "Planet Bollywood: Indian Cinema Abroad," Desai chronicles the ways in which second- and third-generation South Asians consume and rework images of diasporic Indian identity through Indian cinema. As these essays demonstrate, old categories that demarcate local from international, immigrant from native, and "original" from fusion hardly suffice to describe this current global climate.

The article "Model Minorities Can Cook: Fusion Cuisine in Asian America" interrogates the category of "global fusion." As Anita Mannur looks at the consumer-friendly marketing of Asian culture through food, she finds far-reaching and disturbing implications for liberal multicultural rhetoric. In "PAPPY'S HOUSE: 'Pop' Culture and the Revaluation of a Filipino American 'Sixty-Cents' in Guam," Vicente M. Diaz brings historical global flows into a personal focus as he takes up the term "Pappy" to reveal a legacy of colonization and imperialism in Guam, the Philippines, and the American South.

Cultural Legacy and Memories

Despite the insistence in popular culture on the new and cutting edge, it remains inextricably linked to history. While mass-produced culture invites us to share in a world devoid of the weight of history, the authors in this collection make clear that history, whether national, cultural, or familial, always informs and shapes both the production and reception of popular culture. However, history does not exist as some unchanging and essential reality. Indeed, history both dictates and is dictated to by cultural formations. The project of recovering history that runs throughout the articles does not simply midwife a fully formed past. Instead, like Foucault's genealogies of history, these authors reshape Asian American history while simultaneously revising contemporary conceptions of Asian America.

In the first two essays of Part II, Victor Bascara and Christine So explicitly address historiography and the practice of remembering a shared past. Bascara's "'Within Each Crack/A Story': The Political Economy of Queering Filipino American Pasts," borrows from queer theory to envision a Filipino American history that values, without valorizing, the early bachelor communities of Filipino male laborers. Through a reading of Asian American poetry, literature, and film, Bascara asks whether reading familiar histories through a new lens can revive the critical subjectivities and agencies of those near-silent men. In her essay, "A Woman Is Nothing: Valuing the Modern Chinese Woman's Epic Journey to the West," Christine So also turns to literature to examine the recent explosion in transnational Chinese women's historical fiction. As she analyses the narratives and global popularity of such works, So argues that history functions as another character in these novels, helping the reader negotiate a global capitalist present. With Hye Seung Chung's "Between Yellowphilia and Yellowphobia: Ethnic Stardom and the (Dis)Orientalized Romantic Couple in *Daughter of Shanghai* and *King of Chinatown*," we turn from literature to 1930s Hollywood cinema and to some of the earliest examples of Asian American stars. By placing the films and star personae of Anna May Wong and the Korean American actor Philip Ahn in historical context, Chung accounts for both their surprisingly sympathetic and active portrayals and for the cross-textual readings by the film's Asian American audiences.

Local audiences' readings of their own representation in the American mainstream media culture is at the center of Morris Young's essay "Whose Paradise? Hawai'i, Desire, and the Global-Local Tensions of Popular Culture." Through the controversy over the use of "pidgin" English in the television series "The Byrds of Paradise," Young implicates popular culture in the negotiation and struggle over local identities as he traces the development and expression of a distinctly Hawaiian sensibility. Rebecca Chiyoko King-O'Riain takes up a different struggle over local cultural identity in "Miss Cherry Blossom Meets Mainstream America." By tracing the controversies that periodically arise within and over Japanese American beauty pageants, King illustrates how changing notions of idealized beauty reflect the shifting and elusive nature of Asian American identity. Through this reexamination King also demonstrates how neglected cultural forms can revise our view of history as a simple progression from oppression to liberation.

The second section concludes with the recovery of repressed histories both personal and political. In "How to Rehabilitate a Mulatto: The Iconography of Tiger Woods," Hiram Perez investigates the erasure of history in the marketing of the "Cablinasian" Tiger Woods. By reinserting Woods into America's fraught racial history, he reanimates the symbolic and political meaning of Woods as an American icon.

Ethnicity and Identification

In the previous section, the authors examined the cultural economics of history and addressed how the constructed nature of history influences personal and public perceptions of beauty, sports, and even family genealogies. As these essays suggest, race and its cultural meanings remain at the core of globalizing media flows and their local receptions.

Race, as we all know, is a social construct, a mass fantasy in which we all participate, yet it persists as a constant material force as well as a visceral and lived reality. This section focuses on the means by which this "reality" is enacted, enforced, and debated through the varied reception and consumption of race and ethnicity. As a field of study, spectatorship has been slow to enter the mainstream of ethnic studies. While gender studies has embraced the concept, particularly in relation to cross-dressing and drag, acceptance by race theorists has been stymied by both practical and political considerations. As Elaine Kim has argued, the emphasis on reception comes at a time when race has finally been recognized as a material force in the lives of racial minorities and an emphasis on performance threatens progressive political moments deeply rooted in identity. Indeed, the search for authenticity as well as an authoritative voice to challenge the racial construction of Asians as a wedge group or "model minority" in American society has long been a motivating force in the creation of Asian American studies (see *The Big Aiiieeeee!* eds. Chin et al.). However, just as essentialist ideas of Asian American racial identity are being dismantled (see Josephine Lee's *Performing Race and Ethnicity,* and Kandice Chuh's *Imagine Otherwise: On Asian Americanist Critique*) so too are calls for singular notions of a seamless and authentic cultural expression of that identity.[3] Rather than reading cultural representation for their positive or negative (authentic or inauthentic) portrayals, the authors in this section emphasize the ways in which these representations function to reiterate, challenge, transform, and/or create cultural norms.

The essays in this last section tackle an array of concerns including cross-racial identification, the invention of an "alternative" Asian American identity, debates about Asian American authenticity, and challenges to the "model minority myth." In "Bruce Lee in the Ghetto Connection: Kung Fu Theater and African Americans Reinventing Culture at the Margins," Amy Ongiri reevaluates the popularity of Asian culture and martial arts in seventies black urban culture, offering new insights into this historically media-savvy but untapped consumer market. Along the way, she challenges traditional understandings of the cinematic "black-Asian connection" and its implications for contemporary media culture. The cybercitizenship created by and for Asian Americans is the subject of Lisa Nakamura's essay "Alllooksame? Mediating Visual Cultures of Race on the Web." In it, Nakamura reviews and theorizes the extent to which Asians can articulate their identities in the newly created transnational and performative space of the Internet.

LeiLani Nishime's "Guilty Pleasures: Keanu Reeves, Superman, and Racial Outing" builds on the earlier discussion by examining how multiracial Asians reshape theories of racial classification. In her readings of Keanu Reeves and the television drama "Smallville," Nishime explores how the pleasures of "outing" race in cases where it is not apparent illuminates understandings of multiraciality and the stakes of identity for their consuming spectator.

The relationship between knowing and seeing the visual aspect of race informs the production of knowledge about race and culture in the previous chapters. Jane Park also examines performance and identity, but this time through music. In her essay "Cibo Matto's *Stereotype A*: Articulating Asian American Hip Pop," Park traces the marketing and critical reception of the group Cibo Matto as an Asian novelty act in the U.S. hip hop music scene, contrasting it with the band's own visual, textual, and tonal self-representations. The essay reveals popular reception as itself a cultural struggle through Park's analysis of Cibo Matto's stylistic engagement with the stereotypes of Asian American women.

The cultural construction of a model minority through a manufactured sound is also addressed in Shilpa Davé's "Apu's Brown Voice: Cultural Inflection and South Asian Accents," where she maps out how ethnic accents produce racial and class hierarchies within the South Asian American and Asian American communities. Focusing on the character and performance of Apu from *The Simpsons* Davé introduces the practice of "brown voice" to elaborate on how vocal representations re-create additional stereotypes.

In the concluding essay, "Secret Asian Man: Angry Asians and the Politics of Cultural Visibility," Tasha G. Oren reevaluates Asian Americans' presence as both actors in and consumers of mainstream media in the shadow of the "model minority" myth. As Oren reads media portrayals of angry Asians against public expressions of rage, she revises familiar stereotypes with an appraisal of how anger is a mobilizing cultural force that fosters social and political awareness and alliances.

The essays collected in *Asian American Popular Culture* address a new phase in Asian American studies of media and popular culture by defying the long-standing practice that has kept thematic concentrations on the local, global, mainstream, and historical at a discreet, politically charged distance. It broadens the scope of inquiry by emphasizing the diversity and interaction within and across ethnic, cultural, and national categories. As all the essays in this final section argue, to recognize the fluidity of race in its cultural and popular incarnations is to recognize its political nature. By situating cultural practices in time, geography, and genre, the authors bring together the dynamic indeterminacy and the solidity of "real politics" to this current moment in our cultural life. As this collection is also an invitation to further research, we look forward to the next one.

NOTES

1. Lisa Lowe, *Immigrant Acts: On Asian American Cultural Politics* (Durham: Duke UP, 1997); David Eng, *Racial Castration: Managing Masculinity in Asian America* (Durham: Duke UP, 2001); Peter Feng, *Identities in Motion: Asian American Film and Video* (Durham: Duke UP, 2003); Josephine Lee, *Performing Race and Ethnicity* (Philadelphia: Temple UP, 1997); and David Palimbu-Liu, *Asian/Americans: Historical Crossings in a Racial Frontier* (Stanford: Stanford UP, 1999).

2. Aihwa Ong, *Flexible Citizenship: The Cultural Logics of Transnationality* (Durham: Duke UP, 1999).

3. Kandice Chuh, *Imagine Otherwise: On Asian American Critiques* (Durham: Duke UP, 2003).

Part I

Globalization and Local Identities

Chapter 1

Trance-Formations

Orientalism and Cosmopolitanism in Youth Culture

Sunaina Maira

Images and sounds of Asia emerged to mark the "cool" edge of U.S. popular culture in the 1990s in ways that express the contradictions of economic and cultural globalization, immigration, and racialization, contradictions that speak to the particular positioning of Asian Americans at this historical moment. In the late 1990s, for example, South Asian motifs and music became particularly visible in the latest manifestation of "Asian cool" at a time when South Asian immigration to the United States was growing rapidly, with an increasing number of South Asian labor migrants working in low-income jobs. South Asian American youth were justifiably ambivalent about this "appropriation" of South Asian cultural symbols, from henna "tattoos" and decorative "bindi jewels" to the images of Hindu deities on T-shirts and lunch boxes.

Yet the commodification of South Asia in mainstream youth culture is not just about contestation over cultural authenticity and ownership; it also brings to light deeper issues of race relations in the United States, the inequities of economic globalization, and rising anti-immigrant sentiment —all heightened after the events of September 11, 2001. I have focused elsewhere on the meanings of this cultural commodification of "Asian cool" for South Asian American youth (Maira 2000), yet not much work has been done to carefully examine what it means for white American youth to consume these symbols of "otherness." Asian icons are often used by white (or other) American youth to signal their "alternative" approach to mainstream popular culture, as with neohippie subcultures that have reinvented the sixties' fascination with India.

I want to focus here on what this manifestation of late capitalist Orientalism reveals about the national and global imaginaries re-created in U.S. youth cultures at the turn of the millennium and, in particular, reflect on the implications of the adoption of South Asian iconography by dance music subcultures. Are notions of Orientalism, cosmopolitanism, and globalization, much discussed in cultural studies and Asian American studies, relevant to these phenomena? If so, how can the "local" and "global" structures of feeling expressed in these youth subcultures help us rethink these paradigms and understand the contradictions of citizenship and consumption today?

Electronic Dance Music and Goa Trance

Electronic dance music is a large and continually expanding musical genre and dance subculture, having evolved from Detroit techno, Chicago house, and New York garage/disco parties as well as European electronic music experiments, notably in Germany (Collin 1997; Reynolds 1998; Shapiro 2000; Silcott 1999). In brief, the story of raves begins, most recently at least, in England where Chicago house music was transformed by clubbers in the 1980s into what was called acid-house, an Ecstasy-driven, all-night dance culture (Thornton 1996). Travel is a key motif in this subculture. It has always been at the heart of the evolution and narration of raves: it was British tourists in Ibiza, Spain—on routes that would later include India, Nepal, and Thailand—who helped import a casual and communal club ethos to England in the late 1980s and early 1990s.

Transnational travel and cultural globalization continues to thread itself into the story of rave culture's entry into the United States. The first full-blown raves on the East Coast were hosted by deejay Frankie Bones in Brooklyn in 1989 after he attended house parties in Britain (Champion 1997; Reynolds 1999, p. 144). On the West Coast, a group of British expatriates drawing on rave's "techno-pagan" dimension hosted parties on northern California beaches that offered a cyberhippie consciousness through a vision of dance as ritual and the deejay as "digital shaman" (Silcott 1999, pp. 58–59; Reynolds 1999, p. 156). In southern California, British expatriates jump-started a party culture that mutated into its local manifestation of outlandishly spectacular and highly fashion-conscious events, some held in the desert; in the early nineties, these parties were reportedly unusually racially mixed (Prince and Roberts 2001; Reynolds 1999, pp. 159–160).

Trance music has been called "the Esperanto of electronic dance music" by dance music critic Simon Reynolds, who claims that in the late 1990s it was the "most popular rave sound in the world" (1998, no page). Trance is growing in appeal in the United States and offers a "populist, accessible alternative to the experimental abstraction of hip rave styles such as techno and drum and bass" (Reynolds 1998). Trance has a more melodic sound within the spectrum of electronic music subgenres, characterized by what Reynolds calls "recognizably human emotions and a warmly devotional aura." Goa trance is the faster, "fiercer" version of trance music (140 bpm and up), first popularized by raver-tourists re-creating the Ibiza paradise on the beaches of Goa, India—historically a sixties' hippie haven—and later circulating as a "viral, 'virtual' presence across the Western world" (Reynolds 1999, pp. 175–176).

I was initially intrigued by "Goa trance" because it seemed to be the enactment of a late-twentieth-century Orientalist fantasy. But the meanings of Goa trance are more complex than I had thought. My own understandings of Orientalism in practice, particularly in the context of globalization, have changed in response to my research. To interrogate the nature of the Orientalist imaginary in Goa trance, one has to situate the music in the particular local contexts in which it is embedded and produced.

The Rave Subculture in the "Happy Valley"

In western Massachusetts, where my research is situated, the rave scene is minimal compared to urban centers in San Francisco, New York, Orlando, and the Washington, D.C.–Baltimore area. Yet there seems to be a community of "party kids" in the Northampton-Amherst area who travel to raves up and down the East Coast. This is not surprising given the large college population attending institutions such as the University of Massachusetts, Amherst, and Smith College and also the demographic makeup of the region, for electronic dance music is a largely white, middle-class youth subculture. The "Happy Valley" of Western Massachusetts, as the area is called with an equal measure of affection and derision, has a predominantly white population with a very visible neohippie culture. Apart from the small Cambodian American community in the Northampton-Amherst area and the Vietnamese immigrant community in Springfield, there is only a transient population of Asian American youth attending the area colleges. Trance fans find out about parties in the region by word of mouth or from fliers and websites. This subculture is inherently no-madic, and the large parties are generally held not in clubs but in visually and digitally enhanced auditory environments created in ice-skating rinks, amusement parks, barns, and fields. The notion of space, and thus of com-munity, is mobile and fluid but at the same time focused and circum-scribed by subcultural ideologies about authenticity and virtuosity.

Deejay Kalyx is one of the young owners of The Grow Room, an elec-tronic music store in Amherst that sells vinyl as well as dancewear and that has become a meeting spot for (aspiring) deejays and party kids. Kalyx spins trance at parties in Cambridge and New York and observed that Goa trance itself has fragmented, with many local variations in sound and tempo across the various sites it has produced. Gavin, a producer of trance parties in Amherst and New York, describes Goa trance as the traditional label, now interchangeable with "psychedelic trance" (or psy-trance) for a sound that has an "arpeggiated synth-line" and is "very chaotic," with "lots of sounds and noises moving in and out of each other," which Reynolds calls "mandala-swirls of sound" (1999, p. 176). The mystical imagery is not coincidental: Goa parties have a "cyberdelic" aura, or what Kalyx calls a "supertribal" vibe, with images of Hindu gods and symbols forming the standard visual iconography of psy-trance fliers. The parties do not use strobe light or traditional shadowy club lighting but ultraviolet or "black" light that reflects off the dancers' fluorescent clothing. Women often wear nose rings or bindis, the Indian forehead ornament, and according to the promoter of the well-known Tsunami trance parties in New York, "they look like goddesses, infused with the spiritual energy of India" (cited in Reynolds 1999, p. 208). Ravers and promoters alike suggest that a particu-lar Orientalist, or at least spiritual, overtone was key to Goa trance's emer-gence in the United States, connected to the return to house in dance music in recent years and the fringe status of psy-trance within rave cul-ture. Hien, a young Vietnamese American man who grew up in Worcester and has been going to dance parties for several years, said insightfully: "I think, you know this is probably like Orientalism at its lowest common denominator. Basically, Goa trance has nothing to do with, trance itself has nothing to do with Southeast Asia or India. . . . It's funny because when house became popular, a lot of people reinvented trance just to be this all mystical, and Oriental, and Southeast Asia like, to set themselves apart from house, to make it seem more like spiritual, or more psyche-delic."

Many observers as well as participants describe trance music as "a religion" and its fans as "tribally devoted to the scene." This attitude was evident among the people I spoke to. Like fans of other music genres, they felt passionately about the music. The underground nature of the trance scene appeals to those tired of the commercialism of the mainstream parties and the influx of younger clubbers who they say are primarily drawn by the drugs rather than the music. Both deejays and dancers like what they perceive as the "underground" nature and spiritual vibe of the trance parties compared to the increasingly expensive, large-scale raves that are attracting high school students.

In fact, Hien points out that the name "rave" itself is no longer used by insiders, because of the mainstreaming of the subculture and the negative attention it has drawn in the mass media: "Raves are like the ideal. But nowadays, being called a raver kind of has a lot of bad connotations. Because when you're a raver, you're trying to be underground, you're trying to do lots of drugs and stuff. That's why a lot of people now call themselves party kids, not ravers." For Hien and other "party kids," there is a clear sense of belonging to a youth subculture that has to keep renaming and re-creating itself in order to remain true to its own vision and distinct from the mainstream, even if doing so is not sanctioned by the law. Issues of authenticity and subcultural capital are preeminent in the hierarchies that undergird belonging in this subculture, as I have elaborated elsewhere (see Maira 2003).

In this subculture there are two ways to gain subcultural capital and advance in the social hierarchy: skill as a dancer or connections as a drug dealer. The issue of drug use is highly contested. All the people I spoke to were ambivalent about its role in the party culture, expressing their concern that drugs had given their subculture a bad rap, so to speak, and had overshadowed what to them was most important and unique about parties: the music and the dancing.[1] Dance is an extremely important element in this youth subculture. Apart from hip hop—from which it draws several stylistic and kinesthetic features—dancing is perhaps the most heavily prized, even fetishized, art form in raves. Hien was himself a member of a dance crew, a collective of young men from western Massachusetts who danced together at parties and who had joined the group by invitation.

There is an understanding among the youth I spoke to that the party subculture is particularly generational, that individuals spend a few years in the scene and then eventually move on, either burned out on the drugs or unable to maintain a lifestyle compatible with being in the workforce. For the mostly middle-class party kids the cover charges for these events are expensive, not to mention the drugs, and attending parties requires a schedule that allows for the travel to and from and "recovery" afterwards. But there are certainly those who struggle to find the time and economic resources to participate consistently in the subculture. So for many, the party scene can be viewed as fulfilling the role of a traditional youth subculture (Clarke et al. 1976), of providing a liminal space where youth can participate in shared rituals that create a sense of collectivity but that they ultimately leave when they enter adulthood and the larger social and class hierarchy.

However, the question I am interested in addressing here is not the traditional subcultural lynchpin of resistance or subversion, but the work of Asian iconography in raves. This preliminary research leads me to ask questions about the relation of youth, specifically U.S. party kids, to the postindustrial nation-state in an age of globalization and at a moment when the Asian and U.S. economies are ever more intertwined, as is apparent from the role of Asian (and Asian American) sweatshop labor and imported Asian commodities (Louie 2001; Skoggard 1998).[2]

I draw on the multilayered structure of Goa trance in offering a preliminary analysis, conceiving of my samples from the interview narratives as layered into two tracks: one, the theme of technology, modernity, and Orientalism; and two, tensions between cosmopolitanism, consumption, and citizenship.[3] In fact, this multilayered structure models that of Goa trance itself.

Track I: Technology, Modernity, and Orientalism

Noah, an articulate and thoughtful young man who grew up in Northampton, has traveled to trance parties in New York and throughout New England. He believed that the very long, "low-frequency sound waves" of the heavy bass have a neurophysiological affect on dancers that is responsible for creating an altered state of being, in addition to or even apart from the influence of drugs. The idea of consciousness-altering rituals involving music and dance that simultaneously subvert and reinforce the social order is obviously an old one. What is new in these contemporary rites at raves is the notion that one can be simultaneously modern, or even postmodern, and premodern. Some have called this techno-shamanism, which for the so-called E-generation is not as paradoxical as it might appear. Gavin, who producers Spectra parties and is based in Amherst, explained why he used Mayan images on his fliers:

> Trance is the fusion of the newest technology available with the oldest rhythms available. People who come to the parties are very computer-literate, they are using technology to awaken their senses. The Mayans were very advanced for their time, and they were also very spiritual. The vibe at parties is very tribal. . . . it's very modern but also the oldest thing people have been doing.

Trance parties rely on digital technology and a postmodern aesthetic based on sampling, but they also distinguish themselves by their ritualistic performance and staging; live acts feature not only deejays but also drummers and fire artists who perform with fireballs and firesticks. Successful party producers such as Gavin pay special attention to the visual decorations, which include not just the digital displays found at other parties but also installations of fabric and banners that react to the UV light. "Om" symbols and images of Hindu deities are also common; in fact, Hindu iconography is so standard for trance fliers that Gavin turned to Mayan imagery to try to distinguish his own graphics from those of other party promoters. Rather than expressing a simple postmodern nostalgia that looks back on a moment in a distant past, trance participants claim that their music and dance *are* a representation of primordial experience and embody the surfacing of collective memory through the mediations of a deejay-shaman. The technology of electronic dance music and trance parties is seen as offering a way to connect with a heightened consciousness via visions of "other" spaces or times. Perhaps, then, this is a performance of Orientalism that is both spatial and temporal (see Maira 2003 on notions of time).

Tribal techno and trance offer white American youth a way to reimagine themselves through racialized, and even globalized, notions of otherness. Noah had just returned from a party in New Hampshire when I spoke to him for the first time, and he described the outfit he had worn: a white dress with "Chinese characters" that glowed in the black light. He reflected, "So when I came into the costume, I take on this other persona. And that's what a lot of people do, they go there to see things, do things, that they can't in their everyday life. So I just wanted it to help step outside of myself." This description could be read as a classic performance of

Orientalism but in our conversation it became clear that it was not the Chineseness of the characters per se that helped Noah take on another persona but the experience of being in what he calls a "costume" and notably in one that he had altered for himself, of performing in an altered light.

Yet it is also true that trance parties draw heavily on mystical-psychedelic symbolism based on Hindu and Buddhist imagery. Fliers for the Synthetic Sadhu parties in New York feature images of Ganesh, Om symbols, and yes, meditating sadhus, with one flier depicting a controversial photograph of Mike Myers as a Hindu deity. Noah's response to these fliers was that they were appealing simply because they were colorful and psychedelic, but he did not seem to consume the Indian iconography through an exoticist lens.

The evocation of India seemed to have meaning for Noah largely as a way to geographically situate the genealogy of the music, the name "Goa" leading him to believe that Goa trance was actually a music produced by Indians. This is perhaps where the Orientalism of trance might seep into the imaginaries of American youth, for as Hien says: "I wish I knew why they chose that name Goa trance. . . . Maybe they wanted to mystify trance further, by adding this element of Goa, this foreign world, you know." Noah also acknowledged that such naming was part of consumerist packaging, saying, "It's the label that has to be put on it. Our culture is so much about the label." During the course of our conversation he realized that Goa trance was really produced by tourists and drew very few Indian followers. This was a revelation to him but he did not seem disappointed, remarking: "Now I understand why people from your country would be offended by this, you know. I mean, maybe they don't like being represented in this electronic music." When I asked Hien how he felt about ravers using Asian symbols or style, he said, "I think it's funny how a lot of people have kanji tattooed on them, and they don't even know what it means. I shouldn't talk, because I have Japanese kanji tattoos!" However, Hien did not see this appropriation of Asian iconography as problematic. He thought that some non-Asian American women actually looked very attractive in the Chinese or Vietnamese clothes that became a popular fashion trend in the late 1990s. Clearly, the responses of youth to Asian iconography vary by ethnicity, gender, and class and are contingent and contextual.

Indeed, in thinking about the complex meanings of Orientalism in my research, it occurred to me that my presence as a researcher had as much to do with the production of Orientalism as these young people's own understandings. They learned that there were no Indian people in trance, but *I* was there. I was both dissolving the myth of the Indian authenticity of Goa trance and simultaneously embodying an Indian subject who, after all, had grown up in India and could be presumed to be authentically Indian, claiming to know about the origins of the music and its relation to India. Needless to say, I did not embark on this project with the intention of setting the cultural record straight about Goa trance, but neither did I assume the role of the traditionally detached researcher who listens, but never comments or responds. This was a complex but always illuminating process, for notions of authenticity and Orientalism, mine and theirs, collided in sometimes unexpected ways.

The thoughtfulness of the young people I spoke to forced me to think more carefully about the interpretive models and theoretical assumptions I was bringing to the research, to really listen to what it was they were saying (Lipsitz 1999), though of course there are moments when it is important to move between listening to "native ethnographers" and analyze critically what is not being said or brought into focus. This dialogic approach underscores the value of using ethnographic methods in cultural studies that go beyond the study of media as cultural texts and speaks to the larger debate about the strengths and shortcomings of youth culture studies in the United States, where a focus on youth culture abstracted from the lived experience of youth themselves has sometimes seemed to be the dominant approach (Grossberg 1996; O'Connor 1996; McRobbie 1997), and also to the value of developing truly interdisciplinary or transdisciplinary methodologies in Asian American studies. My ethnographic subjects forced me to think about how my questions were embedded in our relationship and to consider difficult ethical and political questions about representation. I was concerned not only about representations of India but also about how my subjects' investments and opinions would be described for a largely academic audience that would, it is safe to say, not be composed primarily of ravers. For those immersed in critical ethnography it is a cliché to say that research is coproduced, within limits, and that it is contingent and conjunctural. But we are still grappling with the shape of the new knowledges produced through reflexive ethnography and their implications: substantive, epistemological, and political (see Maira 2003).

In this project, for instance, the reflexivity of my research relationship complicated my own understanding of Orientalism and its relation to cosmopolitanism. Recent work on Orientalism that refines Edward Said's

(1978) framework offers useful ways of thinking about the production of Orientalism in turn-of-the-millennium U.S. youth culture. Meyda Yegenoglu revisits Said's distinction between the "unanimity" and "durability" of the "latent structure" of Orientalism, as opposed to the "apparent contradiction and heterogeneity" of its "manifest content," and astutely concludes, "To insist on the unity of Orientalist discourse is not to claim that it is a monolithic block. But, if the legacy of Orientalism is with us today, and if it has been able to survive despite the collapse of empires, it is because it has articulated itself differently in each instance" (1998, pp. 71–72). Holly Edwards, curator of the exhibition "Noble Dreams, Wicked Pleasure: Orientalism in America, 1870–1930" (2000), conceptualizes Orientalism as "multivocalic," evolving, and conflicted (2000, p. ix) and, in similar vein, Lisa Lowe has examined "orientalist representations overlapping with rhetorics of gender and class" (2000, p. 325). If Orientalism is multivocalic, however, it is also self-reflexively evoked and ambiguously produced by scholars and critics in relation to research subjects.

Track II: Cosmopolitanism, Consumption, and Citizenship

I returned to talk to Noah, having decided that I needed to explicitly discuss the politics of representing constructions of "difference" in the subculture. I explained to him my understanding of Orientalism, the construction of the "East" as opposed to the "West" in Edward Said's (1978) framework. Noah's response was:

> You bring up East and West, and . . . stuff like that, and it's hard for me to think about that. And I don't know why that is. You know, I've always lived in the West, . . . but for me, the music is a worldwide thing and that's why it's so important to me because I feel that it's a force that can connect us all, regardless of our origins, our gender, our physical characteristics, . . . That's the only way that I try to talk about it, with most people, as a unifying force. . . . With our different languages, our different cultures, and all these differences, to me it really looks like . . . the roots of something we can all connect to.

For Noah, the categories of "East" and "West" were less important than a particular notion of cosmopolitanism in the face of an acute awareness of social differences, a belief in electronic music and dance as offering a universal language that could cross national and cultural boundaries. Raves are a global cultural phenomenon, and trance parties are drawing youth in countries as far-flung as Japan, Hungary, Mexico, and Australia. Lee, a young woman who has been to parties across New England, said that the theme of "we are one world, one people" is very evident in Goa trance. Fliers for raves and dance music albums often talk of "one planet" and depict a world map. Yet, interestingly, the theme of nation and of nationalism persists. A New York City rave in 2001 promoted by a production company called "Stuck on Earth and Unity" had a flier entitled "One Nation," with an image of the Statue of Liberty against a red, white, and blue backdrop. A trance album has the telling title "TranceGlobalNation" superimposed on an iconic globe represented by latitudinal and longitudinal meridians. In some instances, the category of nation is used to imagine the planet. The party subculture is for some an imagined community with horizontal, affective ties like the nation described by Benedict Anderson (1983), except it is now a "global-nation."

The contradictory discourse of trance, which seems to override national identity and simultaneously evoke the nation as the model for a global community, particularly through its discourse of universalist humanism, appears cosmopolitan. Bruce Robbins proposes that "actually existing cosmopolitanism," rather than an older, romantic notion of universalism, arises out of "an ethos of macro-interdependencies, with an acute consciousness (often forced upon people) of the inescapabilities and particularities of places, characters, historical trajectories, and fates" (Rabinow, cited in Robbins 1998, p. 1). In this model, cosmopolitanisms are not only plural and "come in different styles and sizes," but they often work in support of nationalisms (Robbins 1998, p. 2). Yet the concept of cosmopolitanism is ambiguous: what, exactly, is this "cosmopolitical" space that is "beyond," yet still yoked to, the nation that manages to allow room for critiquing what Robbins calls a "dangerously reinvigorated U.S. nationalism"—certainly a pressing question in the wake of September 11, 2001 (Robbins 1998, p. 13)?

Clifford's cautious and careful appraisal of cosmopolitanism is useful in thinking about its role in global dance culture. He writes of "discrepant cosmopolitanisms" as occupying just one position along a "continuum of sociospatial attachments" from neighborhoods and cities to national communities and cross-border affiliations. He notes, "You do not, of course, have to leave home to be confronted with the concrete challenges of hybrid agency" (Clifford 1998, p. 367). It is in this sense that rave culture is

cosmopolitical, for it has provided a social arena and a specifically auditory and sensory medium for young people to negotiate with and, more
commonly, accommodate to the demands of nationalisms that are increasingly imbricated with globalization. These negotiations, Clifford real-
istically concludes, have more to do with hopes for "survival and ability to
articulate locally meaningful, relational futures than with transformation
at a systemic level" (367). This assessment of the politics of rave culture is
far more useful than the largely abstract focus on the "politics of disen-
gagement" in other writings on rave (Borneman and Senders 2000). The
politics, or cosmopolitics, of rave culture is clearly ambiguous, but if raves
are apolitical, they are still one way in which young people engage with
notions of the local and the impact of the global, by imagining different
kinds of community—sometimes through Orientalizing imagery—and
using different languages of affiliation which are not necessarily subversive
or even inclusive.

The politics of race and class affect different participants in the subculture differently, in accordance with their relation to U.S. nationalism
within this globalized imaginary. This became apparent to me in the story
of an Indian American woman at her first trance party, narrated for me by
Becca, a young woman from Northampton who has been going to dance
parties for several years. Anita's parents had migrated from India, and
Becca says:

> her parents were very poor when they moved to the United States, they lived
> in a one-room attic with a bunsen burner and a stove . . . and now they're
> very wealthy, you know, they made it in America. I don't even know what
> they do, but they both make lots and lots of money. And Anita said that as a
> child, when she was going back to India, she was just so hurt and so grieved
> by the poverty that she saw around her . . . that she turned away from it and
> she didn't want to be a part of it. . . . And so for many, many years she ab-
> solutely rejected [identification with India] and she sheltered herself in
> American culture.

Anita finally decided to visit India again when she was twenty because,
Becca said, she wanted to "figure out where I came from and who I am because of it." Before she left, Becca invited her to attend a psy-trance party
in Washington, D.C., describing it to her as featuring music that "came out
of India" that had changed her brother's life and helped him to find "a part
of himself." Anita went to her first rave dressed in a sari and was "enrap-

tured" by the party and the music. According to Becca, the music catalyzed a sense of ethnic pride, for Anita came away feeling, "I'm so proud of my people . . . who created this amazing, beautiful music that's touching people's lives." Anita not only felt she had rediscovered India before her trip there but she reportedly wanted to move to San Francisco because of its vibrant dance party culture. Interestingly, her adoption of a sari seems to suggest the use of a "costume" to perform a different kind of story about one's self, distinct from the everyday, that might have as much to do with (self)-Orientalization as did Noah's white outfit.

This fascinating story shows the ways in which Asian American participants in this largely white, middle-class subculture can use the music to negotiate their own class anxiety by thinking not beyond nation but very much through the ideas of nation, and perhaps also global-nation, to recast or repress questions of global economic inequities. Anita was able to claim pride in "her people" because Becca had framed trance music through a narrative about its presumed origins in India and its transformative possibilities for white American youth. This fantasy and misrecognition of India provides a site of redemption for middle-class American youth grappling with the meanings of immigration and globalization in their own lives. The meanings of this experience are obviously very different for Anita and Becca, and Anita's experience is filtered through her friend's telling of it, leading to questions about the importance of this particular narrative for Becca herself.

This story about Anita can, in fact, be read as another instance of a reflexive, multivocalic Orientalism in which ethnic subjects find themselves by turning to "the East" and American youth negotiate their own cultural and material anxieties through narratives about "other" places. It also suggests that the location of the United States as a site from where people imagine or talk about cosmopolitanism has to be made explicit, as does the invisibility of U.S. national identity. The positioning of differentially racialized and classed subjects within the United States must be taken into account, as must the varied meanings of cultural and political imperialism, when thinking about notions of cosmopolitanism produced by American youth, as opposed to German or Japanese or Mexican youth (García Canclini 2001; Russell 1992).

The ambiguous relation between nation and planet in rave culture, as in global-nation, is also perhaps a way of coming to grips with the close link between the nation and globalized capital that is clearly at work at parties attended by an international rave community that can afford to travel around the world. The young people I spoke to all said that the parties they went to tended to be more diverse with regard to nationality than to race or class, attended largely by middle- to upper-middle-class youth from the United States but also England, Japan, Sweden, South Africa, and even Morocco.[4] Parties are expensive to attend even for local participants, requiring disposable income to buy a ticket, which often costs up to thirty to forty dollars; drugs (twenty to twenty-five dollars for a pill of "E"); bottled water; parking; and gas for road trips. Noah remarked that he was often unable to go to parties because he could not afford them, working as he does as an "entrepreneur" for his father's small multimedia business. Black and Latino youth are generally absent from the scene, though this varies by location and music genre. Lee observed that there were actually "quite a few" middle-class Asian Americans (generally Vietnamese, Chinese, Japanese, and Filipino Americans) at raves in the Amherst area and that they tended to be from predominantly white towns where, she says, "their culture was similar to my culture."

Yet this middle-class suburban cultural style in turn draws from the fantasies of other lifestyles. Hien points out that the style in rave culture shifted in the late 1990s from the blissful, childlike imagery of candy ravers with lollipops and pacifiers to the "ghetto style" adopted by "wannabe gangsters." Fantasies of class and race, evoking Asian iconography but also black or Latino style, thus become intertwined in the cultural consumption of this music and dance, suggesting the ways in which young people negotiate their relationship to the nation-state through the varied practices and ideologies of cultural citizenship in popular culture.

Conclusion: Youth and Citizenship

Néstor García Canclini writes that "the habits and tastes of consumers condition their capacity to become citizens" and argues that "for many men and women, especially youth, the questions specific to citizenship, such as how we inform ourselves and who represents our interests, are answered more often than not through private consumption of commodities and media offerings than through the abstract rules of democracy or through participation in discredited legal organizations" (2001, pp. 119, 5). This is strikingly true of the discourses of nation and globalization that emerge from this preliminary study of electronic music and rave culture. The adherents of trance music share a "sociality constructed primarily in

relation to globalized processes of consumption" and participate in a definition of nation, or global-nation, that is fundamentally "an interpretive
community of consumers" (García Canclini 2001, pp. 43–44). García Canclini's analysis is useful for grounding the notion of cosmopolitanism and,
importantly, nationalism in social practices of consumption and focusing
on the specific relationship of global markets to cultural production and
consumption.

Raves are spectacles that are very much intertwined with the leisure industry and the targeting of youth as a niche market, even if psy-trance
parties are going underground and trying to distinguish themselves from
commercialized events. In fact, the ideal of the truly underground party is
itself part of the larger commodified structure of leisure and the market
economy. Becca said, "America's so focused on capitalism, so focused on
money, that it makes sense you know [that] they messed it up, they've
messed up the party scene." These critiques linking nation and capital by
youth emerge very much from *within* the sphere of popular culture. While
it is important to think of alternatives to privatized models of citizenship
in the face of the dismantling of the welfare state, these alternatives cannot
be located in some pristine space outside cultural consumption. García
Canclini's framework suggests that we need to be more attuned to the new
forms that citizenship takes in an era in which relations of social belonging are "steeped in consumption," while simultaneously pursuing efforts
"to reform the state," "to reconceptualize the public sphere," and to realize
"the right to participate in the remaking of the system, that is, to redefine
the very arrangement in which we desire to be included" (2001, p. 21; 154–
155). Placing consumption in relationship to citizenship allows us to realize that the desires and needs of young people invested in this space are
part of larger structures of ("local" and "global") feeling being expressed
through an increasingly commodified popular culture (Evans et al. 2000,
p. 161). The communitarian desires expressed through raves are on a continuum of manifestations of political subjectivities that have been transformed over time by the impact of global migration, new media, changing
labor markets, and consumption practices.

While the Asian iconography in trance music, or in youth subcultures
more generally, may allow U.S. youth to tap into Orientalist fantasies, my
preliminary research also suggests that their notions of national identity
or of cosmopolitanism take understandings of citizenship and globalization into the cultural realm. These subtle and sometimes contradictory expressions have not been fully explored by theorists of globalization who

have yet to take into account the responses of young people to these major structural shifts. Looking critically at the work of Asian motifs in youth popular culture will allow Asian American studies scholars and antiglobalization activists alike to understand the particular questions about affiliation and justice that youth are grappling with in their everyday lives. This is particularly crucial after the events of September 11, 2001, when questions of citizenship and racialization have taken on even more urgent meaning for Asian, particularly South Asian, Americans and Arab Americans. More work is needed to understand how notions of "one world" have fractured or morphed in U.S. youth culture since 9/11. For it is apparent that the Orientalization of Arabs, Muslims, and South Asians remains a powerful political rhetorical tool for justifying U.S. foreign policy, perhaps more potent than ever, as images of "backward" Afghan women and "fanatical" Muslim youth suggest. We live in the belly of the empire, and it behooves us to embrace the solidarity of oneness and the potential of collective gatherings without falling under the spell of historical amnesia, as the political trance of the new McCarthyism would have us do.

NOTES

I wish to thank all the people I interviewed for this essay, particularly "Noah" and "Becca" for their generosity and support, the editors for their thoughtful comments and suggestions, and Jeff Melnick for his feedback on a longer version that appears in the *Journal of Popular Music Studies*.

1. This is in large part why I have chosen not to reproduce the focus on drug use of earlier writings on rave culture; the role of chemical substances in enjoying, and even inspiring, the music is certainly important, but less attention has been paid to the social meanings of dance music for youth and the connection between raves and the politics of the nation or globalization that shape the context in which young people make sense of and produce this music.

2. Asian American youth are clearly becoming increasingly aware of the links between race politics and commodification, as was apparent from the protests in spring 2002 of Abercrombie and Fitch's racist caricatures of Asian Americans on T-shirts made by sweatshop labor in the U.S. territory of Saipan, a Pacific island. However, reports suggest that most protests focused on issues of racial representation rather than economic injustice.

3. I did this research in spring and summer 2001, during which time I did eight interviews with young people involved in the electronic music party scene as participants, producers, and deejays. I also talked to several other people informally

about the subculture and learned a great deal from my undergraduate students at UMass, Amherst, particularly those in my course on youth cultures.

4. More research is needed on the relationships between globe-trotting Asian ravers and U.S., especially Asian American, party kids, and on trance subcultures in Asia itself.

REFERENCES

Anderson, Benedict. 1983. *Imagined Communities: Reflections On the Origin and Spread of Nationalism.* New York: Verso (1991 edition).

Austin, Joe, and Michael N. Willard. 1998. *Generations of Youth: Youth Cultures and History in Twentieth-Century America.* New York: NYU Press.

Basch, Linda, Nina Glick Schiller, and Cristina S. Blanc (eds.). 1994. *Nations Unbound: Transnational Projects, Postcolonial Predicaments, and Deterritorialized Nation-States.* Amsterdam: Gordon and Breach.

Borneman, John, and Stefan Senders. 2000. "Politics without a Head: Is the 'Love Parade' a New Form of Political Identification?" *Cultural Anthropology* 15(2): 294–317.

Champion, Sarah. 1997. "Fear and Loathing in Wisconsin." In *The Clubcultures Reader: Readings in Popular Culture Studies,* edited by Steve Redhead, 94–105. Oxford, UK, and Malden, MA: Blackwell Publishers.

Clarke, John, Stuart Hall, Tony Jefferson, and Brian Roberts. 1976. "Subcultures, Cultures, and Class." In *Resistance through Rituals: Youth Subcultures in Post-War Britain,* edited by Stuart Hall and Tony Jefferson, 9–79. London: Hutchinson, in association with the Centre for Contemporary Cultural Studies, University of Birmingham.

Clifford, James. 1998. "Mixed Feelings." In *Cosmopolitics: Thinking and Feeling beyond the Nation,* edited by Pheng Cheah and Bruce Robbins, 362–370. Minneapolis: University of Minnesota Press.

———, and George Marcus (eds.). 1986. *Writing Culture: The Poetics and Politics of Ethnography.* Berkeley: University of California Press.

Cohen, Phil. 1997. *Rethinking the Youth Question: Education, Labour, and Cultural Studies.* Durham: Duke University Press.

Collin, Matthew. 1997. *Altered State: The Story of Ecstasy Culture and Acid House.* London: Serpent's Tail.

Edwards, Holly. 2000. "Curator's Preface," and "A Million and One Nights: Orientalism in America, 1870–1930." In *Noble Dreams, Wicked Pleasures: Orientalism in America, 1870–1930,* viii–x, 11–57. Princeton: Princeton University Press.

Evans, K., I. Taylor, and P. Fraser. 2000. "Shop Til You Drop." In *The City Cultures Reader,* edited by Malcolm Miles et al., 158–162. New York: Routledge.

Fikentscher, Kai. 2000. *"You Better Work!" Underground Dance Music in New York City.* Hanover, NH: Wesleyan University Press/University Press of New England.

García Canclini, Néstor. 2001. *Consumers and Citizens: Globalization and Multicultural Conflicts.* Minneapolis: University of Minnesota Press.

Groove. 2000. Directed by Greg Harrison. Sony Pictures Classics, in association with 415 Productions.

Grossberg, Lawrence. 1996. "Toward a Genealogy of the State of Cultural Studies: The Discipline of Communication and the Reception of Cultural Studies in the United States." In *Disciplinarity and Dissent in Cultural Studies,* edited by Cary Nelson and Dilip Gaonker, 131–169. New York: Routledge.

Lipsitz, George. 1999. "Listening to Learn and Learning to Listen: Popular Culture, Cultural Theory, and American Studies." In *Locating American Studies: The Evolution of a Discipline,* edited by Lucy Maddox, 310–334. Baltimore: Johns Hopkins University Press.

Louie, Miriam C. 2001. *Sweatshop Warriors: Immigrant Women Workers Take on the Global Factory.* Cambridge, MA: South End Press.

Lowe, Lisa. 2000. "Turkish Embassy Letters." In *Orientalism: A Reader,* edited by Alexander L. Macfie, 324–325. New York: NYU Press.

Maira, Sunaina. 2000. "Henna and Hip Hop: The Politics of Cultural Production and the Work of Cultural Studies." *Journal of Asian American Studies* 3(3): 329–369.

———. 2003. "Trance-Global-Nation: Orientalism, Cosmopolitanism, and Citizenship in Youth Culture." *Journal of Popular Music Studies* 15(1): 3–33.

Malbon, Ben. 1999. *Clubbing: Dancing, Ecstasy, and Vitality.* London: Routledge.

McRobbie, Angela (ed.). 1997. *Back to Reality: Social Experience and Cultural Studies.* Manchester: Manchester University Press.

O'Connor, Alan. 1996. "The Problem of American Cultural Studies." In *What Is Cultural Studies? A Reader,* edited by John Storey, 187–196. London and New York: Arnold.

Prince, David, and Todd Roberts. 2001. "Mad Hatters, Map Points and Ecstasy Freaks: The Secret History of the L.A. Rave Scene." *Spin* 17, 10 (October): 90–100.

Reynolds, Simon. 1998. "New Invader on the Dance Floor." *New York Times,* November [e-mail from author].

———. 1999. *Generation Ecstasy: Into The World of Techno and Rave Culture.* New York: Routledge.

Robbins, Bruce. 1998. "Introduction, Part I: Actually Existing Cosmopolitanism." In *Cosmopolitics: Thinking and Feeling beyond the Nation,* edited by Pheng Cheah and Bruce Robbins, 1–19. Minneapolis: University of Minnesota Press.

Russell, John. 1992. "Race and Reflexivity: The Black Other in Contemporary

Japanese Mass Culture." In *Rereading Cultural Anthropology,* edited by George Marcus, 296–318. Durham: Duke University Press.

Said, Edward. 1978. *Orientalism.* New York: Vintage.

Shank, Barry. 1994. *Dissonant Identities: The Rock 'n Roll Scene in Austin, Texas.* Hanover, NH: Wesleyan University Press/University Press of New England.

Shapiro, Peter (ed.). 2000. *Modulations. A History of Electronic Music: Throbbing Words on Sound.* New York: Caipirinha Productions.

Silcott, Mireille. 1999. *Rave America: New School Dancescapes.* Toronto, Canada: ECW Press.

Simonett, Helena. 2001. *Banda: Mexican Musical Life across Borders.* Middletown, CT: Wesleyan University Press.

Skoggard, Ian. 1998. "Transnational Commodity Flows and the Global Phenomenon of the Brand." In *Consuming Fashion: Adorning the Transnational Body,* edited by Anne Brydon and Sandra Niessen, 57–70. Oxford, UK: Berg.

Stewart, Kathleen. 1992. "Nostalgia: A Polemic." In *Re-Reading Cultural Anthropology,* edited by George E. Marcus, 252–266. Durham: Duke University Press.

Thornton, Sarah. 1996. *Club Cultures.* Cambridge, UK: Polity Press.

Visweswaran, Kamala. 1994. "Betrayal: An Analysis in Three Acts." In *Fictions of Feminist Ethnography,* 40–59. Minneapolis: University of Minnesota Press.

Yegenoglu, Meyda. 1998. *Colonial Fantasies: Towards a Feminist Reading of Orientalism.* Cambridge and New York: Cambridge University Press.

Chapter 2

Making Transnational Vietnamese Music

Sounds of Home and Resistance

Kieu Linh Caroline Valverde

Since the arrival of the largest exodus of Vietnamese to the United States in 1975, *Viet Kieu*[1] popular music production has evolved in interesting ways. Led by enthusiastic individuals and catapulted by technological advances, members of the overseas Vietnamese population have successfully created a global music industry.[2] Heavily influenced by exile and anticommunism, *Viet Kieu* music has a special blend of nostalgia that appeals not only to the members of the diasporic communities but also to the residents of Viet Nam. Inversely, more *Viet Kieu* singers are braving the scrutiny of being labeled communist by the overseas community to return to adoring fans in Viet Nam. How and why is it that people are able to make meaningful transnational musical connections across borders despite the difficulties of resettling in a new land and the duo-political influences and oppressions emanating from staunch anticommunist groups in the United States as well the communist government in Viet Nam? Despite fear of reprisals from both sides of the ocean, *Viet Kieu* musicians continue to work in environments of cultural control and restrictive censorship to bring their music to global audiences. How they manage to maneuver though the social and political constraints imposed on them is most interesting.

Unlike many of my *Viet Kieu* compatriots, I grew up with many musical influences. My mother raised me listening to Latin dance music. I also gravitated toward 1950s Motown tunes and the easy sounds of Nat King Cole and Johnny Matthis in elementary school and moved toward modern rock sounds such as INXS and Roxy Music in high school. Because we rarely had Vietnamese music at home, my exposure to Vietnamese American music culture began as a hybrid cultural product in the form of the European New Wave invasion of the 1980s. The sounds of CC Catch, Joy, and others played frequently at the Vietnamese American clubs. Along with this music was the occasional Vietnamese song that had been translated into English.

My real introduction to Vietnamese music came while listening to the Vietnamese American band, 17th Parallel.[3] The four male, one female band played its own compositions in English and Vietnamese but also covered mainstream American and Vietnamese tunes. It played versions of well-known *Viet Kieu* singers and composers such as Tuan Ngoc and Duc Huy, respectively. My interest in Vietnamese music was sparked by 17th Parallel's ability to jam like the rock bands I was used to seeing on MTV while belting out Vietnamese lyrics instead of English ones.

From there, my curiosity about "home country" music grew. I began seeking contemporary classic songs by Trinh Cong Son sung by Khanh Ly. I later began listening to hybrid Vietnamese-jazz productions by such artists as Tuan Ngoc. Tuan Ngoc has described his music as an almost purely American music with its special brand of rhythm, harmony, and melody. The only difference is that he uses Vietnamese instead of English lyrics in his singing. But even with these new musical interests based on combining the American style with Vietnamese words, it seemed clear that Vietnamese American music was not evolving, and I would have to reach across the ocean to satisfy my curiosity.

I had the opportunity to live in Ha Noi in 1993, and it was there that I found an array of traditional to contemporary music with creative arrangements and fantastic vocals. Upon my return to the United States from Viet Nam in 1993 and 1996, *Viet Kieu* relatives, who wanted to sample the new diverse sounds from the homeland, quickly took my tapes away. By the early 1990s, I had already begun seeing Vietnamese products such as Trinh Cong Son's songs sung by his then-protégé, Hong Nhung, in the music stores in San Jose, California. Thus I knew Viet Nam's music had potential for mass appeal. This mass appeal had modest beginnings but it took off in a number of small pockets within our Vietnamese American community. Similarly, *Viet Kieu* music has since infiltrated the markets and entertainment venues in Viet Nam.

In this chapter, I discuss how conditions in Viet Nam and abroad influenced the production, dissemination, and consumption of contemporary popular Vietnamese music. Though the political ideology of the

Vietnamese government and the *Viet Kieu* communities often restricted free, innovative, and collaborative music projects and the dissemination of the productions of its members, individuals and groups still managed to fine clever ways to produce and release their works. I document this struggle and enterprise by discussing popular Vietnamese music history since 1975, highlighting the voices of musicians, producers, and consumers in the United States and Viet Nam. I also discuss three well-known music production companies, Paris by Night Thuy Nga Productions (PBN), Trung Tam Asia, and Kim Loi and a network of independent *Viet Kieu* musicians, Bflat, to illustrate the transnational culture flows and forms of collaboration and influences between Vietnamese American and Vietnamese music makers.

Though this chapter involves looking at music data from Viet Nam and in the Vietnamese communities in the United States, I am not taking the strict musicologist route to analyzing this data. Rather, I try to understand the psychological motivations and sociological processes of those who produce and consume the music and the way it affects the lives of people in Viet Nam and in the diaspora. As Stephen Blum suggests, this type of ethnomusicological investigation serves to "shed new light on human creativity on the fundamental importance of musical skills in human adaptive responses" (Blum et al. 1991: 1).

Origins and Synthesis to 1975

Tan nhac or modern music began with the French presence in the early nineteenth century. French music initially came through the church, followed by the military shortly after its takeover of Ha Noi in 1873 (Gibbs 1998). The new French foreign injections of popular songs were made even more popular by talking movies and ballroom dancing (Gibbs 1996). Though French chansons[4] heavily influenced the early modern popular music style in Viet Nam pre- and post-1975, eventually Vietnamese composers would find their special brand of popular music by incorporating a variety of foreign and domestic influences. Vocalists who popularized this music included Khanh Ly and Thai Thanh among the "sang" singers, and Thanh Tuyen and Che Linh, among others, for the "binh dan" or "sen" listeners.[5]

In the following decades, Vietnamese also listened to western popular favorites of the 1960s and 1970s. This included the French singer Christophe and rock icons such as Elvis Presley, the Beatles, and Rolling

Stones (Gerke and Tuyen 2000). Nguyen Thanh Duc, Vietnamese journalist and cultural critic, claimed that before 1975, "Broadcast stations had the American music that the youth of Sai Gon liked to hear. Furthermore, the city was lined with bars that frequently played music from the United States."[6] The early popular-music scene was made up of a combination of influences from abroad and within the country.[7]

Politics and Culture in Transition

> As part of expressive culture, music is a mirror that migration studies have yet to hold up to the refugee experience, and forced migration is a key that ethnomusicology has yet to turn to to gain entry into another world that music inhabits. (Reyes 1999a: 3)

After 1975 refugees and immigrants from Viet Nam were initially concerned with adapting to their new home. This was also true of musicians. However, it was not long before Vietnamese music spread throughout the newly burgeoning Vietnamese American communities. Music at this time had more meaning than just entertainment; it also served the important role of connecting refugees and exiles to the homeland they thought they had lost.

In the initial 1975 refugee flight, unanticipated departure meant that most refugees left with little more than the clothes on their backs. Not many thought of bringing music with them. Thus, in the early years the few with music items such as records and tapes exchanged their wares with others in the community. During the late 1970s and early 1980s, those with previous experience in the music industry in Viet Nam reestablished their trade in the United States.

At this period Thuy Nga Productions, a pre-1975 music house, continued to produce music in France. The company's owner, Mr. To Van Lai, participated in the rebuilding of the company. With a keen sense for the diasporic market, Lai created a division of Thuy Nga called Paris by Night (PBN). Lai found that the refugees in Paris were alienated and he wanted to find a solution. "After working all day, they [*Viet Kieu*] want to be able to sing, dance, whatever in the evening. Paris by Night is based on the desire for this type of leisure distraction."[8]

Though its production center was outside the *Viet Kieu* music center of southern California and to a smaller degree northern California, Thuy

Nga Productions hoped for a global Vietnamese diasporic music invasion. Along with records they began producing music videos in 1989. This has proved to be the most profitable and influential direction Thuy Nga has taken to date. Success was so quick that within a few years Lai had moved their headquarters to Orange County, California. PBN has been operating from that location ever since (December 29, 1995, *Orange County Register*). Though it capitalized on the new video technology, the content of early PBN recordings still focused on Vietnamese songs that had been written before 1975.

The global Vietnamese diasporic population numbered approximately 500,000 in 1975. This number increased to about 1 million in 1990 and 2 million in 2000. Because the Vietnamese market has always been relatively small, Vietnamese overseas music sales were minute compared to the mainstream recording industry. The ethnic minority industry considered a 15,000-unit seller a success. But however modest the beginning, the profits were in the millions and that in turn allowed for the employment of large numbers of performers, composers, and producers. By 1995, over thirty music-related companies alone occupied the four-square-mile area of Westminster and Garden Grove of southern California known as "Little Saigon" (Marosi 2000).

In the first decade after the fall of Sai Gon, pre-1975 music was the staple of the Vietnamese American community. Considering the circumstances of the *Viet Kieu* departure from Viet Nam and their desire to hold onto their history and sense of nationhood, it was no wonder that music from the war years continued to have a popular following long after the war had ended. So popular was this genre of maudlin ballad that some have called Vietnamese American popular music "culture in a bubble." Indeed, for over a decade after 1975, the same songs—western or Vietnamese songs that were popular in the nightclubs of Sai Gon during the Viet Nam war—were still being heard in coffee shops and nightclubs and sold in music stores.

The "nostalgia" for a homeland before communism remains strong especially for first-generation *Viet Kieu*. This could explain why the musical taste of so many remains with the familiar. Even fifteen years after the demise of Sai Gon, the music of the pre- and war periods evoked fond memories of their lives back in Viet Nam. Music that evoked nostalgia was soon accompanied by new music about a lost nation, patriotism, and the refugee experience. These nationalistic songs conjure up images of a glorious past and speak of returning to the homeland. One of the more popular tunes in this genre is Pham Duy's "1954 Cha Bo Que—1975 Con Bo Nuoc" [The Exiles of a Father and His Son]. The song speaks of how a father had to leave the communist-controlled north in 1954 for the south and twenty years later his son had to flee Viet Nam altogether for the same reasons.

In her 1995 article on Vietnamese American music, Adelaida Reyes observed an abundance of what she termed "love" and "sad" songs. She attributed the popularity of these songs in the exiled Vietnamese American community to two factors: their desire to preserve a culture they perceived the Communist Party had destroyed and as an act of resistance, since these types of songs were prohibited in the Socialist Republic of Viet Nam (Reyes 1999b: 212–216).[9]

It seems, then, that the thing that comforts the community in exile is also what keeps it from creating new sounds. The dependence on the old pre-1975 songs in musical repertoires persists to this day, and few venture to write and sing new songs. Anticommunist pressures also prevent people from creating pieces outside the culturally and politically demarcated lines. These factors threaten the future of Vietnamese American music production or the bursting of the "cultural bubble."

Thien Do, a long-time musician in the Vietnamese American community, offers his interpretation of this phenomenon: "Innovation is not considered a virtue in the creation process. Most people strive to copy their teachers as best they can, not create their own works." Historically, Vietnamese composers and singers were two separate groups. But with the rise of modern popular music, composers performed their own works. Artists like Pham Duy and Trinh Cong Son began their careers by performing their own compositions. New singers would only sing songs they knew the audience approved of. "It is not worth it to the singers to take career risks by singing something new—essentially not giving a new composer opportunities to be heard. So, nothing new gets heard,"[10] Thien explains.

Underlying this nostalgia is a strong anticommunist perspective. I argue that this single ideology has been central to every facet of Vietnamese American life, including their institutions, political organizations, and cultural production. In the early years, if the cultural *Viet Kieu* gatekeepers perceived anyone falling out of line with these views, they would pressure the person or group to take a stronger anticommunist stance. Truc Ho, *Viet Kieu* director of Asia Productions, exemplifies this attitude:

> The main purpose of Asia is to gap the bridge between the young and old generations. We try to promote to the new youth. If they want to sing about love and human rights for Viet Nam, I will help them. But if they want to sing about communism, I will not produce them. (Truc Ho)[11]

Not everyone in the community or music industry is as strongly anticommunist. For them, music transcends politics. As long as the music is good and the artists can find an audience, their music is promoted. For example, Nguyen Thanh, who owns Kim Loi Productions, openly produces and distributes music by Vietnamese artists. As his work involves direct relations with Vietnamese artists and officials, he faces constant harassment from anticommunist groups in the United States. They phone his store and home to threaten him and protest in front of his store and at the concerts he produces. At one point, they even attempted to burn down his San Jose, California, store (Nguyen Thanh).[12]

Along with exile music, the Vietnamese American community is also interested in the music of the west. For example, *Viet Kieu* also enjoyed disco in the 1970s. In the 1980s, it was European new wave music that found a long-standing niche in the overseas community. A musician speaks of that time:

> New wave was so good, and we could handle listening to it and playing it. It was like CC Kat, Modern Talking, Bad Boy Blue, and a whole bunch of other bands. We [Vietnamese Americans] grabbed whatever worked and made it our own. I had a band, and we played this stuff because it was the only way to get to play [for a Vietnamese American audience]. (Phu Nguyen)[13]

Attracted by the heavy synthesized music and easy to understand lyrics, *Viet Kieu* found Eurodisco especially appealing. Groups that could not find a market in the mainstream American audience were still able to pack ten-thousand-seat stadiums full of Vietnamese Americans in places like San Jose and Anaheim, California (Lull and Wallis 1992: 217, 231).[14]

The popularity of *Viet Kieu* music lasted well into the mid-1990s, penetrating the black market in Viet Nam and impacting the culture of the citizens there. How did this happen, given that the Vietnamese government maintained such tight control over cultural production in the country? While Vietnamese Americans were *relatively* free to develop their cultural identity, Vietnamese in Viet Nam were dealing with the aftermath of the war and the poverty and confusion that followed afterwards. The new government found cultural production an important tool for nation building. However, it was heavily monitored by the socialist regime. But despite state control, the Vietnamese still managed to assert their own independence in terms of what they chose to consume.

The new leadership felt that sad songs would dampen postwar morale and believed that the songs needed to be lively and to praise the heroes of the revolution and their love of the newly reunified nation.[15] Hence melancholy love songs that were popular in South Viet Nam during the war were prohibited after the war (Marosi 2000; Nguyen Thanh Duc, interview 2001).

As Taylor Philip noted in his article, "Music as a 'Neocolonial Poison' in Postwar Southern Vietnam," music was heavily targeted for reform (Philip 2000).

In the late 1970s, an urgent and sustained attempt was made to understand the mysterious hold the "former" way of life continued to have over the southern population. Many of the unfamiliar attributes of life in the South—such as consumerist lifestyles and popular music—were subject to exhaustive scrutiny, as they had come to be seen as indexes of the southern Vietnamese people's domination by the former enemy. The distinctive characteristics of the popular music associated with "U.S. neocolonial culture" were argued to be part of a plan whose pernicious intent had purportedly been to stifle the Vietnamese people's revolutionary spirit and their consciousness of being oppressed. (Philip 2000: 100)

Though exerting heavy control, government officials could not monitor all its citizens. As time went on, people found ways to listen to the music of their choice. As Tran Dieu Hanh explains:

[Government restrictions] lasted for five years [since 1975]. In 1982 I began hearing some western music like ABBA being played in public places. We were freer to play western music by the mid-1980s. But not until late in the 1980s did I hear pre-1975 music played in public places. Also, we got some cassettes from overseas Vietnamese around 1986 or 1987 and were exposed to new wave and other new pop styles. Maybe others got it earlier, but I got hold of these cassettes at this time. Then in 1996 I immigrated to the United States.[16]

When I conducted research in Ha Noi and Sai Gon in 1993, I witnessed the power of the black market and how it allowed Vietnamese citizens to keep up with consumer trends, including illegal music acquisitions. Though the Vietnamese government attempted to stop black market activities and illegal purchases of foreign products (*do hai ngoai*) through enforcement campaigns, Sai Gon residents watched foreign movies openly in 1993. Paris by Night videos and other tapes and CDs from the overseas Vietnamese community could be found openly in the shops of Sai Gon and covertly in Ha Noi.

Saigonese residents were captivated by *Viet Kieu* music and especially Paris by Night videos. Most of my respondents from Sai Gon at that time much preferred the music of the overseas community over their own, claiming they had the best singers and the most professional performance videos. They thought the PBN shows looked glamorous and modern compared to what they thought of as unsophisticated look of the Vietnamese musical productions. Families could not wait for the next installment of music videos to arrive from the United States. Sai Gon residents' musical consumption in many ways mirrored that of the *Viet Kieu* community in the United States. Like their overseas counterparts, those in Sai Gon also enjoyed live shows with performers singing the old pre-1975 classics—be it *nhac tien chien* (pre-Indochina war music), American pop tunes, or Pham Duy songs.

The novelty of *Viet Kieu* music declined with the growing popularity of local favorites like Hong Nhung, Thanh Lam, My Linh, and Phuong Thanh. By the mid-1990s, I observed that *Viet Kieu* music seemed stagnant, whereas Vietnamese music was perceived as innovative. Of course many still enjoyed the tunes from abroad, whether from the *Viet Kieu* community or elsewhere, but they were not the runaway success of earlier years.[17]

During my field work in 2002, I observed a rather stark transformation in Sai Gon. Already familiar with the "Vietnamese music invasion"[18] phenomena, I was still taken back by the new popularity of *Viet Kieu* singers in Viet Nam. Apparently, with the help of the Committee for Overseas Vietnamese, a handful of *Viet Kieu* performers were allowed to sing regularly in Viet Nam and were even billed side by side with Vietnamese singers (Thanh Thuy).[19]

Doi Moi, Viet Nam's 1986 open market campaign, supposedly brought about a more relaxed atmosphere for international exposure to and exchange of culture production. However, whenever the Vietnamese government feels threatened by competing cultural productions, it imposes a systematic crackdown on the creation and dissemination of these products. For example, the intermittent anti–"social evils" campaigns were set up to curb western and *Viet Kieu* influences in Viet Nam. Such "social evils" include drug abuse, prostitution, gambling, drinking, and having Western consumer values (Barr 1997).[20]

In 2000, the nationwide 09/2000/CT-TTg went into effect, leading to more campaigns to impose cultural censorship and control. Examples included inspectors seizing 120,194 tapes, 84,054 CDs, 30 tons of printed matter, 690 video recorders, and 16 gambling machines, as well as deleting 23,000 square meters of "illegal advertisement hoarding" (*VNS*, August 30, 2000).

The intimidating tactics of anti–"social evil" campaigns were intended to send the message that Viet Nam is an authoritarian state and consuming anything but official, government-sanctioned Vietnamese cultural products will be seen as a threat to its fragile national identity. Foreigners had to tread carefully if they wanted to continue living and working in Viet Nam. And locals had to be extra careful, or they could lose their means of livelihood or face imprisonment. As Blum and his colleagues suggest,

> We must judge institutions by the extent to which their policies enhance or diminish the freedom of all whose lives they affect. The unity of modern music history comes from the universality of claims to fundamental human rights, which can be realized only through continual dialogue and argument. (Blum et al. 1991: 3).

Even under this kind of cultural control, people found ways to listen to the music they enjoyed. And because there were such inconsistencies in what could be heard and produced, musicians still managed to express their creativity—albeit under some censorship. The next section will discuss how, despite the erratic government crackdowns, there has been some loosening of rigid censorship and allowance made for burgeoning musical productions from Viet Nam since 1999. So widespread is this phenomenon outside Viet Nam that it has been called the "Viet Nam music invasion."

Production, Distribution, and Technology

In the summer of 1999, I heard the music of one of the most famous Vietnamese singers, Thanh Lam, playing loudly at music stores in San Jose's Lion Plaza commercial center, the heart of the Vietnamese American community in the Bay Area. Vietnamese music was appearing in the most unlikely places—like weddings. At a 2000 Vietnamese VNHELP (an American humanitarian group) fundraiser in San Jose, California, nearly half of the songs played had been composed by post-1975 Vietnamese composers, yet no one in the audience so much as flinched in the audience.

In 1999, browsing through the music stores of Phuc Loc Tho shopping center, the largest Vietnamese American shopping area in Orange County, California, I discovered that music from Viet Nam occupied nearly the same number of stalls as *Viet Kieu* music. When I visited the music shops in 2001, I found *Viet Kieu* and Vietnamese music products, from CDs to videos to karaoke discs, next to each other without any distinction. The lines between music from Viet Nam and that originating in the Vietnamese American community are being blurred every day. This takeover of the diasporic market by Vietnamese music from Viet Nam is fascinating. Why the sudden appeal of music from a country that many of its exiles still mistrust?

Many believe that having over 70 million people accounts for Viet Nam's larger talent pool. Others believe that a lack of creativity by *Viet Kieu* artists and poor management by *Viet Kieu* producers has resulted in low-quality *Viet Kieu* music. And some say that the soul of music lives most strongly in Viet Nam than among the *Viet Kieu*. Whatever the reason for the widespread popularity of Vietnamese music from Viet Nam, the year 2000 marked the undisputed moment when we witnessed its dominance beyond Viet Nam. For the first time since 1975, *Viet Kieu* music no longer reigned either in the diaspora or in Viet Nam. A *Los Angeles Times* survey of more than twenty-five Vietnamese American music stores in 2000 showed that sales of *Vietnamese* music had increased from 30 percent to 70 percent since the height of its popularity in 1995. It has also been observed that *Viet Kieu* music does not sell as well as its Vietnamese competitors (Marosi 2000). Is the music coming from Viet Nam here to stay? Will it contribute to the growth of the *Viet Kieu* music industry? Or does its presence and ascendance signal the end of *Viet Kieu* music?

In 2003, the idea of listening to music produced under the Socialist Republic of Viet Nam hardly seems that provocative. However, there are still many in the Vietnamese American community who will never accept music that originated in communist Viet Nam. Some of them boycott everything related to Viet Nam, from refusing to return to their home country, to sending remittances, even to consuming goods from there. They see everything, even cultural productions, as propaganda tools of the Vietnamese socialist government. So they boycott music from Viet Nam, criticize Vietnamese American singers who work in Viet Nam, and protest Vietnamese singers when they perform in the United States. They see material cultural products from Viet Nam as a threat to the dominant anticommunist cultural ideology of the exiled Vietnamese American community. For them, these products are a social evil that require them to launch a de facto "social evils" campaign to stop things from Viet Nam from infiltrating the Vietnamese American population.

When it comes to music, no production house is safe from anticommunist scrutiny. Even the popular PBN suffered under Vietnamese American censorship. In celebration of Vietnamese mothers, in 1997 Thuy Nga released "Ca Dao Me" [Mother's Folk Song], number 40 in the PBN series.[21] Though it was another highly anticipated PBN video, its contents soon proved too controversial for the anticommunist groups in the Vietnamese American community. The controversy involved images of a South Vietnamese military helicopter in battle followed by Vietnamese families running from burning villages. Anticommunist groups like "the Front"[22] claimed that this depicted the South Vietnamese military as perpetrators of pain and suffering. They (and others) carried out a full campaign to demand an apology and a recall of all 40 PBN videos. *Viet Nam Insight,* the Front's newspaper, posted letters of protest throughout the Internet, targeting overseas Vietnamese readers.

> Paris by Night 40's mistakes, especially the portion that portrayed a one-sided story about the Vietnam War in which it presented the people's sufferings and casualties as caused by the U.S.-backed South Vietnam's military action without any showing of the communist North Vietnam's atrocities, have aroused anger among the anti-communist Vietnamese community overseas (Tran Chan 2000).

Bowing to community pressure, PBN wrote a public apology and edited the offensive sections of its video for trade. The lesson was clear: de facto censorship in the Vietnamese American community will stifle any new music that seems to threaten its anticommunist ideology. Because images shown in beloved video productions like PBN can come under fire, artists and producers are careful not to cross the line.

Such censorship extends to controlling *Viet Kieu* artists' livelihood. For example, due to general curiosity about the home country, improved work conditions in Viet Nam, and the additional competition of the "Viet Nam music invasion," a handful of *Viet Kieu* artists have opted to perform in Viet Nam despite heavy criticism from the anticommunist groups in the United States. One of the first *Viet Kieu* to return to Viet Nam was Elvis Phuong in 1996. Under the direction of Kim Loi Inc. he created the personal homecoming music video *Ta On Doi, Ta On Nguoi* [Thanking Life, Thanking Humanity] Kim Loi #8 that same year. For this effort, eleven of his shows were canceled when he returned to the United States (Elvis Phuong).[23] The point of the protest is that cultural collaboration with Viet Nam is not acceptable.

Despite the ostracism of anticommunist factions in the community, more artists are choosing to work in or visit Viet Nam every year. They include Hoai Linh, Ngoc Anh, Thanh Ha, and Anh Tu. Some have also decided to make Viet Nam their home, at least for about half the year. They include Elvis Phuong, Trisie Phuong Trinh, and Huong Lan. The push factors in the United States include the shrinking market. Overexposure in the Vietnamese American community means that artists cannot find work as they once did. This makes the pull factors in Viet Nam more attractive. There, *Viet Kieu* singers are still a novelty and are already known to the general population through pirated CDs and videos. As long as artists can move beyond harassment tactics such as threatening phone calls, slanderous statements, and the boycott of their products, they are free to work in Viet Nam. Another incentive is the fan base in Viet Nam. Most people I spoke to in the music industry agreed that musicians just want to perform and do not care who or where their audience is so long as they can put on a show for their fans.

Until 2000, attempts to have Vietnamese singers perform in the United States were met with heavy anticommunist objections. In 2000 a Vietnamese singer had the courage to perform publicly in the United States. Sponsored by Kim Loi, over three hundred people gathered at the opulent Athletic Club in San Jose to watch Cam Van perform. People heard of the show either by word of mouth or through the radio stations. I coaxed my rather reluctant aunt and grandmother to attend the show with me. They told me that though they would love to see Cam Van, they were afraid to go because of my grandmother's age and health problems and the possibility of violent protestors. But we went anyway, and were happy to find familiar faces from San Jose's Vietnamese American community gathered there. Young and old, everyone sat listening to the diva belt out her tunes as they had drinks and caught up with friends. Nguyen Thanh, the organizer of the event, thought the night had been a success, but not for the reasons anticipated:

> She [Cam Van] was so lucky no one protested her. She was crying for joy that she was able to perform in the U.S. She was the first Vietnamese to perform in the U.S. [if you do not consider Thanh Lan in 1994]. We promoted her concert on Vietnamese radio and in the *San Jose Mercury News*. Tickets were going for $50, which is cheap compared to the $100 we were going to charge for the East Coast concert. Lots of radio and newspaper reporters were there last night.

On the heels of a series of successful 2000 and early 2001 concerts with Vietnamese singers from Viet Nam, Nguyen Thanh of Kim Loi promoted another concert in August 2001. I attended this historical production featuring Lam Truong and Cam Van from Viet Nam as well as Yvonne from the United States. Held at the Sun Theater in Anaheim, the two thousand or so protestors matched the number of those in attendance. But unlike the other events that were protested, at this one the audience was protected by security. Although the attendees had to drive through streets lined with protesters, they were protected and shielded within their cars. The drive past the mob lasted less then ten seconds, and when they emerged, they were met by a fleet of riot tanks and police cars. At the end of the concert the guests were escorted to the back of the theater and led out of the parking lot, half a mile away from the protesters. Some people in the community actually condone the censorship of cultural products from Viet Nam, or what I have called the *Viet Kieu* community "social evils" campaign. But when it comes to music, the trend is toward freedom of choice.

Transnational Strategies of Viet Kieu and
Vietnamese Producers, Singers, and Musicians

When we look at the *Viet Kieu* music industry, we see that only since 1996 have the *Viet Kieu* returned to Viet Nam and openly performed there. As we saw in the previous section, anticommunist protestors made it impossible for Vietnamese citizens to perform in the United States at this time. Only in 2000, after the "Viet Nam music invasion," did we see Vietnamese performing in the United States.[24] But even before the exchange of performers, songs, technology, and ideas were being shared. This next section discusses the underground connections that created cultural bridges then, presently, and in the future.

There is a misconception in the Vietnamese American community that a clear distinction can be made between Vietnamese diasporic music and Vietnamese music. Just the opposite is true, as being Vietnamese American also means that one has fluid connections with things coming from Viet Nam.[25] A prominent *Viet Kieu* music producer told me that although he limits his contact with Viet Nam, his need for new materials has led him to find ways to diversify his company's musical repertoire. He explains how he avoids criticism from the community while working with composers in Viet Nam:

> The community does not complain because they cannot differentiate which song comes from a Vietnamese composer and which one from an overseas Vietnamese composer. Singers will be criticized because you can see their faces, but songs are harder to figure out because you can't see the face of the composer.

Producers on both sides of the ocean are anxious to find ways to keep the Vietnamese and Vietnamese American music industry strong. They do so by studying their advantages and disadvantages. Currently, Viet Nam has a larger number of strong vocalists and composers. Additionally, labor for everything from staging to video direction is much cheaper in Viet Nam than in the United States.

In the United States, Vietnamese Americans still dominate music production in the areas of technology and style. Being located in one of the richest and most technologically advanced nations in the world, the Vietnamese American music industry has had access to the best production technology available. Able to learn and experiment liberally in the techniques of arranging, it is years ahead of its Vietnamese counterpart. Even musicians starting out can have an affordable mini-studio in their own home. They can lay tracks and create music at their leisure. By contrast, Viet Nam's music industry has very limited access to such equipment and training.

Many Vietnamese singers are aware of these discrepancies. After a successful concert with My Linh and Tran Thu Ha, two leading Vietnamese divas, sponsored by the *Viet Kieu* humanitarian relief organization VN-HELP, Tran Thu Ha noted the advantages of working with *Viet Kieu* musicians:

> I had these preconceived ideas about *Viet Kieu.* I thought they were basically losers because of the few that came back to Viet Nam and created a bad reputation for the others. But when I arrived here, my hosts were very kind and the audience was very receptive. Now I'm meeting with local *Viet Kieu* and mainstream musicians and producers to work on collaborative projects. I'm thoroughly impressed with what I've seen. I'm so proud of the *Viet Kieu* community for what they have created in the United States in such a short time. My views have totally changed. (Tran Thu Ha)[26]

The United States also dominates in "style," although this is a subjective attribute. Some of the most widely known pop music comes from the U.S. mainstream. This is the kind of music that Vietnamese singers, young and old, like to imitate. In the area of Vietnamese-language songs, Vietnamese from the new generation grew up watching PBN and the glamour that went with each show. The organizers of PBN spared no expense to create and maintain a stylistic, high-end look. As owner To Van Lai explains, "Each song of the video has its own background that costs a lot. Just background alone cost $70,000 to $80,000 and the lighting costs $100,000."

Music production can get quite costly, especially in the United States. For this reason, many Vietnamese Americans have opted to produce their videos or music in Viet Nam. There are numerous benefits to doing this. The location is exotic and can evoke nostalgia. The Vietnamese American community is fascinated with things from the home country. They give the videos a fresh look and are available at a fraction of what it would cost *Viet Kieu* directors to produce in the United States. Additionally, *Viet Kieu* and Vietnamese singers now have the option of performing on opposite sides of the Pacific and hence of broadening their market and fan base.

Musicians can compensate for the shortcomings on both sides by using ideas and resources from the other. *Viet Kieu* and Vietnamese in the music industry have been known to do this for some time. Though communist zealots in the community present an obstacle to such collaboration, it occurs regularly. Similarly, though the government of Viet Nam likes to regulate all cultural production, it cannot stop the collaborations either. Hence the music industry has continually created a cultural bridge between Viet Nam and the Vietnamese diasporic communities despite the external obstacles placed in its way.

Collaboration will inevitably bring about some creative changes and help revitalize the Vietnamese and Viet Nam music industries. Many musicians lamented the dearth of original compositions, arrangements, and performances. Vietnamese Americans who have ventured to create their own music cannot find a market in the Vietnamese American communities. Nguyen Phu, a musician who composes and sings his own work, is a rarity in the community. His struggles for acceptance had to do with growing up with hybrid cultural influences. "I didn't appreciate Vietnamese music until I was fifteen or sixteen. I used to listen to American music. When I hung around with the Vietnamese was when I learned to appreciate the lyrics." His compositions are unique for the blatant Saigonese pronunciation of his songs. Like the English and Irish who prefer American English pronunciation, Vietnamese pop standards prefer the northern Vietnamese accent. But Phu takes chances and his band Phuong attempts to play in the edgier style of rock and roll. For these reasons, they cannot find a large enough market in the community.

Bands like Phu's rarely get the support of the major Vietnamese American production houses. Duy Tran, a sound engineer and musician, complained, "I've lost faith in Asia and PBN because they have the power to make change happen but they won't do it." Responding to the lack of support for young bands, Duy Tran and others formed B-Flat:

> PBN has brainwashed the *Viet Kieu* community here to understand what is good. As a result, we musicians have no chance to have our original works accepted. Our 17th Parallel band was really hated by the community, and that had a lasting impact on me. So, my work with B-Flat is to support artists. Artists are very vain, and I know this. I always push the artists be-

cause it's the only way to help them pursue their art. In my compilation work with B-Flat, there are lots of bands that have broken up, but I want to help them feel inspired to take up music again.[27]

B-Flat's first compilation, "What the *Pho*," included eclectic Vietnamese American music ranging from new wave to hard rock. According to Duy, B-Flat's new compilation, *No MSG*, has two purposes: "to create good music and to promote up and coming musicians. I want to see how far these groups can go. I know SYG, ESL, Phu, Y Nhi, and my band, Superseed, are good and very serious." Both compilations consist of original musical works. Writing and performing one's own material is still very rare because the number of people actually creating new music in Viet Nam and in the diaspora is low. Duy still hopes for a rock and roll scene but sees the community in Viet Nam and abroad as falling somewhat short of this.

The future of popular Vietnamese music, both in this country or abroad, depends on several factors:

1. An easing up of (overseas) community and (Viet Nam) government pressures to produce politically correct songs.
2. Open collaboration between artists and producers from both countries—the United States and Viet Nam.
3. Training the audience to accept new sounds.
4. Shedding the idea that new music is bad or that innovation is not good.
5. Having confidence in one's work.
6. The promotion of young singers and composers who have a different sound by established music production houses.

These factors require a transnational effort. Even if individuals and groups succeed in developing a unique Vietnamese popular style, there will still be many external forces to deal with, most importantly copyright infringement laws. "The lives of musicians are simultaneously based in economics and aesthetics, and their production is both symbolic and concrete" (Glasser 1995: 8). In reality, the artists' works are not protected even when strict copyright laws are in place. Artist after artist predicted that copyright infringement will lead to the demise of the Vietnamese music industry. Still, the problem will be moot if there are no new materials to copy.

Conclusion

> Without the empowerment gained through music, it is impossible to keep
> the past alive in the present, or to recognize and respond to the realities that
> are transforming the present into the future. (Blum et al. 1991: 9).

Modern Vietnamese music has survived and evolved through the years. It
has done so because a brave few individuals decided they would create,
produce, and disseminate music transnationally despite the political and
social pressures from Viet Nam and the Vietnamese American community
in the United States. Furthermore, though U.S. policies strictly regulated
contact between Vietnamese Americans and those in Viet Nam in the early
years following the war, transnational music flows continued. Music culture transcends the boundaries of nation-states not only because of politics but because of musicians who create products which those in the diaspora and in Viet Nam want to consume. Viet Nam's influence runs very
much the same way. To protect communist ideology, Vietnamese governments made every attempt to block pre-1975 music, which they deemed
foreign or foreign-influenced. Government restrictions continued after reunification but so did people's desire to listen to different kinds of music,
including music from the *Viet Kieu* communities.

The Vietnamese American community's need to maintain a culture of
anticommunism and hold on to its memories of a glorious past also
greatly affected *Viet Kieu* music creations and production. Anticommunist
ideology not only added to the "culture in a bubble" phenomenon, it also
inhibited open collaboration between musicians in Viet Nam and those in
the diaspora. But while Vietnamese Americans complied with the dictates
of the anticommunist groups and its ideology, they were curious about
music being created in Viet Nam. Businesspeople also saw opportunities
for the expansion of musical products in the *Viet Kieu* market in the
United States. Increased travel and connections with the new culture productions in Viet Nam also exposed the *Viet Kieu* to musical changes.

These transnational culture flows cloud the distinction between *Viet
Kieu* and Vietnamese music. I believe continued collaboration and support are needed in both places to create a new blend of music. Furthermore, reacting to the sometimes static and formulaic *Viet Kieu* music,
artists in the Vietnamese diaspora have formed networks to share their
creations outside the old *Viet Kieu* groups. B-Flat, which is one such net-

work, offers an alternative space for original creations. The future for diasporic and Vietnamese music looks bright. All these different sites and styles of music production will give the consumer more choices in the future. *Viet Kieu* music connections will become more diverse because of the transnational links to Viet Nam.

NOTES

1. I choose to use the term *Viet Kieu* to refer to (1) the overseas Vietnamese population; (2) the Vietnamese living outside Viet Nam who have received most of their formal education abroad and continue to work outside Viet Nam; (3) Vietnamese who have adopted another citizenship but who live, study, work in, or visit Viet Nam. In using *Viet Kieu,* I intend no disrespect to those who take special offense to the term. However, I find it linguistically correct and useful in my work to apply this term to the overseas Vietnamese population.

2. Viet Nam's civil war in the 1950s and the involvement of the superpowers at the time, namely, the United States in the south and U.S.S.R. and China in the north, caused decades of instability in Southeast Asia. The second Indochina War or Viet Nam War, as it was called, ended with the defeat of the South Viet Nam military and saw the start of the largest exodus of refugees (125,000) from Viet Nam on April 30, 1975. By 1999, approximately 1.75 million Vietnamese had resettled in numerous Eastern and Western countries. Of these, the United States took some 900,000, while Canada, Australia, and France resettled over 500,000. Additionally, 250,000 Vietnamese were permanently resettled in China and another 100,000 left for other resettlement countries (INS 2001). As of December 2000, one of Viet Nam's agencies estimated that there were approximately 2.7 million Vietnamese nationals living in more than one hundred countries and territories worldwide, including more than 1 million in the United States (*VNA*, December 4, 2000). According to the U.S. 2000 Census, the Vietnamese number 1.1 million in the country. In California the number is 447,032 of 33,871,648 residents or 1.3 percent of the state's population. In the Bay Area Vietnamese Americans number over 150,000, and in the city of San Jose alone, they account for 8.8 percent of the population or 78,842 (2000 Census).

3. Do Chi Thien, one of the founders of the band, gave the band the name 17th Parallel. Using the metaphor of the demarcation point between northern Viet Nam and southern Viet Nam created by the Geneva Accords, Thien wanted to show that the band was at a midway point incorporating musical styles from different influences (Do Chi Thien).

4. Chanson is defined as a French song, usually secular, such as a satirical cabaret song of the twentieth century.

5. *Vietnamese music, female producer.* Personal interview, Sai Gon, Viet Nam, February 9, 2001. My translation.

Vietnamese popular music has a number of informal categories. Though widely used by music makers and consumers alike, there is no consensus on the true definitions of each. I identify the following categories:

1. *nhac sang*: Music created by trained composers and singers. It tends to sound like jazz.
2. *nhac sen*: Easy listening songs with simplistic lyrics and soft melodies.
3. *nhac que huong, nhac binh dan*: Songs with a folk-country appeal.
4. *nhac tre*: Pop songs mostly targeted to youth.
5. *nhac quay, nhac rock*: Fast-paced rock and roll-inspired music.

6. *Vietnamese journalist for Tuoi Tre newspapers and cultural critic.* Personal interview, Sai Gon, Viet Nam, January 31, 2001. My translation.

7. Because popular music is a relatively new phenomenon in Viet Nam, many of those who began the movement in Viet Nam are still alive today. In fact, because the memories of this period are so fresh in the minds of these pioneers, they have successfully continued producing and evolving outside Viet Nam.

8. *Vietnamese American, founder of Paris by Night.* Orange County, June 16, 2000. My translation.

9. For the younger *Viet Kieu* generation—those who were raised or born in the United States—listening to melancholy music is not so appealing. Like other young people, they are attracted to mainstream popular music or renditions of that music in the Vietnamese American music scene.

10. *Vietnamese American musician and writer.* Personal interview, Oakland, California, August 15, 2001.

11. *Director of Asia Trung Tam, Vietnamese American music production house.* Phone interview, Orange County, California, June 27, 2001. My translation.

12. *Vietnamese American founder and owner of Kim Loi Music Productions.* San Jose, California, December 9, 2000. My translation.

13. *Vietnamese American musician.* Phone interview, Orange County, November 18, 2000. My translation.

14. In the 1990s, mainstream ballads and rap joined the list of favorites. Even though music performances included popular western songs, the specific favorites of the community, Vietnamese standards, and some new compositions gave Vietnamese American music a distinctive flair.

15. It is with some irony that by the mid-1990s love was one of the few themes that composers were allowed to liberally write about and singers perform, though sex was still considered taboo (Nguyen Thanh Duc).

16. *Middle-aged Vietnamese woman who later immigrated to the United States.* Personal interviews, April 5, 1993, Sai Gon, Viet Nam; February 29, 2001, San Jose, California. My translation.

17. For many *Viet Kieu* musicians, the turning point where they began to take post-1975 Vietnamese music seriously began with the release of My Linh's CD *Tieng Hat My Linh* [The Voice of My Linh]. One song in particular stuck out, "Tren Dinh Phu Van" [On Phu Van Peak]. This song was unique because it took many traditional elements—the instrumentation and vocal styling—and put them in a modern context. *Viet Kieu* musicians had not yet attempted this fusion with such wondrous results.

18. Richard Marosi may be credited for having referred to the new popularity of Vietnamese music in the Vietnamese American communities as "Vietnam's musical invasion." This phrase appeared in his article, "Vietnam's Musical Invasion," *Los Angeles Times*, August 8, 2000.

19. *Vietnamese music, female producer.* Personal interview, Sai Gon, Viet Nam, February 9, 2001.

20. For example, the government decrees 87/CP and 88/CP of 1995 were enacted to regulate "the business and circulation of films, video tapes/discs, audio tapes/discs, and sales and rentals of publications; cultural activities and services in public areas; advertising, writing and installation of sign boards."

21. PBN videos are chronologically numbered as they are released. Forty means it is the fortieth video in the PBN video series.

22. The National Front for the Liberation of Viet Nam (NFLVN), also known as *Mat Tran Quoc Gia Thong Nhat Giai Phong Viet Nam* or the Front, is an anticommunist group created after the Viet Nam War by Vietnamese exiles (most from the former South Viet Nam military) with the express purpose of retaking Viet Nam by force or any other means.

23. *Popular Vietnamese American male singer.* Personal interview, Sai Gon, Viet Nam, June 2, 2002.

24. Though Vietnamese entertainers were unable to perform in the United States until 2000, they were able to do so in countries such as Germany and Australia years before.

25. For example, a musician who works in the music industry in southern California told me about the collaborative effort that had gone into creating the so-called "Vietnamese music invasion." For instance, one of the earliest and most influential artists of this "invasion" sold her music to a *Viet Kieu* producer to be remastered and distributed in the United States and Viet Nam. In fact, more than one music house owns the copyright to Vietnamese music. Such collaboration has occurred since at least 1995 and possibly earlier. This is not made public because music producers do not want to be accused of being communists.

26. *Popular Vietnamese female singer.* Personal interview, Berkeley, California, October 30, 2002.

27. *Viet Kieu sound engineer and musician.* Personal interview, Oakland, California, April 2000.

REFERENCES

Barr, Cameron W. 1997. "Vietnam's New War: 'Social Evils," *Christian Science Monitor,* September 24, 1997.

Blum, Stephen, Philip V. Bolman, and Daniel M. Neumen. 1991. Introduction to *Ethnomusicology and Modern Music History,* Stephen Blum, Philip V. Bolman, and Daniel M. Neumen eds. Urbana: University of Illinois Press.

Chan, Tran. 2000. *Vietnam Insight* editor (the Front), phone interview by the author, March 11.

Gerke, Frank, and Bui Tuyen. 2000. "Popular Music in Vietnam," December 17, 2000. http://www.hkn.de/english/culture/1999/vietnam/Ezine/Popmusic.

Gibbs, Jason. 1996. "A Musical Instrument Workshop in Hanoi." *Experimental Musical Instruments* 12:1.

———. 1998. "Whac Tien Chien: The Origins of Vietnamese Popular Songs." *Destination Vietnam: Things Asian: Explore the Cultures of Asia* (June/July).

Glasser, Ruth. 1995. *My Music Is Not My Flag: Puerto Rican Music and Their New York Communities, 1997–1940.* Berkely: University of California Press.

Lull, James, and Roger Wallis. 1992. "The Best of West Vietnam." In *Popular Music and Communication,* James Lull, ed., 217–231 Newbury Park, CA: Sage.

Marosi, Richard. 2000. "Vietnam's Musical Invasion: The Popularity of New Songs from the Homeland Has Widened a Political and Cultural Divide between Young People and Older Generations Who See It as Mere Propaganda." *Los Angeles Times,* August 8.

Philip, Taylor. 2000. "Music as a 'Neocolonial Poison' in Post-War Southern Vietnam." *Crossroads: An Interdisciplinary Journal of Southeast Asian Studies* 14:1, 99–131.

Reyes, Adelaida. 1999a. "From Urban Area to Refugee Camp: How One Thing Leads to Another." *Journal of the Society for Ethnomusicology* 43:2 (Summer/Spring): 1–10.

———. 1999b. *Songs of the Caged, Songs of the Free: Music and the Vietnamese Refugees Experience.* Philadelphia: Temple University Press.

This essay originally appeared as "Making Vietnamese Music Transnational: Sounds of Home, Resistance and Change," in Amerasia Journal 29:1 (2003). Reprinted with permission by the UCLA Asian American Studies Center Press.

Chapter 3

Planet Bollywood
Indian Cinema Abroad

Jigna Desai

India, the largest producer of feature films globally, produces almost twice as many films as Hollywood. Bollywood, Bombay's Hindi-language cinema, is not only nationally popular, but also one of the most important in the world. Bollywood is a global cinema that positions itself against the hegemony of Hollywood. Unknown to many Westerners, Bollywood films have been familiar for many decades to viewers in the Middle East, East and Southeast Asia, and East Africa. More recently, Indian films have become increasingly popular in transnational migrant and diasporic South Asian communities. As part of world communications, these films produce economic, cultural, and social ties between the Indian homeland and its diaspora.

Indian films have been successful in gaining the attention of not only the first generation, but also second- and even some third-generation viewers. Popular Bollywood films like *Taal, Lagaan,* and *Kabhi Khushi Kabhie Gham* (*K3G*) have grossed from one to three million dollars in U.S. markets alone. In Britain, they have sometimes surpassed the box office receipts of Hollywood films.[1] Currently the largest market for films outside South Asia is in the United Kingdom, the Middle East, the United States, Australia, and Canada, all locations with large migrant populations.[2] The overall popularity of films has been fostered by South Asian migrant audiences viewing them at home (via video cassettes, satellite television, and DVDs) and in theaters. Films, televised serials, and music in many languages, including Hindi, Punjabi, Tamil, and Telegu, have increasingly circulated in the diaspora and elsewhere. Cultural products, especially films in their many forms and live performances (variety shows with Bollywood performers), greatly contribute to first-generation migrants "staying in touch with the homeland," and also lead to exposure and interest among second-generation South Asians in the diaspora.

The popularity of Bollywood films among second-generation South Asian Americans is a recent phenomenon. Indian films have been present in U.S. South Asian communities at least since the 1970s. However, for the most part these films were popular with first-generation migrants but less so with their second-generation children. In the mid-nineties, a number of factors led to an increasing consumption of and interest in Indian films abroad. The political economy of globalization facilitated flows of technology, people, and cultural commodities, thereby creating specific pathways by which film productions from India became available to expanding migrant and other populations in the Middle East, Africa, Europe, Australia, Asia, and North America. Furthermore, with increasing remittances and investment opportunities in India due to the liberalization of its economy, many diasporic communities became potentially more significant to the political economy of India. I argue that this led to shifts in the cinematic representations of the diaspora as well as the popularity of these films in the diaspora. Consequently, these representations appealed to second-generation viewers.

In the United States, the circulation of Bollywood cultural products has resulted in the popularity of Hindi cinema with second-generation South Asian Americans who are becoming acquainted with it for the first time. The impact of the Bollywood film and music industry in the 1990s has created a new language of cultural identity and affiliation among second-generation youth in the United States. Focusing on Indian films and their consumption, this essay attempts to keep the cultural texts and the meanings and uses associated with them in constant tension. Consequently, I argue that cinema not only reflects and produces relations between diasporas and nation-states, but that it also significantly contributes to processes of diasporic identity formation, and thus is central to thinking through pleasure and power and how they impinge on the diasporic constructions of South Asian American subjectivity. As part of a larger project linking research on the cultural politics of representation in Bollywood cinema and its reception and consumption by second-generation South Asian American youth, this essay is based on interviews with approximately sixteen South Asian American youth from New York and New Jersey during the fall of 2001.[3]

Films

References to Bollywood appear in many forms in U.S. popular culture, ranging from music videos and television to films (for example, *Ghost World, Moulin Rouge,* and *The Guru*). Nevertheless, this popular cinema is often unappealing to viewers unfamiliar with its content and aesthetic forms that derive from diverse Indian sources, including Parsi theater and Hindu performance. A dominant form of Indian cinema is the *masala* (mixture) film. These three-hour films are often identifiable by their all-encompassing forms that include elements of comedy, (melo)drama, action, romance, and music that do not fit Western aesthetic expectations. In particular, the recent increased emphasis on elaborate and often extradiegetic song and dance numbers, usually six to eight per film, often pose difficulties for Western viewers. Other Indian films, such as those of Satayajit Ray, have been visible in the West through the category of high culture and art cinema in the United States, but popular Indian cinema, for the most part, has been seen as kitschy and unrefined.

According to most scholars, Indian films were made as early as 1899 with the first Indian feature—the mythological *Raja Harishchandra* by Dhundiraj Govind Phalke—appearing in 1913. Since the 1970s and 1980s there has been an increased global consumption of Indian films in and out of the diaspora. Even during the early years of Indian independence in the 1950s when Indian cinema was primarily a national cinema, it was a popular non-Western cinema and circulated not only in the diaspora but also in such places as Russia and China. Nevertheless, the cinematic representation of the South Asian diaspora in Hollywood or Bollywood is recent. Appearing on the margins of a few Bollywood films, nonresident Indians (NRIs) were typically depicted as corrupt and Westernized. There were few depictions of the South Asian diaspora prior to the recent spate of Bollywood films and the emergence of films made by and about South Asian diasporans such as Gurinder Chadha and Nisha Ganetra.

Located in a precarious position between Bollywood and Hollywood, diasporic films[4] attempt to translate and marry elements of both Hollywood and Bollywood primarily for viewers in the economic North. For example, British filmmaker Gurinder Chadha's next project is *Bride and Prejudice* starring Bollywood star Aishwarya Rai, coupled with an unnamed Hollywood actor. Inspired by the success of foreign language sensation *Crouching Tiger, Hidden Dragon* and South Asian diasporic films in

English like Mira Nair's *Monsoon Wedding* and Chadha's *Bend It Like Beckham*, recently Bollywood films like *Lagaan* and *Devdas* have attempted a crossover into Western markets. Bollywood cinema itself has sought to reach Western filmgoers by capitalizing on its presence in countries with South Asian migrant viewers. In England, Hindi films have consistently dominated the foreign film market due to the large presence of South Asians. This crossover success hinges on luring with diasporic and Indian films not only first-generation South Asian fans into theaters, but also second-generation South Asians and non–South Asians.

The Indian film industry is well poised to produce films that will appeal to multiple audiences. Frequently, different films are popular in India than in the diaspora. For example, *Ghadar,* an anti-Pakistani and anti-Muslim film, was immensely popular in India, breaking box office records, while its patriotic narrative seemed of little interest to many diasporic viewers. The Hindi film industry distributes films based on a territory model that divides India into six major territories, with the overseas market (primarily the United States and United Kingdom) counting as a seventh territory. Generally, the significance of this seventh territory fluctuates as a result of an advantageous currency rate rather than the number of viewers, with certain types of films, such as romances and family dramas, doing better than others in the diaspora. Hence, the Indian film industry is characterized by flexibility in its ability to target different viewers and audiences by making and circulating a wide range of films that will appeal to cab drivers in New York and rickshaw drivers in Mumbai as well as to second-generation engineers and agricultural laborers.

By the mid 1990s, the Indian film industry was beginning to seriously attend to the presence of the diaspora not only in its accounting ledgers, but also in the reformulated national imaginary. Until recently, Bollywood films frequently employed the West (for example, Switzerland) as a beautiful and exotic foreign backdrop documenting and displaying the production costs of a film. But seldom did the films concern themselves with the subjectivities, experiences, or oppressions of those who lived elsewhere. In fact, whenever diasporic characters did appear, it was often as a foil to the "heroic" non-Westernized protagonist. They often represented the dangers of Westernization resulting from simple physical displacement from the homeland. These earlier films featured characters who had lost their connections to India, its "traditions," and their families by virtue of their presence in the decadent West. Thus, NRIs were often depicted as immoral, corrupt, and unchaste, that is, as westernized in films such as *Purab aur*

Paschim. From about 1995 to the current moment (2005), Bollywood has concerned itself with producing films with diasporic audiences in mind.

Whereas diasporic films such as *Masala, Mississippi Masala, My Beautiful Laundrette, Chutney Popcorn, East Is East,* and *Bend It Like Beckham* undertook the "burden of representation" in response to the lack of diasporic experiences in films, recent Indian films such as *DDLJ* and *Aa Ab Laut Chalen* have sought to identify and fill that void by constructing narratives that tell the stories of those who are no longer in India. Bollywood narratives of diasporic experiences assume that nostalgia is a central driving force for consumption and viewing; they also assume that cultural retention (loss of culture) due to deterritorialization and displacement is a central concern for migrant viewers. Unlike South Asian diasporic films, they are rarely concerned with issues of location, racism, or citizenship faced by those in the diaspora, concentrating instead on representing and reinforcing the transnational ties between the homeland and the diaspora through the maintenance of "traditional" Indian values. Consequently, seeking to appeal to diasporic audiences, NRI characters now appear in Bollywood films as heroic and uncontaminated. The film narrative has shifted from depicting the West as an always contaminating and corrupting place to being just another location inhabited by the Indian nation. In other words, displacement no longer necessarily functions as a marker of loss of Indianness. Some of the films effectively attempt to detach national "culture" (values, traditions, and identities) from territory, thus reincorporating the diaspora into the Indian nation.

The consumption of Indian films abroad has had a large impact on the film industry itself, as the industry has noted the profitability of the diasporic markets in comparison to the domestic and international (nondiasporic) ones. Specific economic, political, and social connections between the diaspora and the nation-state have been frequently imagined by Bollywood. In these recent reformulations, the deterritorialized members of the nation became imagined not only as an integral part of the nation, but also as the overseas saviors of the Indian economy. Cultural narratives and identities attesting to such connections were fostered by state policies and popular discourses, including those present in Bollywood cinema.[5] In its recent discourses about dual citizenship, the state has imagined and constructed the diaspora, constituting India as the spiritual home of the fragmented and deterritorialized part of the nation living abroad. These discourses portray the nation as able to negotiate these distant but powerful transnational communities located primarily in the West by attempting to (re)incorporate them into the fold of its cultural imaginary. Thus diasporas are constituted by the nation not so much as outsiders to Indian culture, but inversely, as insiders removed. The diaspora appears central to the construction of national identity due to its transmission of transnational economic and cultural capital in favor of the state. Moreover, this capital enables the diaspora to affect the conception, production, and distribution of Indian films.

This reincorporation into the imagined community of Indian is also significant to understanding why we might want to understand these films and their consumption as diasporic rather than immigrant, where the latter implies a disavowal and detachment from the place of migration in favor of acculturation and assimilation to the place of residence.[6] On the other hand, the diaspora suggests the possibility of transnational affiliations to the homeland. The "classic" definition of the diaspora, based on the Jewish model, presumes that dispersal is due to forced exile from a homeland to which a "people" desire to return eventually. Recent usages of the term are less stringent and refer simply to the migration of an ethnic community, albeit with some connection to the perceived homeland. In my usage, the term diaspora implies and reflects the multiple and complex economic, cultural, social, linguistic, and political transnational relations between migrant communities and their homelands. Cinema is a central feature of these relations.

In viewing the South Asian diaspora as an active and lucrative market as well as necessary investors, the Bollywood film industry now reimagines NRIs as deterritorialized cultural citizens. Recent films have emphasized the possibility of "maintaining one's Indianness or Indian values" in the material West. Many Bollywood films engage in this specific contestation; they attempt to wrestle with the question of what it means to be Indian, pedagogically illustrating this through a conflict between a good NRI and a bad NRI. In fact, recent films such as *Pardes, Taal, Dilwale Dulhaniya Le Jayenge, Kuch Kuch Hota Hai, Mohabbetein, Yaadein, Aa Ab Laut Chalen, Kaho Na Pyaar Hai,* and *Kabhi Khushi Kabhie Gham* all feature some NRI characters who remain "Indian at heart" while being Western in terms of wealth.[7] Many of the films specifically highlight the Western designer clothing, palatial dwellings, and expensive sports cars of the characters and their high consumerism. They suggest that it is possible to be in the West and be Indian, a narrative that is of significance to not only first-generation, but also second-generation South Asian American viewers. Furthermore, this portrayal corresponds well to the discourses of the nation-state that also herald the NRI. Almost without exception NRIs are now portrayed as sometimes wealthier than Indians in India but no different culturally from them. Indianness is now determined less by geopolitical location than by the performance ("maintenance") of cultural and "traditional Indian values" that encapsulate the "real India."

Much has been written on past and contemporary Bollywood and Indian vernacular films and their relevance to Indian nationalism. The provocative work of Madhav Prasad (2000), Ashish Rajadhyaksha (1994), and Sumita Chakravarty (1993) locates Indian cinema at the center of the formation of the nation. Additionally, Rachel Dwyer's (2000) recent scholarship explicates the role of cinema as the dominant form of Indian public culture, in the formation of the culture of the cosmopolitan middle class in India. Furthermore, my earlier project, *Beyond Bollywood* (2004) focuses on South Asian diasporic cinema rather than on Bollywood and Indian films abroad. In relation to the Indian media, Patricia Uberoi (2001) and Purnima Mankekar (1999b) have probed the general viewing practices of Indian audiences, while Marie Gillespie (1995) and more recently Rajinder Dudrah (2002) examine the consumption and viewing practices of British South Asians. These types of analyses have barely begun to be considered in the case of South Asian Americans and their consumption of Indian films. Very few scholars have investigated the recent emergence of representations of the diaspora within Indian cinema and their relevance to Indian and diasporic nationalism.[8]

Therefore, in analyzing these films, it is necessary to go beyond describing the ways in which diasporic locations such as the United States, United Kingdom, and Europe are imagined by the films, and to understand and explicate how the diaspora functions in the formation and imagination of Indian national identity. A larger analysis of the ways in which Bollywood imagines and represents the Indian diaspora, in particular the population designated as nonresident Indians (NRIs) in relation to its political, social, and economic contexts is required. Furthermore, scholars must also recognize that films and viewing practices go beyond analyses that focus primarily on nationalism and national identities.

Indian and South Asian Identities

For many, Indian films have provided the language of a shared South Asian identity in diaspora. Across different diasporic locations, in many sites, Bollywood has articulated the "South Asianness" that is common and necessary to formulating imagined communities. In terms of second-generation South Asian Americans, it fosters social belonging, familial connections, transnational ties, linguistic fluency, and cultural knowledge. South Asian American social norms require that cultural authenticity and fluency be performed for social belonging. One primary way to indicate this is through the consumption of Bollywood films. The films are often read as cultural capital marking authentic Indianness in the service of constructing South Asian American identities in the diaspora. In these cases, the viewing of films is both a performative and pedagogic act, one in which South Asian Americans learn what it means to be Indian and South Asian American, and simultaneously perform their South Asian American identities.

Of course, the shared consumption of commodities is a marker of community belonging and membership in many youth cultures. Within South Asian American youth culture, it is not only the consumption of films that is significant, but also the consumption and production of other related transnational commodities such as (film) music, (film) fashion, and food. However, I maintain that film is unique in the ways it constructs a shared South Asian diasporic identity. Indian films have a significant impact on second-generation South Asian American youth, even on those who seldom watch films, because they provide much of the vocabulary for understanding culture, authenticity, the nation, and cultural difference.

In the popular Indian American film *American Desi*, for example, the male protagonist is depicted as an assimilated or white-washed Indian American who has changed his name from Krishna to Kris and avoids socializing with other Indian Americans, especially those he designates as Fresh Off the Boats (FOBs). In the film labeled a "coconut"—brown on the outside, white on the inside—Krishna is portrayed as denying his Indianness by refusing to join the South Asian American student organization, eat Indian food, speak an Indian language, and watch or appreciate Bollywood films. While one of his roommates hangs a poster of the Bollywood actress Rekha on the wall, Krishna disavows any connection to such nonsense. Specifically, his inability to comprehend the language, aesthetics, or sentiment of Hindi films marks him as someone who shuns his culture and therefore cannot "get the girl." In one particular scene where he has volunteered to watch Bollywood films with his romantic interest to select songs and themes for the upcoming student association fête, Krishna alienates her further by ridiculing the films, their musical sequences, and their melodrama. Later, he participates in student association cultural events to prove himself worthy of the relationship. Desire for an Indian, or "desi," woman provides the motivation for his transformation and integration into South Asian American social communities.

American Desi posits that consuming Bollywood films is a sign of cultural belonging for South Asian Americans. The Bollywood films are a venue to learn not only what is Indian, but more importantly what is Indian American. Thus viewing Indian films has performative and pedagogical functions. *American Desi* constructs a Hindu normative world in which all South Asians, including minorities (here, Muslims and Sikhs), are united in part by their consumption of Bollywood films. For second-generation youth, ethnonational and religious identities do not conflict with the formation of the larger identity of a South Asian American articulated in the language of Bollywood cinema.

As several scholars have noted, college is a crucial time for identity development, especially among migrant and racial minority communities. It is also a time in which the ways in which youth produce and consume culture shift and change. In studies of South Asian American racial and ethnic identities, scant attention has been paid to the consumption and impact of one of the most influential cultural media of South Asian diaspora in the United States, namely, film. Of course, the cinema is not the only site in which identity issues are worked out. Music and religion play significant roles, as do other forms of cultural community such as student organizations, as Sunaina Maira (2002) and Khyati Joshi (unpublished manuscript, no date) have argued. Films, however, play a central role in identifying what is desi about desi cultural values for many South Asian American youth. Moreover, youth are producing new identities and new meanings that are shaped by and reshape the cultural politics of South Asian America through their practices of meaning making and consumption. These youth have created elaborate public spaces and cultures that engage the politics of their locations. Maira writes that many produce discourses that suggest that they reformulate what might have been seen as bifurcated or binary worlds into a third or hybrid space. She notes that nostalgia and cool are critical categories that mark the significant boundaries of authenticity and group identification in much of second-generation South Asian American discourses.

As in *American Desi,* watching films signifies membership and belonging for many college-age South Asian Americans, as it marks shared racial and ethnic identity in the United States. Consuming Indian films is what makes them South Asian American, even for some who are not Indian. Many of the respondents in this study indicated that they began to socialize primarily with other South Asian American youth when they entered college and became involved with South Asian American student groups. For Hamid, a Muslim male who is Pakistani Canadian and attends an elite private university, those who constitute much of his social community are the members of South Asian student organizations that he joined for the first time after he entered college.[9] Earlier in his life, he had socialized primarily with white Canadians and found Bollywood films stupid, preferring to play his Gameboy while his parents watched the films. But he reevaluated his position once he joined the college groups and experienced a gap in his social exchanges. Hamid wondered what he was missing out on when his friends talked about the movies and he did not want to "be left out or left behind." In contrast to other subjects who prefer to watch the films alone, for Hamid watching films is a public and social endeavor in which he discusses and argues about their meaning dialogically with others, participating in the process of imagining India as a shared social act. Watching and discussing the films with his male South Asian American friends provided him a sense of belonging. In the South Asian diaspora, this rhetoric of cultural difference articulated in gendered terms reemerges most commonly in relation to ethnic and racial identities.[10]

While these films are Indian, for some South Asian American second-generation youth, they create the means for a broader South Asian identity. Hamid comments that watching Indian films gives him a connection to Pakistan, as he does not differentiate between Pakistani and Indian culture. He indicates his awareness of the seeming incongruity of this comment by saying, "I like identifying with the culture by watching Indian movies. He [his Pakistani friend] started laughing. And I said why are you laughing. I said that they were the same country forty years ago." For Hamid, Bollywood cinema is neither Hindu nor normatively Indian but signifies a general South Asian culture to which he feels strongly connected through the consumption of the films. Rather than create distinct South Asian identities, Hamid binds more tightly together the idea of a shared South Asianness that is characterized by cultural difference, not internally within South Asia, but between South Asia and the West. He finds refuge in the unchanging cultural difference he associates with Indian films and South Asia.

The South Asian cultural traditions depicted in the films are identified with the time before independence and partition, thereby creating an insider status for cultural communities. Furthermore, these traditions and values are read as markers of cultural difference from the West. This pan-national and pan-religious South Asian American identity is frequently mobilized in opposition to Western identification or assimilation. In both *American Desi* and participants' responses, South Asian American or desi identity signifies difference from dominant white American cultural norms. The tradition versus Western binary underlying many of the participants' responses has its roots in colonial discourses and anticolonial Indian nationalisms.

Like Hamid, Vijay Mishra argues that Bollywood cinema constructs an "Indian diaspora of shared cultural idioms" (2002: 238). In contrast to Mishra and *American Desi,* I suggest that the consumption of the diaspora is not so unified or unitary and that differences within South Asian diaspora communities are significant and cannot be erased by a solitary understanding of the "Indian diaspora." Moreover, lack of attention to gender, sexual, linguistic, regional, religious, or ethnic differences reifies the North Indian (sometimes Punjabi) Hindu normativity that underlies the construction of India in Bollywood cinema. Bollywood's heteronormative and Hindu-normative vision of India and the Indian diaspora ignores these significant other differences.

Bollywood films, despite their heterogeneity, are frequently Hindu-, Hindi-, North Indian-, and heteronormative. Thus, they construct a very particular version of India usually unquestioned by South Asian Americans. However, several second-generation youth indicated very thoughtful analyses of the normativities and hegemony of Bollywood cinema. Ginder, a second-generation American Sikh woman at a large state university, was critical of the Hindu supremacy of the films, especially in relation to depictions of Sikhs in India.[11]

> Punjabi movies don't really come out much but in Hindi movies you'll always see Sikhs as like the comic relief, just the stupid guy, the butt of all the jokes. The Sikh culture as well as the Hindu culture, they are sort of blending. And so I can't say they really misrepresent them, but they don't put an effort to show them in a good light either. When you have a movie like *Mission Kashmir* with the one Sardar [Sikh] in it, who's like one of the soldiers. He's the guy who's scared shitless and he's peeing in his pants. . . . That bothers me . . . when you know that they have such a good tradition, good military tradition, the one Sikh in the movie you represent him like that. You show him as being a coward when every other soldier in the

movie is the brave one and is taking all the risks and doesn't care about dying.

Jagjit, a second-generation Sikh American male at an elite private university, also commented on this particular scene in *Mission Kashmir,* which suggests that the film and its depiction of Sikhs has had a large impact. He observes that Sikhs in India are an oppressed minority and that these films play a significant role in that oppression:

> I've seen many movies where Sikhs are portrayed, I'd say like blacks were in . . . the Jim Crow period of the United States, . . . as sort of the scapegoats, the people to make fun of. . . . The people are just the losers and you know, they're the weirdos on the side. . . . And that's probably been my biggest gripe with the movies. And same with my brother, and my dad too. We all see that the more recent movies, like for example there's this movie called [*Mission Kashmir*] or something where there is this Sikh soldier I believe who is like standing on a landmine and he like pisses in his pants or something, right? And that really hurts the Sikh community, big time. Because he's like the only Sikh in the whole movie. And he turns out to be a complete loser. And nobody in the whole—what is it, one billion people in India?—knows who these Sikhs are. They just know that they're some minority group and we're immediately getting a horrible rep as portrayed in this movie.

Significantly, Jagjit compares the portrayal of Sikhs with the racial oppression experienced by blacks in the United States when describing how he sees the representation of Sikhs in dominant Hindi cinema. Marie Gillespie (1995) in her study of British Asians writes that viewers tend not to participate in the communal or fundamentalist politics of the homeland nation-state. Her reading suggests that diasporic viewers do not have differentiated spectatorships regardless of other kinds of difference in relation to a generic diasporic South Asian consumption.

Jagjit and Ginder indicate quite the opposite, suggesting that second-generation South Asian American youth, especially those who are a religious minority (in this case Sikh) in India, view films with these differences in mind. The participants' responses indicate less interest in furthering communalism in the sense of claiming a homeland, but clearly refer to these politics. They view these films with little nostalgia or as articulations of a shared *Indian* cultural idiom. In fact, quite the opposite seemed to

occur, in that the films' negative portrayals of Sikhs reinforce their understanding of the oppression suffered by Sikhs in India and encourage their
distance from an identification as Indian or Indian diasporic. Instead,
both their responses indicate that they have strong conceptions of a racialized ethnoreligious Sikh identity that is threatened by Indian national narratives.

Conclusion: Nostalgic Viewing

In its song "Brimful of Asha," the British Asian pop music group Corner-
shop associates pleasure, comfort, and hope with the diasporic viewing of
Bollywood cinema:

> There's dancing
> Behind movie scenes
> Behind the movie scenes
> Sadi Rani
> She's the one that keeps the dream alive
> from the morning
> past the evening
> to the end of the night
> Brimful of Asha on the 45
> Well it's a brimful of Asha on the 45

Suggesting that films and film music construct and satisfy structures of
feeling identified as nostalgia for the homeland, the lyrics affirm that
"dreams" of everyday struggle, of comfort, and of belonging are kept alive
by the musical recordings of film musicians and singers such as Asha
Bhosle and Lata Mangeshkar. In the song, these female singers are
personified as maternal figures of the absent motherland who provide migrant communities sustenance in the struggle for survival and hopes of return. Many assume that the films provide comfort or familiarity as emblems of national homeland culture to homogeneous audiences who consume them nostalgically.

U.S. and other South Asian diasporas with increasing capital are influ-
encing the production and distribution of films, as the film industry recognizes that diasporas are no longer peripheral markets and the state seeks
further investment and remittances from deterritorialized nationals. The

rapidly expanding Indian capitalist economy profits from the diasporic audiences who in turn maintain economic connections by reifying Indian culture. Critiques of diasporic consumption suggest that NRIs have sequestered the film industry from its properly national moorings in service of its own fantasies. Some films, like *3KG*, with their emphasis on "loving and honoring family" as the primary traits of being Indian seem made primarily with the overseas market in mind. These fantasies consist of Hindu-normative paeans to the family as nation and are rampant in many films, not just *3KG*. In this sense, deterritorialized Indian identities are fostered through narratives of family and longing that are popular with youth. Thus, the consumption of films (and other media) is frequently seen as reuniting and healing the migrant deterritorialized nation and its homeland culture.

Additionally, the gender- and heteronormative narratives of the films are thought to appeal to diasporic audiences. The danger of Western contamination and corruption to the diasporic male is often staved off by the incorporation of the traditional and culturally authentic Indian woman. Thus, many of the narratives literally marry the diaspora to the nation by joining a male NRI protagonist with an Indian heroine. The heroines often embody Indianness and are charged with maintaining the loyalties and connections to nation, family, and culture for the men who might be separated from these concerns due to the need to make money in capitalist society.

The NRI viewer is presumed to watch Bollywood films in order to produce an idealized India that satisfies the needs less of the country "left behind" than those of the everyday. Hindi films are seen as providing narratives of desire and fantasy. Diasporic audiences, however, are assumed to be passive and nostalgic consumers of Bollywood cinema and televised serials who homogeneously desire one vision of India. Most viewers are seen to consume the films as prefabricated transnational commodities providing comforting and familiar emblems of normative social values neatly wrapped in packages of glossy celluloid.

Simple conceptions of nostalgic viewing have been offered but cannot and do not provide adequate explanations for consumption and reception. Some scholars have reductively suggested that Indian films bring together a linguistically and culturally diverse community. First-generation immigrants remain nostalgic for their home country, and these films—no matter what their quality—can be very emotionally satisfying. In most discourses of the diaspora, nostalgia, longing, and loss are central themes that define diasporic subjectivities and experiences. Assessing the impact and function of Indian cinema raises questions of viewership and consumption in much more complicated ways than these explanations suggest. However, while most analyses of the consumption of Indian cinema assume simple nostalgia as the primary impetus for viewing films, this essay suggests that this narrow and essentialist explanation has too long been used to describe heterogeneous, contradictory, and complex viewing practices. While nostalgia induced by physical displacement is commonly used to explain the popularity of these transnational cultural products among first-generation migrants abroad, this explanation does not interrogate what the viewer is nostalgic about nor does it distinguish between forms of nostalgia that characterize South Asian diasporas, especially in relation to other categories of social difference such as gender, sexuality, class, religion, and generation. Thus, more attention must be paid to the differentiated viewing and interpretative practices of South Asian Americans to examine what specific forms of nostalgia are produced and their relationship to Indian national filmic production.

NOTES

I thank Khyati Joshi, Shilpa Davé, Tasha Oren, and LeiLani Nishime for their helpful comments on this essay. The research was funded and supported by the University of Minnesota's President's Faculty Multicultural Research Award and single semester leave.

1. The British Film Institute provides detailed accounts in its annual *BFI Film and Television Handbook.*

2. See http://meadev.nic.in/media/films.htm and Vijay Mishra's *Bollywood Cinema.*

3. This fieldwork was done in collaboration with Asian American studies scholar Khyati Joshi. We conducted semistructured interviews. Additionally, we also did a limited amount of participant observation by attending youth activities such as cultural performances and dance events. The interview protocol followed a semistructured format, enabling us to build a conversation around a series of open-ended questions on formalized topic areas. Our questions reflected areas of interest to the research participants in an open and direct way.

4. I identify diasporic films as those films focused thematically on South Asian diaspora, especially those with South Asian diasporic writers and/or directors. Therefore, certain films (such as *The Sixth Sense, What's Cooking,* or *Elizabeth*) made by South Asian diasporic directors are marginalized in this discussion, while

others (such as *Seducing Maarya* made by Singaporean Canadian Hunt Hoe) could be included.

5. This project began as a counterpoint to my previous work in which I analyze constructions of the diaspora and the homeland in South Asian diasporic cinema. I became interested in the increasing popularity and impact of Indian films on diasporic groups and identities. I also began to note a shift in the way the Indian diaspora was being represented in Indian cinema and became interested in the construction of the diaspora by the homeland.

6. Cultural studies theorists have posited the diaspora as an oppositional theoretical concept in relation to the nation. In these formulations, the diaspora challenges the "natural" connection between a place and a people that is articulated in exclusionary national narratives.

7. Two directors, Subhash Ghai and Aditya Chopra, have been particularly influential in producing films that reflect these kinds of narrative shifts. Ghai's "trilogy," *Pardes, Taal, Yaadein,* and Chopra's *Mohabbetein, Dilwale Dulhaniya Le Jayenge,* and *Mujhse Dosti Karoge* have been highly popular.

8. Purnima Mankekar (1999a) and Vijay Mishra (2002) are two exceptions.

9. The pseudonyms chosen here reflect the gender, regional, ethnic, linguistic, and/or religious qualities of a person's name.

10. Although I do not have the space to elaborate here, I also posit that especially for those South Asian Americans who occupy a privileged class position, cultural difference is contested and negotiated through gender and sexual norms as well as food, religious, and linguistic practices. For working-class South Asian Americans, racial and ethnic identities are often more clearly visible and identifiable.

11. These representations and her learning about Sikh history have influenced Ginder's decision to work on human rights issues in the future.

WORKS CITED

Chakravarty, Sumita. *National Identity in Indian Popular Cinema 1947–1987.* Austin: University of Texas Press, 1993.

Desai, Jigna. *Beyond Bollywood: The Cultural Politics of South Asian Diasporic Films.* New York: Routledge, 2004.

Dudrah, R. K. "Vilayati Bollywood: Popular Hindi Cinema—Going and Diasporic South Asian Identity in Birmingham (UK)." *Javnost: Journal of European Institute for Culture and Communication* 9.1 (2002): 9–36.

Dwyer, Rachel. *All You Want Is Money, All You Need Is Love: Sex and Romance in Modern India.* New York: Cassell, 2000.

Gillespie, Marie. "Sacred Serials, Devotional Viewing, and Domestic Worship: A Case-Study in the Interpretation of Two TV Versions of the *Mahabharata* in a

Hindu Family in West London." In *To Be Continued . . . Soap Operas around the World*. Ed. Robert C. Allen. New York: Routledge, 1995, 354–80.

Joshi, Khyati. "Immigrant and Second-Generation Students and Religion." Unpublished manuscript, Fairleigh Dickinson University, n.d.

Maira, Sunaina. *Desis in the House: Indian American Youth Culture in New York City*. Philadelphia: Temple University Press, 2002.

Mankekar, Purnima. "Brides Who Travel: Gender, Transnationalism, and Nationalism in Hindi Film." *Positions: East Asia Cultures Critique* 7.3 (1999a): 731–61.

———. *Screening Culture, Viewing Politics: An Ethnography of Television, Womanhood, and Nation in Postcolonial India*. Durham: Duke University Press, 1999b.

Mishra, Vijay. *Bollywood Cinema: Temples of Desire*. New York: Routledge, 2002.

Prasad, M. Madhav. *Ideology of the Hindi Film: A Historical Construction*. Oxford: Oxford University Press, 2000.

Rajadhyaksha, Ashish, and Paul Willeman. *The Encyclopedia of Indian Cinema*. New Delhi: Oxford University Press, 1994.

Uberoi, Patricia. "Imagining the Family: An Ethnography of Viewing *Hum Aapke Hain Koun*." In *Pleasure and Nation: The History, Politics, and Consumption of Popular Culture in India*. Ed. Rachel Dwyer and Christopher Pinney. New York: Oxford University Press, 2001, 309–29.

Chapter 4

Model Minorities Can Cook
Fusion Cuisine in Asian America

Anita Mannur

In a recent episode of the Food Network show, *$40 a day,* the host, Rachel Ray, traverses the multiple culinary spaces of New York City to accomplish her goal of eating well without exceeding her daily budget of forty dollars. During the lunch portion of the show, Ray finds herself at *Tabla,* an upscale fusion Indian restaurant in midtown Manhattan. She opts to dine in the Bread Bar, at the lower level and less expensive section of the restaurant. On the show, chef Floyd Cardoz prepares a "Vegetable Frankie," an Indian-style burrito—spicy vegetables rolled up in an Indian flatbread that has been coated in egg and pan fried—showcasing the type of culinary fusion typically featured on *Tabla*'s menu. As Ray leaves the restaurant, ready to discover New York's next culinary treasure, she comments, "Chef Floyd Cardoz's menu is a perfect example of what is so great about New York dining—its ethnicity, its diversity." Rachel Ray's comments about *Tabla*'s version of fusion cuisine echoes common sentiments about this cuisine: the notion that it is truly "American" because it melds the immigrant palate to mainstream tastes.

If fusion is heralded as the democratic melding of cuisines, it is largely because it is a type of culinary multiculturalism that seems to challenge the rigidity of national boundaries and fixity. It is seen as the apparent tribute to successful multiculturalism in the United States—different ingredients come together to create something new—and it is often described as a fusion of different national styles, so that, for instance, one finds cookbooks or restaurants that offer ways to combine one national cuisine with another. With the emergence of new restaurants in Boston,

Memphis, New York, and New Orleans, Asian American fusion cuisines have been garnering more national attention and are celebrated as the cuisine of choice for cosmopolitan urban dwellers. A wave that swept through California and the west coast in the 1980s in the form of Japanese-French or Chinese-Italian-French restaurants, fusion cuisine began making a mark on east coast culinary culture in the 1990s. Beginning in the late 1990s and continuing into the early millennial years, fusion cuisine restaurants have been proliferating in metropolitan cities, and are now also becoming a presence in smaller U.S. towns and cities.

The burgeoning popularity of fusion cuisine in urban metropolises can be understood as part of the trend toward high-income gentrification within certain sectors of the urban landscape in global cities such as New York, London, and Tokyo. Saskia Sassen (1991) usefully explores the types of class differentials that sustain the demand for "cuisine," rather than "food" (341) in these urban spaces. She describes this emergent class of "spenders," high-income workers with a propensity to spend rather than save or invest their disposable income, as important players in the market for highly priced goods and services. She connects their consumption patterns and demand with the presence of an immigrant working class, often from Asia and the Caribbean, hypothesizing that "economic inequality in major cities has assumed distinct forms in the consumption structure, which in turn has a feedback effect on the organization of work and the types of jobs being created. There is an indirect creation of low-wage jobs induced by the presence of a highly dynamic sector with a polarized income distribution. It takes place in the sphere of consumption (or social reproduction)" (285). Sassen describes this type of "high-income gentrification" as labor intensive. "Behind the gourmet stores and specialty boutique," she argues, "lies an organization of the work process that differs from the self service supermarket and department store" (285). Gentrified classes in these cities that demand varied cuisines in restaurants exert a new type of pressure on the service sector that makes it necessary for Asian immigrants, for instance, to satisfy the demand of high-income gentrified workers located amid the "new cosmopolitan work culture" (341). In the late 1990s, fusion cuisine experienced a boom, with new restaurants opening their doors to restaurant goers demanding varied and innovative approaches to cuisine.

But as a new class of restaurant goers emerges, a new type of cooking show has also emerged on television. In particular, the Food Network has brought fusion cuisine into living rooms in Middle America, and nonurban centers. But the show that has made fusion cuisine an Asian American phenomenon is that hosted by Ming Tsai, the Asian American poster boy of cooking. Tsai's fusion cuisine show, *East Meets West*, has catapulted him into popularity, earning him accolades in the food and beverage industry as well as a large fan base. The far less visible but equally interesting on-screen presence of Padma Lakshmi, host of the show *Padma's Passport*, provides additional food for thought in conceptualizing the relationship between Asian Americans and fusion. Although it may be too soon to claim that fusion cuisine is an Asian American phenomenon, the fact that two prominent Asian Americans who embody the model minority stereotype dish up fusion cuisine on their respective cooking shows, week after week, warrants close analysis. With this in mind, I explore how Ming Tsai and Padma Lakshmi's respective cooking shows espouse a politics of assimilable fusion: a politics of culinarity that celebrates fusion cuisine because of the seeming ease with which Asian American personalities assimilate the tastes of their "ethnicity" with mainstream culinary fare.

Fusion cuisine's tendency to meld and assimilate difference into a coherent whole can be usefully contrasted with definitions of liberal, inclusive multiculturalism. According to Lisa Lowe, multiculturalism "assert[s] that American culture is a democratic terrain to which every constituency has equal access and in which all are represented, while simultaneously masking the existence of exclusion by recuperating dissent, conflict, and otherness through the promise of inclusion" (1996: 86). Heeding Lowe's cautionary remarks about multiculturalism, this essay argues that it is important to understand the sociopolitical conditions that render fusion possible when analyzing the popular presence of Asian American culinary culture in the mainstream media. I juxtapose the work of two ambassadors of Asian American culinary culture who currently host cooking shows on the Food Network, Ming Tsai and Padma Lakshmi, to explore how the public performance of racialized gendered national identity maps onto the public performance of culinarity. While the history of fusion cuisine is different from that of race in the United States, the rhetorical strategies used to describe fusion as a form of culinary multiculturalism can be better understood by placing it in the context of the racial and ethnic debates about diversity, difference, and assimilation in the United States without necessarily creating a homology between race on the one hand and culinary practices on the other. In juxtaposing the rhetoric of fusion cuisine with the rhetoric of popular and legal discourse around race and ethnicity in Asian America, I debunk the myth that fusion culinary discourse can be separated from the political terrain on which consumers of fusion cuisine are located.

Chopsticks and Forks: Ming's Culinary Quests

Ming Tsai, author of the award-winning cookbook, *Blue Ginger* (1999)—named for his restaurant in affluent Wellesley, Massachusetts—and host of the Food Network shows *East Meets West* and *Ming's Quest*, is the face of fusion cuisine in Asian America. *East Meets West*, one of the first cooking shows to showcase fusion cuisine hosted by an Asian American, promises to combine the best of both worlds, "Eastern" and "Western." Breaking with the earlier mold available to Asian American cooking show hosts, most notably Martin Yan, Ming Tsai presents cuisine in innovative ways, attempting to chronicle the diverse ways in which Asian tastes can mingle with the "American" palate. The "East-West" fusion cuisine he presents on the half-hour show is a combination of "Western" cuisine infused with Asian spices and herbs. Dishes such as "Tea-Smoked Salmon with Wasabi Potato 'Latkes' and Fuji Apple Salad" or "Asian Lacquered Poussin with Hoisin Lime Sauce" are just some of Tsai's fusion culinary offerings. But what exactly is fusion, and how do shows like *East Meets West* espouse its high-class ideals? Norman Van Aken, who takes credit for having invented the term "fusion cuisine," defines it as "a harmonious combination of foods of various origins." Offering the more precise term that circulates in the restaurant industry, Andrew Dornenburg and Karen Page define fusion as "a melding together of the cuisines of more than one country" in a single dish.[1]

Ming Tsai offers a slightly different take on fusion cuisine. According to him "'so called' fusion cooking produces chaos on the plate and in the mouth. This results from not respecting a culture's ingredients and the traditional techniques that turn them into wonderful eating. Successful East-West cooking finds just the right harmonious way to combine distinct culinary approaches. When a dish is not just new—but better—when I can find a superior way to celebrate oxtail's earthiness, say, or the deep sour tang of preserved lemons, and then join the two—that's real East-West cuisine."[2] Tsai's definition, however, is still coated in terms of the promise of inclusion; as a colleague commented, rarely do we see "true" fusion on the show. Ming Tsai will often prepare a dish, and then pour lychee honey over it, as if that superficial coating with a purportedly

Asian ingredient makes for fusion.[3] In almost all the recipes included in his book, as well as on the show, Tsai muses on how ingredients from the "East" can make "Western" cuisine better, alerting us to the uneven flows between "East" and "West."

Like many of the cooking shows that have begun to gain popularity on the Food Network, the chef is a central part of the show's narrative. Ming Tsai is presented as a young, cosmopolitan Asian American subject who does away with traditional boundaries between "East" and "West," making him a formidable ambassador for fusion cuisine. He is equally at home in both worlds—a point driven home by the thirty-second opening sequence to the show. It begins with Tsai attired in white "Oriental" garb sitting in lotus position with his eyes closed, apparently doing yoga. Accompanying this shot is slow, serene instrumental "Oriental" music. The music abruptly changes, and we are brought into a fast-paced contemporary "American" world that shows Tsai clad in sporty whites, playing racquet-ball. This change in scene is accompanied by a change in music. The serene music gives way to a more energetic and lively music (with Asian undertones), suggesting that, in addition to moving spatially from a spiritual Asian place to a multicultural United States, we have moved forward in time. In the next few shots Ming Tsai is seen selecting spices, produce, and meat in the Asian market and the American grocery store. He is then seen riding his bicycle down the streets of Boston's Chinatown and pulling up to a suburban home in a sports utility vehicle. The shot closes with Ming Tsai in traditional clothing. As he rises, he brings his palms together, and the camera cuts to the words "East Meets West" with chopsticks and a fork symmetrically framing the words. In this short sequence, Ming Tsai is portrayed as a remarkably dexterous character. Because he moves in and out of stereotypically "Eastern" and "Western" worlds he can presumably be relied on to create true fusion between east and west. Ming Tsai personifies fusion, and *is* what happens when east meets west—or so this sequence would have us believe.

While the opening sequence highlights Tsai's ability to travel rapidly between east and west, it also places him within a classed framework. He is depicted in a series of leisure activities—yoga, squash, shopping, driving an SUV, riding a bike for pleasure rather than as a mode of transportation —that complement his interest in the gourmet-style cuisine showcased on *East Meets West.* Through his cooking shows, as well as his restaurant, he can provide the type of cuisine demanded by his young, high-income, gentrified customers because he is socially and economically on par with them, and with those who consume fusion cuisine. At the same time, he is not exactly breaking bread with his clientele. He cooks for them, he looks beautiful for them, and he performs for them. To this end, selling Ming Tsai as a model minority is a crucial ingredient in making Tsai successful. Eric Ober, president and general manager of the Food Network, begins his afterword to Tsai's book by asking, "How many Yale graduates with engineering degrees and professional squash careers go on to win an Emmy award? Then again, how many of them have their own award winning restaurants?" (Tsai and Boehm 1999: i) as if to suggest that Tsai is the model minority extraordinaire, or as *A. Magazine* put it, "the Asian American poster boy of cooking."[4]

Ming Tsai is presented as the all-American male who chooses to make culinarity a vocation. Starting from humble beginnings in Dayton, Ohio, where he excelled in his studies, he went on to receive an Ivy League education, earning an engineering degree and a hotel and restaurant administration degree. Then he trained at prestigious cooking schools and restaurants. Ming Tsai thus embodies the model minority stereotype. He is upwardly mobile, well assimilated, does not talk about unpleasant racial experiences, and apparently seems to have made it in the United States.

Unlike the traditionally effeminized and desexualized Asian American, Ming Tsai exudes charisma and sex appeal. *People* Magazine included Ming Tsai on its list of the "Fifty Most Beautiful People in the World" for the year 2000, describing him as a "Chunk"—chef as hunk, a phrase coined by Heidi Diamond, an executive at the Food Network, Ming Tsai's employer. His fans have also been quick to pick up on his sexual appeal; in addition to watching the show to see how Ming Tsai creates culinary fusion, fans are interested in seeing Ming. On the Food Network fan forum devoted to Ming Tsai, for instance, one fan articulately comments, "Ming is a talented babe with a great personality :o) Woo Hoo." Another notes, "Wow I love this show!! Plus he looks Hot in that one pair of shorts he wore when he went to Hawaii!! (sorry I can't help it I think he's hot! And not a bad cook there!!)" and another fan poetically waxes, "I believe Ming is a great chef with a vast knowledge of gastronomy, he has a great show in which the viewers learn a lot, and he is cute to boot." To some of his Asian American fans, this is cause enough for celebration. One fan comments, "I'm very proud of you and your heritage, you are a great example of good breeding," while another notes, "He is quite good looking . . . more than that, he's extremely talented, I think people need to see more positive examples of asian men, he's very smart also. You know he graduated from Yale."[5]

If *East Meets West* portrays Tsai as the assimilated model minority who can bring both worlds—"Asian" and "American"—together, his newer television show *Ming's Quest* adds another dimension to his onscreen persona, casting him as the "American" who enjoys the great outdoors and has time for fun and relaxation. Unlike *East Meets West*, this show takes place outside the studio kitchen, in a range of on-site locations including Bali, Indonesia, Hawaii, and Northern Vermont. The show portrays Ming Tsai as equally at home on the range and behind the kitchen range. In his quest for "better" food, Ming Tsai pushes the frontiers of cooking, searching and hunting—that most masculine of activities—and transforms wild creatures such as Balinese duck, Alaskan blue mussels, or Vermont trout into delectable dishes, fused with the tastes of the "East." Not only can he travel between East and West, but he can do so while maintaining a solid masculinist image.

At one level the show breaks with the stereotypical image of Asian cooks. Ming Tsai is not the bumbling idiot who prepares egg foo young and chop suey and cannot speak English. Nor does he conjure up images of the offensive "heathen Chinee" stereotypes that have long been associated with Asian American men who cook, nor for that matter does he resemble his most immediate predecessor Martin Yan who speaks in heavily accented English and seems an irreducibly foreign and desexualized comic character. He is presented as the future of America—a figure who takes the "best" of the east and incorporates it into his Western culinary offerings. In this way, Ming Tsai emerges as the model minority chef who inhabits a newer stereotype—that of the hyperassimilated, attractive, and yuppified Asian American who seamlessly integrates into American cultural life.

"Sexy Dishes": Padma's Passport

If Ming Tsai emerges as the all-American man who understands and who belongs in a multiethnic America, Padma Lakshmi, the other Asian American who appears with some regularity on the Food Network, is presented as a new breed of American for whom race is irrelevant because she embodies the vision of a transnational multicultural America. On the cover of her cookbook, *Easy Exotic: Low-Fat Recipes from Around the World*

(1999), is a photograph of sumptuous fruit hanging in clusters from a fruit vendor's cart. Posing in front of the fruit is a woman with dark hair that falls to her shoulders. The cover image combines food and sensuality with exoticism and suggests that the book will offer easy strategies for consuming delectable images of alterity. But the female figure centrally positioned on the cover of the book is racially ambiguous. Although her name, Padma Lakshmi, suggests that she is ethnically South Asian, her light skin and dark hair frame her as "exotically ethnic."

In the opening pages of the book Padma shares nostalgic memories of growing up and learning to cook in the company of female relatives in South India, thus establishing her connection to Indianness. The division of the book into sections on Spain, France, Italy, India, Asia, and Morocco (in that order), however, undercuts notions of rigid nationality while still using national categories. Deliberately situating itself at the crossroads of national culinary culture, the cookbook is not engaged in producing a national narrative that seeks to understand how and where the chef fits into a vision of a multicultural United States. Rather, the text produces a flexible, transnational narrative marking Padma Lakshmi's emergence as a cosmopolitan and mobile South Asian American subject who travels easily between cultures and nations. Her public image on Internet websites, cooking shows, and in her cookbook, *Easy Exotic,* frames her as part of a class of young and mobile South Asian Americans raised in the United States who are not bounded by classed notions of citizenship and national belonging; she effortlessly slides in and out of ethnic and national contexts while consistently maintaining a purportedly exotic ethnic appeal.

Although Padma Lakshmi, a model, actress, and host of a cooking show, does not own her own restaurant, she is more of a media presence in public cultural circuits than South Asian restaurateurs, or established chefs and culinary authors such as Madhur Jaffrey and Julie Sahni. Her background in modeling, her ability to speak five languages (European and South Asian), and her racially ambiguous appearance position her as a formidable ambassador for (Indian) fusion culinary culture. Her cooking show, *Padma's Passport,* a segment of *Melting Pot,* is described as "a culinary passport to the rich heritage of our country."[6] Like her cookbook, the show claims to break down national boundaries. Generally organized around a specific topic, either showcasing types of food to be consumed and prepared for special occasions and outings such as picnic lunches, light summer fare, and aphrodisiacal food, each episode creates culinary fusion by juxtaposing dishes from disparate national culinary cultures.

Unlike many other culinary show hosts, including industry stalwarts such as Emeril Lagasse, Ming Tsai, or Martha Stewart, Padma does not navigate the kitchen with ease. Using metal utensils on nonstick pans, emptying the blades of the food processor into the saucepan along with the blended sauce, turning a blender on with the lid open are all culinary faux-pas made by Lakshmi during the half-hour show that airs on the *Food Network.* Using campy humor to detract from her apparent inability to navigate the kitchen, her comment, "I *do* know how to use this" punctures a moment in the narrative when she struggles to fit the lid to a blender. Such moments attest to her discomfort in the kitchen, at least in the onscreen version of the kitchen.[7] For the most part, vegetables, fruit, and meat are presliced and spices and herbs are heaped on a plate in the correct quantities—all that is left for her to do is to chop and slice the occasional vegetable and then assemble the dishes and present a completed version of the dish to eager viewers at home. So, if viewers are not tuning in to see culinary wizardry, what is the appeal of this show?

Judging from audience comments posted to the on-line fan forum for *Padma's Passport,* viewers are not watching the show merely to learn about the intricacies of Indian, Spanish, French, or Moroccan cuisine; they are tuning in to watch Padma. As one fan on the Food Network's on-line fan forum gushes, "Padma is awesome. And I'm not just saying that because I'm a guy. I mean she can cook, present herself articulately, yet be revealing all at the same time. What an Indian foxx. [*Sic*] Oh yea, and the foods she cooks look slammin'. Why not show more, and I do mean more of Padma; Please!" Another fan writes, "Padma is the best and sexist girl on TV, keep up the good work baby doll, everybody loves you."[8] Transformed into a latently sexualized object by her on-line fan base, Lakshmi's good looks and "ethnic-exotic" appeal are an integral part of the show's narrative. In producing a palatably exotic version of alterity, Padma herself becomes one of the main ingredients of the show. Like the food she prepares on the show, she herself is commodifiable, consumable, and desirable.

Reinforcing the idea that she is one of the consumable ingredients of her book dished up for hungry viewers, tantalizing images of sumptuous food alternate with images of Padma Lakshmi seductively kneading pastry dough or shopping for vegetables in body-hugging clothing. Lakshmi's image on the show is also deliberately sexualized. Typically, she wears revealing outfits—leather pants, short T-shirts exposing her midriff, tight sleeveless dresses, low-cut blouses—not typically associated with the "sensible clothing" style of most Food Network stars. Audiences tuning in to see Padma are also consuming other images of Padma Lakshmi present in cyberspace. Numerous websites (primarily based in Italy, where Lakshmi worked as a model) catalog photographs of her work as nude model.[9] These overtly sexualized images of Lakshmi in cyberspace offer an additional point of entry into understanding how and why the conflation of sex, sensuality, and food enhance Lakshmi's popularity. Sexually explicit photographs play up her ambiguous "exoticism," rendering it difficult to read these particular photographs of her solely in terms of any particular national, racial, or ethnic background.

Fan groups have been quick to notice Lakshmi's sex appeal. At the time of writing, there were three discussion groups hosted at yahoogroups.com devoted to Padma Lakshmi: Padma Lakshmi's Lotus Oasis (1,441 members), the Padma Lakshmi Fan Club (1,076 members), and Padma Lakshmi (27 members).[10] But unlike many on-line discussion groups devoted to discussing specific ideas about the show or the host, these groups feature minimal discussion. When the rare conversation does take place, it is often to alert other members that Padma Lakshmi is making an appearance on a television show, or that new photographs—usually partial or full frontal nudes—have been uploaded to the website. Indeed, the primary feature of each group is the extensive section of photos archived in the "photos" section of each website. As access to such features is limited to members only, one has to have membership in the particular group to download images of Padma Lakshmi. Most subscribers opt to be anonymous and while this prevents them from posting messages to the group, it does not prevent them from accessing the photos. By their own admission (via postings), the subscribers are not interested in cooking, or in creating a larger on-line community.

When aspects of *Padma's Passport* are discussed, the focus is entirely on Padma's appearance. As one subscriber writes, "Padma on the food network . . . on the show "Melting Pot" today! She wore skintight leather pants with a skintight shirt that showed her tummy and no bra! Her breasts were hanging out every time she bent over to cook something. She made food for lovers/ aphrodesiac [sic] foods! And at one point was licking chocolate off her finger! You've got to see her live!" (October 11, 2001, Padma Lakshmi's Lotus Oasis discussion group). Such voyeurism is unusual, as subscribers rarely share details about their observations in this forum. In part this is because most subscribers remain anonymous and are therefore prohibited from posting messages, but it is also a response to the list moderator's call for nonmisogynistic postings. In the introductory message, he writes, "I will update new PICS as I find them and ask you to do the same. I would like to limit the public posts to a 'NOT TOO MASO-GENISTIC' [sic] level. There are other clubs that will be more than happy to fulfill this need of yours!" Thus while the rampant but private consumption of pornographic images is accepted, public discussions of sexual fantasies are strictly prohibited.

Fans may seem to converge in their readings of Padma, but unraveling the often contradictory representations of Lakshmi and Tsai is complicated precisely because they are *both* the "exotic ethnic" other *and* the assimilated model minority. Lakshmi is the alluring temptress who is a cosmopolitan world traveler and still remembers her roots. Ming Tsai is the hyperassimilated Asian American but is also comfortable with his traditional upbringing in an immigrant Taiwanese American family. While the shows have worked against the traditional invisibility of Asian American bodies in public culture, the uncomplicated and commodifiable image of ethnicity raises the question of whether inclusive representation that renders race invisible, and even irrelevant, is necessarily positive.

Indeed, the question of race being rendered invisible for new(er) cosmopolitan subjects is the topic of the now (in)famous 1993 *Time* cover with the headline, "The New Face of America: How Immigrants Are Shaping the World's First Multicultural Society." The cover displays the computer-generated image of a woman who, although only 15 percent Anglo-Saxon, has, as Victor Burgin writes, "the appearance of a White woman recently returned from a holiday on the Mediterranean" (1996: 259). Although Lakshmi does not have the appearance of being "white," she bears an uncanny resemblance to the computer-generated woman heralded as the future face of "America" insofar as her South Asianness is never fully fixed. While her name identifies her as South Asian, there is little in her physical appearance that definitively marks her national identity. With a fair complexion, dark hair, and just the right combination of exotically "ethnic" features, she can easily (claim to) pass as a cosmopolitan Spaniard, Italian, or Moroccan. To borrow Victor Burgin's terms, she has the appearance of a mythic exotic beauty that one might encounter on a fabled Mediterranean holiday.[11]

The title of the show, *Padma's Passport,* implies a certain transnational mobility. Watching *Padma's Passport,* viewers are transported to other lands with a host who claims native knowledge of most of the cuisines featured on the show. But lodged within a classed matrix, the passport, so central to the show's narrative, is often only an icon of easy mobility. Undocumented laborers, refugees, both political and economic, do not always have access to a passport, a legal document that grants them the right to move easily. And for those who have passports, there is also the question of having the stamp of approval and the "correct" visa, or "correct" type of visa, lodged in it. The H1-B visa that grants "temporary skilled workers" permission to work in the United States is considerably different from the H1 visa, the "standard" visa allowing non-U.S. residents and citizens to work in this country. As Amitava Kumar notes, H1-B workers are particularly susceptible to exploitative work practices because of the tenuousness of their position.[12] Temporary skilled workers, refugees, and undocumented laborers thus may not have the requisite passport or means to imagine the pleasures of frequent border crossing.

Padma's mobility is not limited to her ability to travel. Her screen presence also takes multiple forms; her accent and clothing shift strategically to accommodate her different screen personae. When she needs to play the alluring temptress who cooks aphrodisiacal foods, she speaks with just the trace of an accent in a husky voice; when she is playing the dutiful younger woman learning from older South Asians, as in a special episode of the Food Network special, *Planet Food,* on southern India, her accent becomes more "Indianized"; and when she is playing the naive "ditz" appealing to the college fraternity boy audience, she will speak in Americanized English, her voice inflecting at the end of every sentence. Without the slightest hint of unpalatable foreignness—she is conversant in (American accented) English, she knows what men want, she dresses like an "American" (read white)—Lakshmi is part of a group of emerging South Asian Americans for whom ethnicity appears to be an optional adornment.

Clothing styles also take on a very important role in constructing Padma's flexible citizenship. When she needs to perform Indianness she is robed in a sari. When she needs to be the sexy and apparently "unethnic" host, she is attired in tight-fitting leather pants and a short electric blue T-shirt. Just as Padma ethnically adorns herself to fit the circumstances, the food that she prepares (often traditional "Western" fare) is dressed to be more "exotic" and "spicy." Fusion in this sense entails spicing up regular American fare, fusing only the elements deemed desirable and assimilable from the "East," leaving behind all that is deemed undesirable and unpalatable.

"Multicultural Commodified Hosts":
Race, Representation, and Otherness

One may legitimately critique Padma Lakshmi for pandering to Oriental-ist stereotypes and self-exoticization that harken back to early images of Asian women as sexualized objects. It would be more pertinent, however, to ask what makes it possible for a show that many critics have lambasted for showcasing unoriginal dishes to emerge in the late twentieth–early twenty-first century. In the case of Ming Tsai, the critique is even more complicated because Tsai is not a culinary neophyte; he is well versed in the traditions of French, Japanese, and Chinese cooking. He has also re-ceived culinary accolades, including the James Beard Award for Best Chef of the Northeast, in 2002. In an era marked by the emergence of what Toby Miller has dubbed "multicultural commodified hosts," one must go beyond lamenting the loss of a serious celluloid food culture and ask in-stead what has enabled and continues to sustain the presence of these multicultural commodified hosts.[13] What are the terms on which Asian American subjects such as Padma Lakshmi and Ming Tsai are represented in the popular media? And would either Lakshmi or Tsai enjoy such levels of popularity without their youthful "exotic" good looks?

Food writer Sylvia Lovegren dubs the 1990s the "fusion" decade, but her elegy to fusion cooking in American culinary culture makes it apparent that fusion is not exclusively about bringing different types of cuisines to-gether: "In America, we have the bounty and the culinary heritage to cook and eat virtually anything we wish. Whether we choose to nourish our-selves with a meal of frozen fish sticks and fat-free brownies, or with food —whether simple or sophisticated—that is chosen and prepared with love and respect, is up to us."[14] The language of entitlement pervasive here, the notion that "we" pick and choose what "we" want to eat also blurs the dis-tinctions between fusion, assimilation, and appropriation.

But the concept of "appropriation" carries different valence when the chefs, or authors, are of Asian background, as with Tsai and Lakshmi who assume the posture of speaking from "within" their cultural contexts. If fusion cuisine is about combining the best of two national cuisines, on what basis does each chef claim affiliation with a particular national style? For Padma Lakshmi, lived experiences in a particular national space— Italy, India, Spain, France—appear to grant her the "legitimacy" to claim an affiliation with their national cuisines. Ming Tsai establishes his credentials by detailing in his public biography how and why he came to be interested in cuisine. He explains that having parents who owned a Chinese restaurant fed his interest in Asian cooking, "I began by 'cooking East.' My parents were born in Beijing, so I grew up steeped in the joys of the Chinese table. I watched my mom, dad, and grandparents cook and later joined them at the stove at home, and at the Mandarin Kitchen, a Chinese restaurant they owned in my hometown of Dayton, Ohio" (1999: x). In explaining how and why Western cuisine came to him, he makes it a point to mention that he was trained at the Cordon Bleu and pays homage to his various mentors in Paris. He also acknowledges the influence of Chinese American chef Ken Hom, a founding father of "East-West" cuisine, and notes that he spent time in Japan mastering the art of Japanese sushi rice making as well as other intricacies of Japanese cuisine.

But both Lakshmi and Tsai fuse Western cuisine with other Asian culinary styles not covered by either their life experiences or training. Tsai never explains how Indian or Vietnamese cuisine fits into his repertoire and yet he offers recipes for pho and lemon basmati rice. Similarly, Padma Lakshmi never explains how recipes for "Oriental Shrimp Salad," "Thai Chicken Stew," or "Pan Asian Fried Rice" enter her repertoire. While it would be problematic to suggest that Tsai has a natural connection with Chinese cuisine because he is Chinese, or that Lakshmi can unproblematically claim to understand Indian cuisine because she is Indian, it is equally troubling to see that some cuisines appear to merit extensive training before Ming Tsai can claim to be an expert while others do not. They suggest that a knowledge of the range of Asian cuisines seeps through their pores merely by virtue of being Asian. Tsai and Lakshmi claim Asian cuisines as their own, but not with a view to establishing a more inclusive vision of pan–Asian American ethnicity. Instead Asianness, as it filters into their respective culinary styles, emerges as something that they instinctively understand because they are Asian American. How, then, do their culinary practices blur the boundaries between fusion, assimilation, and appropriation?

A more useful way to approach this question would be to ask how their cookbooks and cooking shows allow pan-Asian cooking styles to be appropriated by those of "us" who are looking to add some diversity to our palates. How does the cooking style of each chef suggest that Asianness need not be understood as an unassimilable presence within the United States, but rather as something that can assimilate quietly and subtly into the U.S. culinary landscape? Indeed, how does fusion cuisine blur the boundaries between fusion, an ostensibly democratic coming together of cuisines, on the one hand, and appropriation, actively taking from the ethnic heritages of people of color, including Asian Americans, and divesting cultural production of any racialized, or classed implications, on the other?

Assimilation, particularly the notion of assimilating quietly, cannot be divorced from the study of race and ethnicity in Asian America. The term assimilation is historically significant in terms of legislation and the juridical mechanisms regulating the racialization of Asian Americans. In the early years of the twentieth century, for instance, numerous Asian groups were excluded from American citizenship because they were deemed "unassimilable." In the context of a legal historical understanding that Asians are unassimilable because they are racially different, what does it mean to describe cuisine in laudatory terms precisely because it is so readily assimilable? Lessons from Asian American and U.S. history show us how Asian Americans negotiate this position of "otherness." Recent furor over national loyalty and security in the drama surrounding the Wen Ho Lee case, the spy plane incident in Hainan, and the current profiling of Arabs and Arab Americans, Muslim Americans, and South Asian and South Asian Americans suggests that a fear of the "other" can be strategically mobilized to position Asians as the perpetual outsider in America who can pose a threat to the sanctity and safety of the American citizenry.

Yet it is true that in recent years Asian Americans have been praised (in contrast to blacks and Latinos) for having "assimilated" so well. Asian Americans are the model minority because they are hard workers, they do not make a fuss, and are not loud. It is thus significant that fusion chef Raji Jallepalli defines her cooking as a "rather quiet melding of vastly different cultures, philosophies and cooking techniques" (2000: 3), echoing the idea that Asians can assimilate subtly, but positively, into the American racial landscape. On the culinary landscape, or culinary-scape, Asian spices and food need not be considered foreign and alien because, given the "right" approach it is possible to bring "exotic" flavors from the east into familiar dishes. Similarly, Ken Hom praises Ming Tsai in the following terms, "He represents both East and West. He has adopted and blended their better aspects. As a chef and television personality, he is ideally suited to assist in the amalgamation of these different culinary traditions" (ix). Ming Tsai can be relied on to create fusion because he lives in both worlds.

In his cuisine, then, foreignness is broken down into easily digestible units that can leave one feeling satisfied for having enjoyed a culinary adventure without having had to leave home, in a figurative sense.

It becomes possible to sample a taste of the "other" without really having to confront what it is that makes Asians different; more specifically, it downplays the importance of larger historical and social issues that have brought Asians to America and also elides the fact that much of the food, if sampled in a restaurant, might be prepared by persons who are not necessarily given full access to citizenship. Focusing on how the taste of Asia can assimilate into America is thus one way to elide larger issues that might in fact suggest that working-class Asian Americans do not always enjoy the rights and privileges afforded to the younger high-income gentrified subjects that they serve, albeit invisibly.

In the name of encouraging the mainstream to cook responsibly and to respect other cultures, how do these chefs assume the posture of the native informant who will unravel the secrets of the "East" to literally render them more palatable? While it is encouraging that Lakshmi and Tsai offer strategies that allow Asian cuisine and flavor to be thought of as nonforeign, it is also important to ask about the terms on which fusion is made possible, and by extension, when fusion is rendered difficult, if not simply impossible. In many of the fusion cookbooks that have come to dominate the fusion cooking market, there are unwritten rules about what ingredients can be fused and what the end product must look like. As Ming Tsai observes, fusion cuisine is by no means a random process of combining various ingredients to create a new product. Rather, there is a highly ordered pattern as to what "counts" as authentic fusion cuisine.

One such dish is the ubiquitous crème brûlée that appears in many fusion cuisine restaurant menus and cookbooks. Tsai comments, "few eating pleasures are greater than a mouthful of this creamy custard with its crackling caramel topping. Everyone loves the combo. There are many flavored crème brûlées around—I've seen them spiked with tea, with lemongrass, with ginger, with coffee and with fruit. When it comes to this incomparable dessert, however, I'm a purist: classic is best. And this version is classic classic" (1999: 254–55). He goes on to say, "I'd be lying if I said that this is a true East-West dish: the vanilla beans from the South Pacific are as close to Asia as this dessert gets. In any case, try to get Tahitian beans—they're particularly plump and fragrant—though any fresh vanilla beans will do." Tsai suggests that his "classic classic" version is not authentically fused but lends an "exotic" touch to his dish. It is thus subtly but significantly "exotifying" precisely because it is only fusion in a nominative sense.

Ultimately, if that end product must always be understood within the framework of crème brûlées, ragouts, cassoulets with a palatably foreign or exotic touch, as is often the case, I must question whether this is fusion, or merely an attempt to show how well Asianness assimilates to the tastes of haute cuisine. I am not troubled by hybrid cuisines, but rather by the terms of hybridization. Smoking poussin on sandalwood chips and serving it with Israeli couscous may indeed be considered an example of French passion fused with Indian flavors because it sits comfortably within the American culinary landscape, but again, it must be asked, who has the option of buying *poussin* and smoking it on sandalwood chips? Or for that matter, who has the ability to recognize that Ming Tsai's Tahitian Vanilla crème brûlée is "classic classic," as he puts it? Specifically, how does class intervene to enhance the cultural capital of these types of cuisine? To extend this argument further, who is able to recognize how each new dish has created a "better product," or to recognize how a "classic" French dish has been improved? The consumer is the one acquainted with such fineries of the palate and the one with the financial resources to buy sandalwood chips with which to smoke the fish.

These new(ish) cuisines are not for people on a limited budget, but for people who have the resources—both temporal and financial—to invest in such ventures. Pierre Bourdieu describes consumption as "a stage in a process of communication that is an act of deciphering, decoding, which presupposes practical or explicit mastery of a cipher or code" (1984: 2). Consuming fusion cuisine, then, can only have meaning for those who have the cultural know-how; if we think of fusion cuisine as a form of artistry, it "has meaning and interest only for someone who possesses the cultural competence, that is, the code into which it is encoded . . . A beholder who lacks the specific code feels lost in a chaos of sounds and rhythms, colours and line, without rhyme or reason" (2). The call to perform a version of Asianness that appears to be authentic and stamped with the seal of approval of the native informant is certainly present in both cases. On the one hand it is admirable that Lakshmi and Tsai have created a niche for their cooking styles and that they are not tied to an essentialist notion of what it means to be Asian in the diaspora. At the same time, what forces are at play in dismantling the borders between national cuisines?

The "arrival" of Asian fusion restaurants and the popularity of cooking shows such as *East Meets West, Ming's Quest,* and *Padma's Passport* have been read as signs that Asian Americans have "made" it. They are stories that attest to the success of Asians in America. But to read the popularity of fusion Asian cuisine as a mark of arrival is troubling because this type of fusion cuisine is self-consciously described as a "rather quiet combining of vastly different cultures" and is thus aligned with the laudatory rhetoric that praises Asians for assimilating quietly into American culture. Quietly combining suggests that the mixing of Asianness and "Americanness" is best when it is subtle, silent, and unobtrusive.

In an extended argument against calls for diversity that do not endorse an assimilationist view of ethnicity, Roger Clegg, general counsel for the anti–affirmative action group, the Center for Equal Opportunity, argues, "It's fine to eat different kinds of food and to have pride in one's ancestors. But in matters of language and our civic culture—as well as, more broadly, our manners and morality—assimilation should be the goal. An America that is multiracial and multiethnic, yes. *Multicultural, no.* E pluribus Unum: *Out of many, one*" (2000). Clegg's failure to distinguish between "multicultural" Americans rehearses an all too familiar argument about racial and ethnic difference presupposing that the only useful contribution that can be made by people of color is in the culinary world. People of color and immigrants are welcome in "America" provided they assimilate to the norms and expectations of a white, English-speaking, United States. Moreover, Clegg implicitly suggests how people of color should "enter" the American racial landscape: like good "model minorities," Asians should "enter" quietly and unobtrusively, adhering to that old ideal, *E pluribus Unum*: out of many one. While Tsai and Lakshmi do not necessarily create one out of many, their respective approaches to cuisine make it possible for an assimilatory version of fusion to emerge. Moreover, neither cooking show instructs viewers how to cook with culinary unmentionables such as dog, or gizzards, or culinary "oddities" such as yogurt and rice; they deal exclusively with wholesome ingredients, strictly adhering to the realm of what is considered palatable.

In promoting a vision of fusion, something is always left out of the equation. But the ingredient that is "left" out cannot merely be ignored. While further research needs to be done on what counts as fusion and what is left out, it is significant that the cookbooks with the most cultural capital in the world of fusion cuisine in the United States allow for a combination of white and Asian, but implicitly disallow fusion between other "colors" or races. The impossibility, until very recently, of imagining black-Asian fusion cuisine in the cookbook market suggests that in many cases fusion is only acceptable when it incorporates cultural markers of whiteness.[15] While numerous forms of Chino-Latino fusion restaurants (Chinese-Cuban, Chinese-Puerto Rican) owned by Caribbean immigrants of Chinese origin can be found in New York City, few of these are considered upscale enough to be serving "cuisine" and most do not command the high prices charged by "recognizable" fusion restaurants such as *Blue Ginger* in Boston, *Sara's* in New Orleans, and *Tabla* in New York. Chino-Latino and Indo-Pak-Bangla "fusion" restaurants and eateries are generally owned and patronized by working-class immigrants who do not fit easily within the stereotype of the upwardly mobile model minority. These establishments produce cheap fast food, not cuisine per se. Certain types of fusion are considered "cuisine" while others are dismissed as mere forays into poor eclectic food. Increasingly, fusion cuisine as offered by chefs such as Ming Tsai is part of the upscale culinary market, commanding higher prices than "merely" ethnic restaurants.

Ming Tsai and Padma Lakshmi, then, are in the unique position of being the new denizens of this culinary culture. Unlike the figure of Apu on the *Simpsons,* Martin Yan, or *Bonanza's* infamous houseboy Hop Sing, Padma Lakshmi and Ming Tsai exist within an economy of desirability. Their foods are desirable, and they are too. Although it is premature to fully assess the implications of their respective approaches to cuisine, the narrowcasting of these images propels the study of race within circuits of popular culture that demand that we develop new methodologies to think about the alignment of food, sex, race, and gender in Asian America.

NOTES

1. Andrew Dornenburg and Karen Page, *Becoming a Chef* (New York: Van Nostrand Reinhold, 1995), 22.

2. Ming Tsai, *Blue Ginger: East Meets West, Cooking with Ming Tsai* (New York: Clarkson Potter, 1999), 1.

3. I am grateful to Mana Hayakawa for making this observation.

4. Lan N. Nguyen, "The Ming Attraction," *A. Magazine: Inside Asian America* (February/March 2001), 31.

5. http://forums/foodtv.com, May 22, 2002.

6. http://www.foodnetwork.com/foodtv/show/0,6525,MP,00.html, October 29, 2001.

7. This is an approximation of a phrase used by Lakshmi during a show in which she struggles to blend fruit.

8. http://forums.foodtv.com, October 20, 2001.

9. http://isidoro3.interfree.it/padma.htm, October 31, 2001; http://www.maxim .it/fantasie/67/, October 31, 2001.

10. This is based on figures collated on June 17, 2002.

11. Lauren Berlant offers a useful analysis of this *Time* magazine cover. See "The Face of America and the State of Emergency," in *Disciplinarity and Descent in Cultural Studies,* eds. Cary Nelson and Dilip Parameshwar Gaonkar (London: Routledge, 1996), 397–438.

12. Amitava Kumar, "Temporary Access: The Indian H-1B Worker in the United States," in *Technicolor: Race, Technology and Everyday Life,* eds. Alondra Nelson and Thuy Linh N. Tu (New York: NYU Press, 2001), 76–87.

13. Toby Miller, "Screening Food: French Cuisine and the American Palate," in *French Food: On the Table, on the Page and in French Culture,* eds. Lawrence R. Scheher and Allen T. Weiss (New York: Routledge, 2001), 221–228.

14. Sylvia Lovegren, *Fashionable Food: Seven Decades of Food Fans* (New York: Macmillan, 1995), 421.

15. The appropriation of black urban styles, reggae and hip-hop by Asian American youth exemplifies a very different type of fusion marked by an overt attempt to address how the experiences of black Americans bear on the racial formation of Asian Americans. See, for example, Vijay Prashad's *Karma of Brown Folk* (2000); Shankar and Srikanth, "Crafting Solidarities," in *A Part Yet Apart:* South Asians *in Asian America* (1998: 105–126); Prashad, *Everybody Was Kung Fu Fighting: Afro Asian Connections and the Myth of Cultural Purity* (2001); and Sunaina Maira, *Desis in the House: Indian American Youth in New York City* (2002).

BIBLIOGRAPHY

Berlant, Lauren. "The Face of America and the State of Emergency." In *Disciplinarity and Descent in Cultural Studies.* Eds. Cary Nelson and Dilip Parameshwar Gaonkar. London: Routledge, 1996, 397–438.

Bourdieu, Pierre. *Distinction: A Social Critique of the Judgement of Taste.* Trans. Richard Nice. Cambridge: Harvard University Press, 1984.

Burgin, Victor. *In/Different Spaces: Place and Memory in Visual Culture.* Berkeley: University of California Press, 1996.

Clegg, Roger. "Why I'm Sick of the Praise for Diversity on Campuses." *The Chronicle of Higher Education.* July 14, 2000. http://chronicle.com.free/v46/i45 .45b00801.htm, September 7, 2000.

Dornenburg, Andrew, and Karen Page, *Becoming a Chef with Recipes from America's Leading Chefs.* New York: Van Nostrand Reinhold, 1995.

"East Meets West—American BBQ—Chinese Style." Host, Ming Tsai. Food Network. June 13, 2002.

"East Meets West—Bean Sprouts: A Tsai Family Business." Host, Ming Tsai. Food Network. December 1, 2001.

"East Meets West—East Lightens West." Host, Ming Tsai. Food Network. November 25, 2001.

"East Meets West—East West Winter Desserts." Host, Ming Tsai. Food Network. December 17, 2001.

"East Meets West—Ming and His Blue Ginger Sous Chefs (Budi, Bear and Amy)." Host, Ming Tsai. Food Network. January 17, 2002.

"East Meets West—More Cooking with Mom and Pops." Host, Ming Tsai. Food Network. October 8, 2001.

Fairchild, Barbara. "America Goes Global." *Bon Appetit.* September 2001, 42.

"Forums and Chats: Food Network." February 20, 2001. http://forums.foodtv .com.

Gabaccia, Donna. *We Are What We Eat: Ethnic Food and the Making of Americans.* Cambridge: Harvard University Press, 1998.

Jallepalli, Raji, and Judith Choate. *Raji Cuisine: Indian Flavors, French Passion.* New York: HarperCollins, 2000.

Kumar, Amitava. "Temporary Access: The Indian H-1B Worker in the United States." In *Technicolor: Race, Technology and Everyday Life.* Eds. Alondra Nelson and Thuy Linh N. Tu (New York: NYU Press, 2001), 76–87.

Lakshmi, Padma, and Georgia Downard. *Easy Exotic: Low-Fat Recipes from Around the World.* New York: Hyperion/Talk, 1999.

Lovegren, Sylvia. *Fashionable Food: Seven Decades of Food Fads.* New York: Macmillan, 1995.

Lowe, Lisa. *Immigrant Acts: On Asian American Cultural Politics.* Durham: Duke University Press, 1996.

Maira, Sunaima. *Desis in the House: Indian American Youth in New York City.* Philadelphia: Temple University Press, 2002.

Melting Pot. October 29, 2001. http://www.foodnetwork.com/foodtv/show/0,6525 ,MP,00.html.

Miller, Toby. "Screening Food: French Cuisine and the American Palate." In *French Food: On the Table, on the Page and in French Culture.* Eds. Lawrence R. Scheher and Allen T. Weiss. New York: Routledge, 2001, 221–228.

"Ming's Quest—Alaskan Blue Mussels Quest." *Melting Pot.* Host, Ming Tsai. Food Network. May 31, 2002.

"Ming's Quest—Duck Fruit Bali Quest." *Melting Pot.* Host, Ming Tsai. Food Network. June 9, 2002.

"Ming's Quest—Mexican Agave/Cactus Quest." *Melting Pot.* Host, Ming Tsai. Food Network. April 28, 2002.

"Ming's Quest—Turkey Cranberry Quest." *Melting Pot.* Host, Ming Tsai. Food Network. November 23, 2001.

"Ming's Quest—Vermont Trout Quest." *Melting Pot.* Host, Ming Tsai. Food Network. April 5, 2002.

Nguyen, Lan N. "The Ming Attraction." *A. Magazine: Inside Asian America.* February-March 2001, 30–33.

Okihiro, Gary. "When and Where I Enter." In *Margins and Mainstreams: Asians in American History and Culture.* Seattle: University of Washington Press, 1994, 3–30.

Ong, Aihwa. *Flexible Citizenship: The Cultural Logics of Transnationality.* Durham: Duke University Press, 1999.

Ozawa v. United States. 260 US 178. Supreme Court. 1922.

"Padma Lakshmi." June 17, 2002. http://groups.yahoo.com/group/PadmaLakshmi.

"Padma Lakshmi Fan Club." June 17, 2002. http://groups.yahoo.com/group/PadmaLakshmifanclub.

"Padma Lakshmi's Lotus Oasis." June 17, 2002. http://groups.yahoo.com/group/PadmaLakshmislotusoasis.

"Padma Lakshmi: Indiana de etnia Tamil" October 31, 2001. http://isidoro3.interfree.it/padma.htm.

"Padma's Passport—Aphrodisiacal Foods." *Melting Pot.* Host, Padma Lakshmi. Food Network. October 1, 2001.

"Padma's Passport—Casual Buffet." *Melting Pot.* Host, Padma Lakshmi. Food Network. March 29, 2002.

"Padma's Passport—Indian Feast." *Melting Pot.* Host, Padma Lakshmi. Food Network. December 7, 2001.

"Padma's Passport—Heartbreak City." *Melting Pot.* Host, Padma Lakshmi. Food Network. March 27, 2002.

"Padma's Passport—Light Luncheon." *Melting Pot.* Host, Padma Lakshmi. Food Network. March 28, 2002.

"Padma's Passport—Hot 'n' Spicy." *Melting Pot.* Host, Padma Lakshmi. Food Network. December 3, 2001.

"Padma's Passport—My Mother's Kitchen." *Melting Pot.* Host, Padma Lakshmi. Food Network. October 12, 2001.

"Padma's Passport—Picnic Gathering." *Melting Pot.* Host, Padma Lakshmi. Food Network. March 25, 2002.

"Padma's Passport—Vegetarian Specialties." *Melting Pot.* Host, Padma Lakshmi. Food Network. March 26, 2002.

Prashad, Vijay. *Everybody Was Kung Fu Fighting: Afro Asian Connections and the Myth of Cultural Purity.* Boston: Beacon Press, 2001.

———. *Karma of Brown Folk.* Minneapolis: University of Minnesota Press, 2000.

Sassen, Saskia. *The Global City: New York, London, Tokyo.* Princeton: Princeton University Press, 1991.

Shankar, Lavina Dhingra, and Rajini Srikanth, eds. *A Part Yet Apart: South Asians in Asian America.* Philadelphia: Temple University Press, 1998.

"South India." *Planet Food.* Food Network. December 31, 2002.

Tsai, Ming, and Arthur Boehm. *Blue Ginger: East Meets West, Cooking with Ming Tsai.* Foreword by Ken Hom. New York: Clarkson Potter, 1999.

"Il vizio de Padma" October 31, 2001. http://www.maxim.it/fantasie/67/.

Chapter 5

"PAPPY'S HOUSE"
"Pop" Culture and the Revaluation of a
Filipino American "Sixty-Cents" in Guam

Vicente M. Diaz

Preface: From a Long Line of Diazes[1]

Hilario Diaz was an indio from Iba, Zambales. He hung with the big boys because as an *herbolario,* Hilario possessed folk knowledge that impressed the *illustrados,* and had practical applications for the nationalist march against the imperialists. Hilario's son, Vicente, extended the lineage as a highly decorated freemason and through advanced *cartillas.* And then Vicente's eyes met those of Bibiana Valero, a fellow educator and a staunch mestiza, who mandated that Vicente first convert to Catholicism, and renounce his affiliation with the Church's sworn enemy. From his decision, and her satisfaction, came Ramon, the first son, who received a law degree from the University of Santo Tomas and a commission in the Philippine Army just before the Japanese invasion and occupation. A survivor of Bataan (because he ate his *mongo* beans, as our version of child psychology would have it), Ramon left the Philippines in 1949 in search not simply of the legendary American Dream but for a place to build a career interrupted and shaped by war, and also for a place to raise his young family. In Guam, Ramon discovered an island similar enough in climate and culture to the Philippines, and sufficiently far enough from a domestic situation that had, according to his wife Josefina, become too much like a battle zone. His move to America, or rather where "America's Day Begins," as Guam is popularly known, was a salvage operation for Ramon's upstart family. So too was *Pappy's* eventual naturalization as an American "sixty-cents," as he punned, ambivalently, his new status as an American "citizen."

Besides the injunction to finish one's mongo beans, among Pappy's most solid convictions is the maxim "blood runs thicker than water." I have inherited this tenet, but mediated by upbringing in postwar Guam, intellectual training, and most recently, fatherhood of my own, I would like to trumpet a new generation of Diazes but with a qualifier: blood may run thicker than water, but the flow that counts is neither genetic nor racial, but narratological in constitution.

This essay takes stock of my stock, especially as it circulates through indio and mestizo displacement in Filipino, Spanish, and American acts of remembering, and as mediated in filial stress and tension in post–World War II Guam.[2] Here, I yearn not merely for a spot in what Vicente Rafael calls the "differentially articulated locations of Filipino-ness," but for a more culturally appropriate, and culturally appropriated, way to engage

Fig. 5.1. Lolo Vicente Diaz [from *Vestiges of War*].

Fig. 5.2. Lolo Vicente and Lola Bibiana and Familia [from *Vestiges of War*].

the perimeters of that highly local and well-entrenched battleground called one's *familia*.³ My approach will be personal, familial, one aim of which would be to illustrate just one moment in the ambivalent character of colonial discourse.⁴

Pappy's House

Years ago, while Pappy was still on the bench, I chanced upon a friend, a cop, who asked about his welfare. My friend had been detailed several times to monitor Pappy's house in the Kaiser subdivision in Dededo, on account of an escaped convict. Now he had an opportunity to address a

Fig. 5.3. Judge Diaz, Superior Court of Guam
[from *Vestiges of War*].

curiosity: "Your house must be really nice in the inside, huh?" His question
alluded to the incongruity of a prominent judge living in a rather rundown, low-cost tract home. It was like, "What's up with your house, man?"
I confessed that the house was the same in the inside as it was on the outside, but he didn't believe me, and he departed still convinced that the ex-
terior of the house was a ruse to downplay in public what he thought was
in fact the material wealth and prosperity of a prominent citizen.

In fact the inside was not only as *magulu* (messy) as the outside, it was
worse: bubbled ceilings, stained carpetry, pocked linoleum. In our *comedor*
(dining room) sat rickety chairs and a table whose susan had become too
lazy to swivel due to piles of books, legal pads, and bills. By the time Pappy
and Mammy moved next to Marilen and Pascual, the house brimmed

with fifty years of things from ten children and more grandchildren. In the final days, Pappy's house was like a tomb, sighed Mammy: dark and cooped up. But if it be likened to a tomb, let it be the famous one on the eve of Redemption, for the house also carried half a century of the woman's crosses to bear it all.

Half a century earlier, Mammy and Pappy moved to Guam. In the mid-1960s they finally settled into what was then one of Guam's first public housing subdivisions built specifically to accommodate residents who had lost their homes to Supertyphoon Karen ("the Killer") of 1962, and more importantly, the first government-funded, all-concrete, no-nonsense typhoon-proof homes. This important moment in Guam's postwar history of urban development also coincided with the influx of Filipinos, and later, of Micronesians, in search of the proverbial pie in America's "westernmost" territory. But for the majority of the Filipinos, Kaiser Dededo would be renamed "Tagalu land," or "Little Manila," even though the hordes were neither exclusively Tagalog nor from Manila.[5]

But Kaiser Cement and Steel represented more than security and calm during subsequent typhoons, the real causes for bubbled ceilings and stained carpets.[6] It also concretized Pappy's determination to be a good provider. Eventually, the surrounding overgrowth bespoke Pappy's epic struggle to convert a barren sea of *cascajo* (crushed coral) or limestone

Fig. 5.4. Kaiser, Dededo, 1967 [from *Vestiges of War*].

Fig. 5.5. Battling outside the court [from *Vestiges of War*].

into a green lawn, another unsuccessful emulation of American (or was it prewar Filipino?) suburbia in Guam. If anything, Pappy's yardwork only paved the way for the bush's return with a vengeance: planting seedlings (never fun) gave way to futile cycles of weeding and mowing. Yard maintenance, like housework inside with ten children, escalated quickly into a full-scale war to keep nature at bay. And though he fought valiantly, often armed with pumps of pesticides, Pappy, like modernity displaced in the tropics, lost most of the skirmishes.

But Pappy's concern with exteriority was not restricted to the surface appearance of the house. He also sought to regulate our public image.

And, like nature, we too resisted things like *camisetas* (T-shirts) that were supposed to absorb our perspiration; or globs of pomade, later brylcream, designed to hold our indio (read: magulu) hair. In the postwar interethnic tension that was mounting in Guam too, we would learn to quickly control, if not disguise, our pinoy accents as well. In this milieu an unmarked (I mark it here) "standard American English" canon would make great strides in washing out vestiges of linguistic and cultural difference and carving out for itself, with ambivalent and even eager assistance from Chamorros, Filipinos, Micronesians, and other Asians, the privileged position as the lingua franca.

Pappy's gaze penetrated the surface, too. He was infamous for speaking his mind, the accent notwithstanding. All had to "mark" his words (never "minced"). This was especially true when it came to morality, of which there were only two kinds: right and wrong. Carlitos would inherit, and contest, Pappy's moral mathematics thus: "There are three kinds of people in the world: those who can count and those who can't!"

Fig. 5.6. With Mammy [from *Vestiges of War*].

Of Riffs and Rifts

Kaiser Dededo was Pappy's "jackpot," as he once put it to me. For me, though, the house (now) is simply rundown. And like my Lolo Hilario (Pappy's Pappy's Pappy) at the end of the last century, a century later I too am feeling a bit up*routed*.[7] At a time when rap music snags all the pop music awards, a "house" is not just a home, but a coming together of people who are cool, with whom you prefer to "hang," as the hip hop brand of twenty-first-century pop culture puts it. In need of a more "down home" (visceral) theory and method, I sample rap's riffs to address the colonial legacy of my rifts, and my desire to proceed with a difference.

Hip hop, cousin to "rap," originated in black street culture in New York, and later in California '*hoods* (neighborhoods) like Crenshaw, Compton, and Carson City (Tony's way of pronouncing the Spanish word for underwear).[8] Hip hop has also become *down* (acceptable) among Filipino and other Pacific Islanders, whose own hoods, like the John and Maryann Carr-hood in Fullerton, rank among the fastest growing communities in California. Of course, hip hop and rap have roots in Jazz and Blues, with roots of their own in the legacies of African slaves in the Americas. But in this cross-cultural mix I contend that the relationship between Pappy, pop, former slaves, and displaced indios such as Chamorros and Filipinos, have deeper implications than understood by trendy scholarly traffic in pop culture. *Know what I mean?* Let me ground some of these stakes, or routes, by returning tactically to my roots.

Pappy [Papi]

"Pappy" is the Patriarch of Todos los Diazes. In an argument with Marilen not long ago, Pappy was adamant about men's natural status as heads of families and societies, that women should be subservient. Len countered that even *Pappy* didn't raise her like that. I got into it too, and interrogated him over where he got this so-called natural law. His answer was "from Mama," Lola Bibiana, the matriarch by all accounts. My pointing out the peculiar notion of patriarchy-derived-from-matriarchy met with Pappy's pointing out the inferiority of my American education.[9]

Nonetheless, the word "Pappy" is one of those terms whose universal variation is slim enough that the objects they signify appear to be natural, like the idea of patriarchy as a natural law. The striking phonetic similarities between Europe's "Papa," the Middle East's "Aba," Oceania's "Apa," and Chamorro "Tata," tempt us to conclude that their signified, the English "Father," like patriarchy, is indeed rooted in nature. Or if not in nature, then in the divine. Allow me to digress tactically on another onomatopoetic word with equally mythic reach and dwelling power: Pappy's *pedo*. Pedo is what Todos los Diazes "throw" (*tira*, or, in Tagalog, "*ai, bastus!*"), which our in-laws across the states decry as "fart," which Chamorros in the House might perform as *do'du*, and for which Tony would need to change his Carson City. Of course, there is no law, natural or divine, requiring that the word for the odoriferous miasma be uniform in sound. For example, in the Micronesian island of Pohnpei (homeland of Lolo Miguel),the appropriate term is *seng*, which explains why our Pohnpeian relations giggle at the late Karen Carpenter's pop tune that goes:

> *Seng*
> *Seng* a Song
> *Seng* out Loud
> *Seng* out Strong!

Speaking of *anima*, Todos los Diazes will not forget the time in our lives when we laughed at, nay, rejoiced in, Carl's successful bids to fart at will. How the release of gas entrapped in his cancerous colon, cause of great agony, could be music to our ears. Two years after his death, memories of Carl's effort to heal our bodies with laughter become sacred; their dwelling power, recontextualized and now culturally syncopated, remixed, so to speak, can also be regarded as a sort of postnatural folk remedy. Go on, try it, with my Pohnpeian tongue, and seng the Carpenter song again. Seng out loud. Seng out strong. And continue the verse that follows, but with memories of your special person's last(ing) days with us:

> Seng of Good Things Not Bad
> Seng of Happy, Not Sad.
> (Join me, won't you? La La La La La . . .)

The digression is the point: terms like "Pappy," and like his pedos for that matter, have an interestingly wide circulation in time and space, and have original meanings that can be remade, and can be remade in the interest of tapping sources of authority, or even deflecting their reach. With these pedo-principles in hand, let us return to the American deep South for a particular brand of pop culture to illustrate the additional value, and deeper mess, of "Pappy's House."

[Papi]

The term "Pappy" is common in the American South, but with a twang, as [Paa-PEE]. For me, Paapee conjures up two interrelated images: Colonel Sanders, and old black men fishing the Missouri River (Maribel and Tom's hood) as escaped slaves. But between the two images of white and black Paapees is an unevenly experienced history of slavery and race relations that still manages to produce the term Paapee as the name of the father for both black and white folks alike.

Fig. 5.7. Mammy and Pappy [from *Vestiges of War*].

Now, how a single term of endearment for "the father" can be embraced by black and white folk alike is an interesting question.[10] But how to account for the term's presence in our *boondocks* tropical neck of the woods? The answer lies in the intertwining of racialized, gendered, and sexualized histories of European imperialism and native responses thereto, and how these transactions are shaped by, and in turn, further shape, notions of parental authority. In our case, the one-two punch of Spanish and American rule, and our embrace of key terms like "padre," "Papa," and "Daddy" would produce hybrids like "Pappy." It is in these political processes of creolization that we can better understand what Chamorros in the House call *Kostumbren Chamorro*: Chamorro customs and practices, couched heavily in Spanish Catholicism, whose own arrival in the Marianas was actually a hybrid form of "Mexican" and "Filipino" mixtures, which were historical and cultural hybridities themselves.

And like Filipino or Mexican "culture," Chamorro *Kostumbre* also reactivates older native values and principles such as *taimamahlao*. Like *walang hiya*, to be labeled taimamahlao is to be reproached big time: to be charged with having "no shame." And in Guam, to be called taimamahlao is to be likened to an *Amerikanu*. Whatever the added (or subtracted) value, terms like mamahlao reveal indigenous histories of unequal relations of power and authority, later recharged through Euro-American colonization and native responses thereto. *Bueno*. But how are these hybridities here linked to those there, in the American deep South? Consider first the southern "Paapee" in relation to the southern "Maamee."

Pappy and Mammy

Like Paapee, the term Maamee is also used by blacks and whites alike. And like Paapee, there are also pop images for Maamee. Recall Colonel Sanders, the quintessential southern gentleman. In his younger days we might imagine him as a dashing officer, quick to defend, even to death, the honor of his woman, the southern belle, the debutante. I imagine southern Paapees as former Confederate soldiers. It is in the name of women, children, money, and nation, that men go to war, and in this context, it is the Civil War's contest between rebels defending the honor and the economy of the South against Yankees defending the integrity of a northern-conceived (and female-engendered) nation.

Fig. 5.8. "More Like His Dad Everyday" [from *Vestiges of War*].

But if for the white South the image of the father is Colonel Sanders, I concur with Barbara Christian that the white image of the mother is not a white woman, but the ubiquitous *black* momma best imaged in Aunt Jemima of pancake and syrup fame.[11] This particular Maamee, whose apron and bandanna symbolize domestication and labor, is the one who attends exclusively to the domestic needs of the white estate. According to Christian, the recurring figure of the nurturing, caring, black Mammy, is what enabled the narrativization of such archetypical white identities as chivalrous southern gentlemen and debutante belles, and their epic romance and tragedy set in the deep South.[12] Christian argues that in the literary, as in the social texts of the region, Aunt Jemima shouldered the brutal actualities of life, for "in the mythology of the South," she writes, "men did not fight duels or protect the honor of a woman who was busy cooking, scrubbing floors, or minding children, since the exclusive performance of this kind of work precluded the intrigue necessary to be a person as ornament." In marking the inextricability between racialized and gendered images of self and other here, Christian also illustrates the deep links between popular culture and histories of colonization. But you might still ask, unconvinced, what the interconnections are between those Paapees and Maamees, and ours. Let's ask the children.

Picaninnies One and All

In the South, and then beyond, the term "picaninny" referred initially to the children of slaves, and later became the metonymic reduction of all blacks in the belief that they were naturally inferior and infantile. White authority, in terms of benevolent parenthood, is at stake here. Though these sentiments are not exclusive to the deep South, nor to the United States, it is useful to trace the term and its actions here for a moment.

After the Civil War, and as an integral component of its national reconstruction, the United States began to lay claims to the globe. The nineteenth century's end, America believed, was its destiny's crossroads: it had survived political and economic collapse, and was witnessing tremendous technological advancement and social upheaval, particularly through the perceived hordes of uncouth immigrants from both sides of the continent. America also believed that it had reached some limits, like land and wilderness, whose transformation was the stuff of progress, whose taming was the mark of its genius. At this time, America's *homies* (peers) *barcada* (mates), like Germany, France, and Britain, had already been taking over the 'hood, as Spain had for three hundred years, except that Spain now couldn't *hang* (keep up). And so in 1898 America evicts Spain with stolen rap riffs like *Cuba Libre!* but in ways that exempted Cuban insurgents, and later, Filipino *insurrectos,* from their own presumed national destinies. But what does all this have to do with picaninnies, and picaninnies with us? *Todos.* When the United States beat Spain and snatched Cuba and Puerto Rico over there, and the Filipinas and the Marianas over here, American publications would run cartoons that consistently depicted their peoples, us! as little black children, as picaninnies.

Interestingly enough, the term picaninny, once thought to be the province of the deep South, but now elevated to national and international

Fig. 5.9. The children [from *Vestiges of War*].

assertions of American supremacy, turns out to be none other than the anglicized contraction of the Spanish term *pequeño niño!*[13] And what is pequeño niño but an earlier strategic articulation of the Spanish *Imperio's* own racialized pecking order, beginning at the top with *peninsulares,* followed by displaced *criollos,* then by even more confused *mestizos* whose vexed indio heritage is always either debased or ennobled in colonial or postcolonial versions of domination.

For Spain, the colonial regulation of money, gender, race, sexuality, language, and identity took place within, among other institutions and practices, the *Patronato Real,* a bureaucratic apparatus which for many reasons failed to ensure the integrity of the monarchy's will across the Atlantic and Pacific. According to Vince Rafael, the Patronato Real was modeled on the idea of a "patron-client" relationship between God and the King, which was replicated between the King and his surrogates, and the surrogates' surrogates dispersed throughout the far-flung empire.[14] Rooted in the idea of the benevolent law of God the Father, the term "patron" also shaped the identity of His principal client and/or offspring, the King, and sought to regenerate itself through the downward and outward flow of the royal patronage system. Transposed across cultures, this Spanish brand of paternalism produced the idea that Spaniards were white parents to indios figured as dark children, or pequeño niños, or their Anglo-American cousins, the picaninnies, in need of proper guidance and upbringing. But the critique of postcolonialism also shows us that the power of colonialism is more magulu (messy) than unidirectional or monolithic. That colonial discourse also insinuates itself in indigenous discourses of power and vice versa, so that its power and effects become epic in their multiple modes of regeneration. With this particular genealogy, it should also become our legacy to contend with the Man (or Woman) in our house, however we define that house.

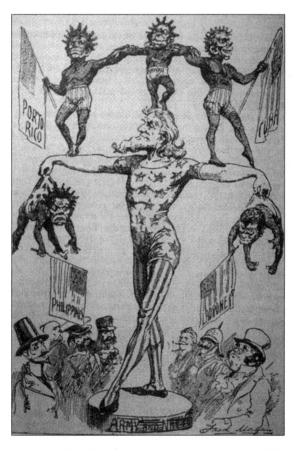

Fig. 5.10. "Uncle Sam's Newly Caught Anthropoids" [from *Vestiges of War*].

Pappies in the House

In a summer seminar on the legacies of the Spanish, Filipino, Cuban, American War of 1898 organized and conducted by Virginia Dominguez and Jane Desmond at the University of Iowa's Obermann Center for Advanced Studies, I was presented with an *ethno-op* (ethnographic opportunity) to ask other historically and culturally informed pequeño niños from Cuba, the Philippines, Hawai'i, Puerto Rico, and Kansas, about "Pappy." Pappy, I discovered, was not one. His Houses, many. At least for us heirs to ongoing histories of Euro-American colonialism (and who is not?). My sheepish question, "Who is Pappy?" elicited specific names, including, for the men, their own. One answer was a corrective: "Not who is Pappy, but what is Pappy?" Not surprisingly, I discovered that Pappy had multiple and deep meanings that ran the gamut from a term of deep affection for one's father or one's son, to the term for an acquaintance ("hola Pappy!"), to cat calls ("Hoooy Pappppppy!"), to steamy talk between hot lovers ("oooh pappppeeee"). In this unscientific survey, Pappy was alternately a figure of authority, a helpless boy, a stud, a spoiled brat, and a lover. One informant, a woman, replied: "Me. I'm Pappy."

Though Pappy is intensely personal, he is also inside every one of us in a way that makes him an intensely collective, public, historical artifact precisely through his meanderings. Moreover, Pappy's historical and cultural multiplicity is just one example of the multiple meanings that have been made of figures and terms of imperial authority, whose structures consist as much in the gaze of authority as in the festive and, at times, irreverent and subversive play of meaning remaking by diverse peoples subject to that authority. And, if that be the case, particularly as compounded in this so-called age of globalization, then the critical question becomes not who is Pappy but that first raised by my friend, the cop: "What's up with *your* house?"

NOTES

1. This subtitle and the genealogies within it are inspired by Cherrie Moraga, "A Long Line of Vendidas," in *Loving in the War Years* (Boston: South End Press, 1983). This essay is dedicated to Tina and Nicole, and especially little Gabriella, who demands that the subject of this essay be grounded. All photos, unless other-

wise noted, are from the Diaz collections. Special thanks to William Hernandez and Lawrence Cunningham for slide reproductions.

2. Guam is an "unincorporated territory" of the United States, a euphemism that obfuscates its actual status as a colony of the United States. A former Spanish colony that was treated as an offshore province of the Philippine command, Guam was seized by the United States at the outbreak of the misnamed Spanish-American War in 1898 and has been held as a possession since then. The indigenous people of Guam (and the surrounding Mariana Islands) are called "Chamorros," and are said to have settled these islands from Southeast Asia beginning about four thousand years ago. Like all Oceanic languages, the Chamorro language belongs to the Austronesian group.

3. I remain indebted to Vicente Rafael's analyses of and relentless skirmishes with nationalist discourses in their multiple forms. The quote is from his analyses of affect and nationalism in "'Your Grief Is Our Gossip': Overseas Filipinos and Other Spectral Presence," *CSST Working Paper 111,* University of Michigan, October, 1996. On the broader condition of Filipino colonial and postcolonial displacement, see Vicente Rafael, ed. *Discrepant Histories: Translocal Essays on Filipino Cultures* (Philadelphia: Temple University Press, 1995), and Yen Le Esperitu, "The Intersection of Race, Ethnicity, and Class: The Multiple Identities of Second-Generation Filipinos," *Identities,* 1:2, 1–25.

The people mentioned in this essay are either siblings, in-laws, and extended family members who comprise what we affectionately refer to as "Todos los Diazes," now living in Guam, across the fifty states, in places like Australia and probably the Middle East, as balikbayans or OCWs, as critically distinguished in Rafael, "'Your Grief Is Our Gossip.'"

4. Bhabha's notion of the ambivalence of colonial discourse first published in Homi Bhabha, "Of Mimicry and Man: The Ambivalence of Colonial Discourse," *October,* 28 (1984): 125–133.

5. Of the total population of Guam in 1996 (156,302), the Filipino population comprised 23 percent and was the second-largest ethnic group next to the indigenous Chamorros (42 percent). Other major groups were: "Caucasians" (14 percent), which included white American and other Europeans, "Other" (13 percent), which included East Asians like Japanese, Chinese, Taiwanese, Koreans, and so on, and finally, "Micronesians" (7 percent), which referred to islanders from the surrounding island nation-states (the Republic of the Marshall Islands, the Republic of Palau, and the Federated States of Micronesia) which entered into "free association" with the United States in the 1980s and 1990s, and whose terms provided unrestricted travel and residence between these islands and American territories and states like Guam and Hawai'i. Population estimates are from Ron Stade, *Pacific Passages: World Culture and Local Politics in Guam* (Stockholm: University of Stockholm, 1998), p. v.

These demographics were a cause for alarm among many Chamorros, an "ethnic" group that dropped below 50 percent of the total population for the first time since the 1980s. Depending on who you talk to, the Chamorros are either "a minority in our own homeland" or "the biggest ethnic group" in the island, a significant gap in description and perception that captures (and fuels) the growing sense of social tension in a society that is widely and uncritically categorized as "American." In this social setup, pun intended, Filipinos are often stigmatized as leading the charge of aliens in the process of dispossessing Chamorros of their land and jobs, in spite of (or perhaps precisely for) the long history that Chamorros and people from the Philippines have maintained since Spanish times. For a sense of the asymmetrical relations between Filipinos and Chamorros within the asymmetrical relations of Spanish and American colonialism, see Vicente M. Diaz, "Bye Bye Ms. American Pie: Chamorros and Filipinos and the American Dream," *Isla: Journal of Micronesian Studies* 3:1 (Rainy Season 1995): 147–160. For a productive, if provocative treatment of the construction of cultural and ethnic identity in Guam, see Stade, *Pacific Passages.*

6. For the social expenses of Kaiser Cement and Steel in California, see Mike Davis, *City of Quartz: Excavating the Future in Los Angeles* (New York: Vintage, 1992).

7. For a general critique of the routedness of culture and the culture of travel, see James Clifford, *Routes: Travel and Translation in the Late Twentieth Century* (Cambridge: Harvard University Press, 1997). From the Pacific, see Teresia Teaiwa, "Yaqona/Yagoqu: Routes and Roots of a Displaced Native" *UTS Review* 4:2 (1998), and "Loosing the Native," paper presented at the Eleventh Conference of the Pacific History Association, Hilo, Hawaii, July 1996. See also Vicente M. Diaz and J. Kehaulani Kauanui, "Native Pacific Cultural Studies on the Edge," special issue of *The Contemporary Pacific* 13:2 (fall 2001); Vicente M. Diaz, "Sacred Tensions: Navigating Tradition and Modernity," in *Micronesian Educator* (Mangilao: University of Guam Press, 2001), and *Sacred Vessels: Navigating Tradition and Identity in Micronesia* (1997: 30 mins.), coproduced with Christine Taitano Delisle.

8. For cultural histories, see the essays in *Microphone Friends: Youth Music and Youth Culture,* edited by Andrew Ross and Tricia Rose (New York: Routledge, 1994).

9. My American education, in the disciplines of history, anthropology, and political theory have also fed me a steady stream of tenets and axioms like the notion that precontact island societies were "matrilineal" in kinship and social structure, in which an individual's identity and resources are reckoned through "the mother's" (and not the father's) lineage. David Schneider's critical cautions notwithstanding, notions such as "matrilineality" continue to serve as deep markers not only of the exotic, but as determinants of native authenticity: where patriarchy and patrilineage, especially as introduced by western imperialism, take root, authentic local culture disappears. Among other things, this essay is part of an ongoing bid for the recovery of purity, but especially purity and innocence through

valorized ideas of matrilineage or matriarchy. On Schneider, see David Schneider, *American Kinship: A Cultural Account* (Chicago: University of Chicago Press, 1980). On kinship in Oceania, see David Schneider, "Conclusions," in Mac Marshall, ed., *Siblingship in Oceania* (Ann Arbor: University of Michigan Press, 1981), 389–404. For a most recent assessment of kinship in Micronesia, see Mac Marshall, "'Partial Connections': Kinship and Social Organization in Micronesia," in Robert C. Kiste and Mac Marshall, eds., *American Anthropology in Micronesia* (Honolulu: University of Hawai'i Press, 1999), 107–143.

10. One answer is found in the way a particular postbellum African American discourse of racial "uplift" appropriated and replicated a social order that upheld white paternalism. See Kevin Gaines, *Uplifting the Race: Black Politics and Culture in the United States since the Turn of the Century* (Chapel Hill: University of North Carolina Press, 1995). On the other hand, see M. M. Manring's wide-ranging and insightful analyses of the durability of the figure of Aunt Jemima in the making of authority for black and white folks. M. M. Manring, *Slave in a Box: The Strange Career of Aunt Jemima* (Charlottesville: University of Virginia Press, 1997).

11. *Black Feminist Criticism* (New York: Pergamon Press, 1985).

12. Again, see Manring's *Slave in a Box*.

13. I thank Kelvin Vellez-Santiago for pointing this out.

14. The foregoing draws from Vicente Rafael, *Contracting Colonialism: Translation and Christian Conversion in Tagalog Society under Early Spanish Rule* (Durham, N.C: Duke University Press, 1993).

Reprinted from *Vestiges of War: The Philippine-American War and the Aftermath of an Imperial Dream, 1899–1999*, edited by Angel Velasio Shaw and Luis H. Francia (New York: NYU Press, 2002).

Part II

Cultural Legacy and Memories

Chapter 6

"Within Each Crack/A Story"

The Political Economy of Queering Filipino American Pasts

Victor Bascara

Prologue: Queer Epiphanies

It turns out all lonely people are the same.
——Fai (Tony Leung) in Wong Kar Wai's film *Happy Together* (1997)

Near the end of Wong Kar Wai's *Happy Together,* Fai, the film's long-suffering and pragmatic protagonist, spots Ho (played by the late great Leslie Cheung), his ex who has again turned to a life of hustling. After their final breakup, he discovers Ho in a public restroom in Buenos Aires. A year earlier, they had gotten stranded in the Argentine capital while on vacation; they parted company, reunited, and then parted again. In the lavatory, Fai was shocked to find himself in the same space as Ho, although he was there for some anonymous sex himself.

At that moment, he has an epiphany that leads to a chain of events that resolve the story: he finally makes his pilgrimage to the Iguazu waterfalls, finally leaves Argentina, and finally returns to Hong Kong, where he is on his way to a reconciliation with his father at the end of the story. He narrates this epiphany to us in voice-over: "It turns out all lonely people are the same." This sentiment characterizes both the triumph and the tragedy of queer identification: the dialectic of both profound alienation and sustaining community.

This essay looks at a famously lonely, alienated, and forgotten community of people—the manongs, or early waves of predominantly male Filipino immigrant laborers. This essay assesses the extent to which contemporary conceptions of loneliness and community, such as that articulated by Fai, resonate with and resemble the manongs. I argue that such queer revisionism allows us to hear and see the manongs anew. Now that we can see them with these new eyes, what do we actually see? Queer revisionism is a wedge into a critique of political economy. We can see that identity-based oppression is never very far from identity-based exploitation. Yet, at the same time, in the history of liberalism and capitalism, oppression and exploitation are not necessarily equivalent and interchangeable. In order to make this argument, we can trace the emergence of queer identity in Asian America and examine the uses to which queer identity has been put in Asian American historical revisionism. The argument then queers the bachelor communities of Filipino men, not necessarily to discern sexual practices or even desires, but rather to examine the ways in which a queered understanding of the manongs reveals critical subjectivities and agencies that might not otherwise have been visible. In apprehending the political economy of queering Filipino American pasts, queerness can be used as a vehicle for discerning class consciousness, because queerness was both a means of legitimating exploitation and a site for imagining critical alternatives to conventional practices of community. But first, how and why did we begin to see queerly?

I. Ubiquitously Queer: The Love That Loves to Speak Its Name

To the casual observer who is even mildly aware of recent social and cultural transformations, the sodomitical implications of "within each crack/a story" are not lost. This phrase would not escape the snickers of Beavis and Butthead, who have been so oddly influential in the queering of popular culture. Precious little escapes the cringing gaze of interpretations looking for multiple entendres, especially when a phrase is positioned specifically to provoke such readings. Queer studies and gay and lesbian studies have a long tradition of provocative phrases: "Anal/Rope," "Is the Rectum a Grave?" "Looking for My Penis," "Live Sex Acts," "This Bridge Called My Crack," to name a few.[1]

In the tradition of inventive reading practices, we can pose the Gayatri Spivak question—"Can the subaltern speak?"—in order to read forms of speaking that issue from locations previously unimagined as sources of representation.[2] The title of this essay comes from the ending of Virginia Cerenio's poem, "you lovely people" (1983). The poem is not ostensibly about buggering. Yet it is precisely this against-the-grain meaning that makes Cerenio's rendering of manongs so suggestive.[3] It is of course important to remember that her poem is overtly about the figure of the manong, those early Filipino immigrant laborers who were "schoolboy cooks / militant farmworkers / pineapple canners / fish piecers / gold miners / navy shoeshiners / poolhall hustlers." After this litany of occupations, the poem can resolutely declare: "now we are all manongs." And the poem further concludes, "ay, manong / your old brown hands / hold life, many lives / within each crack/ a story." The cracks of old, laboring hands are the cracks that tell stories. Yet they can also be understood as the cracks through which we can recognize alternative social practices, alternative modes of pleasure and community that emerged out of the *material* conditions of the manongs.

For at least a decade or two, queerness has had a profound impact on discerning and valorizing alternative forms of socialization, both current and historical. The truly wondrous possibilities of this new perspective have led to mildly utopian visions of liberal tolerance made possible by a generous contribution from the universal queerness of postmodernity. Indeed, we're here. We're all queer. And we all have gotten used to it: from David Geffen, the gay dollar, Act Up, *Queer as Folk,* Ellen Degeneres, *Will and Grace,* and fag-hag Margaret Cho to gay-friendly episodes of *Everybody Loves Raymond* and *The King of Queens* on famously family-friendly CBS. Queerness is pervasive, as befits any commodity. So the slogan declares: "We are everywhere."

In spite of these transformations and recognitions, a relatively new question has been heard with increasing frequency and loudness: how, if at all, does queering productively intersect with critical race theory and historical materialism? In other words, how does "We are everywhere" intersect with "Now we are all manongs"? How does a queering of Asian American pasts contribute to a critique of political economy? There have been a few compelling formulations of that connection and, with the unmitigated triumph of globalization, the time is ripe for such a link to be made more explicit.[4] This essay, then, seeks a marriage of Lisa Lowe's notions of Asian American cultural politics with the radical potential of queer theory as a historical methodology.

Nayan Shah's generative notion of "queer domesticity" can be used to characterize pre-1965 communities of Filipino laborers. Following Shah's use of "queer domesticity" to explain forms of socialization in early twentieth-century San Francisco Chinatown, the manongs are a resonant and related formation. Shah also asserts that the queering of those communities is not so much a way of valorizing gay and lesbian identity as it is a wedge of critique into the capitalist development that both occasioned those communities and better enabled and legitimated their exploitation in the service of capitalist development.

> The analysis of "queer domesticity" emphasizes the variety of erotic ties and social affiliations that counters normative expectations. Rather than viewing the term *queer* as a synonym for homosexual identity, I use it to question the formation of exclusionary norms of respectable middle-class, heterosexual marriage. The analytical category of queer upsets the strict gender roles, the firm divisions between public and private, and the implicit presumptions of self-sufficient economies and intimacy in the respectable domestic household. (Shah 2002, 13–14)

In readings of works of Asian American and Filipino American cultural politics, as well as examining period sources and historiography of the waves of Filipino immigrants to the United States, this essay narrates the stories found in the proverbial cracks. These stories tell a tale of how they fell into and are emerging from those orifices of the past and present.

II. "Difficult Remembering": Heroes of Queer History

Perhaps the central enabling insight of *Immigrant Acts,* Lowe's definitive study of Asian American cultural politics is the following: "It is . . . in culture that individuals and collectivities struggle and remember and, in that difficult remembering, imagine and practice both subject and community differently" (1996, 3). "Difficult remembering" well describes the act of recognizing queer pasts that can emerge from Asian American critique. Although her book does not explicitly take up the queering of Asian American pasts, Lowe's formulations of what the past reveals, particularly vis-à-vis a narrative of gendered racialization and capitalist development, can provide a welcome jolt of both political economy and historical materialism into the queering of history.

Toward this objective, we need to make queer *economic* sense of alternative forms of domesticity in historical understandings of pre-1965 waves of Filipino immigrants to the United States. Through an analysis of the ways in which dominant and emergent histories characterized Filipino communities, we can grasp a rationale for queer social formations that register the hostilities facing these little brown siblings and may indeed provide a blueprint for alternative forms of mobilization today. That is, by understanding the dialectic of queerness and Filipino immigrant labor, the limits of current forms of engagement with exploitation become more visible and new possibilities emerge.

Especially since the 1980s, the cultural and political work of scholars and activists has been central to making these limits and alternatives visible, by elucidating the links between race, labor, gender, and sexuality.[5] One of the most influential essays emerging from the new social movements of the 1980s is Richard Fung's much-anthologized "Looking for My Penis."[6] As with Ronald Takaki's guiding metaphor of "a different mirror" for revising dominant histories, Fung also reads a looking glass in which he cannot quite see himself reflected back. His mirror, however, is contemporary gay pornography. Fung's essay is required reading for anyone wanting to understand both the capabilities of cultural studies as well as the breathtaking sense of possibility that the 1980s presented to emergent subjectivities and communities.

The even more effective piece was Fung's film, *Dirty Laundry,* which has the earnest subtitle, *A History of Heroes.* This part-narrative, part-documentary assembles reenactments, interviews, and dramatizations. The result is a series of acts of historical recovery that contemporary queer subjectivities perform on the past. The protagonist, Roger Kwong, is a journalist riding the Canadian rails, trying to write a feature on the model minority on his new-fangled word processing device that fits atop his lap. He also carries with him a framed photograph of his great-grandfather, who had worked on the construction of the Trans-Canadian Railway.

Through a series of accidental moments involving a variety of fluids ending up on our hero, the past becomes queered. The epiphany occurs when a conductor's careless act results in the dropping of the framed portrait and the revelation of a hidden photograph. In that second portrait we see two men: Roger's great-grandfather and another unidentified Chinese man. Their hands are touching.

The conductor, a Chinese man who is presumably an immigrant, explains to Roger that in China men are affectionate with one another in that way. Eventually, Roger and the conductor physically pleasure each other in unambiguously sexual ways, both on and off camera. The film sets up a parallel between the cruising that Roger and the conductor perform and the cruising that Roger performs on the photograph. And so

Roger's "gay-dar"—the popularized concept used to describe a radar-like sensitivity for detecting disruptions in heteronormativity—is recalibrated to rethink overseas Chinese pasts of community and labor as the site and occasion for queer domesticity. Fittingly, the video ends with Roger writing a magazine article about that very subject.

Intercut with this drama are sexperts who describe the historical conditions of bachelor communities of Chinese laborers. Nayan Shah and other historians flesh out the possibility and probability of queer domesticity in the bachelor societies. It is both ironic and fitting that Fung's protagonist is a biological descendant of a member of these notoriously childless social formations. As Shah elaborates in his book, these communities were the Other against which Victorian domestic units felt their legitimacy and centrality. Through against-the-grain readings of archives, particularly those emerging out of the discourse of public health, Shah discerns the ways in which categories like bachelor society, and even gay and lesbian, may be inadequate to describe the practices and subjectivities of these Asian American men and boys.[7]

Both Fung's article and film emphasize acts of reading and interpretation, primarily from analyses of the dominant archive of statutes and popular record, but also from occasional flashes of evidence from the Chinese themselves. The film dramatizes what follows from his abortive penis (and phallus) search: both a critique of normativity and the newly recognizable alternative practices that also made that critique possible. Fung's film and article are efforts to excavate subaltern epistemologies. But the film more explicitly follows through on what the article can only gesture toward: a critique of political economy.

These epistemologies are subaltern because they went unrecognized by modernity and its official past. These persons and practices only become visible after a change in consciousness. This change equips the present to see those communities only as traces of a lost world. *A History of Heroes* is effectively an instruction manual and model for historical recovery made possible by the emergence of new social movements. (And, in the spirit of "Looking for My Penis," the movie involves two Asian men having sex, albeit without a "money shot" or even a full monty shot.)[8]

III. Little, Brown, and Company:
Sons, Brothers, and Fictive Kinship

Fung's video explicitly queers Asian North American pasts. It is a post–Stonewall era text, if I may invoke the customary watershed of gay identity.[9] Through Roger's analysis of the photographs, Fung's video reads texts against-the-grain to find the queer subalternity of Chinese immigrant labor in the nineteenth and early twentieth centuries. There remains an archive of evidence awaiting that scrutiny to rethink the ways in which Asian American pasts have, or have not, been understood. The archives of Filipino American history are just such an object for this methodology.

Even within Asian American studies, the conception of Filipinos as forgotten, and forgetful, is canonical.[10] It has customarily and persuasively been argued that this amnesia is an epiphenomenon of the amnesia around U.S. colonialism in the Pacific at the turn of the century.[11] In particular, the invisibility of Filipinos in American history has occurred because of the incommensurability of Filipino history and U.S. nationalist ideology. The institution of America's official national culture was not equipped to recognize the presence of colonies and colonial subjects, outside of the thirteen slave-holding bourgeois settlements on the east coast, peopled by English expatriates. Colonies are what the United States used to be, not what America would aspire to acquire. And so, visions of America's colonialism in the Pacific ironically evaporated in the face of its actual realization.[12]

More generally speaking, the lack of conventional institutions and mechanisms of reproduction have led to the practical and conceptual disappearance of bachelor communities. That is, Filipinos had fallen out of familial and national structures that would have otherwise ensured their legitimacy and recognition. Yet people nonetheless have recourse to these conventional models of kinship: for example, the old timers are called *manongs* or older brothers. In *Bontoc Eulogy,* Marlon Fuentes claimed—presumably to granting organizations in the era of family values and multiculturalism—that the subject of his film was the search for his lost grandfather. That claim is wonderfully dubious.

And one of the irresistible historical nuggets that contemporary Asian American and Filipino American revisionism points to is the "Manilamen," sixteenth-century sailors aboard Spanish galleons who jumped ship and settled in what is now Mexico and the Southern United States.

Cerenio's poem invokes these sailors: "indios / on spanish galleons / to new orleans / revolutionary pirates." The assertion that "we are not new here" is especially well-served by the evidence. Yet as we are dealing with evidence more suited to the archaeologist than the historian,[13] the notion that there is a substantial and continuous familial link between those colonial subjects and today's neocolonial subjects is almost absurd, despite the claim by some Filipinos and Latinos to high quantities of Spanish blood.

Still, as a model for how to discern usable pasts, the Manilamen may actually turn out to be the rule rather than the exception. Until the post-1965 era, Filipino American communities were not exactly conventional domestic units. A history of antimiscegenation laws and wide gender imbalances ensured that conventional forms of reproduction—literal and figural—were not easy to come by. Alternative social structures and models emerged, producing and reproducing informal economies of both commerce and desire: bachelor societies, prostitution clientele, taxi dancing, antimiscegenation laws, and the like. Aside from widespread isolation and invisibility, a fraternal order dominated.[14] A horizontal brotherhood rather than a parent-child model was the idealized social ordering. Indeed, the parent-child model would have been the relationship between the United States and the Philippines. Even though the phrase often used to describe that colonial relationship is "little brown brothers," it has more closely approximated "little brown children."

Yet for the early waves of Filipino immigrants, there would be very few little brown children. This is not to say that conventional kinship was not a powerful force; domestic bliss was a dream deferred. What happened to that dream? Did it dry up like a raisin in the sun, fester like a sore, and then run? Or did it sag like a heavy load? Or did it *explode*? Domestic bliss dried up for some who died embittered. It sagged for others who sought alternative means of sociability and leisure in a world unwilling, or at least unenthusiastic about recognizing their existence. And it certainly exploded, as the uprisings in the wake of the closing of the International Hotel in San Francisco in the 1970s demonstrated.[15]

Until the epistemological transformations of queer studies, these communities were looked to with pity for the presumed loneliness, and mourning for the presumed disappearance, of manongs. The queering of Filipino American pasts has taken forms ranging from explicit analyses of "gay Filipino men" to portraits of presumably lonely men looked at with downcast eyes. Yet we cannot rescue these men from the fact of poverty and exploitation by valorizing a queerness that they did indeed embody and practice. Our appreciation of the queer domesticity of these men allows us to see a connection to older modes of exploitation that teach us how they may indeed persist.

Thus we can see how these men are both exceptional and paradigmatic. They are exceptional because they lived lives that, for the most part, history and their own moment little noted. They were, in Raymond Williams's useful terms, "residual" rather than "dominant," the vestiges of an earlier historical moment that found their exploitation legitimate or at least manageable.[16] But they are paradigmatic because they were also an "emergent" formation that may have tragically arisen to dominance.

IV. *"A Mere Filipino, an Eater of Wild Dogs": The Queering of Cheap Labor and the Cheapening of Queer Labor*

Filipinos have been both a rationale for and a disruptive force in American civilization. R. Z. Linmark's poem, "They like you because you eat dog," tracks this very idea. The poem formally employs repetition and inventory. It catalogs the various reasons why Filipinos—ultimately unnamed in the poem—serve the American civilizing mission by being those in need of civilization. In the history of Western conceptions of Filipinos, the consumption of canine meat has long served as the dividing line between the civilized and the noncivilized worlds, from titular dog eaters of Luis Cabalquinto and Jessica Hagedorn (1990) to the sensational Igorots at the 1904 St. Louis World's Fair. Importantly, this difference must be understood in relation to the possibility of reform. The forms of difference that Linmark enumerates are presumed to be ultimately assimilable. Filipinos are, in the biblically charged phrase from Stanley Karnow, "in our image":[17]

> They like you because you're a copycat, want to be just like them.
> They like you because, give it a couple of more years, you'll be just like them.

The trajectory from diner-on-man's-best-friend to "copycat" nicely sums up the colonial project of the Americans in the Philippines.[18] Immediately following the above-cited lines, the poem ends with an ominous rhetorical question: "And when that time comes, will they like you more?" The presumed answer is no. Cultural difference has served important economic functions for the cheapening of labor; that is, such laborers do not require a living wage because they are a lesser form of being for whom life is cheap. The middle section of Linmark's poem articulates the rationale for exploitation:

> They like you because you're a potato queen.
> They like you because you're one hell of a gardener.
> They like you because you work three full-time jobs—scraping greasy floors, scouring pots and pans, and scrubbing toilet bowls.
> They like you because you're a walking cholera, hepatitis, and TB.
> They like you because you're a minimum-wage.
> They like you because you have maids back home.
> They like you because you're a doctor there and a nurse's aide here.
> They like you because you say you have a college degree but they say it's only the equivalent of a ninth grade American Education.

Filipinos are multitalented, loyal, and inexpensive. They are a labor force made exploitable—in current parlance, "flexible"—by the needs of capital and its culture. Historically, being flexible has meant practicing a queer domesticity that conventional domesticity both needs and repudiates. Ideologically, conventional domesticity needs these alternatives to legitimate its own practices.[19] And economically, conventional domesticity needs these alternatives because it takes an immense amount of work to maintain a Victorian household, and alternative families facilitate cheap labor.[20]

A canonically Asian American rendering of this idea can be found in the curious emergence of a Filipino man in prewar California: Marpo Hummingwing, from Hisaye Yamamoto's 1951 short story, "Yoneko's Earthquake."[21] Yet this strangeness and controversy actually becomes an opportunity to read for queer pasts. In Asian American history, Japanese Americans have the exceptional condition of having been able to form relatively conventional domestic units, if picture bride and war bride marriages and plantation families are considered to be forms of conventional domesticity. In any case, persons of Japanese ancestry had nuclear families at a far higher rate than did persons of other Asian ancestries. But this is not necessarily a virtue.[22]

In her story, the titular seismic activity occasions a social upheaval for a Japanese American nuclear family. The patriarch of the Hosoume clan becomes incapacitated by a downed power line. As King-kok Cheung usefully notes, Yamamoto's stories, in their unflinching portrayals of domesticity, critique the position women are forced to occupy in the family.[23]

The presence of Marpo is both necessary and disruptive to the domestic economy of the Hosoumes. He is a material necessity for the cheap labor he provides, but an ideological anomaly because of that fact. That is, he shows that the family may not be an adequate institution to meet its needs economically, or even emotionally. Marpo is a fascinating father-figure to the Hosoume children and, one infers, a husband-figure to the gorgeous Mrs. Hosoume (Yamamoto 1998, 49, 52). As Mikhail Bakhtin said, "the servant is the most privileged witness of private life" (1981, 125), that is, one who most readily sees both the attraction and the contradictions of domesticity.

After the earthquake, trouble ensues when Marpo effectively takes the place of the incapacitated Mr. Hosoume. Even before the earthquake, the Hosoume children were very fond of and fascinated by Marpo. After the trembler, he comes to run the household and, apparently, has a love affair with Mrs. Hosoume. He has been incorporated into the family. When Mr. Hosoume begins to sense that Marpo has "forgot[ten] his place" (Yamamoto 1998, 54), the result is domestic violence.

> *"Nama-iki, nama-iki?"* said Mrs. Hosoume. "How dare you? I'll not have anyone calling me *nama-iki!"*
>
> At that, Mr. Hosoume went up to where his wife was ironing and slapped her smartly on the face. It was the first time he had ever laid hands on her. Mrs. Hosoume was immobile for an instant, but she resumed her ironing as though nothing had happened, although she glanced over at Marpo, who happened to be in the room reading a newspaper. Yoneko and Seigo forgot they were listening to the radio and stared at their parents, thunderstruck.
>
> "Hit me again," said Mrs. Hosoume quietly, as she ironed. "Hit me all you wish."
>
> Mr. Hosoume was apparently about to, but Marpo stepped up and put his hands on Mr. Hosoume's shoulder. "The children are here," said Marpo, "the children."
>
> "Mind your own business," said Mr. Hosoume in broken English. "Get out of here!"
>
> Marpo left, and that was about all. (53–54)

Marpo is a disruptive presence in the conventionality of the Hosoume household, but also a source of structure, inspiration, and desire. Even after Marpo has left, matters come to a head when Mr. Hosoume criticizes Yoneko for wearing nail polish with the put-down "You look like a Filipino." Mrs. Hosoume responds with an account of the lengths to which she had gone in her youth in Japan to color her fingernails. She describes, with quasi-ethnographic detail, the process of carefully wrapping her nails so that the pigment could set overnight. Her narrative is so compelling that Yoneko is transfixed by the telling, as well as the attractiveness of her mother. In offering this narrative, Mrs. Hosoume indicates a convergence between Japanese and (presumed) Filipino identity. (The nail polish had actually come from a neighboring girl of French descent.) She comes across as siding with a Filipino.

Eventually the story shows us how the demands of normative social ordering lead to the abjection of Marpo. He is replaced by "an elderly Japanese American man," who is no threat to Mr. Hosoume's masculinity. Marpo's ultimate betrayal and displacement of Mr. Hosoume is his apparent affair with his wife. The main evidence we have of this is an engagement ring that Mrs. Hosoume accepts but passes on to Yoneko (who loses it). At no point does the story say that Marpo gave it to her. The only other evidence we have is the presumption that Marpo would indeed want to marry Mrs. Hosoume and that she may have gotten an abortion or miscarried. Marpo falls through the cracks in representation. As with so many forgotten Filipinos, we do not know what became of this manong after he had outlived his welcome.

V. "Now We Are All Manongs": Alienation and the Condition of Postmodernity

The writings of Bienvenido Santos have been instrumental in using literature as a record of the lives of the manongs. The alternative social formations they make visible demonstrate a queer sensibility, that is, a sensibility critical of conventional norms of domesticity. With this interpretive framework in mind, the figure of Marpo—whose name we never really know because "Marpo Hummingwing" is simply what Yoneko *thinks* his name is—does not fully disappear as he departs the Hosoume household. He simply could not be assimilated into a conventional domestic unit because of the threat he posed to patriarchal authority. Indeed that may have been the source of his attractiveness to Mrs. Hosoume. But he remains an elliptical character because he flits in and out of a conventional domestic unit, not unlike the hummingbird his name seems to invoke.

Santos's stories, such as "The Day the Dancers Came" and "Scent of Apples," help us to see what might have happened to Marpo and his ilk, because they focus on the lives and loves of the pensionados. Santos's story, "Immigration Blues," picks up the life of Alipio, a manong who is a widower and has long since retired. He is desperately lonely, isolated from human contact since his wife passed away. An old friend's wife's sister is looking for a green-card marriage and the aged Alipio is a fine candidate for the job.

At first Alipio resists the idea; he worships the memory of his late wife. The women conceal their motives because their efforts are rooted in the idea of companionate marriage, which he initially rejects. But as the story progresses, they all begin to come around to a new conception of marriage that is newly legitimate. Alipio begins to see the memory of his sainted wife as much more resonant with the Zafra women's hopes. Mrs. Zafra says, "Here's my sister, a teacher in the Philippines, never married, worried to death because she's being deported unless something turned up like she could marry a U.S. citizen, like I did, like your first wife Seniang, like many others have done, are doing in this exact moment." Alipio is won over by this explanation, referring to the situation as "lightning striking the same fellow twice." He can only respond with his catchphrase, "God dictates." Contravening convention and law, Alipio is happy to perform domesticity because that performance is indeed the real thing for him.[24]

Turnabout is fair play. He has an unapologetically mercenary disregard for conventions of domesticity and companionate bonds. He dons his INS status like a Rolex or a BMW, not as an exception but as the rule. Just as law had been historically used against the manongs to produce their abjection, it is now being turned around in his favor. As post-1965 history has shown, family reunification is largely responsible for the unprecedentedly large numbers of Asian immigrants since the lifting of restrictions.[25]

Asian American history has been shaped by the recruitment of Asians as "cheap" labor and the exclusion of Asians as unassimilable.[26] Immigration policy has been de facto labor policy. The limitations on naturalization and immigration mollify both the demands of white capital and white labor. This odd compromise has resulted in a century and a half of queer domesticity that continues to take new forms. While the backbone of the economy continues to be the nuclear family—an idea whose time has passed—queer domestic units continue to cheapen labor for capital. Historically, gay and lesbian identity has often served as a reason for exclusion, but more recently it has been a potential basis of asylum.

In Cerenio's poem, a queer reading renders cracks in a laborer's hands as cracks in a gluteus maximus. Remembering labor history and political economy, those cracks become cracks in their hands once again. But with an appreciation for alternative ways in which those cracks can be understood, we can grasp the subaltern subjectivities that become recognizable as sites of resistance and pleasure, of a life, there and then.

For bachelor societies, queerness is acquired through projection, something retroactively discerned rather than deliberately mobilized around. At this point queerness has veered into a very broad definition, encompassing anything that eschews the radically uninhabitable ideals of heteronormativity. And thus the weak utopianism of queerness becomes apparent. The important difference between a too-easy "strategic use of essentialism" is the idea that queerness here functions more as a subaltern formation. That is, as a subaltern formation, queerness is necessarily that which had functioned as a basis of exploitation, not valorization. It was a condition to be repudiated, if not exterminated. Queer domesticity for the manongs can only be understood as a historical relic rather than as something that modernity and liberalism can tolerate or even champion as a manifestation of vaunted diversity. This is not to say that valorization does not have its uses but rather to argue the importance of discerning a genealogy of those celebrations out of a history of legitimated exploitation.

The dialectic of pity and valorization has long served new social movements; indeed those are often the conditions of a group's emergence into mainstream recognition. What we may now enjoy as the shiny new Embaracadero, conceals a history of displacements. It is like watching hot dogs get made: we may enjoy the finished frankfurter, but we would rather not see the process. Remembering the manongs reveals the history of the defeat of their legitimacy to remain downtown. Recognizing their lifestyles as queer importantly valorizes and relegitimates their lives, despite that displacement. That mix of pity and valorization is there, if we know how to recognize it.

When sympathetic Sheriff Richard Hongisto of San Francisco declares, at the beginning of Curtis Choy's 1983 documentary, *The Fall of the I-Hotel,* that these old-timers are unambiguously "pathetic," he is simply articulating the position that capitalism has carved out for them. After the Chinese and the Japanese, they were the third wave of Asian labor recruited for menial work which found itself phased out of the new economy. They face and succumb to the threat of eviction because the plot of land on which their residence hotel is located is to become, à la Joni Mitchell, a parking lot.

Yet the I-Hotel was no paradise. There can be no romanticizing the conditions of poverty in which these manongs lived. The dialectic of pity and valorization is a cultural framework that serves capital's need for cheap labor and national culture's need for its erasure; they are dinosaurs for whom the latest phase of capitalist development feels no obligation. They are in dire straits because they lack public and private safety nets; the only result is a violent confrontation between developers and demonstrators. The manongs are a residual formation that the state and national culture no longer recognize as worthy of handouts.

Similarly, the 1984 documentary, *Dollar a Day, Dime a Dance*, in no way romanticizes the lot of bachelor manong communities. These elderly men —many of whom continued to work in the agribusiness fields of the Central Valley well into their seventies—tell on-camera tales of the Watsonville Riots, their being cheated at dancehalls, their compulsive gambling, their service in World War II, their persistent dreams of going "back home" and finding a wife. The film ends with one of the manongs reminiscing about a Chicana girlfriend he had in his youth. He tells us that he used to serenade her with his rendition of "Mexicali Rose." He sings for us as the film ends.

The assignation of gay identity is clearly inappropriate. Even queerness seems an odd fit because so many never really surrendered their dreams of conventional domesticity and cling to nostalgic memories of having been "ladies' men." The film continually shows sepia-toned photographs of sharply dressed manongs, enjoying each other's company and that of a few predominantly non-Filipina women.[27]

In the political and cultural circumstances in which they lived, they rarely ever embodied normative domesticity. But they lived. They formed alternative institutions by companioning each other. In the twenty years since the making of that film, one can only presume that but a handful survived into their nineties. Perhaps none are left alive, considering the harsh conditions of a farmworker even for someone in the prime of his or her youth. The label of "queer domesticity" to describe the alternative social formations that both served and resisted exploitation becomes a way of allowing us to remember the history of the powerfully lingering lure of impossible middle-class aspirations of nuclear family and domestic hearth. Such aspirations, as the sociological work of Rhacel Parreñas documents, fuel the desires and regulate the satisfaction of those currently under the sway of globalization.[28] In this way, "now we are all manongs." Let's hope we don't get used to it.

NOTES

1. The authors of these pieces are David Miller (1990), Leo Bersani (1987), Richard Fung (1998), Lauren Berlant (1995), and Jose Muñoz (1998), respectively.

2. It should be remembered that Spivak's oft-cited article, "Can the Subaltern Speak?" does conclude on a rather provocative reading of a bit of bodily evidence that seeks to destabilize notions of private, familial rituals and acts of political insurgency: that is, the suicidal body of a menstruating insurgent named Bhuvaneswari Bhaduri (1988, 307–8).

3. There is a terrific proliferation of overtly queer Filipino diasporic culture. For example, Alec Mapa's "I Remember Mapa," the writings of Nice Rodriguez, R. Z. Linmark's *Rolling the Rs,* Nicky Paraiso's cabaret acts (especially his homage to Patrick Adiarte, who played the young Prince Chulalongkorn to Yul Brynner's King), the Kilawin Kolektibo in NYC, the visual art of Paul Pfeiffer and Vince Golveo, the scholarship of Martin Manalansan and Eric Reyes. And the list goes on. The purpose of this essay, however, is to identify queering as a practice done to things not openly gay.

4. The sociological work of Rhacel Parreñas is instructive here. Her analysis of "the international division of reproductive labor" demonstrates how the practice of middle-class domesticity continues to be built upon not only the structural inability of populations—in her case overseas Filipina domestics—to achieve that domesticity, but the continued power of that idea to motivate these women to pursue this work and the pity that liberals feel for them because of this lack. See Parreñas 2002, 61–79.

5. The obvious example would be the work of Angela Davis. See Davis 1983.

6. Fung's seminal essay has appeared in Leong 1995; Eng and Hom 1998; and Yu-Wen Shen Wu and Song 2000.

7. Shah 2002. Jennifer Ting was also an early queerer of bachelor societies.

8. Depicting Asian male sexuality in independent film and video is not absent. See the early work of Quentin Lee, "To Ride a Cow" (1992). On the significance of the "money shot," see L. Williams 1989, esp. chap. 4, "Fetishism and Hard Core: Marx, Freud, and the 'Money Shot,'" 93–119.

9. The work of anthropologist Martin Manalansan IV both queers Filipino American pasts but also Philippinizes queer pasts. One of his informants, Mama Rene, is something of a reluctant legend in the world of gay Filipinos in New York City because she was arrested at the Stonewall Rebellion. See Manalansan 1995.

10. Ronald Takaki, in his influential book *Strangers from a Different Shore: A History of Asian Americans* (1990), thematizes immigrants from the Philippines as "Forgotten Filipinos"; Oscar Campomanes (1995) extends and revises these amnesiac epistemologies by examining this forgetfulness as a process of subject formation under emergent U.S. imperialism.

11. W. Williams 1972, 20; Kaplan and Pease 1994, 3.

12. On American postcolonialism, see Sharpe 1995.

13. The distinction between archaeologist and historian is one that Shah pointedly makes in his revisionist approach to Chinatown. One needs to understand archives as reliquaries, that is, as receptacles of objects having meanings and functions that did not survive to the present in any conventional way. Shah's reliquary is the public health records of San Francisco. See Shah 2002, "Introduction: Public Health, Race, and Citizenship." Also see Foucault 1976.

14. See R. Lee 1999, esp. chap. 1, "Fraternal Devotions: Carlos Bulosan and the Sexual Politics of America," 17–43.

15. A forgotten group of old-timers became a *cause célèbre* in the battle between developers and existing communities as the City by the Bay attempted to adapt to the changing economy by building newer infrastructure for finance and tourism. See Curtis Choy's film, *The Fall of the I-Hotel* (1983; rev. 1993).

16. R. Williams 1977, "Emergent, Dominant, Residual."

17. Karnow 1989.

18. The colonized's penchant for mimicry is a common trope. See Bhabha 1994.

19. Shah 2002, 81–86.

20. Parreñas 2002, "International Division of Reproductive Labor."

21. See Yamanaka 1997; Murayama 1988. Kandice Chuh devotes the introduction of her forthcoming book, *Imagine Otherwise* (2004), to the controversy at the 1998 AAAS conference in Honolulu.

22. "Wartime hysteria" is the official explanation of internment. See the 1991 apology letter from George H. W. Bush that accompanied redress payments to internees.

23. Cheung 1993, 28–30.

24. The dynamic between realness and performativity is a central dialectic of queer studies. See Butler 1990; Reddy 1998; and Thomas 1996.

25. See Okamura 1995, 393.

26. Formative work in Asian American history has established the link between capitalism's need for the cheapest labor possible, usually immigrants, and American racism and xenophobia. See Bonacich and Cheng 1984; Saxton 1971. For the fullest theoretical articulation of this contradiction between the needs of capital to recruit the racialized and the needs of U.S. national culture to exclude them, see Lowe 1996, esp. "Immigration, Citizenship, Racialization: Asian American Critique," 1–36.

27. Fujita-Rony (2003) offers a much-needed history of these early-twentieth-century laboring communities that examines the Filipinas as well as the Filipinos who traveled the migratory circuits of the emerging Pacific Rim.

28. Parreñas 2002, "The Transnational Family: A Postindustrial Household Structure with Preindustrial Values," 80–115.

WORKS CITED

Bakhtin, Mikhail. *The Dialogic Imagination: Four Essays*. Austin: U of Texas P, 1981.

Berlant, Lauren. "Live Sex Acts (Parental Advisory: Explicit Material)." *Feminist Studies* 21:2 (1995): 379–404.

Bersani, Leo. "Is the Rectum a Grave?" *October 43* (1987).

Bhabha, Homi K. "Of Mimicry and Man: The Ambivalence of Colonial Discourse." Chapter 4 in *The Location of Culture*, 85–92. New York: Routledge, 1994.

Bonacich, Edna, and Lucie Cheng. *Labor Immigration under Capitalism: Asian Workers in the United States before World War II*. Berkeley: U of California P, 1984.

Butler, Judith. *Gender Trouble: Feminism and the Subversion of Identity*. New York: Routledge, 1990.

Campomanes, Oscar. "The Empire's Forgotten and Forgetful Subjects: Unrepresentability and Unassimilability in Filipino-American Postcolonialities." *Critical Mass: A Journal of Asian American Cultural Criticism* 2:2 (1995): 145–200.

Cerenio, Virginia. "you lovely people." *Breaking Silences: An Anthology of Asian American Poets*, ed. Joseph Bruchac, 11. Greenfield Center, NY: Greenfield Review P, 1983.

Cheung, King-kok. *Articulate Silences: Hisaye Yamamoto, Maxine Hong Kingston, Joy Kogawa*. Ithaca: Cornell U P, 1993.

Chuh, Kandice. *Imagine Otherwise: On Asian Americanist Critique*. Durham: Duke U P, 2004.

Davis, Angela. *Women, Race, and Class*. New York: Vintage, 1983.

Eng, David, and Alice Hom. *Q&A: Queer in Asian America*. Philadelphia: Temple U P, 1998.

Ferguson, Roderick. *Aberrations in Black: Towards a Queer of Color Critique*. Minneapolis: U of Minnesota P, 2003.

Foucault, Michel. *The Archaeology of Knowledge*. New York: Harper and Row, 1976.

Francia, Luis, and Angel Velasco Shaw, eds. *Vestiges of War: The Philippine-American War and the Aftermath of the Imperial Dream, 1899–1999*. New York: New York U P, 2002.

Fujita-Rony, Dorothy. *American Workers, Colonial Power: Philippine Seattle and the Trans-Pacific West, 1919–1941*. Berkeley: U of California P, 2003.

Fung, Richard. "Looking for My Penis: The Eroticized Asian in Gay Video Porn." In *Q&A: Queer in Asian America*, ed. David Eng and Alice Hom, 115–134. Philadelphia: Temple U P, 1998.

Hagedorn, Jessica. *Dogeaters*. New York: Pantheon, 1990.

Kaplan, Amy, and Donald E. Pease, eds. *Cultures of United States Imperialism*. Durham: Duke U P, 1994.

Karnow, Stanley. *In Our Image: America's Empire in the Philippines*. New York: Random House, 1989.

Lee, Rachel. *The Americas of Asian American Literature: Gendered Fictions of Nation and Transnation*. Princeton: Princeton U P, 1999.

Leong, Russell, ed. *Asian American Sexualities: Dimensions of the Gay and Lesbian Experience*. New York: Routledge, 1995.

Lowe, Lisa. *Immigrant Acts: On Asian American Cultural Politics*. Durham: Duke U P, 1996.

Manalansan, Martin. "In the Shadows of Stonewall: Examining Gay Transnational Politics and the Diaspora Dilemma." *GLQ* 2:4 (1995): 425–438.

———. *Global Divas: Filipino Gay Men in the Diaspora*. Durham: Duke U P, 2003.

Mapa, Alec. "I Remember Mapa." In *O Solo Homo: The New Queer Performance*, ed. Holly Hughes and David Roman, 199–228. New York: Grove P, 1998.

Miller, David. "Anal/Rope." *Representations* 32 (1990): 114–133.

Muñoz, José. "This Bridge Called My Crack: Alternative Economies and Utopian Economies." Paper presented at the American Studies Association Annual Meeting, Seattle, 1998.

Murayama, Milton. *All I Asking for Is My Body*. Honolulu: U of Hawaii P, 1988.

Okamura, Jonathan. "The Filipino American Diaspora: Sites of Time, Space, and Ethnicity." In *Privileging Positions: The Sites of Asian American Studies*, ed. Gary Okihiro, Marilyn Alquizola, Dorothy Fujita-Rony, and K. Scott Wong, 387–400. Pullman: Washington State U P, 1995.

Parreñas, Rhacel Salazar. *Servants of Globalization: Women, Migration, and Domestic Work*. Stanford: Stanford U P, 2002.

Reddy, Chandan. "Home, Houses, Nonidentity: *Paris Is Burning*." In *Burning down the House: Recycling Domesticity*, ed. Rosemary Marangoly George. Boulder, CO: Westview P, 1998.

Reyes, Eric. "Asian Pacific Queer Space." In *Privileging Positions: The Sites of Asian American Studies*, ed. Gary Okihiro, Marilyn Alquizola, Dorothy Fujita-Rony, and K. Scott Wong, 251–260. Pullman: Washington State U P, 1995.

Rodriguez, Nice. *Throw It to the River*. Toronto: Women's P, 1993.

Santos, Bienvenido. *Scent of Apples: A Collection of Stories*. Seattle: U of Washington P, 1979.

Saxton, Alexander. *The Indispensable Enemy: Labor and the Anti-Chinese Movement in California*. Berkeley: U of California P, 1971.

Sayles, John. *Men With Guns and Lone Star*. London: Faber, 1998.

Shah, Nayan. *Contagious Divides: Race and Epidemics in San Francisco's Chinatown.* Berkeley: U of California P, 2002.

Sharpe, Jenny. "Is the United States Postcolonial? Transnationalism, Immigration, and Race." *Diaspora 4:2* (1995): 181–199.

Song, Min. "The Unknowable and Sui Sin Far: The Epistemological Limits of 'Oriental' Sexuality." In *Q&A: Queer in Asian America,* ed. David Eng and Alice Hom, 304–322. Philadelphia: Temple U P, 1998.

Spivak, Gayatri Chakravorty. "Can the Subaltern Speak?" In *Marxism and the Interpretation of Culture,* ed. Lawrence Grossberg and Cary Nelson. Urbana: U of Illinois P, 1988.

Takaki, Ronald. *Strangers from a Different Shore: A History of Asian Americans.* New York: Vintage, 1990.

Thomas, Kendall. "'Ain't Nothin' Like the Real Thing': Black Masculinity, Gay Sexuality, and the Jargon of Authenticity." In *Representing Black Men,* ed. Marcellus Bount and George Cunningham. New York: Routledge, 1996.

Ting, Jennifer. "Bachelor Society: Deviant Heterosexuality and Asian American Historiography." In *Privileging Positions: The Sites of Asian American Studies,* ed. Gary Okihiro, Marilyn Alquizola, Dorothy Fujita-Rony, and K. Scott Wong, 271–280. Pullman: Washington State U P, 1995.

Williams, Linda. *Hard Core: Power, Pleasure, and the Frenzy of the Visible.* Berkeley: U of California P, 1989.

Williams, Raymond. *Marxism and Literature.* New York: Oxford U P, 1977.

Williams, William Appleman. *The Tragedy of American Diplomacy.* New York: Norton, 1972.

Yamamoto, Hisaye. "Yoneko's Earthquake." In *Seventeen Syllables and Other Stories.* Latham, NY: Kitchen Table P, 1988.

Yamanaka, Lois Ann. *Blu's Hanging.* New York: Farrar, Straus and Giroux, 1997.

Yu-Wen Shen Wu, Jean, and Min Song, eds. *Asian American Studies: A Reader.* New Brunswick, NJ: Rutgers U P, 2000.

Chapter 7

"A Woman Is Nothing"

*Valuing the Modern Chinese Woman's
Epic Journey to the West*

Christine So

Gary Krist begins his *New York Times* book review of May-lee Chai and
Winberg Chai's *The Girl from Purple Mountain: Love, Honor, War, and One
Family's Journey from China to America* with the following, "If living in interesting times is the curse it's reputed to be, then few people in history
have been as accursed as the Chinese in the 20th century. . . . Little wonder,
then, that such a turbulent era has inspired so many excellent memoirs"
(2001). The cataclysmic events of twentieth-century China have indeed
captured the attention of Western audiences and publishers. From the revolution against the Manchu dynasty and the Japanese occupation of
Manchuria and Shanghai in the century's first decades, to the rise of Mao
Tse Tung and the Communist Party and the Cultural Revolution and
Tiananmen Square Massacre, the massive upheavals that mark the century
have formed the backdrop for a number of diasporic Chinese women's
narratives that have found an audience in England, Australia, Canada, and
the United States. Memoirs by the aforementioned Chais, Jung Chang,
Leslie Chang, Pang-Mei Natasha Chang, Nien Cheng, and Adeline Yen
Mah, as well as novels by Chung Yun Bezine, Lillian Lee, Leslie Li, Bette
Bao Lord, and Linda Ching Sledge,[1] while certainly varied in terms of
their tone, approach, and stories, all revolve around the same fundamental
conflict: the enormous struggle waged by Chinese women to survive and
triumph during those tumultuous times.

Written primarily by Chinese immigrants to the United States or
Britain or by their daughters or granddaughters, the memoirs in particular

rely on the same general format. Although they might differ in terms of the number of narrators or the date on which the women "escape" China, they are remarkably similar in two respects: first, their focus on several generations of women and the pressures they faced in the "modern" era in particular, and second, their dependence on "History," specifically twentieth-century Chinese history, imagined as a set of objective and agreed upon facts, dates, and political events to function as another character, an overwhelming series of challenges that generations of Chinese women must confront and overcome. The memoirs highlight authenticity and epic history by often incorporating detailed chronologies of national and global events, extensive family trees, and/or maps of China. Often beginning with the early part of the twentieth century, they stress the social changes that occur during the rise of the Republic and of Sun Yat Sen, especially the loosening of social restrictions on women, taking care to emphasize the merging of "Eastern" and "Western" beliefs and the celebration of modernity. They then trace the women's lives as they migrate, either crisscrossing China itself or beyond its borders to Hong Kong, Taiwan, England, and the United States. They almost uniformly highlight their female protagonists' strength in the face of great adversity and subordinate social position. Highlighting the diminished value of women—the first chapter of Pang-Mei Natasha Chang's *Bound Feet and Western Dress* is entitled, "A Woman Is Nothing"—the narratives then emphasize each woman's rebellion against social restrictions and her subsequent economic and social triumphs over the catastrophic events that perpetually threaten her survival.

The proliferation of these texts and the bestseller status in the United States and other countries of such works as Jung Chang's *Wild Swans,* Nien Cheng's *Life and Death in Shanghai,* and Adeline Yen Mah's *Falling Leaves* speaks to the appeal of books that, as Gary Krist points out, recount the travails of the "accursed." The triumph of the oppressed in the face of numerous daunting obstacles is certainly a captivating narrative, and the glimpse into the horrors that result from imperialist invasion, civil war, and a communist regime are particularly tempting to Western audiences, especially given China's role as a Cold War adversary. The memoirs' focus on the empowerment of Chinese women no doubt appeals to the same audiences that enthusiastically consumed Amy Tan's *The Joy Luck Club,* especially given that these texts, like Tan's, enable a notion of universal womanhood, while at the same time leaving intact the imagined essential differences between "West" and "East."[2]

In addition, the historical and "factual" nature of the texts appeal to those in search of a more "personal" and authentic understanding of the political events that have shaped China in the twentieth century. These "facts," however, work in a similar contradictory manner to the representation of women; despite their seeming specificity in terms of names, dates, and locales, they resist naming the economic and political forces that contextualize their experiences. The result is account after account which, although set in China, might take place anywhere, in any nation that has witnessed imperialist invasion, civil conflict, and massive migration in the last century. As a group they serve to reinforce U.S. audiences' desire for shared and universal (that is, liberal humanistic) ideals, and to reassure their readers of a new global landscape which can be mapped in old and familiar ways.

In this essay, I focus on three of these recently published memoirs: Adeline Yen Mah's *Falling Leaves: The True Story of an Unwanted Chinese Daughter* (1999), Pang-Mei Natasha Chang's *Bound Feet and Western Dress: A Memoir* (1996), and May-lee Chai and Winberg Chai's *The Girl from Purple Mountain: Love, Honor, War, and One Family's Journey from China to America* (2001). Written by Chinese Americans about either their own or their foremothers' experiences, they are fairly representative of the genre as a whole and particularly make visible the memoirs' central focus on the value of Chinese women on account of the protagonists' embodiment of both the history and the future of China. The spectacle of the Chinese woman who locates her self-worth against a rigid patriarchal structure becomes particularly resonant when placed against the figure of the diasporic Chinese businessman whose citizenship, as Aiwha Ong makes clear, becomes subject to the demands of global capital. Citing his "flexible citizenship," which "refers to the cultural logics of capitalist accumulation, travel, and displacement that induce subjects to respond fluidly and opportunistically to changing political-economic conditions," Ong explains that "the image of the border-running Chinese executive with no state loyalty has become an important figure in the era of Pacific Rim capital" (1999, 135–136). Equally pervasive and important at this particular moment, I would argue, is the figure of the persecuted Chinese female expatriate, who emerges victorious and whole from the tumultuous, fragmenting, and dramatic events of the last century.

If the Chinese businessman abroad is identified by his mobile ability to accommodate his needs to those of global capitalism, then the Chinese woman in the West, whose mobility responds solely to the shifting political landscape, is defined instead by her emergence from the twentieth century's relentless march toward and through tragedy, upheaval, and alienation. The inability to locate Chinese diasporic men decisively—since their flexibility demands that capital, not national borders, be the primary coordinates for travel—is countered by almost a hyper-identification of Chinese women with nation, its history, conflicts, landscape, chronology, past and future. And yet what emerges from these narratives is not the authors' and narrators' allegiance to a specific nation-state, that is, China, but their embodiment of nationhood generally. In other words, these women become representative of universal and depoliticized notions of history, trauma, geography, migration, family, and home. The women become symbolic of China, which has itself become symbolic of twentieth-century turmoil, and the symbolic value they acquire is as globally transportable as the economic value their male counterparts accumulate.

History as Romance

Adeline Yen Mah's *Falling Leaves: The True Story of an Unwanted Chinese Daughter* especially demonstrates this universalizing of Chinese women's personal history. First published in Great Britain and rising to the bestseller lists there, as well as in Hong Kong, Australia, and the United States, *Falling Leaves* is the memoir of a wealthy Chinese daughter estranged from her family. Featuring exclamatory blurbs from *The Joy Luck Club's* author Amy Tan and Nien Chang, author of *Life and Death in Shanghai*, it juxtaposes the disintegration of the Yen family with larger historical events in China and Hong Kong in the twentieth century. The memoir resembles, in the words of several reviewers, a "fairy tale," and for Nien Chang, a "modern-day Cinderella story." The comparison of Mah to Cinderella is an apt one, given her mother's early death and the subsequent arrival of evil Eurasian stepmother Niang. As her memoir progresses, Adeline becomes increasingly alienated from her family and becomes the victim of progressively more harrowing emotional abuse, culminating in her enrollment in a boarding school in Tianjin in 1948 as her parents flee to Hong Kong. The second half of her memoir, however, charts her struggles to complete medical school in London, and her immigration to the United States where she finds emotional and financial success, although she is never able to effect the longed for reconciliation with her own immediate family.

Chronologically, Mah juxtaposes the rupture of the Yen family with the fragmentation of China as a whole, and the many moves that various family members make to Hong Kong, Canada, Britain, Nigeria, and southern California replicate the experiences of the wealthiest Chinese elite after the communist victory. At the same time, however, by intertwining national and familial history, Mah suggests that the struggles for power and belonging within her own family only replicate the larger battles for dominance and unity within China. The interdependence of national events with the personal struggles of one alienated girl reinforces the epic dimensions of Mah's story even as it brings national events into the realm of fairy tales. The blurring of the forms can be seen in the following passage, which immediately follows new stepmother Niang's conferring English names on the children to replace their Chinese ones. Mah writes:

> Overnight, my sister Jun-pei became Lydia, my three brothers Zi-jie, Zi-lin and Zi-jun were named Gregory, Edgar and James, and I, Jun-ling, was called Adeline. Japanese troops, which already occupied Tianjin and Beijing, were now moving steadily southwards. They met surprisingly strong resistance in Nanking and, in retaliation, went on a terrifying spree of rape, looting and murder. Over 300,000 civilians and prisoners of war were tortured and killed during the Rape of Nanking in 1937 and early 1938 after the city was captured by the Japanese. . . . It's not hard to imagine the tension and turmoil that these momentous political upheavals must have imposed on Chinese family life. (1999, 30)

"History," although ostensibly used to contextualize the significant moments in Adeline's own story, also serves here to reinforce the traumatic invasion of the Yen family by Niang, and to highlight the chaos and shifts in power that threaten Adeline and divide the family. While the historical "facts"—numbers of victims and dates—authenticate and authorize Mah's narrative, her own story transforms Chinese "history" into a tale of "good" versus "evil," devoid of social, economic, and political considerations. Such a rendition universalizes the twentieth century in China, depicting it as a frenzied, tragic era, filled with famine, displacement, destruction, and death. This portrayal of China is becoming almost as ubiquitous as the image of China as the land of Confucius, jade, ancestors, and temples. While such a backdrop of human misery certainly imbues the narratives' heroines with a greater sense of triumph, we must consider, however, why the spectacle of twentieth-century Chinese mass suffering has become an especially powerful symbol in the era of globalization.

These images of mass dispersal and destruction work as reminders of the modern era, an epoch of bombs, advanced weaponry and technology, anguish on a scale previously unheard of. While reading about such trauma may work to reassure Western readers of the comfort and safety within their own lives, the depictions also effect a vision of history, especially Chinese history, as fated and destined. Beyond people's control, Mah's and others' renditions of floods, famines, invasions, wars, as well as communist campaigns such as the Great Leap Forward and the Cultural Revolution, all promote "history" as a series of inevitable events to which the narrators and their families have fallen victim. The chaos of the twentieth century, although unimaginable and seemingly unmanageable, can, however, be overcome through individual will and determination. By distilling "300,000" stories into one personal tale of familial betrayal and alienation, Mah transforms the chaos of the modern era into a reiteration of traditional family values. In the face of mass migrations in the current era (and certainly the populations of the People's Republic of China have particularly come to symbolize an enormous and undifferentiated mass for U.S. peoples), Adeline's efforts even more strongly speak to the power of loyalty, family, and the ties that bind one to one's mother and motherland. Arjun Appadurai notes, "The past is now not a land to return to in a simple politics of memory. It has become a synchronic warehouse of cultural scenarios, a kind of temporal central casting, to which recourse can be taken as appropriate, depending on the movie to be made, the scene to be enacted, the hostages to be rescued" (1996, 30). Twentieth-century China in *Falling Leaves* and in the other narratives of this genre emerges as the historical backdrop of choice for Western readers in their efforts to grapple with present and postmodern anxieties about global migration and dehumanization. Not only can these concerns be displaced onto another time and place, but *Falling Leaves* and other memoirs reassure us of the universality and individuality that can triumph over these forces of mass dispersal and destruction.

Particularly appealing is the central focus on Chinese women's triumphs. Mah's journey from unwanted daughter to enlightened doctor is largely propelled by the mothers, grandmothers, and great-aunts that precede her, and much of her story revolves around women who have rejected traditional definitions of womanhood in China. Mah's great-aunt, purported lesbian and owner of the first women's bank in China, marks the beginning of Mah's narrative. She writes, "At the age of three my great aunt proclaimed her independence by categorically refusing to have her feet bound, resolutely tearing off the bandages as fast as they were applied" (5). Mah's beginning calls forth many U.S. readers' assumptions regarding the oppressed status of women in China, even as she begins with her great-aunt's rejection of that positioning. The strong will of Chinese women becomes the focal point of Mah's narrative, and the means by which her audience is able to resolve anxieties about the current global capitalist era. The battle between the pandemonium of globalization and the security of family and nation is particularly played out in the comparison between the memoir's two mother figures—Eurasian stepmother Niang and Adeline's Aunt Baba. Their relationship to Adeline and to each other seems inversely proportional: the less affection Niang bestows upon Adeline, the more Aunt Baba acts as her protector; the more money Niang commands, the less Aunt Baba receives; when Niang flees to and thrives in capitalist Hong Kong, Aunt Baba elects to stay in China and has most of her possessions and property stripped from her. Descriptions of Niang particularly play up her French and Chinese roots, connecting her mixed heritage to her insatiable desire for grandeur. She writes about her stepmother, "Jeanne's taste reflected her mixed origins. She invariably wore western clothes and she wore them well. She liked to be surrounded by French furniture, red velvet curtains and richly textured wallpaper. At the same time, she collected antique Chinese porcelain, paintings and chairs. She liked plants and flowers to scent the hallway, living-room and her own bedroom. Like Grandmother, she smoked incessantly" (29). Niang's ability to surround herself with aesthetic extravagance and her relentless consumption stand in marked contrast to Aunt Baba, who gives up her own financial and personal desires to act as caretaker to Adeline and her brothers and sisters when their mother dies. In addition, when Niang withholds money from her stepchildren and in-laws as a form of punishment, Aunt Baba uses her meager salary to support her father and to provide a small allowance for Adeline.

Mah intertwines Niang's mixed heritage and her control over money in a move that reinforces the link between desire for the West with narcissistic, capitalist excess. She further emphasizes Niang's privilege and mobility, when Niang declares in 1997, "Your father and I are really citizens of the world. If the situation looks bad, we can fly to any country at a moment's notice" (233). Mah thus juxtaposes two models of femininity here: the global capitalist "Eurasian" with flexible citizenship, and the maternal citizen who is inextricably bound to nation. In this paradigm, the global capitalist personifies upheaval, loss of identity, and the disintegration of the nuclear family, and her contrast of Niang and Aunt Baba calls forth two visions of Chinese peoples in the twentieth century, one in which the Chinese diaspora, spurred by money and consumption, abandons family and homeland for the West, and the other in which those in China are subject to persecution, deprivation, and separation from the West.

These competing imaginations of China and Chinese peoples in the twentieth century set the stage for the narrative's final reconciliation between Adeline and Aunt Baba, and on a larger scale, an imagined future reunion of the Chinese diaspora, China, and the West. Even as we have entered a phase in which national borders can no longer contain the flows of capital, culture, and peoples, nations themselves, especially China, continue to serve as specters of the global future. As Aunt Baba herself promises, "The way I see it the nineteenth century was a British century. The twentieth century is an American century. I predict that the twenty-first century will be a Chinese century. The pendulum of history will swing from the *ying* ashes brought by the Cultural Revolution to the *yang* phoenix arising from its wreckage" (226). China thus serves simultaneously as an imagined past and an imagined future for the West, one that documents the mass upheavals and traumas of the twentieth century and at the same time promises a future site for global development and economic profit. Niang's invasion of the Yen family, the dispersal and fragmentation of the Chinese peoples, and the unity of family and nation are all resolved by history's inevitable destination of progress and modernity. The specter of the third world, global capitalist woman, unmoored from nation and family, is firmly banished when Adeline returns to China to sit at Aunt Baba's deathbed. Mah reflects, "In her modest and unassuming way, [Aunt Baba] had guided me towards a spirit of independence which she herself had manifested by rebuffing Niang and remaining in Shanghai. Aunt Baba was not one to dwell on the bitter hardships she suffered during the Cultural Revolution. Love, generosity and humour never left her" (174). Beyond the universal appeal of Aunt Baba's transcendence of hardship lies the triumph of Chinese women; their strength and ability to overcome adversity binds together the twentieth and twenty-first centuries, and enables Western readers to imagine a global culture that incorporates a nostalgia for a past that they never experienced and a future that has already become their present.[3]

History and Modernity

Like *Falling Leaves,* May-lee and Winberg Chai's *The Girl from Purple Mountain* also deploys scenes of mass upheaval as a means to highlight the endurance, value, and empowerment of Chinese women, as well as to position Chinese women as emblematic of the modern and epic sweep of history. In a passage that echoes the rhetoric of *Falling Leaves,* May-lee Chai notes, "[My grandparents] witnessed the fall of the Qing dynasty and the birth of the Republic of China. They then saw the promise of democracy dashed as their country disintegrated into regions controlled by warlords. They survived the Japanese invasion of China, fleeing the Rape of Nanjain in 1937, moving from city to city, one step ahead of the Japanese army. After the Communists won the civil war, they fled to Taiwan, then finally immigrated to New York in 1955" (2001, 9–10). The rise-and-fall, to-and-fro movement here is reinforced by the multiple perspectives from which the story is told. Alternating sections, May-Lee Chai and her father Winberg Chai attempt to unravel the life of Winberg's mother, and May-lee's grandmother, Ruth Mei-en Chai, and in so doing effect a sweep across generations and continents, moving back and forth from present to past, and from the United States to China.

May-lee and Winberg Chai's efforts to excavate Ruth's story suggests that wholeness can be achieved by reconciling these oppositions in time and space. Winberg explains, "It is my duty to try to understand my mother, to seek answers. To ignore the past is too much like forgetting. And to forget the past would be to dishonor my parents" (7). May-lee echoes her father's emphasis on the importance of piecing together the past. She questions her lack of knowledge beyond the "official story" she has been told. She writes, "But nothing in the official version of the story of their lives helped me to understand my grandmother" (11). And she admits, "I despaired of ever understanding anything" (19). The question of "understanding," of making coherent what seems insensible, becomes a crucial element of these memoirs. The chaos of early-twentieth-century China serves as a backdrop against which knowledge of oneself can be achieved. Leslie Bow notes a similar phenomenon in Amy Tan's *The Joy Luck Club.* She writes, "China is portrayed as the location of woman's suffering and America embodies the opportunity for women's choices. Based on this dichotomy, ethnic consciousness is achievable through the following: until the daughters accept their Chinese mothers' lessons about womanhood, they will not understand what it means to be Chinese" (1994, 241). While this is also true to some extent of these tributes to Chinese women's triumph over twentieth-century Chinese history, what is perhaps more relevant in these texts is the way that women's embodiment of history and modernity operate to enlighten their Chinese American descendants and their Western readers. While their suffering does indeed enable Chinese American women's ethnic and feminist consciousness, as my reading of Pang-mei Natasha Chang's *Bound Feet* will demonstrate, it also renders Chinese women synonymous with twentieth-century upheaval; through them, we in the United States are able to more firmly locate ourselves in terms of a global past, present, and future.

That these stories are valuable is established early on and continuously in all these narratives. Ruth's status as an exemplary modern woman is declared almost immediately in the memoir. May-lee introduces her, "My grandmother, 'Ruth' Mei-en Tsao, was one of the first women admitted into a national university in China when the government finally allowed women to attend in 1920" (2001, 10). Winberg Chai also heralds his mother's unique and singular status. "My mother was the most beautiful woman alive in China. Everyone who knew her would tell you so. She was born into a wealthy family, a good family, an old respectable family from the north" (21). The elite status that Ruth is accorded serves to emphasize even further her abilities to rise above the chaos of the turbulent century, and her successive triumphs and unbreakable will enable her to take her place in a long of line of women ahead of their time. For example, in a description of Ruth's mother's rebellion against having her feet bound—a scene strikingly similar to that in Mah's *Falling Leaves* and another in Chang's *Bound Feet and Western Dress*—Winberg writes of his grandmother's reaction, "And in the beginning, my mother's mother cried with lungs that exploded with power, like steam engines. . . . The shrieks continued nonstop for three months, unabated. No one could remember a child with such strength and willpower, especially a girl" (23). The power of Ruth's mother's voice and of Ruth's own beauty and intellect speaks to their refusal to be constrained by the conventional social dictates surrounding women. As Winberg Chai writes about Ruth, "My mother should have been a man" (35).

Such declarations elicit the ultimate transgression and compliment, that she has achieved the social status of men. Simultaneously highlighting the strict demarcations of gender roles in China, that is, Chinese women possess neither power nor value while Chinese men are oppressive and controlling, and extolling the strength of Ruth Chai in her ability to reverse these positions, May-lee and Winberg Chai highlight the figure of the Chinese woman as straddling the boundaries of gender, time, and place. Unlike the Chinese diasporic male with "flexible citizenship," the Chinese diasporic woman does not move across national borders; instead she evokes the specific characteristics of the nation—its history, politics, social structures, and geography—in order to transcend them. Her refusal to be contained by boundaries and limits of any kind allows U.S. readers to imagine that "authentic" Chinese history—verified by dates and locations—is in fact a universal past, filled with every type of suffering and conversely every kind of triumph.

The collapse of borders is once again emphasized in the authors' conflation of the past and the "modern." Despite their look back in time, the Chinese women who are memorialized in the narratives are not situated in an ancient and forgotten era; instead they are almost always described in terms that establish their embodiment of modernity. Ruth's coming of age parallels the rise of the republic, during which "the Chinese character for ocean, *yang*, also came to mean 'foreign,' 'Western,' and 'modern'" (55). In describing Ruth's demand that she be allowed to choose her own husband, Winberg Chai notes, "These were modern times, not the feudal past; there should only be love marriages, no more arranged marriages" (71). And when Ruth's mother finds out that Ruth will attend graduate school in the United States, she approves, saying, "You can be married in America. . . . A modern woman. Just as you always wanted" (73). The modern consists not only of present events in the United States, but paradoxically can also be found in early twentieth-century China. Cut off from its natural progression by the communist takeover of China in 1949, the potential of "modernity" remains intact within the Chinese woman's body, waiting to be excavated by future Chinese American generations.

The abrupt disruption of history is particularly played out in Ruth and Winberg's last visit to their ancestors' graves, before fleeing Nanjing in 1937. At the temple, Ruth promises that Winberg's name and accomplishments will be carved on the polished stone tables, alongside those of previous generations. Winberg, however, writes, "As it turned out, nothing more would be recorded for our family. The war would scatter us all across China and then across the world, and then in the 1960s, the Red Guards would come and destroy the family temple, smashing the statues and the stone steles, setting fire to the bamboo plaques and the rice-paper books recording the history of the Chai family" (151). The dramatic description of the destruction of "history" counters Ruth's and China's forward trajectory toward the modernity of the West. Instead, history and time itself seem to be interrupted by the invasion and the eventual communist takeover. The ideological divide between China and the "West" is thus depicted as a break in time, in which neither past nor future exist, only endless and directionless movement. This figuration of twentieth-century China corresponds with Johannes Fabian's argument that the East is often imagined to occupy an earlier temporal position with respect to the West. Often representing the primitive or the ancient, Africa and Asia thus stand as counterparts and "other" to the modern and progressive "West." *The Girl from Purple Mountain* and other books in this genre re-move China from the opposition and instead position it outside time's continuum.

The opposition between the promise of Ruth's future at the creation of the Republic and the erasure of that future is again emphasized with the destruction of the family home. Built with proceeds from her mother's in-heritance—again stressing matrilineal rather than paternal ties—Ruth builds a house, which May-lee Chai characterizes as "modern." "Not just any house, but the perfect home, the foundation for the rest of her life. Modern. Western. . . . All of my childhood, I'd heard of this miracle house, the best house in the world, my grandmother's modern, American-style brick dream house" (123). When May-lee and Winberg return in 1985, how-ever, the house has fallen into disrepair. In a rundown neighborhood, dot-ted with "tin-roofed shanties and squatters' shacks . . . we found a long nar-row brick house, now sooty-gray and dilapidated, with two brick columns that must have been imposing once but that now seemed merely in need of supports" (123). Upon discovery, Winberg rants, "You've ruined every-thing! Everything is dirt! Everything is poor! The country is poor! You've ruined China! The Communists have ruined everything!" (123). The juxta-position between "modern," "American," and "Western" and poverty, dilap-idation, and communism highlights again the narrative's trajectory from cultural and social promise to economic decline. The book closes with an-other trip to China in which capitalism seems to have taken hold. "Our rel-atives all had refrigerators and color television sets now. The women were wearing skirts and high heels. My father's cousin . . . had received a visa to work in New York at Columbia University. We celebrated with a seventeen-course banquet" (296). The markers of "success" abound, and the narrative ends where it begins, with the image of a changing China, one that is mov-ing to embrace Western cultural values and capitalism.

History and Chinese Women's Value

I turn now to a discussion of Pang-Mei Natasha Chang's *Bound Feet and Western Dress: A Memoir,* in an effort to explore more fully the impact of these narratives on the construction of an Asian American identity and history. Following a format similar to *The Girl from Purple Mountain,* the memoir is told from two perspectives, that of the author, Pang-Mei Natasha Chang, and of her great-aunt, Chang Yu-I, the first woman in China to get a divorce. The narrative again juxtaposes two time periods—the beginning and the end of the twentieth century—and two locales—China and the United States—in order to highlight the struggles that each of the women face. Beginning almost each chapter with her own questions about her place in the family's hierarchy and in larger social and national structures, Pang-Mei Natasha Chang then moves back in time to her great-aunt's struggles to negotiate family and society. She particularly makes parallels between her own efforts to locate a Chinese American identity and her aunt's negotiations of the cultural changes that character-ize early twentieth-century China: the loosening of social restrictions on Chinese women, especially the abandonment of practices such as foot binding, and the increased interaction between China and Western na-tions such as the United States and England. Her great-aunt's fame as the first woman to get a divorce in China, that is, her notoriety for rejecting the role of wife, becomes the primary means through which Pang-Mei herself is able to locate her own identity in a national and international history that primarily revolves around the accomplishments of men.

The act of writing her great-aunt's story presumably serves to disrupt the formal narrative of the Chang family from which Pang-Mei finds her-self alienated. She explains the ways in which the men in the Chang fam-ily have achieved distinction, and how their public triumphs have been the foci of the Chang family narrative. In the respected realms of politics, economics, science, and education, where her grandfather and great-un-cles have joined the ranks of elite history makers as the heads of political parties, banks, and universities, Pang-Mei does not see a place for herself. "While proud of my grandfather and great-uncles, I did not know to what extent I dared identify with them. These were Chang men. Whenever the family talked about my great aunts the Chang women, they praised their successful marriage to educated or wealthy men, and their elegant skills in social situations. . . . I worried where that left me, a first-generation

Chinese-American girl who had never been to China" (1996, 39). Pang-Mei asks here about her own position in the formation of a Chinese nation-state: how can she, as a "Chinese American girl who has never been to China," make an equally big name for herself?

The nation that Chang claims is not the United States but China, a choice that seemingly works against the efforts of Asian American activists and scholars who have labored to assert Asian Americans' roots and rights in the larger U.S. imaginary. Acquiescing to the idea that the United States is not a "country I could call my own," Chang instead turns toward her great-aunt's notoriety as the first divorced woman to claim national status, a move that counters her great-uncles' educational, economic, and social achievements within the national context. To claim one's place in history in the postmodern global era, in other words, does not necessitate, as in the case of writing Asian American history, the establishment of one's po-sition in the economic, social, and political structures of U.S. history, a narrative that has been constructed around and against the "absence" of Asian Americans. Instead it involves linking one's identity to a woman who personifies the "in-between," who moves back and forth across the borders of gender, nation, and time.

Chang closes her narrative with the same symbol with which she opens it, with her great-aunt's cheongsam. She writes:

> I have come now to place two articles of clothing in the trunk alongside Yu-I's. My two wedding dresses. The first, a gown of white chiffon—the stuff of my American childhood fantasies—I wore as I pronounced my marriage vows. The second dress, a full-length silk sheath in bright red, the Chinese color for felicity. Slim, slitted and topped with a stiff, stand-up collar, my cheongsam is modeled after those worn by Yu-I and my mother. When I changed into my cheongsam for my wedding reception, I felt vibrant and proud, at once a filial daughter and self-reliant sister, though I had broken with tradition and married, with my parents' blessings, outside of my her-itage. (211–212)

Although Pang-Mei "breaks with tradition," the narrative ends in a fairly traditional fashion, with a wedding. Even though her great-aunt's public identity revolves around her dissolution of marriage vows, Chang's resolu-tion of Pang-Mei's own marriage "outside of [her] heritage" signifies the dependence of her own racial identity on her nontraditional-yet-tradi-tional position to marriage. Early-twentieth-century China thus emerges as a historical time that captures the "traditional" customs of feudal China —rituals that evoke "the Orient" for a Western audience—while also standing for the revolutionary spirit of the era, the birth of the new republic, the new freedoms for women, and increased interaction with the United States and Europe. As a symbol of this new (precommunist) nation, Chang Yu-I can be deployed as a quintessential Chinese foremother for contemporary Chinese American women, located within a specific history and geography and yet transcending all boundaries of time and place.

Conclusion

And yet, what are the implications of this alignment for Asian Americans? How does turning to China effect a different Chinese American history from a backward glance at, for example, Chinese immigrant women in San Francisco in the 1930s? The locating of our foremothers in China does correspond with the history of Chinese Americans. Due to anti-Asian immigration legislation, Chinese women were restricted from entering the United States. Thus, as Gary Okihiro (1994) points out, many of them were counted upon to maintain home and family in China while Chinese American men labored in California. The social realities of the transnational family even in the early twentieth century continue to support arguments for locating Asian American history outside U.S. borders. At the same time, however, *Bound Feet and Western Dress*, as well as *Fallen Leaves, The Girl from Purple Mountain*, and other narratives like it spurn Asian American history and instead embrace a global "history," in its current postmodern form. They imagine Chinese American women's history not necessarily as a history rooted in the moment of immigration to the United States (even though most eventually conclude in that manner), but instead as one grounded in migration in general, a perpetual state to be inhabited, one that captures the full global capitalist moment. Unlike their male counterparts, they imagine but never quite realize a "flexible cultural citizenship," in which their spectacular strength and determination enable them to enter any nation even as that entry is predicated on their embodiment of China.

While the proliferation of such texts seems to speak to China's continued function as a site for U.S. fantasies about exotic and foreign lands, the narratives also reveal the value of Chinese women's history as a means of negotiating a global capitalist present. Chinese women in these narratives become a means by which we imagine modernity's potential; straddling the boundaries of gender, hemisphere, and time, they stand forever poised on the cusp of the modern era, the realization of which is perpetually deferred by the dramatic events that threaten to overwhelm them. Chinese women's history thus functions as both a marker for the epic past as well as the potential for transformation and realization of worth. Through them, we simultaneously witness our past and our future, the reassurance of our triumph over epic events and the expansive possibilities of global capitalism. Chinese women's history, written also as the history of Chinese American women, becomes global history, not grounded in the United States or in U.S. relations with China, but instead in the disjointed time and space of postmodernity.

NOTES

1. Sau-ling Wong has dubbed these narratives "Gone with the Wind" epics. Wong elaborates, "Virtually all involve a multigenerational family saga interwoven with violent historical events . . . , as well as a culminating personal odyssey across the ocean to the West, signaling final 'arrival' in both a physical and ideological sense" (Wong 1995, 200). Wong's use of the phrase "Gone with the Wind" is gleaned from a reviewer's praise of Linda Ching Sledge's *Empire of Heaven*. Some of the authors that Wong lists as participating in this genre include Bette Bao Lord, Nien Cheng, C. Y. Lee, Linda Ching Sledge, Jung Chang, and Lillian Lee. Alice Cairns (1997) points specifically to first-person accounts of the Cultural Revolution such as Anchee Min's *Red Azaleas*, Jan Wong's *Red China Blues*, Rae Yang's *Spider Eaters*, and Ting-xing Ye's *A Leaf in the Bitter Wind*:

> The essential ingredients are the same. These are true stories, in which the main character/author is an attractive, intelligent woman, struggling to stay morally superior in the political chaos of China. She is usually aided or inspired by a granny with bound feet, a noble mother or an angelic daughter, and held back by a hopeless and/or brutal father. Add to that several hundred screaming Red Guards, the denunciations of once-loyal neighbours and friends, and an uplifting final chapter set in the Free World, and you have the makings of a money-spinner.

2. I echo Sau-ling Wong's argument that *The Joy Luck Club* "allegorizes a Third World/First World encounter that allows mainstream American feminism to construct itself in a flattering, because depoliticized, manner" (Wong 1995, 181).

3. See Frederic Jameson's *Postmodernism, or, the Cultural Logic of Late Capitalism* (1991), and Arjun Appadurai's *Modernity at Large* (1996) for a longer discussion of this postmodern phenomenon.

REFERENCES

Appadurai, Arjun. *Modernity at Large: Cultural Dimensions of Globalization.* Minneapolis: University of Minnesota Press, 1996.

Bow, Leslie. "Cultural Conflict/Feminist Resolution in Amy Tan's *The Joy Luck Club.*" In *New Visions in Asian American Studies: Diversity, Community, Power.* Eds. Franklin Ng, Judy Yung, Stephen S. Fugita, and Elaine H. Kim. Pullman: Washington State University Press, 1994, 235–247.

Cairns, Alice. "Birds of a Feather." *South China Morning Post,* 10 August 1997. sec. Sunday Magazine: 16.

Chai, May-lee, and Winberg Chai. *The Girl from Purple Mountain: Love, Honor, War, and One Family's Journey from China to America.* New York: Thomas Dunne Books, 2001.

Chang, Jung. *Wild Swans: Three Daughters of China.* New York: Simon and Schuster, 1991.

Chang, Pang-Mei Natasha. *Bound Feet and Western Dress: A Memoir.* 1st ed. New York: Doubleday, 1996.

Fabian, Johannes. *Time and Other: How Anthropology Makes Its Object.* New York: Columbia University Press, 1983.

Jameson, Fredric. *Postmodernism, or, the Cultural Logic of Late Capitalism: Post-Contemporary Interventions.* Durham: Duke University Press, 1991.

Krist, Gary. "The Great Leap Backward." Review of *The Girl from Purple Mountain: Love, Honor, War, and One Family's Journey from China to America,* by May-lee Chai and Winberg Chai. *New York Times,* 8 July 2001, late ed.: sec. 7:6.

Mah, Adeline Yen. *Falling Leaves: The True Story of an Unwanted Chinese Daughter.* 1st Broadway Books trade pbk. ed. New York: Broadway Books, 1999.

Okihiro, Gary Y. *Margins and Mainstreams: Asians in American History and Culture.* Seattle: University of Washington Press, 1994.

Ong, Aiwha. *Flexible Citizenship: The Cultural Logics of Transnationality.* Durham: Duke University Press, 1999.

Wong, Sau-ling Cynthia. "'Sugar Sisterhood': Situating the Amy Tan Phenomenon." In *The Ethnic Canon: Histories, Institutions, and Interventions.* Ed. David Palumbo-Liu. Minneapolis: University of Minnesota Press, 1995, 174–210.

Chapter 8

Between Yellowphilia and Yellowphobia

Ethnic Stardom and the (Dis)Orientalized Romantic Couple in Daughter of Shanghai *and* King of Chinatown

Hye Seung Chung

Throughout the 1990s, media scholars writing about Hollywood's representation of Asians have privileged a handful of now-canonized silent films, such as *The Cheat* (Famous Players, 1915), *Madame Butterfly* (Famous Players, 1915), and *Broken Blossoms* (United Artists, 1919), which are continuously recycled in critical discourse.[1] Each of these texts—like their latter-day permutations, including *The Bitter Tea of General Yen* (Columbia, 1933), *Love Is a Many-Splendored Thing* (20th Century–Fox, 1955), *Sayonara* (Warner Bros., 1957), and *The World of Suzie Wong* (Paramount, 1960)—share the theme of interracial romance (or sexual contract) entrenched in the Orientalist imaginary of racialized and gendered others. Discounting the rare exceptions *The Good Earth* (MGM, 1937), *Dragon Seed* (MGM, 1944), and *Flower Drum Song* (Universal, 1960), classical Hollywood films seldom foreground Asian romantic coupling as the central plot element. Furthermore, the blossoming of romance between two "Orientals" in the aforementioned examples is either mediated through the inscription of white actors in "yellowface" or facilitated through a kind of casting apartheid—an all-Asian counterpart to segregationist African American musicals *Hallelujah* (MGM, 1929), *Stormy Weather* (20th Century–Fox, 1943), and *Cabin in the Sky* (MGM, 1944). Capsizing this representational schemata and casting politics, two obscure, critically overlooked Paramount 'B' films—*Daughter of Shanghai* (1937, dir. Robert Florey) and *King of Chinatown* (1939, dir. Nick Grinde)—not only proffer nonstereotyped, upwardly mobile, middle-class Asian Americans as active protagonists but also culminate with the constitution of an Asian romantic duo (self-represented by two Asian American actors, Anna May Wong and Philip Ahn) in place of the traditional Caucasian coupling.

This essay will situate the positive representation of Asian Americans and the formation of the Anna May Wong-Philip Ahn couple in these films within larger sociopolitical, cultural, and industrial contexts, namely, the anti-Asiatic immigration acts, East Asian political conflicts, the cycle of Oriental detective films, and the studio's publicity and marketing of ethnic stars in order to tease out the deeper implications of these anomalous images, which make sense only when the specific historical period in which they were created is thrown in relief. In addition, I will argue that *Daughter of Shanghai* complicates and racially reinscribes the conventional scopic regime of classical narrative cinema by foregrounding Anna May Wong's Orientalized body as a female spectacle, yet simultaneously mobilizing her investigative gaze as an identificatory conduit for the spectator. Furthermore, I will unpack a pivotal scene in the film which manifests the reciprocal specular relation between the onscreen "gaze of recognition" (the two protagonists' shared gaze penetrating the other's masquerade) and the offscreen gaze of Asian American spectators who are capable of recognizing the cross-ethnic masquerade of Oriental stars and actors.

Bad Orientals, Good Orientals: Coolies Go Home!
But Let's Save China

Daughter of Shanghai is an adventure thriller revolving around the exploits of Lan Ying Quan (Anna May Wong), the daughter of a San Francisco–based Chinese art dealer, Quan Lin (Ching Wah Lee), who has been secretly gathering evidence against an alien smuggling ring. Quan Lin is shot and killed after he refuses to cooperate with the smugglers' demands that he employ illegal Chinese laborers. On the night of her father's murder, Lan Ying is introduced to detective Kim Lee (Philip Ahn)—a federal agent assigned to the case—through family friend and patron Mrs. Hunt (Cecil Cunningham). Unbeknownst to Lan Ying and Lee, the benevolent, wealthy art collector is the mastermind of the smuggling ring with ties to Central America. Resolved to bringing justice to the murderers on her own, Lan Ying travels alone to an exotic Port O' Juan saloon run by Otto Hartman (Charles Bickford), Mrs. Hunt's overseas underling, and masquerades as a dancer in the hope of gathering clues about the smuggling operation. At Port O' Juan, Lee reappears, incognito, wearing the clothes of a sailor, and is quickly hired as an interpreter by the captain of the smuggler's ship. After a series of perilous pitfalls and last-minute rescues that demonstrate Lee's intelligence in outwitting the villains, the couple manages to expose Mrs. Hunt and her cohorts, who are then handed over to the police. The dénouement of the film not only brings the mystery to the satisfying resolution audiences have come to expect in classical Hollywood storytelling, but also slyly undercuts this horizon of expectations and reconfigures the racial norm by showing, in the penultimate shot, the triumphant Lee proposing marriage to Lan Ying in the backseat of a car— an iconic, mobile interior for the final romantic fade-out—juxtaposed with the last shot of the arrested white villain, Mrs. Hunt, being whisked away to jail in handcuffs.

Garnet Weston's original story, *The Honor Bright,* from which the film's screenplay evolved, is loosely based on a *Los Angeles Times* article (dated June 4, 1934) about the arrest of a ring responsible for smuggling thousands of Chinese citizens into the United States. An extract from the newspaper article, accompanying Weston's draft, reports that the syndicate ruthlessly murdered aliens by jettisoning them overboard contraband ships when detection became imminent.[2] *Daughter of Shanghai* opens with a montage of newspaper headlines such as "Foreign Horde Floods U.S.," "Human Cargo Payoff Totals Millions!" and "Undercover Coast Smuggling Ring." The ensuing scene shows a smuggler's plane chased by state patrol aircraft. In a fashion similar to that recounted in the *Times* article, the smugglers open the trapdoor of a secret compartment, discharging human cargo into the ocean just before the anticipated seizure. The film continues to condemn the illegal immigration by inserting menacing statistics—in the form of newspaper reports—into the storyline: "Fifty thousand aliens make illegal entry into this country each year." In addition to the negative portrayal of illegal entrants and their smugglers in the story, one of the publicity posters of *Daughter of Shanghai* explicitly attempts to arouse antialien sentiment by directly addressing the audience with a series of didactic questions: "Did you know that thousands of aliens are smuggled annually into the U.S.A? Did you know that blackmailers bleed them to the tune of $1,000,000 a year? Did you know that 100,000 of these illegal entrants are subjects for Relief? Did you know that 3,500,000 more have taken the jobs of American citizens?" (Paramount pressbook 1937). Ironically, in the film this critique of the ignorance of illegal immigrants issues from the mouth of Quan Lin (a Chinese immigrant himself) who tells his daughter that racketeers are importing

> misguided human beings. Among them men of my own blood. . . . They find the victims from all parts of the world—the ignorant, the helpless, who have heard of America. And when these people are finally landed here, they are sold like slaves.

In a previous version of the script, entitled *Anna May Wong Story* and dated September 8, 1937, the upper-middle-class entrepreneur Quan Lin utters a harsher expression, "misguided coolies," stigmatizing underclass illegal laborers of his own ethnicity (Paramount script files). By situating Chinese American males—Quan Lin and Kim Lee—on the side occupied by immigration authorities,[3] *Daughter of Shanghai* not only effectively evades any potentially racist, anti-Sinitic allegations concerning its portrayal of "misguided coolies,"[4] but also erects a distinct demarcation between the "good" Oriental (the assimilated American citizen) and the "bad" Oriental (the illegal immigrant).

In his trailblazing treatise *On Visual Media Racism: Asians in the American Motion Pictures* (1978), Eugene Franklin Wong argues that the passing of the 1924 Immigrant Act (or Nationality Origins Act)—which denied admission to all aliens ineligible for citizenship, thus practically excluding all Asians except Filipinos—and "the subsequent social relief accompanying the end to the Asian immigration problem, gradually provided a psychological incentive and social climate given to the acceptance of an image of a non-villainous Asian" (107–108). Even prior to the 1924 Act, which specifically intended to exclude the Japanese—the only Asian community (besides Filipinos) whose immigration had been permitted on a limited basis under the terms of the Gentlemen's Agreement of 1908 between the United States and Japan—Chinese immigrants had been barred from American shores by a series of exclusion acts passed by Congress between 1882 and 1902.[5] Originally welcomed to the United States as cheap laborers mobilized en masse to excavate California's gold mines and build transcontinental railroads, the Chinese quickly came to be viewed as "yellow peril" coolies usurping the jobs of European immigrants. The anti-Chinese xenophobia was translated, throughout the following decades, into abhorrent cinematic images of emasculated, opium-addicted coolie laborers or derivatives of the archetypal enemy to the white race, Dr. Fu

Manchu. The popularization of the Charlie Chan series beginning with *Charlie Chan Carries On* (Fox, 1931), however, marked a turning point in Hollywood's sinophobic representations. Despite white actors' yellowface impersonations of Charlie Chan's exaggerated, yet stoic, pseudo-Confucian mannerisms, the Chinese detective hero, as Norman K. Denzin points out, "neutralized previous negative images of the Asian-American, and offered to Asian-Americans (and Americans) a particular Americanized version of who they were and who they should be" (1995: 89). Likewise, *Daughter of Shanghai* provides an Althusserian interpellation[6] of an American-born, acculturated, middle-class Chinese identity that is completely distinct from the subaltern class of illegal coolie laborers. The film thus captures the rebound of yellowphilia's predilection for good, likable Orientals against the backdrop of a yellowphobia erected against illegal immigrants. Eugene Wong evaluates the film positively, albeit with minor hesitations: "While failing to explain that given anti-Asian legislation the only way in which Chinese could enter America was through illegal means, *Daughter* was a favorable treatment of Chinese. . . . The combination of Ahn and Wong provided an extraordinarily interesting filmic attempt to develop Asian American characters" (1978: 136–137).

Besides domestic immigration policies, the Sino-Japanese conflict in the East Asian political theater began to influence the representation of Chinese and Japanese in American films. Although pre-Pearl Harbor U.S. government edicts maintained an isolation policy toward Japan's imperial expansion in East Asia (its annexation of Korea in 1910, of Manchuria in 1931, and its subsequent full-scale military aggression against China leading to the outbreak of the Sino-Japanese War in 1937) in order to avoid a direct military conflict with Japan, the American public increasingly sympathized with the Chinese people suffering under the heels of the Japanese.[7] Warren I. Cohen defines the period stretching from 1900 to 1950 as an "era of paternalism" in Sino-American relations (1978: 55). Fostered by American missionaries, journalists, and writers in China, America assumed the fatherly self-image of protector for the peace-loving, defenseless Chinese violated by belligerent Japanese imperialists.

The myth of the American protector permeates pro-Chinese Hollywood films made throughout the duration of the Sino-Japanese War, including *China Girl* (20th Century–Fox, 1942), *China* (Paramount, 1943), *The Story of Dr. Wassell* (Paramount, 1944), and *China Sky* (RKO, 1945), in which white American journalists, merchants, doctors, and officers heroically support, protect, or save their Chinese subordinates. Produced only months after the outbreak of the Sino-Japanese War and released concurrently with the "Rape of Nanking" (the Japanese military's brutal massacre of hundreds of thousands of Chinese civilians in the capital city),[8] *Daughter of Shanghai* indeed manifests, however obliquely, the paternalistic pro-Chinese sentiments of the American populace—without making direct reference or allusion to the war.

Less than two years after the release of *Daughter of Shanghai*, Paramount unveiled another Anna May Wong vehicle, *King of Chinatown*, a gangster film with all the trappings of the genre, yet one that couches a subtextual discourse concerning the relief of wartime China. Not unlike her role in *Daughter of Shanghai* as a wealthy heiress-turned-female detective, Wong again plays a nonstereotypical character. In *King of Chinatown*, she is Dr. Mary Ann Ling,[9] a medical surgeon who saves the life of Frank Baturn (Akim Tamiroff), the film's titular underworld racketeer wounded in a shoot-out. Baturn falls in love with Mary, despite her engagement to attorney Bob Li (Philip Ahn), and gradually reforms under her care. Mary and Bob are involved in fund-raising activities to establish an ambulance unit in war-ravaged China. Baturn is eventually double-crossed and assassinated by his right-hand man, the "Professor" (J. Carrol Naish), who has taken control of his rackets during his absence. In a philanthropic gesture before dying, Baturn endows an honestly earned portion of his fortune to Mary for her Red Cross operations. The final scene shows Bob and Mary, recent newlyweds, on a plane to China. Thus, in *King of Chinatown*, the China relief program is fueled by white money, mirroring America's $25 million aid package to China in the form of purchase credit in February 1939, one month before the release of the film (Cohen 1990: 124).[10] The penultimate scene of the film vocally conveys the paternalistic countenance of America patronizing a weaker nation with relief funds in Baturn's emphatic last words to Mary: "I want you to buy the finest ambulance and equipment you can get. . . . Hurry! Hurry! They need you there. I'll be with you! Hurry! Hurry!" While white humanitarian assistance to China is stressed through reformed Frank's altruistic last will and testament, a politically conscious speech directly referring to the war in China was dropped from an earlier script.

In the early version, dated June 6, 1938, Mary's Chinese father states in his New Year's speech: "Unfortunately, friend, there can be no Happy New Year tonight in our home land—our people are at war, invaded by an enemy nation. There are those who say that this war marks the end of ancient China—they don't know China—that is only the beginning of a new and greater China." In a second script, dated August 1, 1938, his speech is less concrete about China's plight: "The old year has brought all the ingredients of good life to us and our people here in this country. . . . But in the land of my ancestors, no laughter rises above the groans of the sick, the suffering and the oppressed." In the final script, the toast speech is given to Mary and lacks any allusion to the political situation in China: "And may the New Year bring peace to our people and the whole world!" (Paramount script files). This change clearly reflects the U.S. government's reluctance to intervene in East Asian conflicts prior to the Japanese attack on Pearl Harbor in December 1941, as well as Hollywood's avoidance of sensitive subjects that might disturb the State Department or upset overseas markets.[11]

The Oriental Detective Cycle and Ethnic Star Making

As discussed earlier in this essay, 20th Century Fox's profitable cycle of Charlie Chan mysteries inaugurated an Oriental detective craze whose longevity attests to an ongoing fascination with "good" Orientals in the 'B' movie market. Designed as an incentive to draw audiences during the Depression, the double-feature system dug a subversive trench for low-budget, quickly shot, roughly hour-long 'B' pictures where less conventional subject matter and characterizations could pass relatively unscathed.[12] Although the first two Charlie Chan films (a ten-chapter Pathé serial entitled *The House without a Key* [1925] and Universal's *The Chinese Parrot* [1927]) used Asian actors of Japanese descent (George Kuwa and Kamiyama Sojin) as the Chinese sleuth, it was not until the 1931 Fox production, *Charlie Chan Carries On*, with the Swedish immigrant actor Warner Oland in the lead role, that the series began to gather steam and succeed at the box office (Hanke 1989: xii–xiii; Mitchell 1999: xviii).

Oland played Charlie Chan sixteen times for Fox until his death in 1938. Missouri-born actor Sidney Toler replaced Oland, beginning with *Charlie Chan in Honolulu* (20th Century–Fox, 1938). Subsequently, Toler performed in twenty-two Charlie Chan films at Fox, eleven at Monogram studios, and another eleven at Monogram studios (Mitchell 1999: xix). Coincidentally, both Oland and Toler worked with Anna May Wong at Paramount. Oland played Dr. Fu Manchu in three Paramount films including *Daughter of the Dragon* (1931), which stars Wong as the daughter of Fu Manchu. In *Shanghai Express* (1932), he was cast as rebel leader Henry

Chang, a megalomaniac who rapes Wong's Hui Fei and is killed by his avenging victim. Toler played Wong's father, Chinese herbal doctor Chang Ling, in *King of Chinatown*. Upon Toler's death in 1947, Roland Winters inherited the role, appearing in the last six Charlie Chan films produced at Monogram from 1947 to 1949.

Both Anna May Wong and Philip Ahn appeared in Charlie Chan films. Wong played a dancer in *The Chinese Parrot* and Ahn appeared as Charlie Chan's son-in-law Wing Foo in *Charlie Chan in Honolulu* (though masquerading as Chinese, Ahn speaks to Sydney Toler on the phone in Korean during the final scene). Ahn assumed the role of murder suspect Captain Kong opposite Roland Winters's Chan in *The Chinese Ring* (Monogram, 1947). The popularity of the Charlie Chan films led to offshoots in the 'B' mystery genre: the Mr. Moto series at 20th Century–Fox and the Mr. Wong series at Monogram. Peter Lorre portrayed Japanese detective Kentaro Moto, a master of disguise and a jujitsu expert in eight films total, from *Think Fast, Mr. Moto* (1937) to *Mr. Moto in Danger Island* (1939). Moto films were ditched prematurely once Lorre moved to bigger roles and the threat of Japanese fascism in the international sphere undermined the legitimacy of a Japanese hero (Denzin 1995: 100).[13] It is also notable that the Charlie Chan series terminated in 1949, the same year Chairman Mao's Communist Party took over China, effectively sealing off sinophilic representations in Hollywood. Like 20th Century–Fox, another Charlie Chan studio, Monogram, provided an alternative Oriental sleuth, James Lee Wong. Boris Karloff played Mr. Wong in the first five Wong films from *Mr. Wong, Detective* (1938) to *Doomed to Die* (1940). RKO publicity-artist-turned-actor Keye Luke, who played Charlie Chan's "Number One Son" in ten films, was cast as Wong in the last film of the series, *Phantom of Chinatown* (1940). It is ironic that Oriental detective films failed to achieve success and popularity when a real "Oriental" actor played Chan or Wong as in *The House without a Key, The Chinese Parrot,* and *Phantom of Chinatown.* The genre remained the domain of white actors who impersonated slant-eyed, heavily accented masters of murder mysteries as well as purveyors of cryptic proverbs in what Eugene Wong calls a "racist cosmetology" (1978: 40).

Unlike the Chan, Moto, and Wong variations, it is quite extraordinary that the Asian American detective roles in *Daughter of Shanghai*—federal investigator Kim Lee and female quasi-detective Lan Ying—are not only played by real Asian American actors but are also devoid of degrading stereotypes. *Daughter of Shanghai* marked the "third beginning" of Anna

May Wong's movie career, to borrow her own expression (McIlwaine 1937). The first period of her career involves her struggle as a pioneering Asian American screen actress whose talent and beauty were largely subsumed by Hollywood's exoticist racial and sexual imaginary of a "madam butterfly" and a "dragon lady" in such films as *The Toll of the Sea* (Metro Pictures, 1922) and *The Thief of Baghdad* (United Artists, 1924). Disheartened by Hollywood's treatment, in 1928 Wong left the United States for Europe to seek what would become the "second beginning" of her acting career. In Germany, France, and England, she ascended to international stardom, appearing in a variety of lead roles in stage and film productions, fluently speaking all the original language dialogue.[14] In a 1933 magazine interview in London, Wong vociferously critiqued Hollywood's racial typecasting of Chinese:

> I was so tired of the parts I had to play. Why is it that the screen Chinese is always the villain? And so crude a villain—murderous, treacherous, a snake in the grass! We are not like that. How could we be, with a civilization that is so many times older than that of the West? We have our rigid codes of behavior, of honor. Why do they never show these? Why should we always scheme, rob, kill? I got so weary of it all—of the scenarists' conception of the Chinese character. (Okrent 1990)

Back in Hollywood, the biggest disappointment for Wong came when MGM offered her the temptress role of second wife Lotus in the film adaptation of Pearl S. Buck's *The Good Earth,* instead of the lead role of O-Lan. After losing the role of a lifetime to Luise Rainer, Wong again deserted Hollywood to visit her ancestral homeland for the first time, to find out whether she was "playing a Chinese or merely giving an American interpretation of one" (ibid.). Upon her 1936 return from China, Wong signed a new contact with Paramount, which provided her sympathetic roles in a series of 'B' detective and crime pictures between 1937 and 1939 (*Daughter of Shanghai, Dangerous to Know, King of Chinatown,* and *Island of Lost Men*) to vie with 20th Century–Fox for the niche market of Oriental mysteries. As Robert McIlwaine rightly points out in *Modern Screen,* "Paramount is making the [Anna May Wong] pictures, not due to the current conflict in the Orient, but because of the tremendous success of those Charlie Chan features" (1937: 41). Therefore, *Daughter of Shanghai* was the accidental, fortunate offspring of industrial competition, the Oriental detective cycle, and Wong's marketability as a 'B' movie star. In light of the antimiscegenation Production Code, Anna May Wong's portrayal of an active romantic heroine (departing from traditionally coded "lotus flower" or "madam butterfly" images) necessitated the introduction of a new Asian American romantic hero.[15]

Although Keye Luke was initially recommended for the role of male protagonist in *Daughter of Shanghai*'s earlier script,[16] Philip Ahn, Wong's close friend since childhood,[17] landed his first leading role opposite Wong only a year after his debut in the Bing Crosby musical directed by Lewis Milestone, *Anything Goes* (Paramount, 1936). *Daughter of Shanghai* and *King of Chinatown* represent the only romantic lead roles he played among some hundred titles in his filmography. Along with Richard Loo and Keye Luke, Philip Ahn was one of the most prolific Asian American actors to portray a diverse cross-section of roles, from 1930s Charlie Chan flicks to 1970s television series such as *M*A*S*H* and *Hawaii 5-O*. Now nearly forgotten or, at best, remotely remembered as the wizened guru Master Kan in *Kung Fu* or any one of the interchangeably hideous Japanese "heavies" in World War II films, his early career was in fact peppered with dynamic supporting roles such as the well-disciplined aide to Akim Tamiroff's titular general in Paramount's Oriental epic *The General Died at Dawn* (1936); the endearing Chinese guardian Sun Lo who passes fortune-cookie wisdom down to Shirley Temple's moppet in 20th Century–Fox's musical *Stowaway* (1936); and double agent "Hong Kong Cholly" who poses as the pidgin English-speaking sidekick of Larry "Buster" Crabbe's *Red Barry* so as to infiltrate the police in Universal's serial of 1938. His pre-war heyday culminates in the two roles as romantic lead opposite Anna May Wong—a rare opportunity afforded to an Asian American actor. This chance to rise above the level of bit player was short-lived, however; for as Hollywood re-aligned its representational modes with the public consensus of "yellow peril" in the wake of Pearl Harbor and U.S. involvement in World War II, Philip Ahn became increasingly mobilized as a Japanese impersonator (in lieu of Japanese American actors facing internment). He earned such appellations as "the man we love to hate" or "leering yellow monster" while appearing in a number of anti-Rising Sun propaganda films, including *Behind the Rising Sun* (RKO, 1943), *The Purple Heart* (20th Century–Fox, 1944), *Back to Bataan* (RKO, 1945), and *Blood on the Sun* (RKO, 1945).

During wartime, Ahn's proud identity as the son of one of the foremost leaders of the Korean independence movement became the focus of his publicity campaign. Hyping Philip Ahn as the "Oriental Clark Gable," Paramount's 1943 press kit described him as "a much-in-demand actor for wartime Oriental roles. . . . He was alternately an inimical Jap and a friendly Chinese." The publicity material furthermore reported that the actor had "made a solemn pledge to himself" not to take the role of a "Japanese-looking heavy in a Japanese-less wartime Hollywood" because of his personal feelings as the son of Ahn Chang-ho (An Ch'ang-ho), "one of the great Korean patriots, who opposed the Japanese long before the war and died in a Japanese prison camp five years ago" (Philip Ahn clippings file). Ahn Chang-ho was not only a revered anticolonial revolutionary who died of illness resulting from prolonged incarceration and torture by the Japanese, but also a pioneering leader and educator of the first Korean immigration wave to hit American shores.[18] Ahn had five children— Philip, Philson, Susan, Soorah, and Ralph—all of whom were born and raised in the U.S. Born in March 1905, in Los Angeles, Philip was arguably the first Korean American born in the Continental U.S. (Cuddy 1996).[19] One of the oft-asked questions by Ahn's interviewers was whether the death of his father at the hands of the Japanese emotionally affected his portrayal of Japanese characters during the war years. Ahn replied: "True, I hated the Japanese, but I told myself that if I was going to play the enemy, I was going to play him as viciously as I could. . . . I took pride in being the most evil man alive" (ibid.). The patriot's son thought that "making people hate the Japanese was a way for him to actively participate in the Independence Movement of Korea, in which his father had been a great leader" (ibid.).

Philip Ahn's wartime career in Hollywood—his onscreen oscillation between Chinese allies and Japanese enemies—not only registers the imperative of cross-ethnic masquerade as a means of survival for a minority actor working in a mainstream industry oblivious to ethnic differences among racial others, but also reflects the theme of displacement vis-à-vis that era's Korean and Korean American identity politics. In the collective consciousness of Koreans (domestic or overseas), the Sino-Japanese War and World War II functioned as surrogates of the Independence War. For them, the Chinese and American victories symbolized the liberation of their homeland from Japanese occupation. Just as Shanghai and Chunking provided an exilic base for many nationalist leaders (including Ahn Chang-ho) who established a provisional government of Korea and executed their anticolonial activities against Japan, Hollywood offered Philip Ahn an imaginary national space in which he could carry on his father's legacy by partaking in anti-Japanese propaganda. What was forbidden and repressed in contemporaneous Korean films under the strict control of the colonial government could be freely expressed in Hollywood. In *China Girl*, Philip Ahn embodies the very image of his father, a teacher and bell-toned orator as well as a political leader, in his performance of Dr. Young, a dignified Chinese pedagogue who unwaveringly continues to give patriotic lessons to a classroom full of orphans despite the threat to life posed by Japanese bombing. In *China*, he acts as the valiant Chinese guerrilla leader Lin Cho, a cross-ethnic personification of the Korean Independence Army who fought against Japanese troops in China, Burma, and India.[20]

Although Thomas Doherty comments that Philip Ahn "sacrificed ethnic pride to contribute to the war effort as morale-enhancing Japanese villains" (1993: 144), even his most malevolent roles—such as a cruel Japanese officer who tortures Filipino children in *Back to Bataan* or a treacherous American-educated Japanese spy who attempts to ensnare his former classmate into an act of treason in *Betrayal from the East* (RKO, 1945)—circuitously served as an extension of his familial heritage insofar as he was instrumental in giving Japan bad publicity around the world through the hegemonic distribution network of Hollywood films. Away from the camera, Philip Ahn likewise demonstrated his patriotism for both America and Korea by joining the U.S. Army in February 1945, a service which had been long deferred by Hollywood producers who sought his presence in their films.[21] Although his military service and temporary dissociation from Hollywood effectively halted the spate of "hate" mail from enraged movie fans ignorant of his offscreen identity, Philip Ahn's persona became permanently branded with the "bad guy" image due to his iconic presence in World War II propaganda films.[22]

As mentioned earlier, America's post–Pearl Harbor intervention in the Pacific war contributed to the surfacing of the actor's Korean lineage in publicity discourse. Since 1905, when Theodore Roosevelt sanctioned Japanese aggression against Korea in exchange for the United States' monopoly in the Philippines, the American government had disregarded the Korean problem altogether until the Japanese invasion of Pearl Harbor. During the war years, Korea reemerged in American public discourse as an "Exhibit A" of Japanese brutality and as a cautionary tale to the world of what would happen if their nations were snared in the Axis web. American officials began to openly express their support for Koreans suffering from Japanese atrocities, a concern officialized in the 1943 Cairo Declaration in which the Three Great Powers (the United States, Great Britain, and the Republic of China) collectively embarked on a commitment to Korean independence. Accordingly, the studios and media quickly capitalized on

Fig. 8.1. Philip Ahn and Anna May Wong in their
prime. *Courtesy of the Ahn Family Collection.*

Philip Ahn's Korean American identity by actively promoting his patrilineal involvement in anti-Japanese struggles and by underscoring the ethnic subject's double commitment to America's war efforts against Japan as both an American citizen and the son of a renowned Korean national leader.

The situation was completely different prior to 1941. In his prewar career at Paramount, Ahn was promoted as a Chinese actor. Paramount's publicity campaign for *Daughter of Shanghai* includes a short article on Philip Ahn, entitled "Chinese Star Makes Debut in Lead Role," which opens with the following words: "Ever hear of a Chinese who couldn't speak Chinese? Philip Ahn is one!" (Paramount pressbook 1937). By defensively identifying Ahn as an assimilated Chinese not in command of his ancestral language, Paramount's publicity machinery attempted to conceal the true reason behind Ahn's inability to speak Chinese: that he was Korean. The *King of Chinatown* pressbook likewise states: "There are only five or six Chinese actors in Hollywood whose names anyone can remember, and ranking high on this list is Philip Ahn, who is teamed with another popular Chinese star, Anna May Wong, in Paramount's new crime thriller, King of Chinatown" (Paramount pressbook 1939). Ahn's exceptional Korean heritage therefore had to be masked to facilitate a comfortable, homogeneous "Chinese" coupling and assuage mainstream audiences' anxieties about ethnic or racial mixing which might evoke, however remotely, the threat of "white-yellow" miscegenation.

The fan magazine discourse further solidified the myth of an idealized Hollywood Oriental couple by promoting an unverifiable, offscreen romantic union between the two Asian American performers. After Wong and Ahn starred as a romantic couple in *Daughter of Shanghai* and *King of Chinatown*, Hollywood gossip columns predicted the two's engagement. Wong's response to this rumor was, "It would be like marrying my brother" (Okrent 1990). Philip Ahn Cuddy, the actor's nephew, argues that

Fig. 8.2. Hollywood's Oriental romantic couple studies the *Daughter of Shanghai* script with director Robert Florey. *Courtesy of Brian Taves and the Estate of Robert Florey.*

his uncle was indeed in love with Anna May Wong, but was forced to give up hope because Helen Lee, Ahn's mother, did not approve of an interethnic marriage for her eldest son (2001). Neither Ahn nor Wong ever married and both were rumored to be gay, although ethnic newspapers often interpreted Ahn's bachelorhood as the result of his fatherly responsibility for younger siblings as well as his Korean-style piety toward his mother, with whom he lived until her death in 1969, only nine years before he succumbed to a fatal bout with lung cancer.

The Gaze of Recognition as Allegory of Asian American Spectatorship

M. G. Herald's review of *Daughter of Shanghai* on December 18, 1937, offers a satirical comment on the title of the picture:

> No war picture is this. No expedition is made to Shanghai. The only reason for the title apparently is that Anna May Wong, an American-born Chinese, is introduced to the ribald habitués of a tropical island honkytonk as "the daughter of Shanghai—exotic dances." (MPPA Production Code Administration files)

Paramount's interoffice memo from producer Harold Hurley to A. M. Botsford, dated July 14, 1937, shows the studio's desire for an exotic title to sell this Anna May Wong vehicle, which was then nondescriptively entitled *Across the River*:

> I have talked with the Chinese consul regarding the Anna May Wong Story, *Across the River,* and have received his approval on it. We wanted to use the title *Daughter of the Tong* on it, but the consul won't go for it. We will need an action Oriental type title for the picture. (Paramount production files)

Obviously, the studio had a clear vision of two components of this picture: an "Anna May Wong Story" and "an action Oriental type" even before the title was decided on and the characters and the script fully developed.[23]

The Anna May Wong character in the film is not a daughter of Shanghai, but a daughter of San Francisco's Chinatown. As Wong is a third-generation Chinese American, her character Lan Ying is an American-born Chinese who speaks English perfectly. However, in the early part of the film, her American identity is repressed: she has a Chinese name, wears only Chinese traditional dress or cheongsam, and faithfully fulfills her filial obligations to her "honorable" father. Lan Ying first enters the film as a living mannequin wrapped in a Chinese royal robe, which is expressly displayed for Quan Lin's VIP customer, Mrs. Hunt, who initially mistakes her as an "antique." Lan Ying comes to life and identifies herself as "only a modern copy." Pleasantly surprised, Mrs. Hunt comments, "Simply exquisite. You will make a perfect princess." Lan Ying replies, "I'd rather be Lan Ying Quan. Thank you." Mrs. Hunt agrees to pay Lan Ying's quoted price, $2,000, for the Peking treasure. This intriguing sequence highlights the cross-racial specular coordinates between a white female voyeur and an Orientalized feminine body. Mrs. Hunt's dominance as an Orientalist (who has a habit of importing not only *objets d'art* from the Far East but also *Orientals*) is mediated both through her pecuniary power and her readiness to unleash an "imperial gaze." The white woman symbolically solidifies her racial hegemony by interpellating the other woman as the mythic spectacle, "antique" or "princess," the object of her gaze.

Mrs. Hunt is a defiant woman whose spectatorial pleasure in Oriental femininity problematizes the "collusion of the male and imperial gazes" prevalent in classic films (Kaplan 1997: 67). Only four minutes into the narrative, *Daughter of Shanghai* challenges mainstream cinema's normative construction of the white male subject as ideal viewer-spectator by filling that position with a female character.[24] Throughout the narrative, the power positions associated with looking and being looked at are flexible and slippery. Along that line, Lan Ying and Mrs. Hunt's looking relations are reversed: in the end it is Lan Ying who looks *back* at Mrs. Hunt and discerns her guilt. Mrs. Hunt is brought to justice only when the shared investigative gaze of Lan Ying and Kim Lee lays bare her cover as a respected socialite. In the scopic scheme of things, female protagonist Lan Ying plays an ambiguous, dual role. Throughout the course of the film she alternates between the object of the imperial gaze (the passive Asian female spectacle) and the purveyor of the investigative gaze (the active detective woman). Although Lan Ying's subject positioning in *Daughter of Shanghai* is associated with a certain degree of paranoia as she witnesses her own father's murder and enacts perilous masquerades, the racialized female subject commands greater freedom and mobility to escape the constrictive domestic space than home-stuck, would-be investigators in women's films such as *Rebecca* (Selznick International Pictures, 1940), *Gaslight* (MGM, 1944), *Dragonwyck* (20th Century–Fox,

1946), *Undercurrent* (MGM, 1946) and *Secret beyond the Door* (Universal, 1948).[25] Lan Ying's flexible identity-in-process, her oscillation between the passive object and the active subject, becomes the signifying vehicle for a veritable cycle of deorientalization and reorientalization in racial terms.

The first moment of deorientalization occurs when she is emancipated from the traditional role of a Chinese daughter upon the murder of her Confucian father. Lan Ying swiftly changes into Western clothing, takes over her father's business and servants, and freely articulates her critique of the authorities:

> I've seen how the authorities handle things! First there's great excitement—an arrest is expected in a few days—and in a few days, everything's forgotten—until someone else is murdered.[26]

Rebelling against the government's authority bestowed on Kim Lee, thus resisting both white and Asian patriarchy, Lan Ying travels to Central America to investigate Otto Hartman, who operates a smuggling house for aliens at Port O' Juan. Lan Ying eventually masquerades as a dancer named Lily Chen and is hired by Hartman. She is reorientalized as the "Daughter of Shanghai," adorned in an exotic costume and accessories. Juxtaposed with Lan Ying's disguise is that of Kim Lee, who infiltrates the smuggler's ship, *Jennie Hawks,* in the garb of a seaman. He is subsequently hired as an interpreter for the captain, Hartman's partner, after pretending to speak what he claims to be "Russian": "Alpha, Beta, Gamma, Delta, Epsilon."[27] When Kim Lee visits Hartman's saloon with the captain, Lan Ying's dance number hits the spotlight. In the midst of her incense-drenched exotica, Lee and Lan Ying share a series of surprised looks (in shot-reverse-shots: Figures 8.3, 8.4, 8.5)—that I define as the "gaze of recognition." The reciprocating, bilateral gaze mediates an ethically codified ocular transaction which allows each to penetrate the "veil of the other," to see through the other's role-playing and masquerade. Although Kim Lee initially appears to be a surrogate for a white male protagonist (comparable to Cary Grant lasciviously leering at Marlene Dietrich's hot voodoo conga in *Blonde Venus* (Paramount, 1932), the bearer of the gaze which objectifies the erotic spectacle, he himself also becomes an object of Lan Ying's epistemological, knowing gaze which recognizes his own performance.

The two ethnic characters' shared "gaze of recognition" also mirrors the offscreen gaze of Asian or Asian American spectators who are capable of identifying the Korean American actor Philip Ahn's cross-ethnic masquerade

Figs. 8.3–8.5. Gaze of recognition between two Asian American masqueraders.

due to their foreknowledge of ethnic differences between Chinese and Koreans (facial features, surnames) and the ethnic stars' offscreen personalities. The ethnic "reading" competency of bicultural and bilingual spectators enables them to command a differentiated viewing position vis-à-vis
the cross-ethnic masquerade of Oriental actors. This distinguished form
of spectatorship is at times mediated by an ability to discern linguistic
differences. In mainstream American film and television productions, not
only have minority actors been cast in a wide range of cross-ethnic and
cross-racial roles but their languages have also been interchangeably sub-
stituted for one another. For example, Philip Ahn speaks his ancestral language while playing Chinese roles in several productions, including *Charlie Chan in Honolulu*, *The Rebel* (ABC, "Blind Marriage," April 17, 1960),
The Wild Wild West (CBS, "The Night the Dragon Screamed," January 14,
1966), and *I Spy* (NBC, "Carry Me Back to Old Tsing Tao," September 29,
1965; "An American Empress," December 25, 1967). The visual and aural in-
congruities stemming from Ahn's ethnic and linguistic masquerade create
an unintentional narrative rupture, thereby exacerbating spectatorial distance for Chinese-speaking and Korean-speaking audiences who are torn
between the subversive pleasure of ethnic recognition ("knowing better"
than the producers and mainstream audiences) and their unsettling alienation from a diegesis which distorts and misrepresents their cultural identities.

This hypothetical reading position is imbedded within multiple differences, depending on the degree of audience knowledge of and familiarity
with (mis)represented cultures and languages, thus problematizing the
construction of a monolithic "Asian American" or "Asian" spectatorship.
For example, there are exponentially as many Korean Americans who cannot speak Korean as there are Chinese Americans who are unable to comprehend Chinese. Korean-speaking or Japanese-speaking audiences may
identify the Chinese language based on its sonic dissimilarity from their
tongues but may not be able to distinguish the specific differences between
Mandarin, Cantonese, Shanghaiese, and other dialects. South Korean audiences will likely feel that Philip Ahn's command of Korean sounds awkward; they may also notice that the actor has a heavy North Korean accent
(his parents came from a region now situated on the northern side of the
Demilitarized Zone). These ruptures point toward the difficulty of applying a race-based concept of "resistant or oppositional spectatorship" (as
charted out in black spectator studies by such scholars as Stuart Hall
[1980], bells hooks [1992], and Manthia Diawara [1988]) to the particular

case of Asian American viewing positions. Linguistic and cultural differences as well as interethnic political conflicts—especially the imperial
domination of Japan over several nations during the first half of the twentieth century—divide Asian (and Asian American) identities into heterogeneous units. As Peter X. Feng puts it, "the label 'Asian' is not used in Asia
—it is only used in the West" (1995: 32).

What is significant about the given "scene of recognition" in *Daughter
of Shanghai* is thus an extratextual manifestation of a historically specific
alliance between two Asian American stars from different backgrounds
yet united in a common cause against Japanese aggression toward their
respective ancestral lands—an implicit discourse that can only be unrav-
eled by spectators armed with differentiated knowledge(s) and cultural
affiliations. Anna May Wong's patriotism for her familial home country
and anti-Japanese feelings during the Sino-Japanese War was no less
publicized than that of Philip Ahn. According to a 1937 Paramount publicity clip, the actress abandoned her new apartment on the grounds that
its view of a Japanese garden upset her sense of patriotism. The following year, studio press-kits reported that the actress auctioned more than
two hundred outfits, jewelry, and other memorabilia to raise funds for
China (Anna May Wong clippings file). The epistemological gaze exclusively shared by Lan Ying and Kim Lee—the only Asian characters in
the multiracial crowd of the scene—during the *Daughter of Shanghai*
number therefore allegorizes the privileged spectatorial position unin-
tentionally provided for bicultural audiences who possess greater sensitivity to and understanding of interethnic dynamics among Asian American players.

The film's penultimate scene, when Kim Lee proposes marriage to Lan
Ying, presents yet another instance that facilitates ethnic recognition by
foregrounding linguistic difference:

> *Kim*: How would you like to live in Washington?
> *Lan Ying*: Perhaps a change of climate is just what I need.
> *Kim*: Then it's settled.
> *Lan Ying*: Does this mean you're asking me to marry you?
> *Kim*: (In Cantonese, untranslated) What do you think?
> *Lan Ying*: (In Cantonese, untranslated) I am very happy you love me.[28]

Lan Ying's anticipated marriage to Kim Lee and impending migration
from San Francisco's Chinatown to Washington, D.C., signifies the final

deorientalization of the ethnic female subject and her ultimate assimilation into mainstream America. Unlike Lan Ying, Kim Lee enters the film in Western attire—black bow tie and evening jacket—and is never associated with traditional Chinese culture throughout the narrative. Even when he impersonates an interpreter to infiltrate the smuggling ring, the foreign languages he claims to speak are Russian, Italian, Spanish, and Portuguese. As a representative of the federal government, Kim Lee epitomizes the ideal model of an interpellated Asian American identity, which Lan Ying is to share through nuptial contract. Nevertheless, the sudden insertion of an unsubtitled Cantonese dialogue in the curtain-closing moments decisively derails the scene from the conventional romantic dénouement of classic films accompanied by the English-language pact of coupling—sealed with sweet-nothings, a kiss, or an embrace. Mainstream audiences can only guess at what is being said by the new romantic couple, now symbolically transported to an ineffable, yet ghettoized and segregated space. Underneath this inscrutable bonding peppered with "sonic Orientalism" lies yet another masquerade beyond the diegesis: that of actor Philip Ahn who "passed" as Chinese. Despite the overt ethnic bonding between the Cantonese-speaking couple, the knowing spectator can see through the ideological transparency of the dominant cinematic code which erects a homogenizing and interchangeable Oriental other through the politics of cross-ethnic casting and linguistic masquerades.

The scene of the final union furthermore otherizes the Asian American romance by physically alienating and desexualizing the couple. Despite Kim Lee's symbolic power as a representative of law enforcement, the Asian male hero lacks physical prowess, a typical attribute of the white male protagonist. Although Kim Lee uses his intelligence and wits to overcome crises, whenever engaged in a brawl with white males he is decisively disempowered and repeatedly knocked to the ground. His final victory against the ring is achieved through his cross-racial male alliance with Mrs. Hunt's righteous Irish chauffeur, whose flailing fists protect Kim Lee and Lan Ying from the villains. This parallels an early scene in which Quan Lin's razor-wielding, faithful black servant frightens away the smugglers harassing his Chinese master. In each case, the hypermasculinity of working-class, non-Asian males is mobilized to guard the safety and power of emasculated, middle-class Asian males. Thus, the portrayal of Kim Lee and Lan Ying's reserved romantic union lacking in physical bonding serves to contain Lan Ying's subversive female subjectivity and sexuality through the patriarchal authority of Kim Lee, who nevertheless represents an Asian American masculinity less potent than its Caucasian counterpart.

Though at first glance Paramount's *Daughter of Shanghai* and *King of Chinatown* appear to represent little more than a momentary lapse in conventional studio wisdom regarding the representation of Asian Americans, they reflect a unique set of attitudes among the historical, industrial, and cultural sectors the interplay of which is attributed to the portrayal of nonstereotypical ethnic role models to offset the "yellow peril" iconography flooding American screens. Of the two films, *Daughter of Shanghai* goes further in its deconstruction of orthodox textual and scopic strategies and in capsizing the racial status quo by employing active Asian American protagonists and their mutual "gaze of recognition," thereby allegorizing the differentiated spectatorship of bicultural and bilingual audiences. While these films definitely indicate a forward-thinking vision of new identity formation in a minority group, they frequently revert to a less progressive discourse by recapitulating images of a sinister Chinatown, Orientalist female spectacles, and emasculated Asian American males—a discursive contradictoriness consonant with the prewar American public's schizophrenic oscillation between yellowphobia and yellowphilia. That this dialogic interplay of meanings could operate so freely, so flexibly within the economically circumscribed world of the 'B' film is indicative of the subversive potential of this genre during the vertically integrated, stringently censored, classical studio era. Beneath the industry's monolithic veneer of big-budget "house styles" and narrative conformity, this period portrayed a rich array of culturally and politically significant subject matter that remains, to this day, critically overlooked. Equally overlooked has been the significance of the first self-represented Asian American romantic couple in classical Hollywood cinema. The formation of the Anna May Wong–Philip Ahn couple in the late 1930s deserves attention not only as a barometer of the shifting racial and international politics of the period but also as an ideal manifestation of Asian American stardom which today's mainstream media still seems reluctant to duplicate.

NOTES

The author expresses her sincere gratitude to Chon Noriega, David Scott Diffrient, and Brian Taves for reading earlier versions of this essay and providing intellectual support. Thanks also to Susan Ahn, Philip Ahn Cuddy, and Ralph Ahn for generously opening the Ahn Family Collection to me and sharing the memory of Philip Ahn. This project is financially indebted to the Institute of American Cultures Research Grant (the UCLA Asian American Studies Center) and the Plitt Southern Theater Employees Trust Fellowship.

1. Gina Marchetti, Sumiko Higashi, and Robert G. Lee are among the commentators of Cecil B. DeMille's *The Cheat*. Both Marchetti and Lee have also written on *Broken Blossoms*. Nick Browne and Marchetti separately investigated *Madame Butterfly*, starring Mary Pickford. See Nick Browne, "The Undoing of the Other Woman: Madame Butterfly in the Discourse of American Orientalism," in Bernardi (1996); Sumiko Higashi, "Ethnicity, Class, and Gender in Film: DeMille's *The Cheat*," in Friedman (1991); Lee (1999); and Marchetti (1993).

2. See Garnet Weston, *The Honor Bright* (story), April 17, 1937. *Daughter of Shanghai,* Paramount script files, Margaret Herrick Library, Academy of Motion Picture Arts and Sciences.

3. While Kim Lee is an official representative of law enforcement, Quan Lin is a voluntary investigator whose intention is to hand over his collection of evidence to immigration authorities.

4. Joseph Breen, head of Will Hays's Production Code Administration at the time of the release of the film, repeatedly urged Paramount to acquire Chinese government officials' approval of the script in order to confirm its presentability to Chinese audiences. His note to John Hammell of Paramount, dated September 16, 1937, states: "It is our understanding that you have assured yourselves that there will be no objection to this picture by the Chinese government or people." *Daughter of Shanghai,* Production Code Administration files, Margaret Herrick Library, AMPAS.

5. For additional information on the Chinese Exclusion acts, see Hudson N. Janisch's "The Chinese Exclusion Laws: Congress and the Politics of Unbridled Passion" (Kim 1996) and for material on the Nationality Origins Act of 1924 (also known as the Japanese Exclusion Act), consult Lee A. Makela's "The Immigration Act of 1924" (ibid.). Also see the chapters "The Regulation Period (1882–1920)" and "The Restriction and Exclusion Period (1921–1952)" (Kim 1994).

6. I am specifically referring to the concept mobilized by Louis Althusser in his essay, "Ideology and Ideological Status Apparatuses" (1969: 197, 173–177).

7. Eugene F. Wong quotes a public opinion poll from August 1937, which shows 59 percent of American respondents expressing its sympathy for China as opposed to 1 percent who supported Japan, concerning the Sino-Japanese War. In February 1940, 76 percent sided with China as opposed to 2 percent with Japan (1978: 136).

8. *Daughter of Shanghai* was produced between September 20 and October 14, 1937 and released on December 17. A full-scale war between China and Japan was inaugurated in July of that year. On December 13, 1937, Japanese forces entered Republic-era China's capital Nanking (Nanjing), raped at least 20,000 women, and

massacred some 140,000 Chinese civilians and soldiers during a seven-week period. For more information, see Bowman (2000: 65–66).

9. This character was based on real-life San Francisco surgeon Dr. Margaret Chung.

10. The United States offered a similar credit package of $20 million to China in April 1940. In the months following Japan's signing of the Tripartite Pact with Germany and Italy in September 1940, America's credit aid to China totaled $95 million. In May 1941, China became eligible for lend-lease (Cohen 1990: 124).

11. Paramount changed the title of another Anna May Wong film from *Guns for China* to *Island of Lost Men* (1939) in light of the State Department's exhortation not to evoke any reference or allusion to the Sino-Japanese War. The studio additionally confirmed the suitability of the script with its sales manager in Japan. *Island of Lost Men,* Paramount production files, Margaret Herrick Library, AMPAS.

12. The double bill, which by 1935 had been implemented in approximately 85 percent of all U.S. theaters (Cook 1996: 301), consisted of an 'A' picture and a 'B' or 'Program' picture as well as short subjects (cartoons and live action shorts) and newsreels, offering three-hours-plus of entertainment. This "two-for-the-price-of-one" system lasted as a predominant exhibition practice throughout the 1930s and the 1940s until the studios ceased 'B' film production in the wake of the Supreme Court's 1948 Paramount Decree, which forced the divestiture of their exhibition branches. The 1930s marked the zenith of low-budget 'B' film productions, which accounted for nearly 75 percent of the entire movie output of the decade (Taves 1993: 313). One of the most undeservingly neglected 'B' film auteurs is French émigré director Robert Florey (1900–1979) who made an average of seven pictures per year from 1933 to the 1942, working in the 'B' division of Warner Brothers and Paramount (Taves 1987: 8). At Paramount, Florey made two 'B' films with Anna May Wong: *Daughter of Shanghai* and *Dangerous to Know* (1938). Florey is also credited as screenwriter for the Sherlock Holmes film *A Study in Scarlet* (KBS/World Wide, 1933), which casts Wong as a mysterious Chinese widow.

13. A Japanese detective hero reemerges during the Cold War era in Samuel Fuller's *The Crimson Kimono* (Columbia, 1959), in which Korean veteran-turned-homicide-detective, Joe Kojaku (James Shigeta), falls in love with a white woman. After the postwar U.S. occupation of Japan and communist takeover of China, Hollywood switched from being pro-Chinese to being pro-Japanese, producing a bevy of films featuring geishas and Japanese war brides such as *Japanese War Bride* (20th Century–Fox, 1952), *The Teahouse of the August Moon* (MGM, 1956), *Sayonara* (Warner Bros., 1957), and *The Barbarian and the Geisha* (20th Century–Fox, 1958).

14. Anna May Wong appeared in three German films directed by Richard Eichberg: *Die Liebe Eines Armen Menschen Kinds* (a.k.a. *Song,* 1928), *Grosstadtschmerttling* (a.k.a. *The City Butterfly,* 1929), and *Hai-Tang* (1930), the last of which was

made in British and French versions (*The Road to Dishonour* and *L'amour maitre des choses*), both starring Wong. She starred in British films *Piccadilly* (1929), *Elstree Calling* (1930), *Tiger Bay* (1934), *Chu Chin Chow* (1934), and *Java Head* (1934) and performed opposite Lawrence Olivier in the London stage production of *Circle of Chalk* (1929).

15. Although the Motion Picture Production Code of 1930 specifically prohibited miscegenation between white and black characters, in practice the exclusion expanded to other racial minorities such as Asians, Latinos, and Native Americans. See Ella Shohat's "Gender and Culture of Empire: Toward a Feminist Ethnography of the Cinema" (Bernstein and Studlar 1997: 45).

16. William Hurlbut's early version of the screenplay, dated September 8, 1937, has a character description section which depicts the role of Kim Lee (then Duncan Lee) as "an American-born Chinese of the Immigration and Naturalization Bureau of the Dept. of Labor. Educated, poised, well-trained. Capable of playing the part of supercargo and interpreter aboard a tramp steamer. Must be a good actor who can portray courage, humor, sympathy and an attractive youth with whom Mei-Mei [later Lan Ying] can fall in love. Keye Luke would be ideal." Interestingly, Philip Ahn's name is attached to the description of a bit character Ah Fong: "Quan Lin's secretary must be a good actor, suave, courteous and speaking good English. Dressed well. Philip Ahn type." *Daughter of Shanghai,* Paramount script files, Margaret Herrick Library, AMPAS.

17. Anna May Wong and Philip Ahn grew up together as neighborhood playmates in Los Angeles's Chinatown and went to the same school, Central Junior High. Philip Ahn was offered his first screen test by Douglas Fairbanks while he was waiting for Wong (as her ride) on the *Thief of Baghdad* set. Ahn reluctantly turned down the role Fairbanks offered because of strong opposition by his mother (Cuddy 1996).

18. Ahn Chang-ho (pen name: Tosan) and his bride Helen Lee (Yi Hae-ryon) arrived in America in 1902, becoming the first Korean married couple to enter the United States. In California, young patriot Ahn became the first organizer of the early Korean immigrant community. After establishing the United Koreans in America (*Kongniphophoi*) in 1905, Ahn returned to Korea in 1907 to save his country from collapsing and created the New People's Society (*Sinminhoi*), a revolutionary organization. In 1909, a year before Japan's annexation, Ahn escaped from Korea and returned to the United States in 1911 via Manchuria, China, and Russia. Then he unified many Korean associations throughout the United States to form the Korean National Association (KNA) in 1912. The KNA performed diplomatic functions for overseas Koreans and provided Korean education for the children of immigrants. In 1913, Ahn Chang-ho also established the Young Koreans Academy (*Hungsadan*), a leadership training organization, in San Francisco. In 1919, he went to Shanghai and unified the Provisional Government of the Republic of Korea. Arrested by the

Japanese in 1932, Ahn spent most of his final years in prison and under house arrest in Korea until he died from illness resulting from torture and imprisonment in 1938 (Pak 2000).

19. Other historical commentators claim that Ethan Sungkoo Kiehm, the son of Do-sam Kim and Soon-nie Hong who was born on a Hawaii sugar plantation in December 1903, is the first American-born child of early Korean immigrants (Lee, Luke, and Kim 2003).

20. The Korean Independence Army (*Kwangbokgun*) was established in September 1940 as the military arm of the Provisional Government then located in Chunking. With the Japanese attack of Pearl Harbor, the Korean Independence Army declared war against Japan and cooperated with the Office of Strategic Services (OSS) for secret guerrilla plans. They actively helped drafted Korean soldiers escape the Japanese Army on Chinese fronts. They also fought with the Allies on the Burma and India fronts.

21. Among such producers was Cecil B. DeMille, who wrote a letter to the Los Angeles Local Draft Board on January 5, 1943: "We are producing a navy motion picture entitled *The Story of Dr. Wassell*. . . . We have selected Mr. Ahn for an important role . . . the part of "Ping" in the script, which has been in preparation since April, 1942, has been definitely fitted to Mr. Ahn's abilities and any substitution . . . might well be detrimental to the production." Letter from President of Cecil B. DeMille Productions, Hollywood, to Chairman W. W. Dunlap, Local Draft Board, Los Angeles, California, the Ahn Family Collection.

22. Hawaiian-born Chinese American actor Richard Loo was likewise habitually cast as a Japanese villain, appearing in many films alongside Ahn—the two ethnically separate thespians creating a double or mirror image of one another.

23. In Paramount's synopsis of *Anna May Story*, dated July 26, 1937, the names of the major characters are Mei-Mei and Duncan Lee (later changing them to Lan Ying and Kim Lee). In this version, Mei-Mei travels to New York instead of Central America, to investigate the smuggling ring.

24. For more discussions of the privileged male looking positions in classical Hollywood cinema, see Mulvey (1975) and Doane (1982).

25. For a discussion of the paranoid woman's film, see Doane (1991).

26. On November 4, 1939, Joseph Breen's office sent a memo to Paramount, suggesting the dialogue be changed or deleted. Breen expressed his concern that this comment on the inefficiency of the police might provoke local censors. *Daughter of Shanghai*, MPPA Production Code Administration files, Margaret Herrick Library, AMPAS.

27. This scene echoes the episode of Philip Ahn's screen test with Lewis Milestone for his debut film, *Anything Goes*. Milestone, who was looking for a pidgin-English speaker, initially rejected Ahn because his English was perfect. On his way out, Ahn returned and mimicked a heavy accent: "You like . . . aligh. You no likee me . . . aligh. Me no care. Hip sabee? Me go school . . . aligh." Milestone broke into

laughter and said, "Okay. . . . the part's yours!" Don Forbes's *Hollywood Scrapbook* script (November 11, 1938), the Ahn Family Collection.

28. In an earlier script, *Anna May Wong Story,* dated September 8, 1937, the last two lines were in English:

Duncan (Kim Lee): What do you think?

Mei-mei (Lan Ying): I wanted to be sure.

Daughter of Shanghai, Paramount script files, Margaret Herrick Library, AMPAS.

ARCHIVAL SOURCES

Ahn Family Collection. A family-based private collection overseen by Susan Ahn and Philip Ahn Cuddy.

Anna May Wong clippings file, Margaret Herrick Library, Academy of Motion Picture Arts and Sciences (AMPAS).

Daughter of Shanghai, Paramount production files, Paramount script files, Paramount Pressbook 1937, Production Code Administration files. Margaret Herrick Library, AMPAS.

Island of Lost Men, Paramount production files, Paramount script files. Margaret Herrick Library, AMPAS.

King of Chinatown, Paramount production files, Paramount script file, Paramount Pressbook 1939, Production Code Administration files. Margaret Herrick Library, AMPAS.

Philip Ahn clippings file, Margaret Herrick Library, AMPAS.

WORKS CITED

Althusser, Louis. 1969. "Ideology and Ideological Status Apparatuses." Reprinted in Althusser 1971.

———. 1971. *Lenin and Philosophy and Other Essays by Louis Althusser.* New York: Monthly Review Press.

Bernardi, Daniel. 1996. *The Birth of Whiteness: Race and the Emergence of U.S. Cinema.* New Brunswick, N.J.: Rutgers University Press.

Bernstein, Matthew, and Gaylyn Studlar. 1997. *Visions of the East: Orientalism in Film.* New Brunswick, N.J.: Rutgers University Press.

Bowman, John S. 2000. *Columbia Chronologies of Asian History and Culture.* New York: Columbia University Press.

Cohen, Warren I. 1978. "American Perception of China." In Michel Oksenberg and Robert B. Oxnam, eds., *Dragon and Eagle: United States-China Relations: Past and Future.* New York: Basic Books.

————. 1990. *America's Response to China: A History of Sino-American Relations*. New York: Columbia University Press.

Cook, David A. 1996. *A History of Narrative Film*, 3rd ed. New York and London: W. W. Norton.

Cuddy, Philip Ahn. 1996. "Philip Ahn: Born in America." The Philip Ahn Admiration Society website (http://www.philipahn.com).

————. November 10, 2001. An interview with the author.

Denzin, Norman K. 1995. *The Cinematic Society: The Voyeur's Gaze*. London: Sage.

Diawara, Manthia. 1988. "Black Spectatorship: Problems of Identification and Resistance." *Screen*. Vol. 29, No. 4.

Doane, Mary Ann. 1982. "Film and Masquerade: Theorizing the Female Spectator." Reprinted in Doane 1991.

————. 1987. *The Desire to Desire: The Woman's Film of the 1940s*. Bloomington: Indiana University Press.

————. 1991. *Femmes Fatales: Feminism, Film Theory, Psychoanalysis*. New York: Routledge.

Doherty, Thomas. 1993. *Projections of War: Hollywood, American Culture, and World War II*. New York: Columbia University Press.

Feng, Peter X. 1995. "In Search of Asian American Cinema." *Cineaste*. Vol. XXI, Nos. 1–2.

Friedman, Lester D. 1991. *Unspeakable Images: Ethnicity and the American Cinema*. Urbana: University of Illinois Press.

Hall, Stuart. 1980. "Encoding/Decoding." In Stuart Hall, Dorothy Hobson, Andy Lowe, and Paul Willis, eds., *Culture, Media, Language*. London: Hutchinson.

Hanke, Ken. 1989. *Charlie Chan at the Movies: History, Filmography, and Criticism*. Jefferson, N.C.: McFarland.

hooks, bell. 1992. *Black Looks: Race and Representation*. Boston: South End Press.

Kaplan, E. Ann. 1997. *Looking for the Other: Feminism, Film, and the Imperial Gaze*. New York: Routledge.

Kim, Hyung-chan. 1994. *A Legal History of Asian Americans*. Westport, Conn.: Greenwood Press.

————. 1996. *Asian Americans and Congress: A Documentary History*. Westport, Conn.: Greenwood Press.

Lee, K. W., Dr. Luke, and Grace Kim. 2003. "Whispers from the Past." *KoreAm*. Vol. 14, No. 1 (January).

Lee, Robert G. 1999. *Orientals: Asian Americans in Popular Culture*. Philadelphia: Temple University Press.

Marchetti, Gina. 1993. *Romance and the "Yellow Peril": Race, Sex, and Discursive Strategies in Hollywood Fiction*. Berkeley: University of California Press.

McIlwaine, Robert. December 1937. "Third Beginning." *Modern Screen*.

Mitchell, Charles P. 1999. *A Guide to Charlie Chan Films*. Westport, Conn.: Greenwood Press.

Mulvey, Laura. 1975. "Visual Pleasure and Narrative Cinema." Reprinted in Mulvey 1989.

————. 1989. *Visual and Other Pleasures.* Basingstoke, U.K.: Macmillan.

Okrent, Neil. 1990. "Right Place, Wong Time." *Los Angeles Magazine,* May.

Pak, Jacqueline. 2000. "Korea's Moses: An Ch'angho and the Colonial Diaspora." Unpublished speech draft delivered at the University of California, Los Angeles, November 9.

Taves, Brian. 1987. *Robert Florey, the French Expressionist.* Metuchen, N.J.: Scarecrow Press.

————. 1993. "The B Film: Hollywood's Other Self." In Tino Balio, ed., *Grand Design: Hollywood as a Modern Business Enterprise 1930–1939.* New York: Charles Scribner's Sons.

Wong, Eugene Franklin. 1978. *On Visual Media Racism: Asians in the American Motion Pictures.* New York: Arno Press.

Chapter 9

Whose Paradise?

Hawai'i, Desire, and the
Global-Local Tensions of Popular Culture

Morris Young

A few years ago, as I was sitting at the Honolulu International Airport waiting for my flight back to Michigan, I heard another person—clearly a tourist—make the following comment: "Honolulu is like New York City in the middle of the ocean. If you want to see the real Hawai'i you need to go to the neighbor islands." As someone born and raised in Honolulu, I was slightly put off by the remark and even contemplated a response: "What do you mean the *real* Hawai'i?" Of course it became clear that what this person imagined as Hawai'i and what I did were competing ideological expressions of what we understood the function of Hawai'i to be: for him it needed to fulfill a "Mainland" American expectation of idyllic paradise ostensibly free from the ever-increasing forces of global capitalism (as represented by New York City); for me Hawai'i has been a place that has always had to grapple with complicated global and local pressures, trying to manage a fragile economy (once built upon plantations; now dependent on tourism and the U.S. military) while also contending with issues of identity for its diverse residents as well as for the state (or Nation for Native Hawaiians) in its relations with the rest of the United States and the world. A type of schizophrenia, perhaps ambivalence and/or anxiety, becomes the state of things as a place like Hawai'i must deal with the rest of the world.

But the interesting predicament that has emerged in recent years is that the rest of the world must now deal with a Hawai'i that is no longer simply an object of consumption, no longer simply a place where outsiders are actors and the locals are scenery. In this essay I focus on the cultural productions of Hawai'i, particularly in expressions of identity through popular culture. In the history of Hawai'i we have seen a shift in representation and cultural production. Where once the most popular texts about Hawai'i included James Michener's 1959 historical novel, *Hawaii,* or the 1953 film, *From Here to Eternity,* the tide began to change in the 1960s and 1970s when a Native Hawaiian cultural renaissance gathered strength and an interest in the Native Hawaiian language grew. In 1978 Hawaii's Constitutional Convention voted to amend the state constitution to recognize both English and Native Hawaiian as official state languages. In the 1980s and 1990s, the Native Hawaiian sovereignty movement not only created an awareness about the political and social rights of indigenous peoples, but helped to further fuel the interest in and commitment to maintaining the Hawaiian language, an important act of nation building. Also in 1978, the first "Talk Story" conference was held in Honolulu to discuss the emerging production, recognition, and analysis of literature written by Hawai'i residents, resulting in one of the most significant acts in Hawai'i and Asian American literature and literary studies, the creation of Bamboo Ridge Press.

Within Hawai'i, then, various acts "legitimizing" Hawaii's local culture and local languages gained momentum as an audience was cultivated by making local cultural texts available (literary texts, but also musical recordings, locally produced television shows, and the like).[1] Writers such as Lisa Kanae and Lee Tonouchi have published Pidgin literature to wide acclaim in the islands, and to national acclaim beyond Hawai'i, as with Lois-Ann Yamanaka. This pressure from within and the increasing public awareness beyond Hawai'i of Native Hawaiian sovereignty, cultural identity, language politics, and various other social issues[2] has made Hawai'i residents more self-conscious about how representations of Hawai'i are constructed and how these representations are received by a larger public.

Locating/Local Culture

As Arlif Dirlik suggests, the local is "a site both of promise and predicament" (1996: 22). Both Eric Yamamoto (1979) and Jonathan Okamura (1994) have outlined and discussed the emergence and dynamic of Local identity. From the dominance of big business interests and the U.S. military during the territorial years (1898–1959) to early statehood anxiety about "modernity" to the further influence of transnational capital in the 1980s, Local identity has operated to define some sense of community in Hawai'i and defense against outside influence. As Yamamoto argues:

> Changes in social structure, the sense of loss of community, a decline in the quality of life, and the accompanying concern, worry, and desperation, have given rise to a movement by people self-defined as belonging to Hawaii (local people) towards regaining control of Hawaii and its economic, political and cultural future. (106)

Thus while the "promise" of Local identity has provided some protection from what are seen as overwhelming outside structural forces by forging a symbolic site of resistance through the emergence and expression of a collective cultural practice, the "predicament" of Local identity has also become more apparent in this time of economic stress. As Jonathan Okamura has suggested, because of the overdependence of Hawaii's economy on tourism, "it may well be too late for the necessary changes to be initiated that can give power and control to the people of Hawaii" (176).

One response by the Local community to the pressures of outside forces has been to generate culture around language, specifically Hawai'i Creole English (HCE), or Pidgin, as it is known in the islands. Pidgin becomes important to the production of culture because, as Charlene Sato (1991), argues, it is seen as a distinct feature of Local identity:

> However, the recent educational and legal controversies seem to have sharpened the community's sense of HCE as a marker of *local* identity. This historic shift was evident in public testimony before the BOE [Board of Education], which frequently referred to HCE as a vital part of local culture needing protection from harmful influences, in much the same way that the islands' natural resources require protection from land speculators and developers. (Sato 1991: 657)

However, while Pidgin has acquired newfound acceptance and recognition as a cultural product, it still exists if not in opposition to, then at least as secondary to Standard English, with Native Hawaiian emerging as another alternative discourse with real presence and power. The actions of the community to "protect" Pidgin can be seen as resistance to co-optation, or even to the elimination of not just a language tradition but of a culture. As Hawai'i has become linked more closely to the rest of the United States (through the broadcast media and the like), its culture becomes subject to the influence of the larger American culture. It becomes important, then, to rethink the concept of the Local. The changing pressures of contemporary Hawai'i society make it necessary to generate new ideas about what a Local culture will look like. Will it become more "American" as influence from the "mainland" increases? Will it become more global as the world becomes more available? Will it get caught up in the representations of island paradise that have been constructed in the past?

Much of my reading of Local identity is informed by the literary and cultural criticism produced by Hawai'i or displaced Hawai'i writers and critics. The active project of recognizing and producing a literature of Hawai'i has involved the kinds of theoretical issues that emerge out of the larger questions of nationalism, identity politics, and colonial/-postcolonial situations. Darrell Lum, an important Hawai'i writer, has commented that the production of literature in Hawai'i reflects the sensibility of Hawaii's peoples:

> The literature of local writers has a distinct sensitivity to ethnicity, the environment (in particular that valuable commodity, the land), a sense of personal lineage and family history, and the use of the sound, the languages, and the vocabulary of island people. (Lum 1986: 4)

Stephen Sumida, a literary critic who specializes in Hawaii's literatures, further complicates this sensibility by recognizing the vexed colonial relationship between Hawai'i and the "mainland" United States:

> Deeply undercurrent in Hawaii's Asian/Pacific American literatures are influences of local history and place, both of these concepts particularized in such an assertive way that these literatures inherently exercise resistance against presumed national, even mainland Asian American generalities. However easy it may be to see native Hawaiian and Hawaii's Asian American literary works as commodified evocations of a facile image of Hawai'i as paradise, this resistance and, further, the agency of self-definition are all the more vital in these literatures; for unless readers too are freed from tourist, colonial views of the subject, then the subject is bound still to be mistaken. Making matters better or worse for Hawaii's own literary power or its limitations (depending on one's point of view), history and place are not simply two separate elements of a worldview or of a sensibility in Hawai'i, but in Hawaii's island culture *place* is conceived as *history*—that

is, as the story enacted on a given site. (Sumida 1992: 216; emphasis in original)

I quote Sumida at length because his discussion of Hawaii's literature specifically highlights to me the problem of the Local and of location. It is easy to read past the resistance found in Hawaii's cultural texts and to see Hawai'i simply as setting. Sumida is right; in Hawai'i place is conceived as history. The problem is knowing whose history, whose story is being enacted to read and understand Hawai'i as place. Do we hear about the histories of an independent nation taken over by American businessmen who were threatened by the rule of a strong queen? Or are we aware of the extended labor strikes on Hawaiian plantations during the first part of the twentieth century? Or of the two-tier public education system which separated students by the quality of their oral communication, leading to de facto discrimination by race? More likely, outside Hawai'i, people are more familiar with the role Pearl Harbor played in the history of the nation and the rebuilding of Hawai'i to become the fiftieth state, a vacation Paradise that serves the rest of the country. From one perspective we see Hawai'i as a site of struggle, as a complicated arrangement of peoples, cultures, and histories that shape the modern Hawai'i. From the other perspective we see Hawai'i as setting, as a place where the local people are often absent or represented as objects for consumption, where local history is absent and tourist desire and leisure organize the economy.

Performing Paradise

Since the late 1960s, Hawai'i has served as the setting for a number of television series. Often these shows have utilized the characteristic beauty of the islands (lush green mountains and fertile valleys, white sand beaches and blue seas, gentle trade winds and balmy sunshine) and the most recognizable cultural images (hula dancers, surfers, and assorted darkskinned ethnics). The use of Hawai'i in the popular media has occurred throughout the twentieth century, according to Diane Mei Lin Mark (1991), as Hollywood even in its earliest films focused on "the exotic setting, nubile native maidens, *kahunas* (priests), *haole* (foreigner, Caucasian) interlopers, and white man–native woman love plots" which we see continued in later films and television series. While these films and television shows have made Hawai'i central to their stories, they have often not engaged and interrogated the cultural images of Hawai'i constructed for a largely "mainland" and white television audience and have not moved beyond representations which continue to exoticize the place and people.

Even the two longest-running television series set in Hawai'i, *Hawaii 5-0* which ran for twelve seasons, and *Magnum, P.I.* which ran for eight seasons, did little to engage Hawai'i beyond its representation as Paradise.[3] In fact, both shows reinforced many stereotypes. For example, in *Hawaii 5-0*, Detective Steve McGarrett (played by Jack Lord) headed an elite state police unit and was assisted by Danny Williams (played by James McArthur). Both fulfilled the audience's expectation of the hero: strong, handsome, smart, and white.[4] Subordinate officers were played by "natives" of Hawai'i: a Native Hawaiian, a Chinese, and various other dark-skinned figures who never acted without orders from McGarrett or Williams.

The very location of the headquarters of this mythical state police unit was also telling. The unit occupied Iolani Palace, seat of the Hawaiian monarchy until the last reigning monarch was overthrown by an assortment of white businessmen and U.S. Marines in 1893. *Magnum, P.I.* is even more problematic as we see even fewer Hawai'i "locals" represented, and then usually as cocktail waitresses or valets at the yacht club where Thomas Magnum (played by Tom Selleck) would associate with his buddies T. C. (an African American), Rick (the club manager), and Higgins (the British majordomo of the estate at which Magnum lives). Just as the occupied space of the palace is revealing in *Hawaii 5-0*, the spaces that Magnum locates himself in are equally revealing: the yacht club, a beachfront estate owned by the novelist we never see, Robin Masters, and even a red Ferrari. These spaces only act to perpetuate an image of Hawai'i as Paradise, where all white men can enjoy the rewards of material culture. And if lucky enough, like Magnum, they can live rent-free (no small feat in the high-rent market of Hawai'i), and have the use of a high-performance vehicle as well.

Enter *The Byrds of Paradise*, a 1994 midseason replacement on ABC, created by Charles Eglee and Channing Gibson, whose writing credits include *St. Elsewhere*, *Moonlighting*, and *LA Law*. More impressive was the fact that the show was backed by Steven Bochco, who had just successfully returned to serial television with *NYPD Blue*. While there have been other short-lived series set in Hawai'i between *5-0* and *Magnum* and after *Magnum*, none of them captured the imagination of the local community in Hawai'i like *The Byrds of Paradise*.[5] Perhaps the depressed state economy made the prospect of a revived television and film industry so attractive that high-level state and city officials were even willing to personally lobby Hollywood. For example, in a bizarre incident, a worker from a mainland production company was found murdered on the Honolulu waterfront. At first he was thought to be part of *The Byrds* crew, and within hours of the body being found, the Governor of Hawai'i, the Mayor of Honolulu, and the director of the Department of Business, Economic Development, and Tourism telephoned Hollywood executives to assure them everything was being done to solve the murder and to provide additional security on the set.[6]

However, while the economic benefits of *The Byrds* surely contributed to support of the show, it was the larger issue of representation that made it attractive to Hawai'i residents. Though the focus of the show was on a newly transplanted white family from New Haven, Connecticut, the rest of the cast, which included significant roles for Hawai'i actors, was almost entirely nonwhite and recognizably "local,"[7] an important concept in Hawai'i. The faces represented the various ethnic groups found in Hawai'i and were played by "local" actors, not imported ethnics performing "Hawaiian face."[8] The names were "authentic" rather than invented pseudo Polynesian or Asian (which was often the case on *5-0* and *Magnum*). Cultural history and practices were represented accurately for the most part. And perhaps most significantly, the "locals" spoke in the Pidgin dialect found in Hawai'i, even making a political assertion in the first episode that Pidgin is their own language, not merely broken English, and not for outsiders to appropriate. In short, *The Byrds of Paradise* was about contemporary Hawai'i, or at the very least made reference to contemporary Hawai'i and a wide range of social, cultural, and political issues that Hawai'i residents find familiar. It has just as much "real life" significance as *NYPD Blue* and *ER* may have for urban and metropolitan residents or *Everybody Loves Raymond* for middle America.

Nevertheless, there are still problematic moments. The show's premise, for example, is not unlike that of a number of other shows or movies set in Hawai'i: a white family comes to Paradise, is transformed by Nature and the Natives, but is still confirmed in its dominant position as civilized "Western" citizens. The Byrds (Sam, the father, and kids Harry, Frannie, and Zeke) come to Hawai'i to heal after the brutal murder of their wife/mother at a cash machine in New Haven. Sam, a Yale ethics professor, becomes headmaster at the mythical Palmer School although he has no formal training in elementary or secondary education. Throughout the series we watch how the Byrd family slowly but surely adjusts to and is accepted by the local community, from being seen as hated outsiders to being almost local. This setup is almost cliché. However, it becomes complicated when we realize that the show knowingly or unknowingly reenacts the first Christian mission from New Haven to Hawai'i in the early 1800s. Once again, we see "missionaries" in search of redemption appear on Hawaii's shores in order to convert the natives.[9]

The show's school motif is particularly interesting since it clearly reproduces the race and class anxieties found in Hawai'i, despite its ostensible concern with the bridging of cultural gaps. Sam Byrd is named headmaster and given authority simply because of his Yale credentials. The Standard English–speaking Byrd children interact with their Pidgin-speaking classmates. We see another reenactment of Hawai'i history and culture represented by the Byrds living in the headmaster's house, a house that once served as the plantation manager's home. In Hawai'i, English Standard schools were established (in 1924–48) to separate students who spoke Standard English (largely the children of the white population) from those who spoke Pidgin (largely the children of the immigrant and native non-white population).[10] Though Palmer School is a private academy, it reenacts the familiar subject positions of 1920s public schools: White men serve as headmasters and plantation managers; local students become plantation subjects.

However, The Byrds did enjoy much popular support from Hawaii's residents.[11] While certain things may have been exaggerated—for example, many people complained the Pidgin was not accurate, while others pointed out that at least Pidgin was being used; and some said that anti-white feelings were played up too much—people still felt that this show was different because it was just as much a product of Hawai'i as it was of Hollywood. Thus when The Byrds was not renewed for the next season after a run of twelve episodes (a thirteenth episode was never aired outside Hawai'i), the local community saw it as a slap in the face despite the reasons given for its cancellation.[12] What they saw was a show which had made a sincere attempt to engage Hawai'i and its cultures, which were rejected by the rest of the United States. Up until the cancellation the Honolulu newspapers ran numerous articles about the show in anticipation of renewal of the series. But when the show was canceled, both Honolulu dailies ran it as their front-page headline stories with lead editorials. People began a "Save The Byrds" campaign (with a T-shirt printed and sold by a local T-shirt business), and studio and network addresses and phone numbers were printed in the papers. Although this campaign soon fizzled, the attention the show drew in the course of a week was extraordinary.

Hawai'i residents could not understand why a family-oriented show with good production quality was not popular. It had begun to engage the central concerns of Hawai'i residents, although it also had to negotiate the pressures of constructing and fulfilling the "mainland" audience's desire for a "Paradise." Channing Gibson, one of the creators, said in an interview after the cancellation: "We played off some of the things people already knew, and hopefully led people into a more real iconography. We were trying to show realities without bursting everybody's bubble" (Noyes 1994: 40). Thus the show had to balance engaging issues which may have had limited audience interest with creating and reinforcing stereotypes of a Hawai'i which appealed to a larger audience. The question became for whom was Paradise being represented? Or perhaps, in light of the eventual cancellation of *The Byrds,* why did *this* Paradise fail to fulfill the desires of American culture? Some answers were offered in two fascinating and disturbing "letters to the editor" published in *The Honolulu Advertiser,* a local daily paper. First this letter by William D. Nueske:

> I was not surprised that the Hawaii-based television series "Byrds of Paradise" was canceled by ABC.
>
> While "Hawaii 5-0" and "Magnum PI" were successful, long running quality Hawaii shows, *I found "Byrds" to be an empty, plotless, small-talent production that was dominated by biased, Pidgin-talking dunces. Bye Bye Birdies.* (28 May 1994; emphasis added)

The second letter, by Anthony J. Keller, also printed in *The Honolulu Advertiser* (24 May 1994), bluntly described what the writer saw as the necessary exploitation of Hawai'i in order to produce a "successful" television show:

> If the TV networks want to attract viewers, they need to give viewers a beautiful, tropical escape. People can read and watch about their own injustices, crime, political incorrectness and ethnic misfortunes within their own state and hometowns.
>
> When people envision Hawaii they want to see beaches, bodies, and spectacular scenery. Viewers want to vacation (even if only through TV) to the Hawaiian Islands and we should promote that—it's our biggest resource and industry!

The "Byrds of Paradise" tried to pass itself off as a relaxed, family program, *all the while causing many people to feel ignorant and uncomfortable for
not "understanding Hawaii's causes."* Not good for ratings. (Emphasis
added)

While neither of these letters is specifically about Pidgin or the complex
language situation in Hawai'i, they suggest that Pidgin and the increasingly visible cultural practices and lives of Hawaii's residents stood in the
way of presenting a Hawai'i that would appeal to a mainland audience.
Granted, I cannot assume the background of these letter writers, but their
surnames are neither Polynesian nor Asian, and their attitudes are patronizing at best, and either racist or close to it. However, these letters confirm
the problematic space *The Byrds* occupied. As they point out, *The Byrds*
did not present the Hawai'i that people (that is, "Mainland" people) knew
and recognized, or more accurately, imagined and constructed. While
Nueske's vitriolic letter reduces very complex issues to vulgar constructions of race and class (read "biased, pidgin-talking dunces" as nonwhite
and poor or working-class), the reasoning and logic of Keller's letter is remarkable. Keller does not hesitate to acknowledge the exploitation of
Hawai'i, and is even bold enough to suggest that we should promote this
image for economic reasons and deny any "reality" which may damage this
image. Certainly, it would be naive to be shocked by Keller's attitudes
(which are probably shared by the state in its efforts to promote tourism),
or even by the bigotry of Nueske (and countless others who employ race
and class in Hawaii's social relations). As both letters seem to prove, in the
end the show did not fulfill the desire of the larger American audience or
even of a particular segment of Hawaii's population. But the letters also illustrate the letter writers' unease about these representations of Hawai'i
entering into mainstream American culture, for these representations
threatened their own status in Hawai'i and its relationship with the rest of
the United States.

While Nueske and Keller found enough to complain about and felt
threatened by the twelve episodes that were aired nationally, they would
have been even more upset had the "missing" thirteenth episode aired.
After ABC decided not to renew the series for the next season, there remained three unaired episodes. Two of the three were eventually broadcast
during the season finale—now the series finale—creating closure by having the Byrds decide to stay in Hawai'i rather than moving back to New
England and a prestigious college teaching job for Sam. However, one

episode was never shown to a national audience though it was broadcast in Hawai'i.[13]

This "missing" episode was entitled "Da Play Is Da Thing" and focused on Palmer School's production of Shakespeare's *Twelfth Night*. However, there was a twist. The version of *Twelfth Night* they choose to do is a Pidgin version, *Twelf Nite o Wateva*, adapted by local actor James Grant Benton, who served as cultural consultant and Pidgin coach for *The Byrds* and had a small recurring role as the school's custodian (a problematic representation, considering the class and race politics associated with Pidgin).[14] Sam even has a friendly argument with the school's dean of students, Healani Douglas, a "local," over Shakespeare being done in Pidgin:

> *Sam*: Can I say something politically incorrect? Are we sending the right message to the kids allowing them to perform Shakespeare in Pidgin?
>
> *Healani*: You're not one of those Shakespeare purists, are you?
>
> *Sam*: No, no, no. I believe in free interpretation. I saw a production in New York where King Lear's throne was a '57 T-Bird. My point is I just gave one of my Ethics students a "D" for having wall-to-wall Pidgin in a term paper. Now is it my imagination or is there a contradiction in there somewhere?
>
> *Healani*: A paper for an Ethics class is an academic exercise. This version of *Twelfth Night* is an opportunity for the kids to see a classic staged in a popular form of expression many of them grew up with.[15]

While Sam's reaction to Pidgin is sensitive, it is interesting that Pidgin is juxtaposed with Shakespeare, an often cited example of literariness and culture (that is, high culture). More problematic is his simple equation of "wall-to-wall Pidgin" in a term paper with the "D" that he gives the paper. I certainly do not suggest that Sam ignore the expectation (and requirement) of academic discourse in his class, but I hope that his evaluation was based on more than the use of Pidgin and the probable assumptions made about the paper's substance (or perceived lack thereof) because of the use of Pidgin. Healani's reasonable response to Sam's concerns has been absent in much of the debate over Pidgin in Hawai'i. While she recognizes the utility and necessity of Standard English in an academic class, she also recognizes the artistic and even literary value of Pidgin and its significance as a cultural practice and production. Thus she does not privilege one language over another, but recognizes the social value of each and suggests implicitly that it is useful to know both. However, this brief exchange over Pidgin is an indication of a larger cultural anxiety at work in this episode, as in other instances we see the Byrds at the "mercy" of the "natives." The anxiety is Sam's, the outsider to Hawai'i, or of the TV audience, as they find themselves in an unfamiliar position; they are culturally ignorant, rather than the cultural authorities they are used to being.

Other scenes from this "missing" episode also create interesting tensions between "local" culture and "mainland" desire. In one scene, we find Harry Byrd demonstrating his new hula skills to his father and brother and their live-in Hawaiian housekeepers, Manu and Sonny. This new interest in hula is a bit clichéd as Harry attempts to become part of the local culture by practicing its cultural art forms. However, Manu and Sonny are in a position to critique Harry's hula style. That Harry is learning hula in the first place begins to challenge the gender and cultural stereotypes which expect only women to perform hula. And toward the end of this clip, Harry is again practicing his hula but is corrected by Manu when she has to show him the difference between the movements for the sun and a rainbow. Perhaps the most remarkable moment occurs when Harry asks Manu to make a grass skirt for him and she tells him that grass skirts are not really Hawaiian, they're a "made-up thing for tourists." While the positions of cultural authority are reversed in this scene, the television audience is disturbed by the revelation that Paradise may not be so authentic, so innocent, so perfect. It may be "made up" and the "natives" may be pulling a fast one over those who are supposed to be more civilized.

The episode is full of examples of cultural authority being reversed. In another scene, Sonny is a cultural authority on sumo wrestling, explaining the different sumo terms, training his cousin, and cooking ethnic foods. Later, Harry's budding romance with a local girl is interrupted when she begins dating a local boy. Frannie must learn Pidgin in order to be in the play and to "communicate" with her "local" boyfriend. Though the show still returns cultural authority to the Byrds in the end—for example, George the sumo wrestler credits Zeke Byrd for being his spiritual counselor and giving him back his confidence—in my view this particular episode came the closest to fully engaging Hawai'i and its cultures.

Because the roles are reversed we see for the first time that Hawai'i is not merely a setting to which outsiders come to renew themselves or to assume cultural authority. Hawai'i becomes a site where a wide range of issues can be engaged, not limited to what happens on the beach or some other exotic location. It is not surprising, then, that this episode was never seen by a national audience and was only shown in Hawai'i. While *The Byrds* did employ stereotypes and cliché in order to attract a mainland audience, it also began to move toward presenting a more "realistic" Hawai'i. Finally that is why *The Byrds* failed in the eyes of a mainland audience. *The Byrds* sought to present Hawai'i and its people as legitimate actors in their own land, which—sadly—spoiled Paradise for the larger audience.

From Popular Culture to Public Culture

Just two months after the "missing" episode of *The Byrds* was broadcast in Hawai'i, another letter to the *Honolulu Advertiser* created an uproar which resulted in substantial discussion in the Honolulu newspaper of the history, status, and cultural significance of Pidgin. The wide media coverage and public discussion of the merits and demerits of *The Byrds* were a precursor to the very public debate about Pidgin that occurred in the Honolulu media from October 1994 through May 1995. The polite and sensitive exchange between Sam and Healani in *The Byrds* gave way to a more strident tone, set by Jon Hall's letter of 4 October 1994, which began the next round of the "debate":

> Your newspaper should print the real reason why Hawaii public schools are among the worst in the nation: students and teachers speak Pidgin garbage, a version of English which is only useful in slums and gang meetings. Is Pidgin widely used in Hawaii's private schools, mainly attended by "upper-caste" Japanese and European Americans? No. Look at their test scores.
>
> Hawaiian public schools will only improve when this language problem is fixed and the curriculum stops being centered on the Hawaiian sovereignty movement and focuses on the three R's. Case closed.

Hall's letter touched a nerve in the community, to say the least. The tone of the letter was similar to that of Nueske's and Keller's letters in criticism of *The Byrds*. Again, issues of race and class were raised as Hall juxtaposed images of "slum and gang meetings" with Hawaii's private schools. Hall's construction of culture was also limited, like Nueske's and Keller's, as he dismissed the Native Hawaiian sovereignty movement and wrote Pidgin off as a "language problem." Hall, Nueske, and Keller had a very rigid definition of what constitutes "legitimate" cultural practices and texts. In short, for them it was a question of cultural legitimacy.

The response to Hall's letter was passionate. A number of letters appeared on consecutive Sundays in the *Honolulu Advertiser* (9 October 1994, 16 October 1994) in the Focus (editorial) section. They fell on both sides of the debate and maintained the divisive rhetoric employed by Hall. The 30 October 1994 Sunday edition of the *Honolulu Advertiser* featured a half-page commentary by Honolulu writer Thelma Chang on the front page of the Focus section, challenging Jon Hall's characterization of Pidgin as "garbage." Chang also focused on "legitimacy" and the construction of culture in her commentary on Hall's denial of history:

> [A]nyone who bothers to understand the long and vibrant history of Hawaii and its people would recognize the legitimacy of pidgin and its evolution. Its use was crucial at a time when diverse cultures struggled to survive in the Islands.
>
> Then and now, survival included the necessity of creating a traffic of language to understand each other, to bridge different societies and to create a "comfort zone" within a dominant culture.

Chang concluded her piece with an important observation: "Many people who speak Pidgin understand the 'outside' world better than the outside world understands them." The patronizing to racist overtones of those who talk about disadvantaged Pidgin speakers reproduce the subject positions of plantation Hawai'i. What has changed since plantation Hawai'i is a growing awareness of class positions and of what constitutes culture in multicultural Hawai'i. What remains the same, sadly, is the anxiety "locals" feel about how they sound and talk and the social value they attach to their speech.

Despite Chang's thoughtful sketch of the history of Pidgin and its social and cultural value, letters continued to appear in the newspapers reducing discussions about Pidgin to issues of proper usage and "legitimate" versus "illegitimate" culture, and equating Standard English with intelligence. Most frustrating was the misleading suggestion that Hawaii's schools were complicit—if not outright responsible—for promoting the use of Pidgin in the classroom. This issue had been raised in *The Byrds of Paradise* when Sam worried he was encouraging Pidgin by allowing a Pidgin play to be produced at his school. In 1985 the Hawai'i State Board of Education sought to mandate the use of Standard English in the classroom but met with widespread resistance from the community. The board revised the policy in 1987 to simply encourage the use of Standard English. The issue is blurred, being less about providing the best methods for literacy education than about simple discipline and the maintenance of a linguistic and social hierarchy.

The false argument is made that by not banning Pidgin in the classroom Standard English is being displaced and that students, unable to move beyond their Pidgin identities, will remain uneducatable. This argument assumes that unless Standard English is the only language of instruction, students will not be able to learn. It also assumes that Standard English is never present in the classroom, and that both teachers and students operate in a space of Pidgin accessible only to them. In practice teachers and students operate in a complicated space where they understand the rules and practices of various discourse communities. As one twelfth-grade English teacher, Lisa-Anne Lung, wrote in the *Honolulu Advertiser*:

> My students and I are bi-lingual. We speak, write, communicate in different, yet similar languages. Both are equally powerful. My students know when to use "proper" English and pidgin English. I don't agree with "authority" dictating what will or will not be spoken in school. I believe that as long as true learning takes place, no matter what the vehicle, that the student has gained through the experience. (29 January 1995)

Like Healani's response in *The Byrds of Paradise*, this teacher offers a reasonable and responsible answer to those who are concerned about the perceived lack of literacy, and lack of literacy instruction, in the classroom. Though I cannot prove whether this teacher's classroom is typical or atypical, I would venture to guess that like her, most educators are concerned about reaching students who are at risk rather than alienating them further.

Coda: Relocating Paradise

At a time when American popular culture still constructs Hawai'i through films like Disney's animated *Lilo and Stitch* or the historical romance of *Pearl Harbor* starring heartthrobs Ben Affleck and Josh Harnett, with accompanying hit pop song by Faith Hill, an increasing number of cultural productions with Hawai'i locals is reaching across the Pacific and entering the U.S. mainland. When local literary texts like Lois-Ann Yamanaka's

Wild Meat and the Bully Burgers (1996) and *Blu's Hanging* (1998) and Nora Okja Keller's *Comfort Woman* (1998) are reviewed in the *New York Times, Chicago Tribune, Los Angeles Times, Washington Post,* and *Boston Globe,* one has to ask how these texts are received both by mainland audiences and displaced Locals. On the one hand, the Local is no longer self-contained, no longer exclusive, as it enters into global contexts and turns its own gaze upon the mainland. On the other hand, Hawai'i still remains "mysterious," waiting to be explored by the curious who cannot make the distinction between complicated local politics and representations and the grandiose images of Paradise. The reception of these "more" local Hawai'i texts remains problematic because they are still read as exotic, authentic representations of "native" life. However, texts like these have certainly challenged outsiders' expectations. Paradise is relocated when the Local and Global interact in multiple public spheres where a range of participants consume and produce Paradise for their own purposes.

In my own public sphere of Miami University (set in idyllic Oxford and subject to its own romanticized representations), I have used Lois-Ann Yamanaka's *Wild Meat and the Bully Burgers* in undergraduate literature courses as a countertext to the understanding of Hawai'i that my mostly Midwest (and usually all-white) students had of Hawai'i. They read about the poverty and working-class lives of Hawai'i residents and their anxieties and desire for middle-class American (read, white) lives. Without the Waikiki beachfront or the palm trees and surf to support their expectations of Hawai'i in Yamanaka's novel, they are forced to see an unfamiliar Hawai'i. However, the expectations influenced by popular culture and cultural imaginings are so strong that they cannot escape their own belief in this exotic foreign land, a belief elevated to the level of fantasy as many expect never to visit Hawai'i themselves. Much as I have worked with students to complicate their readings both of the texts and of Hawai'i, their lack of local knowledge is a barrier to understanding the fine points of everyday life in Hawai'i.

But as students grapple with and resist this disruptive reading of Hawai'i presented by Yamanaka, or in some cases even romanticize this grittier representation, I also believe that when they encounter Hawai'i through popular culture (whether in film, television, or even a dormitory lu'au), they turn a more critical gaze on this text rather than blindly consuming the blue oceans, white sand beaches, and green mountains. We *should* ask for whom paradise is being constructed and consumed, because there are material consequences for Hawaii's residents as global pressures mount and local communities are faced with an increasingly poor economy and the "price of Paradise." But we should *also* consider how Locals construct and consume Paradise themselves, how they respond to global pressures with their own "nationalist" rhetorics of Local identity or Native Hawaiian nationhood. In our competing desire for Paradise and in our conflicts over representation we often lose sight of the responsibilities and commitments of our local and global communities. We may ask "whose paradise" is being represented but we should also ask, "What's at stake in Paradise?"

NOTES

1. See Stephen Sumida's chapter, "Hawaii's Local Literary Tradition," in his *And the View from the Shore* (1991), for a discussion of the production of cultural texts in Hawai'i.

2. The issue of same-sex marriage was contested in Hawai'i after the Hawai'i State Supreme Court ruled that the state must show a "compelling reason" why same-sex couples cannot be issued a marriage license. In response to the Hawai'i case, states across the United States as well as the federal government have acted to legislate against same-sex marriage. See Helen Zia, "Out on the Front Lines," in her book, *Asian American Dreams: The Emergence of an American People* (2000).

3. For a discussion of other television series set in Hawai'i, see Darrell Hamamoto, *Monitored Peril: Asian Americans and the Politics of TV Representation* (1994).

4. It is interesting to speculate about the subject position of McGarrett. While McGarrett's physical features are clearly Caucasian, they also hint at an exotic quality which places him in an intermediate position between Hawai'i and the rest of the United States. He is darker than the other white characters, and as Christopher Anderson points out, his very dark hair is arranged in an "iconic Hawaiian-wave hairstyle" (1987: 116). Danny, by contrast, is the picture of the all-American hero: he has light brown hair, softer facial features, and an easygoing manner.

5. Since *The Byrds of Paradise* two other television series have been set in Hawai'i. *One West Waikiki* (CBS), starring Cheryl Ladd, entered as a summer replacement (1994) but failed to generate the ratings needed to be considered in the fall lineup or as a midseason replacement. *Marker,* starring Richard Grieco, made its debut in the winter of 1995 on the new United Paramount Network (UPN). Both shows follow the formula of pre-*Byrds* shows and the literature on Hawai'i by "mainlanders": mainlanders come to Hawai'i after suffering a trauma, learn about "non-Western" culture from the natives, and finally heal themselves.

6. See Tim Ryan's account of the murder and response by Hawai'i officials

(*Honolulu Star-Bulletin*, 5 May 1994). See also Tim Ryan, "Hawaiiwood or Bust," in the *Honolulu Star-Bulletin* (13 May 1994) for a discussion of the impact of the film and television industry on Hawaii's economy.

7. The notion of "local" identity is important among Hawai'i residents. In her essay "Between Nationalisms: Hawaii's Local Nation and Its Troubled Racial Paradise," Candace Fujikane discusses the construction of local identity in Hawai'i (particularly through its literature) and the formation of something she terms the "Local Nation." Fujikane suggests that this "Local Nation" is an "imagined" formation (after Benedict Anderson) of the nonwhite ethnic-racial residents of Hawai'i in response to the continental imperial power of the United States (1994: 26).

8. See Diane Mei Lin Mark's essay, "The Reel Hawaii," for a discussion of non-Hawai'i actors being imported for lead roles rather than using "local" actors (1991: 110).

9. In a letter to the *Hawaii Herald* (20 May 1994), Wendy Motooka argues that *The Byrds* is a clear example of the colonialist fantasies of Americans. Motooka points out that issues of race and class are central themes in the show, reinforcing the dominant position of this white mainland family while trying to appear multiculturally sensitive and virtuous.

10. For a fuller discussion of the significance of the plantation and English Standard school in Hawai'i, see Morris Young, "Standard English and Student Bodies: Institutionalizing Race and Literacy in Hawai'i" (2002).

11. The lead female role in *The Byrds*, that of Healani Douglas, was played by Elizabeth Lindsey, a former Miss Hawai'i and now an actress. Many of the supporting roles were filled by Hawai'i actors, most notably Sonny (Robert Kekaula) and Manu (Lani Opunui-Ancheta), the live-in Hawaiian housekeepers, and Crystal Sapolu (Elsa Awaya) and Todd Matsuoka (Todd Yamashita), classmates of the Byrd children.

12. The reasons given for the cancellation of *The Byrds* are fascinating. *The Byrds* had already been placed in a difficult time slot by ABC, running head-to-head with the popular comedies *Mad about You* and *Wings* on NBC, and *The Simpsons* on Fox. After *The Byrds* began its run, CBS counter-programmed with *Christy,* another family-oriented show, and the ratings of *The Byrds* began to decline. Rather than moving *The Byrds* or running a promotion campaign to support it, ABC decided not to renew the show because it believed its fall entry for that time slot would be successful. However, this show, *My So-Called Life,* while critically acclaimed, met with similar ratings disappointment.

13. The "missing" episode was broadcast in Hawai'i on July 28, 1994.

14. The casting of James Grant Benton as the school custodian raises many interesting issues regarding the politics and representation of Pidgin. While a national audience would not be familiar with Benton, a Hawai'i audience recognizes him because of his active role in the community as an actor, comedian, and play-

wright. I point out Benton's role as the custodian because it appears to reinforce the stereotype of the Pidgin speaker—working class and nonwhite. Benton's appearance in this episode of *The Byrds* is full of irony as his character, Mr. Esclavada, can only watch from the back of the auditorium as the play which Benton adapted in reality is directed by a fictional white drama teacher, Brad Hamilton (Victor Bevine).

15. "Da Play Is Da Thing," *The Byrds of Paradise*, ABC Television, KITV, Honolulu, 28 July 1994.

WORKS CITED

Anderson, Christopher. "Reflections on Magnum, P.I." In *Television: The Critical View*, 4th edition. Ed. Horace Newcomb. New York: Oxford UP, 1987, 112–125.

"'Byrds' Canceled." Editorial. *Honolulu Advertiser.* 10 May 1994: A-10.

"'Byrd's' Eye View, part II." *Honolulu Advertiser.* 13 May 1994.

"'Byrds' Protests." Editorial. *Honolulu Advertiser.* 14 May 1994: A-8.

Chang, Thelma. "Revisiting Pidgin." *Honolulu Advertiser.* 30 October 1994.

"Da Play Is Da Thing." *The Byrds of Paradise.* ABC Television. KITV, Honolulu. 28 July 1994.

Dirlik, Arlif. "The Global in the Local." In *Global/Local: Cultural Production and the Transnational Imaginary.* Eds. Rob Wilson and Wimal Dissanayake. Durham: Duke UP, 1996, 21–45.

Fujikane, Candace. "Between Nationalisms: Hawaii's Local Nation and Its Troubled Racial Paradise." *Critical Mass: A Journal of Asian American Cultural Criticism* 1.2 (Spring/Summer 1994): 23–57.

Hall, Jon. Letter. *Honolulu Advertiser.* 4 October 1994: A-12.

Hamamoto, Darrell Y. *Monitored Peril: Asian Americans and the Politics of TV Representation.* Minneapolis: U of Minnesota P, 1994.

Harada, Wayne. "Backing Up Byrds." *Honolulu Advertiser.* 13 May 1994: A-1, A-6.

———. "The Big Wait." *Honolulu Advertiser.* 4 May 1994: C-1, C-4.

———. "Bye-Bye 'Byrds.'" *Honolulu Advertiser.* 10 May 1994: B-1, B-3.

———. "'Byrds'—A Paradise Found, and Then Lost." *Honolulu Advertiser.* 18 May 1994: C-6.

———. "Fans Raise Flap over 'Byrds' Cut." *Honolulu Advertiser.* 12 May 1994: A-3.

———. "Nest of 'Byrds.'" *Honolulu Advertiser.* 5 May 1994: B-1–B-3.

Kanae, Lisa Linn. *Sista Tongue.* Honolulu: Tinfish Press, 2001.

Keller, Anthony J. Letter. *Honolulu Advertiser.* 24 May 1994: A-7.

Keller, Nora Okja. *Comfort Woman.* New York: Penguin, 1998.

Lum, Darrell H. Y. "Local Literature and Lunch." In *The Best of Bamboo Ridge.* Eds. Eric Chock and Darrell H. Y. Lum. Honolulu: Bamboo Ridge P, 1986, 3–5.

Lung, Lisa-Anne. Letter. *Honolulu Advertiser.* 29 January 1995: B-3.

"Mainland Viewers Shoot Down Quality 'Byrds.'" Editorial. *Honolulu Star Bulletin.* 10 May 1994: A-12.

Mark, Diane Mei Lin. "The Reel Hawaii." In *Moving the Image: Independent Asian Pacific American Media Arts.* Ed. Russell Leong. Los Angeles: UCLA Asian American Studies Center and Visual Communications, Southern California Asian American Studies Central, Inc., 1991, 109–117.

Morse, Harold, and Tim Ryan. "'Byrds' Supporters Flock at Rally." *Honolulu Star-Bulletin.* 13 May 1994: A-3.

Motooka, Wendy. Letter. *The Hawaii Herald.* 20 May 1994: A-2.

Noyes, Martha. "Clipped Wings." *Honolulu Advertiser.* June 1994: 38–46.

Nueske, William D. Letter. *Honolulu Advertiser.* 28 May 1994: A-9.

O'Connor, John. "Families on the Move to and from Their Roots." *New York Times.* 2 March 1994: C-22.

Okamura, Jonathan Y. "Why There Are No Asian Americans in Hawaii: The Continuing Significance of Local Identity." *Social Process in Hawaii* 35 (1994): 161–178.

"Pidgin: Da Kine Dispute." *Honolulu Advertiser.* 29 January 1995.

Ryan, Tim. "'Byrds of Paradise' Canceled." *Honolulu Star-Bulletin.* 9 May 1994: A-1, A-9.

———. "Goodbye, Paradise." *Honolulu Star-Bulletin.* 16 May 1994: B-1, B-3.

———. "Hawaiiwood or Bust." *Honolulu Star-Bulletin.* 13 May 1994: D-1, D-3.

———. "Local Officials Rushed to Calm Hollywood's Fears." *Honolulu Star-Bulletin.* 5 May 1994: B-1, B-5.

———. "Save 'The Byrds' Campaign Takes Off." *Honolulu Star-Bulletin.* 11 May 1994: A-1, A-6.

———. "Tears Flow as Byrds Leave Hawaii Nest." *Honolulu Star-Bulletin.* 12 May 1994: D-1, D-4.

———. "'We Were Just Learning the Dance . . .'" *Honolulu Star-Bulletin.* 10 May 1994: D-1, D-3.

———. "Will 'The Byrds' Return to the Nest Next Season?" *Honolulu Star-Bulletin.* 7 May 1994: B-1, B-6.

Sato, Charlene J. "Sociolinguistic Variation and Language Attitudes in Hawaii." In *English around the World.* Ed. Jenny Chesire. Cambridge: Cambridge UP, 1991.

"Save the Byrds." Editorial. *Honolulu Star-Bulletin.* 12 May 1994: A-16.

Suemori, Alan. "'The Byrds of Paradise.'" *Hawaii Herald.* 19 March 1994: A-8.

Sumida, Stephen H. *And the View from the Shore: Literary Traditions of Hawai'i.* Seattle: U of Washington P, 1991.

———. "Sense of Place, History, and the Concept of the 'Local' in Hawaii's Asian/Pacific American Literatures." In *Reading the Literatures of Asian America.* Eds. Shirley Geok-lin Lim and Amy Ling. Philadelphia: Temple UP, 1992, 215–237.

Tonouchi, Lee A. *da word*. Honolulu: Bamboo Ridge P, 2001.

Yamamoto, Eric. "The Significance of the Local." *Social Process in Hawaii* 27 (1979): 101–115.

Yamanaka, Lois-Ann. *Saturday Night at the Pahala Theatre*. Honolulu: Bamboo Ridge P, 1993.

———. *Wild Meat and the Bully Burgers*. New York: Farrar, Straus and Giroux, 1996.

———. *Blu's Hanging*. New York: Farrar, Straus and Giroux, 1998.

Young, Morris. "Standard English and Student Bodies: Institutionalizing Race and Literacy in Hawai'i." *College English* 64.4 (March 2002): 405–431.

Zia, Helen. *Asian American Dreams: The Emergence of an American People*. New York: Farrar, Straus and Giroux, 2000.

Chapter 10

Miss Cherry Blossom
Meets Mainstream America

Rebecca Chiyoko King-O'Riain

Beauty Pageants as a Popular Cultural Form

Denigrated as "low-brow" culture and antifeminist in the past, beauty pageants have been largely ignored within sociology and Asian American Studies. White feminist critiques of beauty and specifically of beauty pageants (Wolf 1991; Bordo 1993) rightly analyze the detrimental effects pageants can have on women. However, they miss some of the subtle details of cultural production, particularly among women of color (King 2001). Recently, however, interest in beauty pageants has been increasing, as they are being seen as important arenas in which diverse cultural meanings are integrated and are given tangible form in the bodies of beauty queens (Callahan 1998; Rogers 1998). Pageants are reflections of larger social forces. For example, gender as a category can be durable and omnipresent, but contextually gendered meanings are fluid and varied (Salzinger 2003). Various forms and patterns of gender can be seen in pageants. Beauty pageants give us a chance to see the place of gender (and in my case study, racial) production in varying contexts. Pageants, though, are also semiautonomous social settings where cultural productions are carried out upon women's bodies themselves and where women's bodies become a focus of community struggle.

Beauty pageants have also been studied as popular cultural realms where the creation of collective cultural meanings takes place. Within beauty pageants, beauty queens are embodied symbols on which racial, gendered, and national meanings are inscribed (Cohen, Wilk, and Stoeltje

1996). I analyze Japanese American beauty queens in Los Angeles, San Francisco, and Honolulu as collective representations of local Japanese American communities.[1] I examine beauty pageants historically to illustrate how local struggles over the meaning of race and gender are shaped by changing community, national, and international contexts. In this racial project pageants are also seen as semiautonomous sites of cultural production where race, gender, and citizenship are constituted. Finally, this essay chronicles the evolution of the concept of citizenship through Japanese American beauty pageants from the 1930s through the 1990s.

I collected my research data by interviewing, following, and working with pageant participants in San Francisco and accompanying them, as a queen committee member, on most of their appearances and trips, including to Los Angeles and Honolulu, from 1995 to 1996. I became interested in this site of cultural and racial production because of the racial rules governing who could participate. These racial eligibility rules fascinated and repelled me, but seemed to me to provide a window into the public, Japanese American community-based discourse about changing racial meanings that I was trying to tap into and study. This provided a case where collective negotiations of race were examinable at both the individual and the community levels. After traveling with and serving beauty queens in many ways, including chaperoning them, carrying chapsticks, hair pins, and other supplies for them, zipping zippers, and marching in parades, I considered myself to be an "almost participant"-observer of the world of Japanese American beauty pageants. They were a perfect form of popular culture through which to see larger struggles over race, gender, and nation.

The Year 1935 to the 1950s, Internment and Beyond: Debates about Nationalism and U.S. Citizenship

Starting in 1935 in Los Angeles, the Nisei Week Festival added the Nisei Week Queen Pageant to draw more people into the festival. The addition of the Queen Pageant reflected the larger goals of the festival, namely, to ease the mounting economic and social tensions between Japanese Americans and the larger white community while trying to bolster the ethnic economy of Little Tokyo. Coming out of the Great Depression, Little Tokyo merchants wanted a way to bring business downtown, particularly encouraging Nisei (second-generation) Japanese Americans to shop in

and maintain ties with their ethnic community. This led to the first staging of the Nisei Week Queen contest. People voted for potential queens by
means of ballots gained when they purchased merchandise in Little Tokyo
establishments. This clever strategy commodified the women in the
pageant to drum up business while also using them to signal to the larger
white community that the Japanese American community was "not a
threat."[2]

The Nisei Week queen pageant in Los Angeles was primarily focused on
representing the Japanese American community to itself under a predominantly white hegemonic gaze. This meant that the Japanese American
women in the pageant were working with white standards of beauty
pageants in mind and re-creating them with a Japanese American twist.
The rationale was that if Japanese Americans, symbolized by the queen,
were seen to be truly American, they could claim to be good and loyal
Americans.

The Nisei Week Queen Pageant and Festival marked the beginning of
the genre of Japanese American beauty pageants in the United States. Nisei
Week queen pageants were an important space for Japanese American
women to make their own claims against hegemonic femininity. Although
they were not allowed to participate in mainstream pageants such as Miss
America, they could at least be Nisei Week queens. Borrowing some elements of mainstream pageantry such as the "question and answer" and
"talent" sections from the Miss America pageant, they decided at times
forgo others, such as the bathing suit competition, omitted in Honolulu
and San Francisco.[3] These local Japanese American pageants were a separate but parallel process (in form and in some content) of claiming the nation. As a queen from the early 1950s said:

> We always had to appear dressed very dressy, in suits and stuff. I made my
> dress out of a yard and a half of fabric with a pattern I copied from the
> Sears catalogue. They gave us nothing from the committee. I was very naïve.
> I just thought that is what you did. I joined a sorority and went to college. I
> wanted to be accepted and I wanted to be very Americanized.[4]

These were symbolic ways of presenting herself in order to be seen as
American. Her behavior as well as her dress focused on acceptance into
mainstream America, for herself and for the Japanese American community. By dressing the queen in western garb and promoting her keen and

usually native-born ability to speak English, the community highlighted the "Americanness" of Japanese Americans. Their push for citizenship and desire for inclusion in the "nation" of the United States were paramount in this era. They hoped that if the queen looked, spoke, and carried herself as an American she would be seen as such by others. This in turn would gain Japanese Americans acceptance in a cultural sphere where they had experienced rejection as "unassimilable aliens" (Takaki 1989). They too could claim to be "All American Girls" by mimicking and adopting hegemonic American cultural values such as innocence, sexual purity, honesty, and caring.

> My dad always said to me, "Sit with your legs crossed and always put your best face forward. You are representing the Japanese American life if you say anything wrong, if you are rude or ungainly or sit with your legs apart, people will think poorly of us Japanese."[5]

As a symbol and representative of the Japanese American community in the wider society, this woman's behavior was subject to social control by Japanese Americans in the name of assimilation. In addition, the larger society was likely to view her as a typical Japanese American girl. Ironically, the creation of separate pageants for Japanese Americans meant that they were also separating themselves further from the mainstream culture whose acceptance they sought. This isolation may have encouraged the exoticization and objectification of Japanese American women in the minds of white America.

However, were the Nisei Week queens "typical Japanese American women"? The pageant may have overrepresented the Japanese American desire to be assimilated and "American." It naturally drew women who were more acculturated and who idealized American cultural forms of beauty, especially those that manifested themselves publicly in the local pageant. The ballot voters, on the other hand, were less assimilated than the pageant participants and were socially oriented to the Japanese American community first and foremost as residents or shoppers in Little Tokyo. The pageants claimed membership in the nation selectively at times— while it was not always necessary to wear a bathing suit in order to be American, pageants themselves were a good way to make the claim. However, these selective appropriations only reinforced the desirable innocence and virtue of "good American girls" of Japanese descent.

In the early days, before World War II, though, it was clear that the primary audience of the pageant and festival was internal to the Japanese American community:

> In the beginning, they [the festival organizers] wanted everyone to come to Little Tokyo. They have always wanted people to come to Little Tokyo. It is just that there weren't a lot of non-Asians that came to Little Tokyo. Before it was all Japanese people at the pageant/festival, now it is half and half.[6]

Before World War II, Japanese Americans in the pageant tried to create a bicultural association of the United States and Japan and bring whites into Little Tokyo (Kurashige 2002). The Issei, first-generation Japanese immigrants, had been denied U.S. citizenship by the 1790 Naturalization Law, and land ownership by the Alien Land Law of 1913. What they could not gain in the legal sphere, they tried to gain culturally by mimicking and adopting American culture, including mainstream popular events such as beauty pageants. Later, after World War II and internment, Japanese Americans tried to integrate into mainstream American culture as quietly as possible; however, their integration was far from complete.

The pageants started well before the World War II internment camps, continued during internment, and started up again shortly after the end of the war. But the post–World War II stigma and the isolation of the community bore its mark on the pageant and those who participated in it. A queen from the early 1950s had this to say:

> When I came out of [the internment] camp I had the same problems as many in high school and college. The la la kind of idea that we really wanted to become American and fit in. Live the American dream. You really wanted to be like a blonde haired blue-eyed kid. It is a real heartache when you think about it now. But this is what happens when you are discriminated against so much, you just want to be assimilated.[7]

Seen as a strategy for assimilation, the pageant was a way to "mimic" mainstream America and to show how "American" Japanese Americans were. The pageants became a site where Japanese Americanness was collectively produced. However, one outcome of the pageant was that Japanese Americans created their own images of beauty and deportment, such as "walking Japanese" with small steps while in kimono, which competed with mainstream ones such as "walking American" in an evening gown with long wide strides and pivot turns. The pageants therefore combined Japanese and American cultural forms, although white American culture clearly dominated. The women in the pageant were supposed to master both forms, though the emphasis was on the evening gown portion and speaking in good, unaccented English. The covers of the program booklets that advertised the pageant/festival and its activities bore pictures of the queen in western garb, usually in an evening dress with a crown, sash, and smile in tow. The covers were glossy and colorful, much like the *Life* magazine covers of the time. Bouffant hairstyles and clumpy false eyelashes reflected some of the mainstream beauty standards of the era.

Nisei Week was different from other city pageants, because of Los Angeles's geographic dispersion, the Los Angeles riots (in 1992), and the pageant's proximity to the Hollywood entertainment industry. Nisei Week was described as a flashier (or more "Hollywood") style of pageant than the others. It had big "Hollywood" style dance numbers, hip, celebrity-designed outfits and gowns, celebrity judges, a "golden circle" of beautiful people, and an audience which could afford to pay more, all of which mirrored the academy awards. Because there were satellite Japanese enclaves for food and goods and it was considered dangerous after the riots to go downtown, outdoor downtown events like the parade had relatively low attendance rates.

The 1970s–1980s: The Battle over Feminism

In the 1970s, Japanese American beauty pageants became an arena in which larger battles in mainstream society were fought and contested. In this era, Japanese American pageants responded to widening awareness of feminist values in liberal cities like San Francisco by omitting bathing suit or fitness competitions and not stating the body measurements of candidates in the program. They also eliminated many of the "beauty"-related judging criteria. The San Francisco pageant, which was started in the late 1960s and early 1970s, was able to sidestep elements of the 1950s patriarchy which had shaped Nisei Week. A Nisei Week queen from Los Angeles in the late 1980s stated:

> I would never have become involved if they had had bathing suits. I think
> half my court would not have become involved had there been bathing

suits. I think they did away with it the year that Lisa Yamamoto won. Lynn Nakamura — she was the one that is credited with being the vocal spokesperson in getting rid of the bathing suits. I don't know what year that was. It must have been the late 70s, early 80s. The whole women's movement happened in the early 70s in the rest of the United States and we sort of came along later. You also have to look at who was in charge then — mostly middle-aged men . . . bathing suits was their favorite part.[8]

Interestingly, the largest and most serious challenge for change, in terms of actually affecting the pageant, came from within the pageant set. Often the participants themselves were the most vocal about not wanting bathing suits, measurements, or anything to encourage objectification by what the girls called the "skebe" (dirty old) men who were organizing or judging it. The interviewee quoted above recognized the Japanese American patriarchy that these "old men" represented, but the women themselves are credited with being strong enough to stand up to them and "get rid of" the bathing suit section of the pageant as unnecessary and sexist. This also reflects the small, community-based, nature of the pageant so that participants were able to mobilize and apply pressure on the organizers to change. Notice, though, that they did not want to get rid of the pageant altogether. Perhaps they saw the pageant as an important outlet allowing Japanese American women to speak out on behalf of other women in their community, as it was one of the few public platforms available to them.

In 1968, in the midst of the Civil Rights Movement, the Northern California Cherry Blossom Queen Pageant was started to choose a queen to reign over the Cherry Blossom Festival held each April in San Francisco's Japantown. Japantown (Nihonmachi) had just been modernized and converted into a commercial rather than residential area, and the festival was created to bring people in so they could patronize the businesses there. The pageant also gave Japanese American women the chance to claim that "Japanese American Is Beautiful," following upon the civil rights theme of "black is beautiful," which claimed that women of color should be found beautiful in their own right without being compared to white standards of beauty. The original organizers saw this as a way to increase business in Japantown as well as a way to share Japanese culture not only with one another but with the larger society as well. It was decided that a queen should be chosen to reign over the parade and festivities and to make visits to other cities representing the Japanese American community of northern California. The queen became a focal center of the festival.

She drew raffle tickets, walked through Japantown in kimono, and greeted important visitors from Japan.

The San Francisco pageant also reflected its more liberal community. The first and only attempt to try to ban pageants altogether occurred in 1988, because the chair of the festival felt it was outdated and sexist. But there was such an outcry from the community that it returned in 1989 in a new format—no beauty judging criteria, career goals as part of the candidates' biographical statements, and no height, weight, or body measurements. Due to increasing awareness of feminism both inside and outside the Japanese American community, the focus had shifted to community and professional service and away from beauty per se as a criterion for the selection of the queen.

The impact of feminism on the pageant in San Francisco was clear from the pageant's decision not to have bathing suits, its attempts to get rid of beauty criteria in the late 1980s, and the cancellation of the pageant itself in 1988. These challenges to the pageant showed that Japanese American women didn't just regurgitate white, mainstream, feminist views. Many felt that feminists were too "out there" and demanding, and too culturally insensitive to be considered Japanese American. They referred to feminism as the "f" word and wanted to "act like feminists" but not be feminists—because ugly feminists were white. As Japanese American women, pageant candidates racialized feminism and gender roles. In their minds, to be Japanese American meant something very different, and less outspoken than white feminists might like.

Of course, some of the most offensive aspects of beauty pageants—such as the bathing suit competition—never played a big part in Japanese American pageants. In this sense, the pageants may have ironically been receptive to the development of feminism while also being influenced by larger feminist debates. The pageant gave Japanese American women a networking opportunity and the short dinner reception gave them a chance to be heard and rub elbows with dignitaries from Japan, politicians, and high-level businesspeople as well as the media and the entertainment industry. These networks helped them to present their ideas and further their professional careers.

Thus the pageants promoted a form of liberal Japanese American feminism which built on the long history of Japanese American women in athletics and politics. But in the pageants it took on a new and more public form. The women spoke outspokenly to push their issues as women to the forefront within the community and refused to toe the "racial" line in order to work for Japanese American progress. Pageant participants now aspired to attend law school and business school, embark on political careers, and speak publicly in support of social and Japanese American causes. Many pageant participants from this era describe the pageant as a platform which centered Japanese American women, allowing them to speak out publicly (thereby going against the Japanese American ethic of modesty) and to appear in public (which some considered very embarrassing or immodest [*hazukashii*], especially if one didn't win). A new type of Japanese American woman was evolving both within the pageant and outside. Again, it was a blend of Japanese American cultural values and practices in a western, some would say uniquely American, kind of beauty pageant.

Many Japanese Americans observers of the pageant were, and still are, strongly critical of the message that Japanese American pageants send to the rest of society and to the young Japanese American women who participate in them. This criticism was strongest in San Francisco and Hawaii. In Hawaii, Terri-Ann Shiroma of Moanalua High School wrote about pageants for a high school journalism contest. The *Hawaii Star-Bulletin* quoted from her winning essay as follows:

> Beauty contests continue to erode years of progress toward achieving sexual equality. Providing pageant winners as standards for young women to emulate and admire encourages them to focus on outward appearances rather than inward cultivation. Eradicating pageants would serve as a momentous step toward ensuring the future health and success of all America's women. (Chang 1996: 1)

Diane Yukihiro Chang of the *Hawaii Star-Bulletin* added, "Contestants are rewarded for pleasing via talents and interview responses deemed to be appropriately feminine. In short, they are reduced to actresses portraying an expected role" (Chang 1996: 1).

In San Francisco too, some members of the Japanese American community criticized the pageants. Mei Nakano and the Women's Concerns Committee (WCC) in San Francisco lobbied hard in the 1980s to get the Japanese American Citizen's League (JACL) to stop sponsoring pageant candidates. Their argument was that as a civil rights organization, the JACL should have a more progressive view not only of race, but of gender as well. But the WCC's campaign to end support for the pageants was unsuccessful as other community members emphasized their importance as a place where Japanese American women could honor alternative models of beauty (Kurashige 2002). Even if Japanese American women could not be Miss America, they could still be honored here. It was a chance to celebrate the beauty and accomplishments of Japanese American women.

Feminism also had an impact on Nisei Week in Los Angeles. The bathing suit portion of the pageant was removed in the 1970s and the impact of white feminist understandings led to a decline in pageant participation. A past participant explained,

> Feminist criticisms of the pageants have made it more difficult to get candidates to run. Fewer women are interested in doing this. A lot of times they are reacting to what they think it is rather than what they will find out it really is. They don't know. And they aren't going to find out because there is a stigma attached to the word pageant. You think of a bubble headed ditzy actress wanna be. Some people said to me "I'm surprised you are interested in that sort of thing," "You are Phi Beta Kappa so why are you running in this pageant?" What does that have to do with anything? I think if someone thinks it is going to help them, it is worth pursuing. For me, my goals were to meet more people in the community and develop more poise and grace. I asked my department chair who was a woman, I asked, "If I participate in this pageant will people question my academic integrity?" and she said, "Not if they are smart. Other people are involved with their church or sports groups. What is the difference?" It is an interest of mine, but it isn't my life.[9]

Feminist criticism was also evident in this story told me by a Nisei Week queen from the 1980s:

> I was with a group of Asian American actresses and they starting teasing me about it. "Is it just thrilling to be Nisei Week Queen? Is it everything you've ever dreamed of?" and I was like, "Excuse me?" They were all laughing, they thought they were so funny. I said, "No, it was something I got involved with because I thought it was interesting and it has been." Then they said, "You must have had so much fun going to all those parties and wearing your crown," and I thought you all are really rude, what gives you the right to judge. Like I am not smart enough to know that they were being facetious. That was a pretty negative experience.[10]

Feminism created tension within the pageants and Japanese American communities at large. While the pageants became a logical target of feminist attack, ironically they also gave rise to a Japanese American feminist ideology. The act of participating in the pageant could be framed as in the above quote, as "bucking the trend," that is, by making a bold, and some would say feminist, move to stand up and participate in the face of strong pressure not to do so.

In the end, both the women in the pageant and the pageant organizers racialized gender roles and feminism simultaneously. These women saw themselves as standing up to change community norms around public space, but they did so in a forum deeply shaped by hegemonic gender ideologies. It is important to remember, though, that with the possible exception of Los Angeles, these beauty pageants were less commodified and provided better access to community networks than mainstream pageants. The participants also had a greater role in shaping the pageants. The Japanese American community was a small pond where the participants became big, publicly known, fish. They spoke publicly and made contacts with many elite members of their community.

The 1990s: Multiculturalism, Multiracialism, and Globalization

In the post–civil rights era of race relations, the certainties of ethnic identity gave way to new concerns in the 1990s. The attacks on multiculturalism as the foundation of ethnic identity politics were reflected in debates about the increasing number of multiethnic queens and their "authenticity" or "legitimacy" as representatives of their local Japanese American communities. This was the era in which debates abounded about the declining significance of race (Wilson 1978), the "overrepresentation" of Asian Americans in higher education (Takagi 1992), racial privacy laws (Millard 2002), and multiple racial responses on the 2000 Census (King 2000). The debates in the community pageants focused primarily on the racial eligibility rules, which limited participation to women who were of 50 percent or more Japanese ancestry in San Francisco and Los Angeles and 100 percent in Hawaii until the 1970s. The increasing incorporation of mixed-race queens resulted in mounting anxiety in the Japanese American community about its "loss of culture."

In the 1980s and 1990s, the pageants became a central venue for debates over "loss of culture" and overassimilation to mainstream culture by the

Japanese American community. With low immigration, an increasingly elderly population, high out-marriage, and an increase in "mixed-race" members, the Japanese American community is currently wrestling with complex issues. The community has shrunk relative to other Asian American communities (Chinese Americans have larger populations in two of the three areas that I studied—Los Angeles and San Francisco) and the larger society (Asians made up less than 15 percent of the total population in the United States in 2000). In 2000, in Los Angeles County the Asian American population was 11.9 percent, and in Orange County it was 13.6 percent. In San Francisco County, the Asian American population was 30.8 percent and predominantly Chinese. And in Hawaii, the entire state was 41.6 percent Asian American, and 9.4 percent Pacific Islander and Native Hawaiian.[11] Mixed-race people have started to make up a bigger part of the Japanese American community, which has changed the dynamics of community membership and understandings of race and ethnicity. Multiracial women embody this tension between shifting Japanese American identities and the norm of whiteness and have sparked heated debate over racial eligibility rules for pageant participants.

This debate over racial rules began most publicly in Los Angeles in the local Japanese-English newspaper, the *Rafu Shimpo,* which discussed "half" Nisei Week queens in 1982. One participant from that era told me,

> We've had some girls who are half Japanese and half various other things, some of them have been more exposed to Japanese culture than some of the girls who are biologically all Japanese. The Posey sisters are both bilingual, but they are half Caucasian. Are they more Japanese than me because they speak Japanese or are they less because both my parents are Japanese? Their mom is from Japan and I am third generation.[12]

Like many, this interviewee questioned how definitions of Japanese American authenticity are being shaped by the relationship between ancestry (race) and culture (ethnicity). The presence of multiracial queens like the Posey sisters highlights the question of who has the right to represent the community as queen. This question had never been asked before because the number of multiracial participants was small. With the increase in multiracial participants, people's attention was drawn to the issue of who, racially, could claim to speak for or represent the community as a whole. The assumption of the link between culture and ancestry was questioned and challenged, if not broken, by the increasing presence of multiracial queens. However, it also took an effort to maintain the race:culture nexus in the pageant setting. If a majority of the community became multiracial, it would be more acceptable for the queen to be multiracial because she would look like the average Japanese American. One participant from the 1980s said,

> They were saying in the papers, "Are we choosing queens based on a western standard of beauty?" and that whole thing. I don't know if it is ethnic integrity or sour grapes.[13]

The racial appearance of the queen was highly correlated in this interviewee's mind with ethnic integrity and authenticity. This debate about mixed-race pageant candidates illustrates the community's growing anxiety about Japanese American assimilation and cultural preservation.

Ironically, community concerns have come full circle from the 1930s. At that time the pageants were a strategy for assimilation, whereas in the 1990s Japanese Americans were asking whether assimilation had gone too far and how they could ensure cultural preservation. This argument was based on a race equals culture equation, meaning that to be a member of the community one must be 100 percent racially Japanese and the culture will follow. However, multiracial participants challenged the either/or dichotomy. They developed their own strategies and conduct as well as identification, thereby problematizing the race-culture nexus. A Cherry Blossom queen from San Francisco in the 1990s said:

> I think if the community wants to survive it's going to have to learn to take in people that maybe it would not have previously. They have to be flexible. A lot people who are biologically Japanese don't care to be a part of what we call the Japanese American community. They don't attend a Japanese church. They don't shop in J-town. They don't eat Japanese food, the whole bit. There are people who are half or a quarter Japanese, not even Japanese, and they want to be part of that. I think you have to be a little less ethnocentric and say if you are interested, we are interested in having you participate.[14]

And in Los Angeles, a 1990s Nisei Week queen said,

> I think they would shut down Nisei Week first though before they would let just someone of any race be queen. Not even thinking that they were being

racist or anything. It would be like "Oh, darn, we ran out of candidates. We faded away." Maybe that would be the time for the pageant to fade away.[15]

The shape of the community changes when borders are opened and the criteria for authenticity is challenged and changed.

Akira "Sunshine" Fukunaga of Honolulu was visiting a buddy in Los Angeles in 1949 when he attended his first Nisei Week Festival. Thinking the festival was a great idea, he returned to Honolulu to start planning the first Cherry Blossom Festival in Hawaii. Sunshine was the first vice president of the Honolulu Japanese Junior Chamber of Commerce (Jaycees) in 1949, and thought Cherry Blossom would be a good project for the Jaycees. "Sunshine explained that this festival could help to perpetuate and promote the Japanese culture in Hawaii, as well as provide members with the opportunity to gain valuable leadership skills."[16] Following the assimilationist tendencies of Nisei Week, Fukunaga adapted the queen pageant to reflect the growing economic and political power of Japanese Americans in Hawaii, which many saw as evidence of their increasing assimilation, this time to a Japanese American elite. Reflecting its sponsorship by the Japanese Junior Chamber of Commerce, the Hawaii pageant is the largest and the best marketed of them all. But due to its geographic closeness to Japan and dependence on Japanese capital, it tends to emphasize traditional Japanese cultural dress and values.

In 1998, Hawaii, the last bastion of racial purity, changed its racial eligibility rules from 100 percent Japanese ancestry to 50 percent. Keith Kamisugi (the president of the Honolulu Japanese Junior Chamber of Commerce, known as the Jaycees) was much criticized for doing so, but he responded:

First and foremost, it was the right thing to do. We always promoted the festival as a representation of Hawaii's Japanese American community, yet the rules barred queen contestants who were not of full Japanese ancestry. It was disturbing that a hapa-Japanese woman could not represent her ethnic community through the festival. At the point where we were close to finalizing the contest rule change, a few people asked if we would still require a Japanese surname, based on the false notion that the queen and court visit to Japanese would be less than ideal if the queen had a *haole* [white] last name. [A few individuals really said this to me.] Absolutely not. A Japanese American woman named Toth is no less or more Japanese than a woman named Matsumoto. Pride in our Japanese heritage does not come from our birth certificate. It comes from our family, our community and our experiences as participants in that culture. I'm gratified that the Cherry Blossom Festival has achieved such diversity in the queen contest. It is a true reflection of our Japanese American community. (Kamisugi 2001: 1)

The issue of authenticity in terms of race and culture continued in Hawaii, as in 1999 there was a part-Chinese participant, in 2001 a multi-ethnic queen with a non-Japanese surname was crowned for the first time, and in 2002 the first part–Native Hawaiian queen was crowned.

Conclusion

In the twentieth century, Japanese American beauty pageants neither "mimicked" mainstream culture nor created a totally new cultural form. Japanese Americans appropriated a mainstream form and adapted it in response to influences from both within and without their community. Fundamentally, Japanese American pageants illustrate Japanese American community struggles from 1935 to the present over national citizenship, gender, and race.

	Struggle	*Strategy*
1950s	Ethnocentric/racist exclusion vs. citizenship (assimilation by mimicry)	Selective appropriation of the "Nation"
1970s	Patriarchy vs. feminism	Claiming public space for women within patriarchal constraints
1980s–1990s	Racial purity vs. porous definition of community/multiculturalism	Problematizing the race-culture nexus

As this table illustrates, the struggles of the early era, both before World War II and directly after it, focused on moving away from the experience of ethnocentric and racist exclusion to trying to claim membership as "Americans." By looking like Americans (whites) in cultural forms such as beauty pageants, Japanese Americans selectively appropriated "American-ness" to further their own inclusion in the nation. Doing so, though, meant embracing western dress, English and mimicking some, though not all, of the components of mainstream "American" pageants. The queens in this era served as symbols of Japanese Americans' ability to assimilate into white America.

In the 1970s, the struggle facing Japanese American communities was how to integrate feminism, particularly mainstream feminism, into a heavily patriarchal society, as evidenced by the mere existence of beauty pageants. I argue that even in this patriarchal cultural form there was room for some women to make feminist claims despite the limitations imposed by the pageant. In fact it was their exposure to feminism, together with their strong commitment to the Japanese American community, that made them stay within the pageant, but assert new feminist notions of womanhood within it.

Finally, the struggle in the most recent era has been over racial purity rules and who constitutes an "authentic" member of the community and therefore a worthy symbol. This debate has created more porous community definitions of membership and with it of community boundaries. Conceptually, it also prompted the community to deal with changing racial demographics by recognizing that the race equals culture nexus must be questioned and challenged. All these issues have been debated in the pageants, thus proving that they are semi-autonomous spaces for strategic action and cultural production. While pageants are a restrictive kind of public space, they can be a venue for a vigorous public discourse about the nature of the nation, gender, and race.

NOTES

1. This research is based on documentary analysis, a year and a half of ethnographic fieldwork in the late 1990s, and sixty in-depth interviews with pageant organizers and participants in Los Angeles and San Francisco, California, Honolulu, Hawaii, and Seattle, Washington.

2. For an excellent and more detailed historical analysis of the context of Nisei Week, see Lon Kurashige, *Japanese American Celebration and Conflict: A History of Ethnic Identity and Festival, 1934–1995,* Berkeley: University of California Press (2002).

3. The bathing suit competitions in Los Angeles were discontinued in the 1970s.

4. Interview with author, Los Angeles, California, March 26, 1996.

5. Interview with author, Los Angeles, California, March 26, 1996

6. Interview with author, Los Angeles, California, March 18, 1996.

7. Interview with author, Los Angeles, California, March 26, 1996.

8. Interview with author, Los Angeles, California, March 18, 1996.

9. Interview with author, Los Angeles, California, April 8, 1996.

10. Interview with author, Los Angeles, California, April 1, 1996.

11. This data comes from the 2000 Census at http://factfinder.census.gov/bf/ _lang=en_vt_name=DEC_2000_PL_U_QTPL_geo_id=04000US15.html.

12. Interview with author, Los Angeles, California, April 1, 1996.

13. Interview with author, Los Angeles, California, March 12, 1996.

14. Interview with author, San Francisco, California, March 1, 1996.

15. Interview with author, Los Angeles, California, March 12, 1996.

16. "History of the Cherry Blossom Festival," from 44th Cherry Blossom Festival booklet (Honolulu, Hawaii), page 16.

WORKS CITED

Bordo, Susan. 1993. *Unbearable Weight: Feminism, Western Culture and the Body.* Berkeley: University of California Press.

Callahan, William. 1998. "The Ideology of Miss Thailand in National, Consumerist and Transnational Space." *Alternatives.* Vol. 23, no. 1: 29–61.

Chang, Diane Yukihiro. 1996. "Beauty Queens Don't Deserve the Adulation." *Hawaii Star-Bulletin.* March 8.

Cohen, Colleen Ballerino, Richard Wilk, and Beverly Stoeltje. 1996. *Beauty Queens on the Global Stage: Gender Contests and Power.* New York: Routledge.

Kamisugi, Keith. 2001. Honolulu Japanese Junior Chamber of Commerce Newsletter.

King, Rebecca Chiyoko. 2000. "Racialization, Recognition and Rights: Lumping and Splitting Multiracial Asian Americans and the 2000 Census." *Journal of Asian American Studies.* Vol. 3, no. 2.

———. 2001. "Mirror, Mirror on the Wall: Mapping Discussions of Feminism, Race and Beauty on Mixed Race Japanese American Women." In *The Sum of Our Parts: Mixed-Heritage Asian Americans,* edited by Teresa Williams-Leon and Cynthia Nakashima. Philadelphia: Temple University Press.

Kurashige, Lon. 2002. *Japanese American Celebration and Conflict: A History of Ethnic Identity and Festival, 1934–1990.* Berkeley: University of California Press.

Millard, H. 2002. "Racial Privacy Act—Be Careful What You Ask For," http://www .newnation.org/Millard/Millard-Racial-Privacy-Act.html.

Rogers, Mark. 1998. "Spectacular Bodies: Folklorization and the Politics of Identity in Ecuadorian Beauty Pageants." *Journal of Latin American Anthropology.* Vol. 3, no. 2 (spring): 54–85.

Salzinger, Leslie. 2003. *Genders in Production: Making Workers in Mexico's Global Factories.* Berkeley: University of California Press.

Takagi, Dana. 1992. *The Retreat from Race: Asian American Admissions and Racial Politics.* New Brunswick, N.J.: Rutgers University Press.

Takaki, Ronald. 1989. *Strangers from a Different Shore*. Boston: Little, Brown and Co.

Wilson, William J. 1978. *The Declining Significance of Race*. Chicago: University of Chicago Press.

Wolf, Naomi. 1991. *The Beauty Myth*. New York: William and Morrow.

Chapter 11

How to Rehabilitate a Mulatto
The Iconography of Tiger Woods

Hiram Perez

"A Real American Story"

Tiger Woods's tongue-in-cheek identification as "Cablinasian" on the *Oprah Winfrey Show* in April 1997 resulted in such contentiousness within the black community that Winfrey followed up later that same month with a program devoted to the "Tiger Woods Race Controversy."[1] Woods's identification as Cablinasian during that interview has more often than not been taken out of context. He relates arriving at that category ("Ca, Caucasian; bl, black; in, Indian; Asian—Cablinasian")[2] during his childhood as a survival strategy against racist taunting and violence, including an incident after the first day of kindergarten when he was tied to a tree and called a monkey and a nigger. However, that moment on *Oprah* when he pronounced the word "Cablinasian" constituted for the multiracial category movement an Amalgamation Proclamation of sorts. Following the program, he was soundly blasted by black media and intellectuals, among them Manning Marable,[3] but such criticism has only deepened the resolve of the multiracial category movement that its ranks are misunderstood and victimized not only by a dominant culture but by other racial minorities, particularly what they regard as a militant, uniracial old guard.

The white parents of biracial (in this case, usually black and white) children constitute the majority of the proponents for the addition of a multiracial category to the census.[4] These parents are attempting to protect their children from what they perceive as the hardships that ensue from identification as black. As Tanya Katerí Hernández explains, "White parents will seize opportunities to extend their privilege of whiteness to non-White persons they care about."[5] Their naiveté lies in the belief that evading the legal classification "black" or "African American" will entirely spare a child from the socioeconomic and psychic hardships common to black people. An examination of the history of passing confirms that the legacy of hypodescent is never eradicated by the act of passing. Part of the insidiousness of racial classification in the Americas, which relies on notions of racial contamination and purity, is the manner in which that one drop of tainted blood assumes a ghostly life, not just in terms of its symbolic quality (by which the threat of invisibility is managed) but by its perpetual return either across generations or, for the subject who passes, at that inevitable moment of confession or betrayal.[6]

I argue that the celebrity of a figure such as Tiger Woods functions to rehabilitate the mulatto in order to announce the arrival of a new colorblind era in U.S. history. Woods's multiracial identity is recuperated as a kind of testimonial to racial progress that simultaneously celebrates diversity in the form of Cablinasianness and the multiplicity that category suggests while erasing the histories of black disenfranchisement, racial-sexual violence, and U.S. imperialism that generate, result from, and entrench the legal, scientific, and popular definitions of race, including each racial component of Cablinasianness and their various amalgamations. The word Tiger Woods chooses to describe his racial makeup effects, ironically, his racial unmaking. As I demonstrate in this essay, Nike advertising, with the exception of the company's very first television advertisement featuring Woods, obliquely references race only to register its insignificance (within the discourse of constitutional color-blindness) or to capitalize (just as obliquely) on racial fantasies about the black body and the Asian body. The Tiger Woods iconography shuttles seamlessly between race consciousness and racial elision. That seamlessness is facilitated by the unlikely union in recent years between the ostensibly incompatible ideologies of multiculturalism and color-blindness. Although multiculturalism and the rhetoric of color-blindness appear to espouse contradictory positions, these philosophies ultimately advance very similar ideologies, as various critical race theorists and cultural critics have already argued. Diversity, as a central goal of multiculturalism, does not transform the economic, legal, and cultural institutions that secure white privilege.[7] Both multiculturalism and color-blindness conceive of racial difference as independent of institutionalized racism. The inconsistencies implicit in the iconography of Tiger Woods (i.e., a celebration of multiraciality that simultaneously heralds color-blindness) become transparent at this intersection of multiculturalism and color-blindness; consequently, the celebrity of Tiger Woods functions ideologically to preserve the status quo, an inviolable institutionalized racism.

In the iconography of Tiger Woods the mulatto becomes a proud product (*sans* irony) of American democracy. In fact, according to this logic, Woods (not just his celebrity, but his very existence) is possible only because of American democracy, hence Oprah Winfrey's reference to Woods as "America's son."[8] Sigrid Nunez's narrator in the novel *A Feather on the Breath of God,* the product of a Chinese Panamanian father and German mother, observes for example that "when I talked about my mother and father people often said things like, 'Only in America.' People called their story 'a real American story.'"[9] A figure such as Tiger Woods hails the success of American democracy and the advent of a multicultural *and* color-blind society. I want to clarify here that I am not attempting with this analysis to address Tiger Woods's personal accountability—or at least that is not my principal concern. By speaking to Woods's transformation into "America's son," I shift the focus of my analysis from an independently acting Tiger Woods to the conglomerate interests informing his iconography. I use the word "conglomerate" to reference both corporate and public interests in Woods as well as the convergence of those interests in the construction of Woods the icon.

For the historian Eric Foner, the period of Radical Reconstruction constitutes an "unfinished revolution": "From the enforcement of the rights of citizens to the stubborn problems of economic and racial justice, the issues central to Reconstruction are as old as the American republic, and as contemporary as the inequalities that still afflict our society."[10] Tiger Woods confirms for Americans that the revolution effected by Radical Reconstruction has indeed been consummated. He is the proof that the inequalities that Foner speaks of no longer hinder racial progress. That he is the product of a black father and an Asian mother provides testament to that progress. Again I want to clarify that I am referring here not to the personal relationship between Earl and Kutilda Woods but to the significance symbolically of that relationship in the production of Tiger Woods's celebrity. According to the fictions of color-blind ideology, Earl Woods's access to the Asian woman's body (the body of a woman who is not black) symbolizes his fully actualized citizenship. How that access to the Asian woman's body for the black man is secured by U.S. military occupation and neocolonialism in Asia remains uninterrogated. Woods's celebrity depends on a eugenical fantasy that stages a disciplining of the black, male

body through an infusion of Asian blood and an imagined Confucian upbringing. The way that Tiger Woods represents racial progress and the ful-
fillment of American democracy is contingent upon both the specific formula of his fractional identity and the institutions of forgetting.

In his book, *Training a Tiger: A Father's Guide to Raising a Winner in
Both Golf and Life* (1997), Earl Woods describes the circumstances that
made possible his marriage to Kutilda Woods: "I also saw the world and, in
two tours of Vietnam as a Green Beret, stared death in the face more than
once. I also met and fought side by side with a Vietnamese officer and
Tiger's namesake, Lieutenant Colonel Nguyen T. Phong. I had become an
information officer years earlier, and it was on one of those information
assignments that I met Tiger's mother, Kutilda."[11] Earl Woods's access to
an Asian wife confirms that a last obstacle to black citizenship has been
eradicated. The notion of women as property underlies much of the an-
tipathy toward interracial unions in both black and white communities.
The white woman, as a form of property protected from black male acquisition, becomes representative of a two-tiered citizenship. For the white
male citizenry, dominion over her body remains a guarantor of white superiority against the encroaching demands of a free, black population. The
tenacity with which the fantasy of the black rapist loosed upon the nation
has embedded itself in the imagination of the dominant culture underscores this anxiety about black male designs on white womanhood. As a
product of a black man and a woman who is not black, Woods confirms
that a final vestige of two-tiered citizenship has been eliminated. That his
mother is Asian and not white makes the interracial relationship between
his parents less objectionable and secures for Woods this symbolic status.
Tiger Woods would not mean the same thing for America if he were the
product of a black man and a white woman. Images of Mariah Carey,
Lenny Kravitz, Halle Berry, Jason Kidd, or Derek Jeter, for example, have
not been mobilized toward the same ends as those of Woods. While the
ancestry of all five of these celebrities has received some media attention,
in none of their cases has miscegenation been imagined to represent the
final actualization of the nation's founding ideals of freedom and equality.

The representation of Woods's multiracial ancestry exploits the stereotype of the black man's superior (suprahuman) athleticism as well as the
stereotype of the Asian American "model minority." The idea of the model
minority has historically been used to blame African American and
Latino/a communities for their own disenfranchisement. The December
1966 *U.S. News and World Report* article, "Success Story of One Minority

in the U.S.," provides one of the earliest articulations of the model minority stereotype: "At a time when it is being proposed that hundreds of billions be spent on uplifting Negroes and other minorities, the nation's 300,000 Chinese Americans are moving ahead on their own with no help from anyone else."[12] Just as model minority rhetoric functions to discipline the unruly black bodies threatening national stability during the post–civil rights era, the infusion of Asian blood together with his imagined Confucian upbringing corrals and tames Tiger's otherwise brute physicality. Some variation of *his father trained the body and his mother trained the mind* is a recurring motif for sports commentators diagnosing Woods's success at golf. Earl Woods has encouraged this fantasy:

> Her teaching methods weren't always orthodox, but they were effective. When Tiger was just a toddler, she wrote the addition and multiplication tables out for him on 3-by-5-inch cards, and he would practice them over and over every day. He started with addition and later advanced to multiplication as he got older. His reward was an afternoon on the range with me. Tida established irrevocably that education had a priority over golf. (Woods 9)

The qualities of Woods's model minority mother compensate for the black man's cognitive deficiencies. In fact, since the stereotype of the model minority secures the normalcy of whiteness by attributing Asian American successes (the evidence for which is often exaggerated and overly generalized) to a biological predisposition toward *over*achievement, the contributions of the Asian mother actually exceed the capacity for white blood and a Protestant work ethic to compensate for black degeneracy. Woods's success at golf, traditionally a sport reserved for the white elite, is in part explained by the logic of eugenics.

The celebration of Tiger Woods as the embodiment of American multiculturalism and racial democracy institutes an instance of "organized forgetting."[13] Oprah Winfrey's celebratory vision of Tiger Woods as "America's son" displaces, for example, historical memories of the bastardized children of white slave owners or U.S. soldiers overseas. Miscegenation as a legacy of slavery is forgotten, as is the miscegenation that has resulted from the various U.S. military occupations in Asia dating back to the late nineteenth century.

Being Tiger/Wanting to Be Like Mike

In one of its first television ads using Tiger Woods's image, Nike presents a montage of children of different races, each proclaiming, "I am Tiger Woods." Nike very astutely capitalizes on Woods's mixed racial heritage in creating a picture of inclusiveness and color-blindness. As Robert Goldman and Stephen Papson argue in their study of Nike culture, "Nike . . . has chosen to foreground race as a category, first in order to draw attention to their association with Tiger Woods, and then doing a 180 degree turn to demonstrate the declining relevance of race as a category."[14] The shots of children of different races located in various geopolitical spaces (in some shots clearly suggesting urban poverty), interspersed with the image of Tiger Woods, documents the democratizing process that Woods symbolizes. Particularly because Woods has succeeded in a traditionally white, upper-crust sport, the advertisement's identification of each of these children as Tiger Woods delivers the children from poverty and racial oppression. Woods's conquest of golf signifies a final frontier of racism. That barrier now vanquished, black, Latino, and Asian children are unshackled from the tyranny of systemic oppression; racial categories become not only obsolete but also retrogressive and dangerous. Goldman and Papson observe, "Remember how *Nike* constructed Barkley in its 'I'm not a role model' ad. Now, *Nike* positions Woods as the ultimate role model. The ad's children don't chant 'I want to be like Tiger Woods,' rather, they state total identification: 'I am Tiger Woods'" (Goldman and Papson 114). This tendency of Nike's marketing of Tiger Woods to reference race primarily as a means for endorsing a color-blind ideology has made Tiger Woods more serviceable to the rhetoric of the multiracial movement than any other mixed-race celebrity.

Tom Petri, a Republican Representative from Fond du Lac, Wisconsin, who served on the congressional subcommittee in charge of the census, tried for several years to enact legislation to introduce a "multiracial" category to the census. Following Tiger Woods's victory at the Masters golf tournament in 1997, Petri renamed the legislation "the Tiger Woods bill."[15] It is not too cynical to suggest that Petri's apparent sensitivity to issues of racial identity is somewhat suspicious. Concerning the general perception of the census by members of Congress, Lawrence Wright clarifies, "the attitude of most elected officials in Washington toward the census is polite loathing, because it is the census, as much as any other force in the country, that determines their political futures. Congressional districts rise and fall with the shifting demography of the country" (46). The introduction of a "multiracial" category undermines governmental structures established to safeguard the equal representation of minorities within a democracy.

Petri's embrace of the multiracial category movement demands closer scrutiny of that movement's ideological underpinnings. The proponents for the addition of a multiracial category on the census and other federal, state, and local government forms base their arguments on four principles: (1) the value of individualism; (2) the elimination of racism; (3) the need for group recognition; and (4) the value of diversity. The claim, very often heard among promoters of a multiracial category, that people should have the right to define themselves, is rooted in notions of American individualism. However, the quality of individualism in the United States is entrenched in notions of property and particularly self-ownership and acquisitiveness. When on June 7, 1892, Homer Plessy challenged both segregation and Louisiana race codes by sitting in a section of a railway car reserved for whites, he discovered that the qualities of self-ownership and acquisitiveness were restricted along race lines. The U.S. Supreme Court agreed with Plessy that "belonging to the dominant race, in this instance the white race, is *property,* in the same sense that a right of action, or of inheritance, is property."[16] Yet, the court was "unable to see" how Homer Plessy, as an octoroon (a person of one-eighth black ancestry), had been deprived of such property.

Nearly ninety years later, under very different circumstances, Susie Guillory Phipps learned the same lesson. Phipps, in the process of applying for a passport, learned that she was classified on her birth certificate as "colored." She sued the state of Louisiana to change her racial status from "colored" to "white" and lost. The U.S. Supreme Court refused in 1986 to hear her appeal. While Plessy's challenge to Louisiana racial codes constituted part of a larger, organized protest against Louisiana's "Jim Crow Car Laws," Phipps's challenge was quite unapologetically an attempt to protect her own property interests in whiteness.[17] According to Neil Gotanda, Phipps reported being "sick for three days" upon discovering that she was classified at birth as "colored."[18] Whiteness functions as a form of property. The tradition of American individualism is very much ingrained in this notion of property. As john a. powell observes, "[g]iven the normative structure of whiteness in the United States, the claim of individualism is often a thinly veiled effort to claim the privileges of whiteness."[19] The multiracial category movement's appeal to American individualism is no exception.

When children of every race can proclaim, "I am Tiger Woods," race becomes insignificant. Woods represents the culmination of the principles of American democracy and the end of racism. The decidedly multicultural flavor of this Nike ad follows on the heels of Woods's first ad for Nike, which portrayed him as an outsider in the predominantly white world of golf. Superimposed over footage of Woods's victory at the U.S. Amateur tournament, the text reads: "Hello world. I am the only man to win three consecutive U.S. Amateur titles. There are still courses in the U.S. I am not allowed to play because of the color of my skin. Are you ready for me?" As Goldman and Papson point out, critics of the ad not only accused Nike of exploiting race consciousness for profit but charged as well that the ad was dishonest since, as Bob Garfield of *Advertising Age* argued, "Tiger Woods was not a victim of racism" (Goldman and Papson 113). Garfield's objection presumes both that Woods's status as an elite athlete and celebrity exempts him from racism and that Woods's success in itself confirms that Jim Crow has irrevocably been laid to rest.

While this first ad emphasized a history of officially sanctioned racial discrimination, the succeeding "I am Tiger Woods" ad ushers in a new era of egalitarianism. James Small, a Nike publicist, responded to the criticism against the first ad by explaining that there are no courses in the United States that would bar Woods from play. The advertisement, according to Small, means to "raise awareness that golf is not an inclusive sport";[20] he explains that we are not to read the ad literally. It turns out that the Tiger Woods represented in the ad whom we mistook for a black man is only a metaphor for the black man. As Goldman and Papson recount, "*Nike*'s public relations director maintained that the ad was not to be taken literally, but as 'a metaphor,' with Woods representing other black golfers" (113). Nike learned from its mistake in this first advertisement and immediately distanced itself from any material, social commentary. Instead Nike executives chose to embrace the richer possibilities embodied in Tiger Woods the metaphor, forsaking the much more disquieting figure of an angry and historically disenfranchised black man.[21]

This backpedaling by Nike executives would be much more amusing if not for the violent forgetting enacted by the "I am Tiger Woods" advertisement, clearly offered up by Nike as a kind of restitution for the race consciousness of the first ad. The refrain of the ad recalls Spike Lee's 1992 film *Malcolm X*, which concludes with black schoolchildren rising from their desks, both in the United States and in South Africa, and pronouncing, "I am Malcolm X." However, the original moment of this spontaneous, black, communal identification appropriated by both Nike and Spike Lee occurs during a mass for Fred Hampton, the twenty-one-year-old head of the Chicago chapter of the Black Panther Party, assassinated during a police raid on December 4, 1969. The mass was conducted by Father George Clements of the Holy Angels Church, who describes the response of Chicago's black schoolchildren to the murder of Hampton:

> I had a mass for Fred, and I was just shattered. I was devastated. And in the midst of this mass I was trying to explain to our children—we had the school children there, all thirteen hundred—and I was trying to explain to them the importance of Fred, and I wasn't getting through—at least I felt like I wasn't getting through. And in the midst of my explanation I just burst into tears, and the next thing I knew here was one of our eighth grade boys—he jumped up and he said "I am Fred Hampton." And then a girl in the sixth grade, she jumps up: "I am Fred Hampton." Another kid in first grade, "I'm Fred Hampton." And before you knew it the whole church, kids were all shouting, "I am Fred Hampton!" And wow! I just felt so wonderful. I felt like, gee-whiz, this death was not in vain at all, because these kids are saying that they are willing to get up here and speak out for liberation, for first class citizenship.[22]

Hampton was slain by local Chicago police using information gathered by J. Edgar Hoover's F.B.I. COINTELPRO program targeting black liberation groups. According to historian Winston A. Grady-Willis, Hoover's counterintelligence program was directed at groups such as the Black Panther Party, the Nation of Islam, and the Student Nonviolent Coordinating Committee and it sought to prevent:

> 1. the formation of a Black political front, 2. "rise of a messiah," 3. violence directed at the state, 4. the gaining of movement credibility, 5. and long-range growth of organizations, especially among young people.[23]

The irony here is appalling. In attempting to remedy its commercial misstep (suggesting that racism still exists in America), Nike invokes the communal reaction to the state-authorized murder of Fred Hampton (no doubt one of the rising messiahs Hoover feared) but perverts it into a slogan for color-blind ideology. Nike's "I am Tiger Woods" advertisement yields its own messianic son, who can deliver the nation from its messy and violent past—announcing the arrival of a fantasied color-blind democracy and obliterating in the process any evidence to the contrary.

This scene described by Father Clements undoubtedly inspires the conclusion of Lee's filmic account of the life of Malcolm X. Lee's appropriation of "I am Fred Hampton" is in itself troubling as evidence of the filmmaker's propensity for finessing black political resistance into successful mass marketing. Lee, comparing the major Hollywood studios to "plantations," justifies his marketing strategy as means to an end for the black filmmaker:

> While we were shooting Jungle Fever in late 1990, I made up an initial design for the "X" cap. I'd already decided I had to do Malcolm X, and marketing is an integral part of my filmmaking. So the X was planned all the way out. I came up with a simple design—silver X on black baseball cap. The colors could be changed later on as the campaign advanced. It looked good. I started wearing it, and we began selling it in our store, Spike's Joint, and in other places. I gave them away strategically. I asked Michael Jordan to wear it, and he has. Then I asked some other stars to wear it and, what can I say, it just caught on. Then the knock-offs started appearing. These X caps are coming from everywhere now. It's raining X caps, X this, X that, *sometimes without the wearers knowing the story behind the X. The word of mouth is beginning to pick up on this already.*[24] [emphasis added]

Lee's candor is astonishing. His proprietary attitude toward Malcolm X's name (after all, "X" becomes a Spike Lee Joint, infringed upon by "knock-offs") contradicts the anticapitalist politics of both Malcolm X and Fred Hampton. More significantly, the value of "X" to Lee as a commodity clearly supersedes the story of Malcolm X and his message. The fact of "word of mouth," insuring box-office success for his film, is more important than "the story behind the X." It is unclear how much irony Lee intended when he entitled his account of the making of *Malcolm X, By Any Means Necessary.* Lee not only contributes to the vacuous sloganization of Malcolm X's call for black liberation but also transforms those words into an endorsement of black capitalism. Spike Lee's long-standing corporate relationship with Nike is well known and difficult to overlook. However, the question of his collaboration with Nike is not necessarily pertinent here. In regard to his choices as a filmmaker, he is already complicit in stylizing and diluting black protest into a form digestible by a mass audience.

Spike Lee's determination to prioritize marketability over questions of ethics and responsibility vis-à-vis the very complicated politics of memorialization opens the door for Nike's corporate assimilation of black resistance and race consciousness. The spontaneous invocation of Fred Hampton by Chicago's black schoolchildren, as described by Father George Clements, is likely inspired by Hampton's own words: "when I leave, you remember I said, with the last words on my lips, I am a revolutionary, and you gonna have to keep on saying that. You gonna have to say that I am a proletariat. I am the people. I'm not the pig." It is an unthinkable perversion of Fred Hampton's legacy that the response of Chicago's black community to his death should be manipulated by a multinational corporation to sell the fiction of America's color-blindness as well as golf shoes.

The "multiracial" figure invoked by Woods's celebrity must be shorn of any historical and material significance in order to consolidate a national fiction of color-blindness. The deracialization of this symbolic mulatto or "multiracial" figure is fulfilled by the identification, "I am Tiger Woods." Woods's service to the fantasy of color-blindness requires a slippage from the material to the metaphorical and a sanctioned forgetting of the legacies of U.S. imperialism and racial oppression. The designation "America's son," although it bears great irony for minority audiences, does not identify a history of racial and sexual violence but rather the availability of Tiger Woods's body for universal consumption. In other words, his celebrity belongs to all of us, but only some of us get to decide what that celebrity can signify. As Lisa Jones protests, "[t]he doors of opportunity that Tiger himself once walked through are shutting, while the nation gloats over him."[25]

The marketing of Michael Jordan also sought to universalize his appeal. As Michael Eric Dyson explains, Jordan has been marketed as "an icon of race-transcending American athletic and moral excellence."[26] The accessibility of the Jordan icon for transracial identification has been encapsulated in the chant, "I want to be like Mike," popularized in the Gatorade advertising campaign. However, this commodification of Jordan for global consumption has not foreclosed race-conscious black identifications. As Dyson observes, "[t]here is also the creative use of desire and fantasy by young blacks to counter, and capitulate to, the forces of cultural dominance that attempt to reduce the black body to a commodity and text that is employed for entertainment, titillation, or financial gain" (Dyson 70). Forms of black cultural expression survive (and adapt to) the commodification of the black body and black culture. These forms of expression remain recognizable to black audiences despite the universalization of the Jordan icon within consumer culture.[27]

The resilience of black cultural expression does not necessarily designate an uncomplicated moment of resistance against the dominant culture. Jordan's articulation of black cultural style has also been successfully exploited by Nike in order to expand its market to the poorest and most marginalized communities in the United States. Dyson condemns not only Nike but also Jordan for his complicity in this project:

> Moreover, while sneaker companies have exploited black cultural expressions of cool, hip, chic, and style, they rarely benefit the people who both consume the largest quantity of products and whose culture redefined the sneaker companies' raison d'etre. This situation is more severely compounded by the presence of spokespeople like Jordan, Spike Lee, and Bo Jackson, who are either ineffectual or defensive about or indifferent to the lethal consequences (especially in urban black-on-black violence over sneaker company products) of black juvenile acquisition of products that these figures have helped make culturally desirable and economically marketable. (Dyson 73)

As golf does not possess the same cachet in urban black communities as basketball, Tiger Woods will never be as marketable as Jordan in black urban centers. The Jordan iconography combines both race consciousness and universalism. The race consciousness is necessary to appeal not only to black urban youth but also to a dominant culture that has redefined its relationship to the spectacle of black athleticism. White men and black men "want to be like Mike" in very different ways. The identification with Michael Jordan by the dominant culture does not circumvent racial difference; instead, it requires and reinforces a fantasy of black masculinity that reduces the black man to a physicality that in the case of Jordan and other black celebrity athletes is simultaneously both superhuman and not quite human. The white spectator desires the superior athleticism essentialized in the black body and remains both attracted to and repelled by that body. Advertising featuring black celebrity athletes typically resists humanizing those athletes. As opposed to representations of white celebrity athletes, advertising images of black athletes such as the Williams sisters, Michael Johnson, Marion Jones, Bo Jackson, and Shaquille O'Neal typically use special effects to emphasize their fantasied superhuman/not quite human capacities.

The manner in which Tiger Woods's celebrity references his racial ancestry functions simultaneously to elide the significance of that ancestry. The cast of multicultural faces pronouncing "I am Tiger Woods" tropes his multiracial heritage while performing an incorporation of that racial heritage that renders it insignificant except as a hallmark of the success of color-blind ideology. The difference between *wanting to be like Mike* and *being Tiger Woods* corresponds to the specific racialized constructions of their celebrity. Jordan's marketing relies persistently on his raced embodiment, while the marketing of Woods references race obliquely only to divest the image of Woods ultimately of any race specificity. Nike's initial campaign, promoting race consciousness, was indeed a misstep. The dominant culture embraces Woods as long as he remains serviceable to a color-blind ideology.

Tiger Woods's celebrity rehabilitates the mulatto to announce the arrival of an era in U.S. history when race will no longer matter. This rehabilitated, amnesic mulatto functions to consolidate a national identity and a national forgetting. Woods's anxious embodiment of a national symbol tellingly represses any Asian constituency. Although Tiger Woods's mother is Thai, she has not figured prominently in the commodification of his image. Commercial interests in Tiger Woods's media image have seized instead on his relationship to his African American father. However, as I have argued in this essay, Kutilda Woods's imagined biological contribution to the construction of "America's son" satisfies more subliminally a eugenical fantasy. The black, male body in this case is disciplined by the influence of a Confucian ethic fetishized as essentially and generically Asian. Tiger Woods is not the model minority but rather the remodel(ed) minority. Nike advertising has of course appreciably shaped the Tiger Woods icon. Hence, while Woods's transcendent celebrity heralds an era of color-blindness, it is still his racialized body being bought and sold.

But America's son is eager to forget. The invisible labor exploited by Nike in Asia materially sustains Tiger Woods's iconic embodiment of racial democracy. Far from being color-blind, the transnational labor of export manufacture is by design both racialized and feminized.[28] It turns out that America's son, ironically a guarantor of American multiculturalism, recalls the classic passing figure; he cannot publicly acknowledge his mother's body—the body of feminized, Third World labor—without compromising his own mobility.

Conclusion: Citizenship as a Form of Property

One of the ironies of Tiger Woods's status as "America's son" and his imagined embodiment of the ideals of American democracy is that, of course, there exists a large Amerasian population sharing a racial heritage very similar to Woods. Yet, far from being celebrated as America's sons and daughters, most of those children of U.S. servicemen and Asian women are in actuality denied U.S. citizenship. I conclude with a discussion of Tuan Ahn Nguyen's legal challenge to section 1409 of the Immigration and Nationality Act because of the way this particular statute reinscribes a tradition of state enforced, racialized bastardy dating back to slavery, a legacy of miscegenation that the Tiger Woods iconography works to forget.

Nguyen v. INS (2001) challenges section 1409 of the Immigration and Nationality Act which stipulates for a child born abroad to one U.S. citizen and one alien parent different criteria for citizenship depending on the status of the mother. If the mother is a U.S. citizen, citizenship is conferred automatically on the child; if the mother is an alien, the child must meet strict criteria in order to successfully apply for citizenship. I also want to return briefly to the *Plessy v. Ferguson* decision in order to complicate the understanding of whiteness as a form of property introduced by Homer Plessy's legal counsel in 1896 and subsequently expounded upon by the legal scholar Cheryl I. Harris in her influential essay "Whiteness as Property" (1993).[29]

As the subtitle to Kimberlé Crenshaw's anthology of Critical Race scholarship suggests, Harris's article is one of the "key writings that formed the movement." Originally published in the June 1993 *Harvard Law Review,* Harris's essay examines how the legal protection of property rights in the United States has historically secured personhood and citizenship while simultaneously maintaining racial oppression. Returning to the *Plessy v. Ferguson* decision, especially Homer Plessy's assertion (corroborated by the Supreme Court) that whiteness constitutes a form of property, Harris delineates the "property functions of whiteness," including "rights of disposition," "right to use and enjoyment," and "the absolute right to exclude."[30] I rely on and agree with Harris's theorization of the property functions of whiteness. My concern is that the centrality of this theory to the critical study of race inadvertently impedes an analysis of race relations that fall outside the (often unspoken) black-white model for racial difference in the United States. Harris's essay provides an example of just such an oversight. Although she provides a close analysis of the language of *Plessy,* she does not extend that analysis to Justice John Marshall Harlan's discussion in his dissenting opinion of the Chinese vis-à-vis white and black citizens.[31] Her examination of the link between whiteness and citizenship extends only to a consideration of the exclusion of blacks and Native Americans from the constitutional guarantees of citizenship: "Race and property were thus conflated by establishing a form of property contingent on race: only blacks were subjugated as slaves and treated as property. Similarly, the conquest, removal, and extermination of Native American life and culture were ratified by conferring and acknowledging the property rights of whites in Native American land" (Harris 278). In order to argue for black enfranchisement, however, Harlan situated the Chinese as duly ineligible for citizenship in opposition to the "citizens of the black race":

> There is a race so different from our own that we do not permit those belonging to it to become citizens of the United States. . . . I allude to the Chinese race. But by the statute in question, a Chinaman can ride in the same passenger coach with white citizens of the United States, while citizens of the black race in Louisiana, many of whom, perhaps, risked their lives for the preservation of the Union . . . are yet declared to be criminals, liable to imprisonment, if they ride in a public coach occupied by citizens of the white race.[32]

Significantly, Harlan's appeal for the guarantees of citizenship on behalf of the black race required that he define the quality of black personhood in contradistinction to that of the Chinese race *and* a propos of black military service. These criteria are relevant then to any historical understanding of U.S. racial formation, especially regarding the role of the Asian body in mediating a perennially compromised black citizenship. This is true not only in regard to Harlan's opposition of Chinese to black and white but also in regard to the foregrounding of the black soldier in his argument. However vexed the history of African American military service—and the disproportionate number of blacks in the U.S. military speaks precisely to a compromised black citizenship—the black soldier nonetheless embodies a hostile, occupying force in the various East and Southeast Asian nations subject to U.S. imperialism. In order to more fully understand, for example, how U.S. imperialism complicates racial dynamics both domestically and internationally, it is necessary to shift the terms of Harris's formulation so that we can evaluate not only the property of whiteness but also the property of citizenship. As *Nguyen v. INS* (2001) demonstrates, citizenship also functions as a form of property that must be protected from ever-encroaching alien hands.

In his work on history and memory, *Lost Narratives: Popular Fictions, Politics, and Recent History,* Roger Bromley asserts, "forgetting is as important as remembering" (12). The symbolic embodiment of Tiger Woods as "America's son" facilitates the kind of "organized forgetting" that Bromley characterizes as a struggle over cultural power. Tiger Woods's iconography revisits a contest over the official narrative memory of miscegenation in the Americas also staged in *Nguyen v. INS* and *Plessy v. Ferguson.* At stake is not only the history of miscegenation but also how we in the present recognize and grapple with its more difficult legacies, including bastardy, shame, forgetting, sexual violence, and the race secret.

The recent Supreme Court decision in the case of *Tuan Anh Nguyen and Joseph Boulais v. Immigration and Naturalization Service* (2001) revives, for example, the tradition instituted by American slavery whereby the child assumes the status of the mother.[33] The ruling is also consistent with the traditions of state-enforced, racialized bastardy variously realized through slavery, antimiscegenation statutes, and U.S. military occupations in Asia. Tuan Anh Nguyen, the son of an American citizen (Joseph Boulais, the copetitioner) and a Vietnamese citizen, was born in Vietnam. In 1975, when he was five years old, Nguyen came to the United States with his father and became a permanent resident. Following his arrest and imprisonment for sexual assault on a child, the Immigration and Naturalization Service began deportation hearings against Nguyen. Although he is the child of a U.S. citizen (Boulais obtained DNA evidence to confirm his paternity), an immigration judge found Nguyen deportable.[34] The Immigration and Nationality Act that governs the acquisition of citizenship requires different criteria, depending on the gender of the citizen parent, for children born abroad to unwed citizen and alien parents.[35] Had Nguyen's mother been a U.S. citizen and his father Vietnamese, he would automatically have qualified for citizenship. Nguyen and Boulais appealed the INS decision on the grounds that the gender-based classification of the statute in question (Title 8 U.S.C. section 1409) violates the constitutional guarantee of equal protection. The U.S. Supreme Court ruled against Nguyen on June 11, 2001, finding that the statutory gender-based distinction withstood equal protection scrutiny, serving "important governmental objectives" (7).

The circumstances leading to Nguyen's deportation—convictions on two counts of sexual assault against a child—threaten to obscure the historical significance of this case. Because the most immediate result of the Supreme Court decision is the deportation of a child molester, the case has not garnered much outrage. Criticism of the decision has also stumbled on this obstacle. For example, while Steve Rissing, writing for the *Columbus Dispatch,* criticizes the ruling as both bad law and bad science, he cannot overcome the hurdle of Nguyen's criminal conviction: "The legal result: deportation. Frankly, I think the punishment should have been more severe."[36] It is perhaps Nguyen's history as a sex offender that allows the Court to seize upon this case in order to uphold the constitutionality of statute 1409. Justice Kennedy, in his majority opinion, notes that the same statute had been challenged three years earlier without resolution in *Miller v. Albright* (1998).[37] Kennedy also cites various conflicting lower court rulings on the constitutionality of the statute. Although Kennedy argues that the presence of the father (Boulais) before the Court singularly distinguishes *Nguyen* from *Miller,* Nguyen's criminal history, even if it did not in fact influence the opinion, impinges on how effectively resistance to this ruling might be mobilized.[38] It is imperative that we look beyond Tuan Anh Nguyen's criminal history in order to assess the implications of this case.

Kennedy's majority opinion in *Nguyen* essentializes maternity while recognizing that paternal ties are necessarily contingent. According to the Court, the Immigration and Nationality Act protects natural ties of the child to the nation conferred biologically by the mater citizen to her offspring. According to Kennedy, the mother's situation is "unique":

> In the case of a citizen mother and a child born overseas, the opportunity for a meaningful relationship between citizen parent and child inheres in the very event of birth, an event so often critical to our constitutional and statutory understandings of citizenship. The mother knows that the child is in being and is hers and has an initial point of contact with him. There is at least an opportunity for mother and child to develop a real, meaningful relationship. (10)

The father's relationship to the child is much less remarkable. Kennedy observes in fact that it is not always clear that "the mother will be sure of the father's identity," a situation that for him merits particular concern in the case of children born overseas. In the context of this decision, the indiscriminate mother who worries him is not the "citizen mother" suckling the potential citizen but rather the alien mother (in the cases of Tuan Anh Nguyen and Lorelyn Penero Miller, respectively a Vietnamese national and a Filipina national). Section 1409 protects national interests:

> Congress is well within its authority in refusing, absent proof of at least the opportunity for the development of a relationship between citizen parent and child, to commit this country to embracing a child as a citizen entitled as of birth to the full protection of the United States, to the absolute right to enter its borders, and to full participation in the political process. If citizenship is to be conferred by the unwitting means petitioners urge, so that its acquisition abroad bears little relation to the realities of the child's own ties and allegiances, it is for Congress, not this Court, to make that determination. Congress has not taken that path but has instead chosen, by means of §1409, to ensure in the case of father and child the opportunity for a relationship to develop, an opportunity which the event of birth itself provides for the mother and child. (12)

By this reasoning, the mother confers naturally upon the child cultural and national identity. The "event of birth" in itself sufficiently establishes the citizen mother's role in mediating national "ties and allegiances." The female citizen is charged with reproducing the nation. Although Tuan Anh Nguyen has resided as a legal resident in the United States since the age of five, his birth to an alien mother renders his national allegiance suspect.

As with the amnesic celebration of miscegenation common to both the multiracial category movement and the iconization of Tiger Woods, the decision in *Nguyen* effaces any history of miscegenation that contradicts constitutional guarantees of justice, welfare, and equality. The miscegenous unions that produce Tuan Anh Nguyen and Lorelyn Penero Miller are made possible by U.S. imperialism. The Court refuses to recognize the state's obligation toward a population of Amerasian children whose existence results from U.S. military occupations in Asia. Without acknowledging any legal or moral obligation by the United States to Nguyen and similarly situated individuals, Justice Kennedy reports, "the year in which Nguyen was born, there were 3,458,072 active duty military personnel, 39,506 of whom were female" (10). Kennedy identifies "the unique relationship of the mother to the event of birth" (9) as the justification for the gender-specific distinctions of section 1409. But the statute is in fact less concerned with extending and validating (in the form of national citizen-ship) the natural ties between the citizen mother and child than it is in ex-cluding from citizenship the Amerasian children of military personnel. Kennedy admits, "[o]ne concern in this context has always been with young people, men for the most part, who are on duty with the Armed Forces in foreign countries" (10). He characterizes these men as "young people" in order to absolve them (and the state) of any responsibility to-ward their children born overseas out of wedlock.

These men apparently do not exercise any racial, patriarchal, or colo-nial privilege in relation to the women residing in the territories that they forcibly occupy. The Asian mother in this instance bears the burden and the shame for miscegenation and its legacy of illegitimacy. She figures as the seductress. The "young men" serving their nation overseas cannot rea-sonably be held accountable for their seduction by indiscriminate foreign women who, after all, regarding their illegitimate claim, cannot even "be sure of the father's identity." With respect to the increased border-crossing resulting from globalization, the *Nguyen* decision also seeks to safeguard the indiscretions of the American tourist and international capitalist. The gender-specific conditions of statute 1409 become a practical considera-tion when one considers, as Kennedy indicates, that "the average American overseas traveler spent 15.1 nights out of the United States in 1999" (11).

This essay seeks to disrupt the amnesic contemporary representations of miscegenation. The case of *Nguyen v. INS* (2001), consistent with the legal treatment of miscegenation dating back to slavery, enforces the con-dition of bastardy on miscegenous subjects in order to exclude similar constituencies (specifically Amerasian children of U.S. soldiers overseas) from the rights and privileges of citizenship. The state-sanctioned bas-tardy implemented by the Immigration and Nationality Act not only dele-gitimizes the child's relationship to the father but also invalidates the child's political membership in the public sphere. *Nguyen* traces how the more difficult legacies of miscegenation, such as state-sanctioned bastardy and sexual exploitation, have not only endured (despite the promise em-bodied by "America's son") but also evolved, protecting national, patriar-chal, and dominant white cultural interests beyond the local onto a global field. An interrogation of the Tiger Woods iconography reveals an unlikely convergence of discourses (including American individualism, con-sumerism, multiculturalism, color-blindness, and eugenics) working like-wise to protect the property interests of both whiteness and citizenship and to preserve the structural transparency of institutionalized racism. I raise the *Nguyen* case to disturb the "organized forgetting" of the nation advanced by Tiger Woods's celebrity.

NOTES

1. "Tiger Woods Race Controversy," *Oprah: The Oprah Winfrey Show,* Harpo Productions, April 29, 1997.

2. "Tiger Woods," *Oprah: The Oprah Winfrey Show,* Harpo Productions, April 24, 1997.

3. Marable criticized Woods as well as Mariah Carey and Paula Abdul for minimizing their blackness: "The litmus test for American democracy has been around the issue of blackness. Tiger's statements are troubling because they seem to minimize his black identity, something that has long been done, in part, to escape racism. Tiger apparently does not understand or minimizes what blackness means and that's what blacks are picking up on." See Denene Millner, "In Creating a Word to Describe His Racial Make-Up, Golfer Tiger Woods Has Also Stirred Up a Round of Controversy among Blacks," *Daily News* (New York), June 8, 1997: 2.

4. See Trina Grillo, "Anti-Essentialism and Intersectionality: Tools to Dismantle the Master's House," 10 *Berkeley Women's Law Journal* 16 (1995). Grillo, a legal scholar, describes her experience at a conference on multiraciality:

> The multiracial movement is not helped by the fact that some of those pressing most vigorously for a multiracial category are the white mothers of children whose fathers are Black. I went to a conference on multiraciality a few years ago that included time for discussion in small groups. There were a number of white mothers of biracial children in my group. The refrain I heard from these mothers was this: "My child is not Black. My child is *golden.*" So it is not simply paranoia that some members of the multiracial movement are perceived as wanting to dissociate from Blacks. (Grillo 26)

5. Tanya Katerí Hernández, "'Multiracial' Discourse: Racial Classifications in an Era of Color-Blind Jurisprudence," *Maryland Law Review* 57:1 (1998): 119.

6. Narratives of passing in literature, film, and popular culture, for example, often pathologize the race confession, building on the pseudoscientific biology of hypodescent. Consider for example the following moment of self-examination by the anonymous narrator of James Weldon Johnson's *Autobiography of an Ex-Colored Man* (1912): "I feel that I am led by the same impulse which forces the unfound-out criminal to take somebody into his confidence, although he knows that the act is likely, even almost certain, to lead to his undoing" (1). James Weldon Johnson, *Autobiography of an Ex-Colored Man* (New York: Penguin Books, 1990). The internalization of the logic of the one-drop rule by mixed-race subjects functions similarly to compel confession (or guard continuously against the imagined inevitability of self-betrayal).

7. As the legal theorist Neil Gotanda argues, "The assumption that it is possible to identify racial classifications of black and white, to consider them apart from their social setting, and then to make those same racial categories the basis for positive social practice is unfounded. Without a clear social commitment to rethink the nature of racial categories and abolish their underlying structure of subordination, the politics for diversity will remain incomplete." Neil Gotanda, "A Critique of 'Our Constitution Is Color-Blind,'" in *Critical Race Theory: The Key Writings That Formed the Movement,* eds. Kimberlé Crenshaw, Neil Gotanda, Gary Peller, and Kendall Thomas (New York: New Press, 1995), 271.

8. "Tiger Woods," *Oprah,* April 24, 1997.

9. Sigrid Nunez, *A Feather on the Breath of God* (New York: HarperPerennial, 1995), 87.

10. Eric Foner, *Reconstruction: America's Unfinished Revolution 1863–1877* (New York: Harper & Row, 1988), xxvii.

11. Earl Woods, with Peter McDaniel, *Training a Tiger: A Father's Guide to Raising a Winner in Both Golf and Life* (New York: HarperCollins, 1997), xv–xvi.

12. "Success Story of One Minority in the U.S.," *U.S. News and World Report* (December 26, 1966), 73.

13. I borrow the term "organized forgetting" from Roger Bromley. He elaborates on the relationship between history and memory: "Forgetting is as important as remembering. Part of the struggle against cultural power is the challenge to forgetting posed by memory. What is 'forgotten' may represent more threatening aspects of popular 'memory' and have been carefully and consciously, not casually and unconsciously, omitted from the narrative economy of remembering." Roger Bromley, *Lost Narratives: Popular Fictions, Politics, and Recent History* (New York: Routledge, 1988), 12.

14. Robert Goldman and Stephen Papson, *Nike Culture: The Sign of the Swoosh* (London: Sage, 1998), 113.

15. Frank A. Aukofer, "Petri Still Seeking Multiracial Category," *Milwaukee Journal Sentinel,* May 18, 1997: 16.

16. *Plessy v. Ferguson,* 163 U.S. 537, 549 (1896). For a discussion of the relationship between race and property, see Cheryl I. Harris, "Whiteness as Property," in *Critical Race Theory,* eds. Kimberlé Crenshaw et al., 276–291.

17. *Jane Doe v. State of Louisiana,* 479 So. 2d 369 (La. App. 1985).

18. Gotanda, 262.

19. john a. powell, "The Colorblind Multiracial Dilemma: Racial Categories Reconsidered," 31 *U. of San Francisco Law Review* 789, 799 (Summer 1997).

20. Goldman and Papson, *Nike Culture,* 113.

21. I do not assume from the content of this ad that Woods is himself committed to eliminating discrimination, at least not at private clubs. He made his attitude quite clear during the 2002 Masters, when he defended the right of Augusta

National to exclude women as members: "They're entitled to set up their own rules the way they want them. . . . There is nothing you can do about it." See Michael·D'Antonio, "Tiger Shoots a Bogey in Social Consciousness," *Los Angeles Times,* July 23, 2002.

22. See *Eyes On the Prize II: America at the Crossroads—1965 to 1985; A Nation of Law? (1968–1971),* pt. 6 (Boston: Blackside, 1989).

23. From U.S. Congress, Senate, *Book III: Final Report of the Select Committee to Study Government Operations with Respect to Intelligence Activities* (Washington, D.C.: S.R. No. 94-755, 94th Congress, 2d. Sess., 1976), 187. Quoted in Winston A. Grady-Willis, "The Black Panther Party: State Repression and Political Prisoners," in *The Black Panther Party Reconsidered,* ed. Charles E. Jones (Baltimore: Black Classic Press, 1998), 363–389.

24. Spike Lee, with Ralph Wiley, *By Any Means Necessary: The Trials and Tribulations of the Making of Malcolm X* (New York: Hyperion, 1992), 21–22.

25. Lisa Jones, "Are We Tiger Woods Yet?" in *Step into a World: A Global Anthology of the New Black Literature,* ed. Kevin Powell (New York: John Wiley, 2000), 50. Jones elaborates, "Lurking behind Woods's coronation in Image America, and the wrangling over his identity, is the nagging truth that black America, circa 1997, is not Tiger Woods. Every day we see federal and state governments chipping away at what Tiger's life really represents: access for those long denied" (50).

26. Michael Eric Dyson, "Be Like Mike? Michael Jordan and the Pedagogy of Desire," in *Reflecting Black: African-American Cultural Criticism* (Minneapolis: U. of Minnesota Press, 1993), 64.

27. Dyson identifies three characteristics of "black cultural style" personified by Jordan: "the *will to spontaneity*" (67); "*stylization of the performed self*" (68); and "the subversion of perceived limits through the use of *edifying deception*" (68) [emphasis in the original].

28. For a discussion of the global feminization of wage labor, see Saskia Sassen, *Globalization and Its Discontents: Essays on the New Mobility of People and Money* (New York: New Press, 1998). "The most obvious reason for the intensive recruitment of women is firms' desire to reduce costs, but there are other considerations as well: young women in patriarchal societies are seen by foreign employers as obedient and disciplined workers, willing to do tedious, high-precision work and to submit themselves to work conditions that would not be tolerated in the highly developed countries" (42).

29. The essay is reprinted in Kimberlé Crenshaw's *Critical Race Theory: The Key Writings That Formed the Movement* (1995). See supra n. 7.

30. While Justice Henry Billings Brown, writing for the majority, agrees with Plessy that whiteness is a form of property, he cannot "see" how Homer Plessy, an octoroon, has been deprived of such property.

31. Neil Gotanda's essay "A Critique of 'Our Constitution is Color-Blind,'" also included in Crenshaw's collection and previously cited here, likewise neglects this aspect of Harlan's argument.

32. *Plessy,* 561.

33. An antimiscegenation statute passed in colonial Virginia in 1662 was the first departure from English common law practice regarding the status of the child in relation to the father: "1662. Act XII. Children got by an Englishman upon a Negro woman shall be bond or free according to the condition of the mother, and if any Christian shall commit fornication with a Negro man or woman, he shall pay double the fines of a former act." Cited in A. Leon Higginbotham, Jr., *In the Matter of Color: Race and the American Legal Process* (New York: Oxford U. Press, 1978), 43.

34. *Tuan Anh Nguyen v. INS,* 533 U.S. 99-2071 (2001). Text available on the Internet at www.supremecourtus.gov/opinions/00pdf/99-2071.pdf.

35. According to Title 8 U.S.C. section 1409, the applicant for citizenship must meet the following requirements if the applicant's parents are unwed and the father is a U.S. citizen and the mother an alien: "(1) a blood relation between the person and the father is established by clear and convincing evidence; (2) the father had the nationality of the United States at the time of the person's birth; (3) the father (unless deceased) has agreed in writing to provide financial support for the person until the person reaches the age of 18 years, and (4) while the person is under the age of 18 years—(A) the person is legitimated under the law of the person's residence or domicile, (B) the father acknowledges paternity of the person in writing under oath, or (C) the paternity of the person is established by adjudication of a competent court." On the other hand, if the citizen parent of a child born abroad is the mother and not the father, the citizenship of that child is guaranteed as long as "the mother had the nationality of the United States at the time of such person's birth, and if the mother had previously been physically present in the United States or one of its outlying possessions for a continuous period of one year." Cited in *Nguyen v. INS,* 4–5.

36. Steve Rissing, "Court's Citizenship Ruling Flunks Basic Biology Test," *Columbus Dispatch* (June 24, 2001), 5C.

37. Lorelyn Penero Miller, the daughter of a Filipina-national mother and a U.S. citizen who served in the Philippines as a member of the U.S. Air Force, filed suit against the Secretary of State (Madeleine K. Albright) following the denial in 1992 of her application for citizenship. Because she was born out of wedlock and did not establish by the age of eighteen paternity by a U.S. citizen, she was ineligible for citizenship according to the Immigration and Nationality Act. The U.S. Court of Appeals for the District of Columbia Circuit determined that "the requirements imposed on the child of a citizen father but not on the child of a citizen mother were justified by the interest in fostering the child's ties with the United States." The U.S. Supreme Court, unable to arrive at a majority opinion

concerning the constitutionality of section 1409, also determined nonetheless that Miller was not entitled to relief. See *Miller v. Albright,* 523 U.S. 420 (1998).

38. In *Nguyen,* Kennedy actually reverses the view on section 1409 that he had expressed in *Miller v. Albright.* Kennedy originally concurred with Justice Sandra Day O'Connor's judgment that although the daughter (Lorelyn Penero Miller) did not have standing to seek relief on the basis of her father's gender discrimination claim, the statute in question could not ultimately withstand heightened scrutiny. Justice O'Connor, who writes the dissenting opinion in *Nguyen,* argued in *Miller* that section 1409 violated equal protection regarding its differential treatment of male and female parents:

> Although petitioner may still assert her own rights, she cannot invoke a gender discrimination claim that would trigger heightened scrutiny. Section 1409 draws a distinction based on the gender of the parent, not the child, and any claim of discrimination based on differential treatment of illegitimate versus legitimate children is not presented in the question on which certiorari was granted. Thus, petitioner's own constitutional challenge is subject only to rational basis scrutiny. *Even though § 1409 could not withstand heightened scrutiny,* it is sustainable under the lower standard. [emphasis added]

Part III

Ethnicity and Identification

Chapter 12

Bruce Lee in the Ghetto Connection
Kung Fu Theater and African Americans Reinventing Culture at the Margins

Amy Abugo Ongiri

In 1974 innovative animation studio Hanna-Barbara debuted a short-lived cartoon series for television based on the exploits of a mild-mannered, albeit lazy, janitor turned kung fu kicking superhero called *Hong Kong Phooey*. Hong Kong Phooey's superhero attributes, which included clumsy kung fu and "jive talk," were activated when he jumped head first into a trash dumpster outside the police station that he was responsible for cleaning. The character was voiced by well-known African American character actor Scatman Crothers, who would go on to gain a certain notoriety during the Blaxploitation era for his participation in the partially animated and incredibly controversial Ralph Bakshi film *Coonskin* (1975). *Hong Kong Phooey* represented one of the last of a series of largely unsuccessful schemes to directly blend the martial arts genre with the Blaxploitation genre in order to exploit an urban African American filmgoers' interest in Asian martial arts culture. The urban African American audience had already provided an essential and lucrative market for mainstream Hollywood studios in its consumption of the cheaply produced, high-return Blaxploitation genre typified by films such as *Shaft* (1971), *Blacula* (1972), and *Super Fly* (1972). In fact, film historian Ed Guerrero credits Hollywood's foray into the production of Blaxploitation films with saving the major Hollywood studios from near financial ruin in the late post-studio-system days of the late 1960s.[1]

Within this formation, Warner Brothers Studio emerged as a leader in the production and distribution of both Blaxploitation and kung fu films.

Besides producing "kung fu in the ghetto" vehicles like *Black Belt Jones* (1974), *Hot Potato* (1975), *Three the Hard Way* (1974), and *Golden Needles* (1974), the studio produced the breakthrough Bruce Lee film *Enter the Dragon* (1973) whose successful multiracial casting of African American karate expert Jim Kelly would lead to the casting of basketball icon Kareem Abdul Jabbar in *Game of Death* (1978). Warner Brothers even coupled with Hong Kong's now legendary Shaw Brothers Studio to place the sequel to its highly successful Blaxploitation film *Cleopatra Jones* (1973) in Hong Kong. Although these ventures proved occasionally lucrative, the major studios were never quite able to capitalize on the popularity of Asian popular culture and the martial arts genre among its urban minority audiences, eventually abandoning such attempts.

It is my contention that the film industry's attempts to capitalize on black interest in martial arts culture failed largely because the film industry, in trying to understand the appeal of these films for this particular audience, failed to understand the complex possibilities for exchange occurring in the reception of Asian popular culture across borders of language and culture and boundaries of genre and production sites. This failure to acknowledge the possibility of complexity in relationship to urban African American audiences' viewing practices of the kung fu genre stemmed not only from a disregard for the artistry of the genre itself but also from the film industry's long history of disregard for the consumption patterns of urban African American audiences. In explaining the appeal of Asian popular culture in the form of martial arts films for a U.S. urban minority audience we can begin to redeem not only a much maligned genre and audience group but also to account for the complexity with which an audience might come to consume and remake what appears to be little more than a formulaic, low-budget genre or "trash cinema."

Long before critics and cult audiences confirmed the importance of the new wave of action cinema from the east, urban African American audiences were busily translating the aesthetic codes and body politics of the first wave of films from Hong Kong with a devotion that rivaled even the most devoted of film fan cultures. While to proclaim that "everybody was kung fu fighting," as the seventies r&b hit claimed, might be to overstate the case, African American interest in martial arts films is an often anecdotally pronounced but rarely explored cultural phenomenon. From Wu Tang Clan's "Shaolin Shadow Boxing" to Allen Iverson's and Marcus Camby's prominent Chinese character tattoos, and the kung fu signifying movement styles of "vogue" innovator Willie "Ninja" and various hip hop artists, African American culture is replete with images drawn from popular cultural representations of Asian and Asian American culture, particularly images drawn from early martial arts film culture. It is my contention that it is possible to give an accounting for the popularity of this genre with an African American audience that extends beyond simplistic assumptions about the ways in which African Americans are capable of reading and translating cultural cues, even within the complications that arise with the transnational migration of popular culture across boundaries and borders.

African American tribute to Asian culture evident in black popular culture goes beyond the forced exotica of something like Jim Jarmusch's recent independent film *Ghostdog: The Way of the Samurai* (2000) in which we are supposed to be startled by the cultural disjunction of a corn-rowed urban black man spouting verses from *The Way of the Samurai*. In *Ghostdog* "oriental," kitschy commodified paraphernalia, litters the screen like so many hiply executed ethnic stereotypes, which also litter the screen. In the film, virtually every sequence contains some seemingly displaced remnant of Asian culture from Chinese Restaurant #1 to the Feng Shui mirror in the gangsters' meeting room or the paperback copy of *Rashomon* that reappears periodically throughout the movie. All these items are meant to evoke, through their distance, a "hip" awareness on the part of the audience. In *Ghostdog,* we are supposed to laugh at the paradox of the gangster's daughter sharing her copy of *Rashomon* with the hired assassin in the same way that we are meant to recognize the humor in the racist Italian American gangster's paradoxical love for black hip hop, particularly the socially conscious group Public Enemy. This is an ironic humor that the characters themselves are always incapable of seeing and in which they could never hope to participate.

I want to propose that, though African American popular culture utilizes much of the same kitschy commodified paraphernalia as a movie like *Ghostdog* or seventies television series like *Kung Fu* and *Hong Kong Phooey,* it operates in a radically different fashion, consuming and then imaginatively creating a film culture in a way that suggests not only the possibilities for a dynamic and resistant spectatorship but also the problem with dismissing certain film cultures because the cinemas to which they are attached are deemed to be beneath serious consideration. For many African Americans throughout the seventies Kung Fu Theater or Black Belt Theater, as it was called in some markets, was staple weekend viewing. Kung Fu Theater rebroadcast the classic and not so classic films of the first wave of Asian-produced action movies, which mostly came from either Shaw Brothers or Golden Harvest studios in Hong Kong (Dannen and Long 10). The exploits of Bruce Lee, the one-armed swordsman, the master killer, and other heroes of the martial arts small screen were as welcome in most black homes as were the exploits of Julius "Dr. J." Erving, Kareem Abdul Jabbar, and Bill Russell. Images of Bruce Lee were at least as popular in many black homes as were images of Martin Luther King, possibly even more so. In fact, in *Planet Hong Kong: Popular Cinema and the Art of Entertainment,* David Bordwell's landmark study of the martial arts genre, he claims it was urban minority audiences that "kept the genre alive into the early 1980s" (84).

When one begins to search for a way to account for the appeal of these truly "foreign" films for an urban African American audience, it is tempting to fall back on assumptions which are always generated around spectatorship and the black film-going audience. The low-budget action film, along with low-budget horror, was traditionally thought by the film industry to be the strict domain of "ethnic" audiences and it would often create low-budget action movies specifically for these audiences (Streible 229). The genre of Blaxploitation came directly out of the industry impulse to target low-budget action and horror films à la *Scream, Blacula, Scream* (1973) and *The Mack* (1973) to an urban, minority audience. It is easy to see the implicit and explicit racist assumptions around the idea that "ethnic" audiences crave violence, cannot sit still for films that highlight interiority or a life of the mind, and cannot "read" a film that is not driven by the most primitive of actions in its narrative structurings. On some level, these assumptions would seem to be borne out by the immense popularity of the kung fu film genre with African American audiences. The genre is, after all, replete with bloody, violent, formulaic, action-driven narrative and visual sequences and the films are as famous for their bad dubbing as for the formulaic stories of honor, betrayal, and triumph, not to mention the much parodied "teacher, they've insulted our school" or "you want to fight, fight me" style dialogue. If you attempt to account for the popularity of kung fu films only through simplistic understandings of the narrative structures of these genres, however, then you are not seeing the full picture. An understanding of the way in which an interest in martial arts films developed among an African American audience must first begin with the understanding that complexity is even a possibility in relationship to both the audience and the films.

When fans of kung fu theater talk about it, their relationship to it, remembrances of it, or attraction to it, they inevitably mention a sequence Golden Harvest's 1974 release, *Fists of Fury*. In this sequence, set in colonized China, Bruce Lee attempts to enter a park that is formally off-limits to the native population. He is stopped by a guard and asked to observe a sign that reads "No Chinese or Dogs." In the sequence's visual and narrative climax, Lee reacts to the sign with characteristic panache by leaping several feet off the ground and shattering it with a single kick. It would be easy to read the attraction to this sequence in a very reductive manner. That reading would go something like "African Americans identify with Lee's character's fight against oppression." This is exactly the argument advanced by Bordwell's discussion of the popularity of the genre among urban African American and Latino audiences who he argues were "inspired by Lee's confrontation with white power" (50). David Dresser makes a similar claim when he makes explicit the link between the Blaxploitation and kung fu genres. He writes: "The appeal of the genre for black audiences is not hard to gauge. Outside of the Blaxploitation genre it . . . offered the only nonwhite heroes, men and women, to audiences alienated by mainstream film and often by mainstream film culture" (38). Of course, these assessments are not exactly *wrong*.

The film was produced in 1974 and appeared in the U.S. market shortly thereafter. There is no doubt that Lee's filmic response to such a blatantly segregationist message as "no dogs or Chinese" would resonate powerfully with an African American audience just a little over ten years after the passage of the Civil Rights Act of 1964. But, in a way, what is striking about this sequence is precisely its uniqueness. Undoubtedly, part of the reason it is remembered so fondly and recounted by so many audiences of seventies kung fu movies is because the overt political aesthetics of the genre itself, veiled political critiques of contemporary governmental policies wrapped around stories of failed dynasties and angry peasants, were largely untranslatable for a Western audience. In this way, the sequence from *Fists of Fury* can stand in for its urban minority audience for an overt political expression that is mostly lacking in other kung fu films of the period.

What then was the appeal for African Americans audience in the formulaic narratives of brothers betrayed, masters and schools insulted, skills sought after and acquired? In a way, the sequence from *Fists of Fury* could be said to make explicit what exactly is implicit in the viewing pleasure of such repetitive narrative and, more importantly, visual formulas for an

African American audience. The most popular kung fu films of the era—films such as *One Armed Swordsman* (1967), *Five Fingers of Death* (1972), *Fists of Fury,* and *Master Killer: The 36 Chambers of Shaolin* (1975)—condensed thematic and visual concerns with justice and self-empowerment into narratives that chronicle the transformation of a protagonist through a regime of physical discipline and rigorous training. Many of the protagonists of the early films, including Bruce Lee, were not just actors but highly regarded martial artists and recognized proponents of various martial arts forms. Meaghan Morris notes that: "Training films give us lessons in using aesthetics—understood as practical discipline, 'the study of the mind and emotions in relation to the sense of beauty'—to overcome personal and social adversity" (10). The early training films are thus studies in the transcendent beauty of the mastery of the body and its assertive possibilities. In this sense it is important to note that *Fists of Fury* is above and beyond all other considerations a *martial* arts film, whose main emphasis is a visual representation of a movement form that was both combative and highly trained and this is a concern whose significance goes far beyond the film's narrative concern with a repressive Japanese colonialism. In his important reconsideration of physical movement in the martial arts action sequences, Aaron Anderson reminds us that "theatrical fights are designed to convey a narrative story of conflict through representational movement" (4). And, furthermore, above and beyond all other concerns: "A theatrical fight is designed to be intelligible to an audience" (4). The stylized action of the martial arts genre readily spoke to an African American audience's history of violence and violation in which acts of spectacularized violence would become the central visual metaphor for African American cross-identification.

Noting that "Black bodies in pain for public consumption have been an American spectacle for centuries," Elizabeth Alexander posits the spectacle of racialized violence at the heart of the historical trauma that is constitutive of an African American identity (92). Alexander argues that spectacularized antiblack violence, which is at once public and experienced as intensely personal, is central to the historical experience of Africans in the Americas, whether it be the violence of slavery, the paradigmatic moment of the lynch scene, or the contemporary moment of the videotaped beating of Rodney King. These spectacularized acts of violence create "blackness" as "an unavoidable, irreducible sign, which, despite its abjection, leaves creative space for group self-definition and self-knowledge" (91). Watching acts of violence, whether they are real or performative, takes on an added significance for African Americans as the collective act of being made to watch and witness acts of violence and violation becomes a way to assert a powerful collectivity and, ultimately, a resistance. The kung fu genre's display of physical prowess and hypertraumatized bodies in pain "convey[ed] a narrative story of conflict through representational movement" that was immediately intelligible to an African American audience that experienced its own history through a collective visual experience of traumatized and transcendent bodies. Alexander writes that the "bodily experience—both individually experienced bodily trauma as well as collective cultural trauma—comes to reside in the flesh as forms of memory reactivated and articulated at moments of collective spectatorship" (94).

Novelist Wesley Brown labels African Americans' ability to take the material and cultural debris of the West and reinvent it the "tragic magic" of black existence. The "tragic magic" of seventies black film culture caused the action genre to be read, reread, and complicated in multiple ways. The action genre of that era was made to negotiate through physical action, violence, and displacement what Elizabeth Alexander terms "the histories our bodies know" (91). The popularity of the action films, in general, among African Americans during the 1970s stood in a direct, but not always progressive, relationship to an African American dialogue with an American culture of violence. Since spectacularized bodily violation was at the heart of black identity, the narrative that the kung fu genre condensed and that was subsequently picked up and read by savvy urban audiences, thus, had everything to do with a popular historiography writ large across the body.

In defining the primary modus operandi of *Enter the Dragon* to be "a type of transnational dreaming," Leon Hunt notes the consequences of the hybridized nature of Bruce Lee's international fame as "bound up with commodifying two Others—violence and the 'Orient,' fused together as mystical bodily harm" (76, 83). African Americans' own mystical body had been configured within the American imagination as both harmed and harming and commodified in a U.S. visual culture context, especially within the genre of Blaxploitation, as both alien to and endemic to a hostile urban American landscape. Narratives in which Ching dynasty–era peasants train their bodies in order to confront an unthinkably hostile environment condensed the concerns with nationalism, justice, and alienation of a rapidly modernizing urban Hong Kong into a nostalgic yearning for an ancient past in which it was possible to imagine the body as a raw tool for the articulation of violent retribution against societal inequities and personal wrongs. Bruce Lee, born in San Francisco and raised in Hong Kong, was the ultimate cosmopolitan urbanite and the vector for a variety of transnational configurations. Lee is, according to Hunt, "a transnational, trans-Pacific" who performs in *Enter the Dragon* by being "a 'mosaic,' everywhere and nowhere, a mobile transnational signifier" (76, 85). For Hong Kong audiences as for urban minority audiences in the United States, the embrace of the "mystical bodily harm" of the kung fu genre had its roots in populist feeling in relationship to changing structures of urbanity in which conditions of commodification, industrialization, and abjection were negotiated.

Hong Kong action cinema initially emerged as a folkloric expression and a popular, postwar phenomenon based on an epic series of films surrounding the legends of contemporary folk hero and martial arts expert Wong Fei Hung, who, according to Law Kar, "taught his disciples kung fu not only to defend themselves but to protect their communities from local thugs and foreign bullies" (65). The Wong Fei Hung series lasted from 1949 to 1970 and was comprised of ninety-nine black and white feature-length films that explored Wong's legacy as a chronicle of struggles and triumphs that were ongoing and cyclical. (The series was, in a sense, extended by new wave films in which Jet Li and Jackie Chan reenact various aspects of the Wong Fei Hung legend.) Wong Fei Hung's elegant displays of martial arts, whether in the popular recent *Once Upon a Time in China* series or the original series, condense, embody, or are emblematic of popular concerns with justice, struggle, popular nationalism, and self-empowerment through discipline and sacrifice (Kar 59–65; Logan 10).

The relationship of early martial arts films to popular expressions of history and resistance was deeply rooted in the tradition of Chinese opera from which it sprang since many of the cinema's stars were originally trained in the intensely physically demanding Chinese opera tradition (Logan 10). From its inception Chinese opera has been linked to popular resistance, literally and metaphorically featuring story lines that often spoke directly to popular feeling on contemporary political and social conditions. In fact, Bey Logan notes that: "When the Ming Emperor was usurped by the Manchu-backed dynasty of the Ching, many famous martial arts masters traveled throughout southern China in the Red Junks that carried opera players" (10). The body as the receptacle with which to register and visually translate metaphorical and literal violation had a long history and context in martial arts films that extended far beyond that tradition into a history of visual representations and negotiations that, in many ways, mirrored African Americans' relationship to a history of spectacularized violence and the body.

Stephen Teo links postwar Hong Kong action film culture to processes of modernization and cultures of urban industrialization. This created an aesthetic expression in which "[t]he low-wage manufacturing base of the economy in the 1970s cultivated a populist type of cinema based on complete identification with working class values" (100). The combination of the populist folkloric narratives that spoke to a burgeoning working-class culture that was urban and industrialized in the language of the body undoubtedly created an instant readability for similarly situated U.S. urban minority audiences. The ubiquitous peasant who would triumph through stringent self-discipline over unthinkable odds in films like *Shaolin Temple* (1982), *Master Killer,* and *Five Fingers of Death* and countless other kung fu films captured and exorcised populist anxiety about the negative odds of the postwar urban reality for an urban black audience as well as for its Hong Kong counterpart.

However, when these aesthetics were directly translated into the idiomatic expression of the black urban ghetto, the emphasis was placed on the artifice of the form as an aesthetic practice rather than the propagation of particular martial arts forms. This was not necessarily a bad thing except when the major studios underestimated what black viewers were seeing in the kung fu genre and represented that mastery over the body as a cartoonish violence that often relied on racist caricatures for humor as epitomized in its worst moments by the *Hong Kong Phooey* series. When the major studios tried to blend the kung fu and black action genres they employed one of two mostly unsuccessful strategies. The first strategy, as in *Hong Kong Phooey, The Dynamite Brothers* (1974), *The Last Dragon* (1985), and *Black Samurai* (1976) was to re-create the kung fu genre in a ghetto idiom that often relied on problematic assumptions about what exactly that should mean. The second strategy was for the studio to take African American models or actors and put them into Asian locales as in *Cleopatra Jones and the Casino of Gold* (1975), Jim Kelly and Ron Van Clief vehicles like *The Tattoo Connection* (1978) and *Way of the Black Dragon* (1978) or the "women in chains" films like *Ebony, Ivory and Jade* (1976).

Seventies African American culture itself was a complex mélange of images and cultural possibilities drawn from sites as disparate and varied as the black cultural nationalist magazines *Black Creation* and *Black World,* popular newsmagazines such as *Jet* and *Ebony,* and televisual culture from

The Jetsons and *Scooby-Doo* to *Soul Train* and *Good Times,* or as Darius James quips, "our parents had jazz, we had cartoons." When African Americans reinvented the kung fu genre for themselves, as in Rudy Ray Moore's independently produced *Dolemite* series, the films did not attempt to simply redo the kung fu genre in blackface or place black characters in Asian locales but instead drew on a black body politics that emphasized black expressive styles through an ironic humor. *Dolemite II: The Human Tornado* (1976) is set both in the city and in the "redneck" south of the early post–civil rights era and comments unambiguously on the potential power of black supermasculinity and the injustice of racial inequities as epitomized by confrontations with the police and the stereotypically ignorant whites who inhabit the film's landscape. In the opening credit sequence, Moore humorously comments on the connection between his film and the decidedly serious signature sequence from *Enter the Dragon,* in which Bruce Lee's character confronts his evil nemesis in a fantastical hall of mirrors. In the sequence from *Enter the Dragon,* which has become one of the most recognizable sequences of the kung fu genre, Bruce Lee has to locate "the real" behind the smokescreen of mirrors that his adversary has created to trap and kill him. He does this through a show of force that aestheticizes not only the physical grace of his movement as he shatters the mirrors but also the injuries he receives as he confronts his enemy's deadly prosthetic hand. The sequence draws an obvious contrast between Lee's perfectly trained, bare-chested body and the imperfect, mechanically manipulated body of his adversary. In contrast, Rudy Ray Moore's less than spectacularly trained body is draped in *Dolemite II* in a floor-length *dashiki* popularized by Black Power–era politics as a signifier of a reconnection with the African past. Moore awkwardly shatters two decidedly unspectacular bedroom-door style mirrors in what appears to be a daily training ritual as he signifies a power that we can only imagine he possesses.

Funkadelic, the seventies funk band suggested in 1971 that if you "free your ass . . . your mind will follow." When Rudy Ray Moore ties his opening sequence to the signature sequence from *Enter the Dragon* he reimagines it in relationship to black vernacular traditions that attempt to wrench the black body from the public spectacle of violence by asserting its very freedom and funkiness. The sequence plays itself out very much like a traditional kung fu training sequence even though Moore's unique "pimp-fu" is obviously lacking prowess, control, or training. This suggests that it is not so much a specific mastery over the body that is important as the recognition that mastery is what ultimately counts. *Dolemite II* is less concerned with an aestheticization of the body through discipline for its own sake than it is with a mastery of the body's expressive possibilities. Moore's chubby, imperfect physique becomes the vehicle through which he can assert a spectacularized power that extends far beyond any demonstration of what his "real" capabilities might be. In this way, African American interest in martial arts film culture, whether it is through the creation of black kung fu films or in the performative appropriation for black body culture of kung fu stylized dance moves or Chinese character tattoos, becomes the vehicle through which African Americans can signify not only a freedom of the body but also assert a raw power and control of the mind. And in doing so they are able not only to improve on a good thing but also to resignify what was good about it in the first place.

In Maxine Hong Kingston's novel *Tripmaster Monkey,* narrator Wittman Ah Sing declares: "Black guys see too many kung fu movies. They think a Chinese-American can go anywhere in the country and have a safehouse where a stranger can be served a family dinner" (255). African American interest in martial arts culture cannot begin to unproblematically define the limits for reading the martial arts genre. It can, however, ultimately confirm the dynamic and transformative possibilities of the act of watching and the potential for the reinvention even of "trash" cinema.

NOTES

This essay benefited from comments by and discussions with Hank Okazaki and Elizabeth Ongiri.

1. The Blaxploitation boom, which began in the mid-sixties and lasted into the late seventies, produced over sixty feature-length black action films. It was part of larger restructuring trends in Hollywood in the wake of the near financial collapse of the major studios in which "the industry's focus shifted to contracting to distribute independently produced features" (83). According to Guerrero, "opportunities opened up for a range of fresh perspectives and aspiring young filmmakers, such as Francis Ford Coppola and Peter Bogdanovich, as well as Gordon Parks, Jr. and Sr., Melvin Van Pebbles and Michael Shultz" (83). Amidst this atmosphere of volatile change, deep restructuring and the opening up of space for the partial articulation of ethnic and minority directors, "Hollywood's belated recognition of the consumer power of the black audience . . . presented itself as a partial solution to the economic crisis in the film industry" (83). Hanna-Barbera Studios also arose out of the financial crisis of the major studios in the late fifties

and early sixties as all the major Hollywood studios scaled back or eliminated animation departments as a cost-saving measure. William Hanna and Joseph Barbera, former animators for MGM, created the studio in response to the dire situation of animators in the post-studio-system days of Hollywood and went on to become the major creators of animation for television throughout the sixties and seventies. *Hong Kong Phooey* represented the always market-savvy innovators' attempts to capitalize on what were seen as important emerging urban African American television audience markets.

WORKS CITED

Alexander, Elizabeth. "Can You Be BLACK and Look at This? Reading the Rodney King Videos," In *Black Male: Representations of Masculinity in Contemporary American Art,* ed. Thelma Golden. New York: Whitney Museum of Art, 1995.

Anderson, Aaron. "Kinesthesia in Martial Arts Films: Action in Motion." *Jump Cut* 42 (December 1998): 1–11.

Bordwell, David. *Planet Hong Kong: Popular Cinema and the Art of Entertainment.* Cambridge, MA: Harvard University Press, 2000.

Brown, Wesley. *Tragic Magic.* New York: Random House, 1978.

Dannen, Frederic, and Barry Long. *Hong Kong Babylon: An Insider's Guide to the Hollywood of the East.* New York: Hyperion, 1997.

Dresser, David. "The Kung Fu Craze: Hong Kong Cinema's First American Reception." In *The Cinema of Hong Kong: History, Arts Identity,* ed. Poshek Fu and David Dresser. Cambridge: Cambridge University Press, 2000.

Fu, Poshek. "The 1960s: Modernity, Youth Culture, and Hong Kong Cinema," In *The Cinema of Hong Kong: History, Arts, Identity,* ed. Poshek Fu and David Dresser. Cambridge: Cambridge University Press, 2000.

Guerrero, Ed. *Framing Blackness: The African American Image in Film.* Philadelphia: Temple University Press, 1993.

Hunt, Leon. "Han's Island Revisited: *Enter the Dragon* as International Cult Film." In *Unruly Pleasures: Cult Film and Its Critics,* ed. Xavier Mendik and Graeme Harper. Surrey: FAB Press, 2000.

James, Darius. "Weird Science." Unpublished manuscript.

Kar, Law. "The American Connection in Early Hong Kong Cinema." In *The Cinema of Hong Kong: History, Arts, Identity,* ed. Poshek Fu and David Dresser. Cambridge: Cambridge University Press, 2000.

Kingston, Maxine Hong. *Tripmaster Monkey.* New York: Vintage, 1990.

Logan, Bey. *Hong Kong Action Cinema.* Woodstock, NY: Overlook Press, 1996.

Morris, Meaghan. "Learning from Bruce Lee: Pedagogy and Political Correctness in Martial Arts Cinema." In *Keyframes: Popular Cinema and Cultural Studies,* ed. Matthew Tinkcom and Amy Villarejo. London: Routledge, 2001.

Streible, Dan. "The Harlem Theater: Black Film Exhibition in Austin, Texas: 1920–1973." In *Black American Cinema,* ed. Manthia Diawara. New York: Routledge, 1993.

Teo, Stephen. "The 1970s: Movement and Transition." In *The Cinema of Hong Kong: History, Arts, Identity,* ed. Poshek Fu and David Dresser. Cambridge: Cambridge University Press, 2000.

Chapter 13

"Alllooksame"? Mediating Asian American Visual Cultures of Race on the Web

Lisa Nakamura

Asian Americans use the Internet more than any other ethnic group in America, including whites.[1] According to data gathered in a 2001 study by the Pew Internet and American Life Report, "fully 75% of English-speaking Asian-Americans have used the Internet. Numbering well over 5 million, these Asian-American Internet users are also the Net's most active users. By comparison, 58% of white adults, 43% of African-Americans, and 50% of English-speaking Hispanics are online" (Spooner 2001). This little-known digital divide between Asian Americans and all other American ethnic groups with regard to Internet use calls into question prior notions of the Internet as a mainly white phenomenon.

Asian American websites, list serves, and on-line forums are the products of an invisible but influential group of American racial minorities: the formulation of the Asian American as the effaced and docile "model minority" both on- and off-line is here replaced by the Asian American as *poweruser,* or part of a digital majority. I am here suggesting that the term poweruser be repurposed from its older meaning, that is, as a technologically savvy consumer and knowledgeable user of personal computers and other consumer electronics. This figuration of a "wired" consumer both hopped up on the drug of hypercapitalism, and endowed with the cultural capital to know his way around cyberspace, implies that social power lies in the ability to purchase and take advantage of the network's advanced features. The reason I wish to recast Asian Americans as powerusers of cyberspace is twofold: first, to do so acknowledges their presence as an on-line force. Indeed, numerous joke lists that circulate via e-mail attest to this self-identification of Asian Americans as avid users of the Internet. For example, one of these, entitled "Eighty-Two Ways to Tell If You Are Chinese," contains an entry that reads, "You e-mail your Chinese friends at work, even though you only sit 10 feet apart." These constitute a useful corrective to digital divide discourse by "casting technology use as one of many aspects of racial identity and practice, rather than vice versa" (Nakamura 2002: 133).

Second and most important, cyberspace functions as a vector for resistant cultural practices that allow Asian Americans to both use and produce cyberspace. Indeed, new media's potential when it comes to Asian Americans has much to do with the powerful ways in which it deploys interactivity to destabilize the distinctions between users and producer, as well as distinctions which serve to rigidify notions of what Asian American "authenticity" consists of. Sites such as Giant Robot's online discussion forum and magazine (www.giantrobot.com) and Mimi Nyugen's blog (www.worsethanqueer.com) work to question the ways in which Asian Americans are falsely represented as "models" of any kind, and do so in ways which put progressive politics, gender, and youth culture into dialogue with considerations of race and ethnicity.

The website that I will discuss in this essay, alllooksame.com, actively works to destabilize notions of Asian identity and nationality in compelling ways that are rendered particularly personal by the user's participation in the site. The site requires the user to guess whether the photographs of Asian faces they are shown are Chinese, Japanese, or Korean, and then calculates the users' score to see if they can accurately tell the difference. Before I begin a close reading of the site, however, I wish to discuss how alllooksame.com is exemplary of a current movement in Asian American critical theory away from essentialist notions of Asian American identity toward a greater recognition of both hybridity and an imperative to "appreciate fully intra-Asian American difference" (Chuh 2003: 13).

In her recent book *Imagine Otherwise,* Chuh constructs a persuasive argument for the "impossibility of understanding 'Asian American' as an unproblematic designation, as a stable term of reference and politics that transcends context" (145). She posits that Asian American studies might have more critical purchase if it were to become a "subjectless" discipline, that is to say, one not defined by the identity or cultural authenticity of objects of study, but rather by its method and critical concerns. If the term "Asian American" is too fraught with internal incoherence to prove useful, and in fact might be doing more harm than good in its insistence on eliding differences between Asian Americans, Chuh is correct in claiming that Asian American studies should find other ways to perform its critique.

The critical study of Asian American new media provides a key opportunity for intervention into a still developing media practice. Even more important, it centers upon the possibility for hybrid and de-essentialized Asian identities that address key contemporary narratives about power, difference, perception, and the visual. Indeed, the distinctive culture of Asian America on-line creates a new representational landscape for issues of identity because it offers what static media lack: interactivity.[2] Interactive media like the web can question identity while building discursive community in ways that other static media cannot.

Likewise, there is a great deal that the study of Asian American critical theory has to offer scholars of new media studies and cyberculture studies. First, failing to examine Asian American on-line culture results in a misreading of the Internet's demographics and representational landscape. Asian Americans are powerusers in both senses of the word, as the Pew Internet and American Life study shows. More important, however, the study of Asian American on-line practices throws a much-needed wrench in the overly simplistic rhetoric of the digital divide. As the 2001 anthology *Technicolor: Race, Technology, and Everyday Life* (Nelson et al.) shows, people of color have long been instrumental in the innovative use and creation of high technologies in a multitude of ways, and their erasure from the digital discourse tends to perpetuate very real power imbalances in the world. And just as important, this figuration of cyberculture as default white tends to demonize people of color as unsophisticated, uneducated, and stuck in a pretechnological past.

In addition, digital divide rhetoric tends to look only at the color of cyberspace's users. In order to formulate a critical practice that takes into account the nuances of participation on-line in terms of identity, power, and race, it is vital to know as well the specific conditions under which new media are produced, consumed, circulated, and exchanged. Interactivity goes both ways as well; websites create users who can interact with them, just as texts create readers. Alllooksame.com's challenging use of interactivity produces a poweruser who is forced to question and eventually discard some essential notions of what it means to be Asian.

There is a tendency in new media criticism to valorize ethnic identity websites that have an overtly progressive political stance as being more culturally "authentic" than others.[3] I chose to examine alllooksame.com because it is a space produced by an Asian designer for an Asian and Asian American audience which debates national and ethnic identities rather than simply affirming them. In addition, alllooksame.com is a comedic site, and thus part of a dramatically underexamined genre which gets next to no critical attention even from net critics.

Dyske Suematsu's' alllooksame.com is a weird, weird site. Interacting with it produces a mixture of guilt, fascination, and a lingering feeling of discomfort. In short, it is uncanny. The initial screen features the familiar iconography of a scantron exam form with its ranks of numbered oval blanks, along with a "welcome" narrative that reads:

> Chinese. Japanese. Korean. What's the difference? Some say it's easy to see. Others think it's difficult—maybe even impossible. Who can really tell? That's what we want to find out. For this first test, we'll show you a series of 18 pictures of CJKs. Select which country you think each is from. When you're finished we'll tell you your score and how you stacked up to others. Future tests will include landscapes, names, architecture, and more. And if you're wondering whether or not to take offense, remember: alllooksame is not a statement. It's a question.

After the user completes a short registration form she is routed to the "test," which consists of digital photographs of young men and women. The form requires the user to click on one of three boxes in order to move ahead in the site: one must guess whether the person in the photograph is Chinese, Japanese, or Korean. After the user has done this for all eighteen images, the site calculates the score; the average score is seven. Users are given the corrected version of their test so they can guess which ones they got "wrong," and are told that they are "OK" if they get a score higher than average.

Suematsu writes that he designed the site "ultimately as a joke" and that he "didn't mean this site to be some sort of political arena." Despite this, as he writes in an essay to the user, "some people felt that this site would promote racism, or that the site itself is racist. Others felt quite the opposite. I was very surprised to receive many emails with encouraging words from Chinese, Korean, and Japanese people. In some ways, I was expecting to upset many of these people." The wide range of responses to the site demonstrates the ways in which this particular kind of interactivity, one which puts the user in the position of a racial profiler of sorts, functions as a nexus for Asians and Asian Americans to actively consider race as an act of seeing. Most important, the low scores that most users get confirm that seeing is *not* believing—the "truth" about race is not a visual truth, yet one which is persistently envisioned that way. This website is an apparatus which deconstructs the visual culture of race. The confusion this entails— users seem to be radically divided as to what the site signifies—provides a unique intervention into the ways in which the visual participates in taxonomies of race.

The most challenging aspect of this, and one which is specifically enabled by this site's interactivity, is that the user is forced to confront her inadequacy in the face of visual "evidence" of race. The low scores that most users get seem to surprise them: in the extremely extensive discussion area of the site where users post their comments, many note that before using the site, they thought they could tell the difference, but their low scores convinced them otherwise.[4] On September 12, 2002, "Annette" posted this particularly thoughtful set of questions to the discussion board:

What does Japanese mean? Does it mean ethnic Koreans, who speak Japanese and no Korean, who are third generation Japanese born? Or is it my friend who is half Japaneese, half Korean who grew up in Puerto Rico?? Well maybe it is the children of a Japaneese and his Korean Bride.

What does Korean mean? Is is people from south western Korea who decended from Chinese in those areas whose names are not Kim and Lee but Chang and Moon??? Or does it mean Koreans who are 1/2 Chinese or Japanese? Nah . . . maybe Korean means the child of a Fillipina (or Chinese or Indonesian for that matter) mail order bride (passing as Korean) and her Korean husband. Then again, they could be those in Uzbekistan forcefully moved there by the Russians 50 years ago, or those in eastern China. What about the Mongolians or Manchurians who came across the border to North Korea . . . Korean??

And just what does Chineese mean? Those Koreans born of Chinese Decent? Or those who have been in Peenang Malasia for over 100 years, who have mixed with the Indians or Malays at some point?? Or does it mean one of the hundreds of recent Chineese labourers to S. Korea.

WHAT IS MY POINT YOU ASK? Well . . . None of these groups are "pure" (ie no mixture or outside influence), nor are they homogeneous. Even among the Koreans who are considered the most homogeneous most inbred in Asia, there has been some mixture . . . that's why it may be difficult to tell . . . but then . . . Is it infact important to tell?????? The world is changing. I for one can't wait for the day when there are so many new groups and categories on the census that they will have to drop the race/ethnicity category.[5]

In the face of empirical evidence of the failure of vision as a means of identifying race, "Annette" redirects the conversation in such a way that the categories themselves are deconstructed. Her comment that race and ethnicity will eventually become uncategorizable, and thus unavailable to empirical analysis, takes the site to its logical conclusion.

Alllooksame.com is a very popular website with Asian Americans.[6] As a result of the site's success, in March 2002 Suematsu was invited to address the Asian American Students Association at Harvard University on the topic of "Asian American community." In his speech, which he reprints on alllooksame.com, he claims to have no interest at all in producing an "Asian American community," asserts that he is not a member of any such thing because he was born in Japan, and goes on to question the importance or relevance of Asian American studies as a discipline and Asian Americanness as a meaningful identity based on anything other than shared racial oppression, the existence of which he professes to doubt. It seems that the default whiteness of web content is so pervasive that these Harvard students were inclined to think that any visual representations at all of Asian Americans on-line constituted an act of community building. But by calling into question what "Asian" is, at least in visual terms, Suematsu is interrogating the basis upon which racial taxonomies like "Asian" are built, and in so doing is producing a community of a different kind. In this, he is "imagining" Asianness "otherwise," to use Chuh's formulation: that is to say, he is envisioning it within his website as a test that can't be passed, or as a set of visual conventions and markers that are less about racial revelation than they are about questioning the status of the "Asian" subject.

By uniting Asian users in the act of deconstructing and questioning their own visual notions of race, alllooksame.com produces a community based on a shared act of interactive self-reflexivity. By discovering that Asian identity is in the "eye of the beholder," as the site asserts, race is detached from biological bodies and reassigned to the realm of the cultural, political, and geographical. Even more to the point, the act of severing the visual as a way of knowing from racial identity addresses a sore point within the Asian American community: that is, racism *between* Asians.[7] In her chapter "Indonesia on the Mind: Diaspora, the Internet, and the Struggle for Hybridity," media theorist Ien Ang explains the ways in which "the dominant discourse of the passions of diasporic identity are being globalized in a dramatic fashion by cyberspace" (2001: 54), and her studies of Huaren (diasporic Indo-Chinese) websites reveals the extent to which they contribute to intra-Asian prejudice. Ang found that "the immediacy of the Internet promoted a readiness to buy into highly emotive evoca-tions of victimization which worked to disregard the historical complexity and specificity of the situation within Indonesia, in favour of a reduction-ist discourse of pan-ethnic solidarity cemented by an abstract, dehistori-cized, and absolutist sense of 'Chineseness'" (69). The site served as a vec-tor for appeals to an "authentic" and essentialized Chinese identity. In this sense, it promoted "ethnic absolutist identity politics" (69). In contrast, al-llooksame.com is a site where racial essentialism can be critiqued in an ac-tive, participatory way with its own built-in apparatus: the test.

Alllooksame remediates several cultural institutions allied with race con-struction in order to comment upon race as a mistaken notion, one that is more easily gotten wrong than right. The site's iconography invokes the scantron exam, a distinctive feature of Western higher education's obses-sion with the empirical, as well as the pictorial convention of the mugshot and the lineup, both connected visually with the judicial and legal system. This confluence of the academy and the police in this site gestures toward the participation of both within the system that maintains racial codes. The site also shows that racial codes come from the user as well as the in-terface or content of the site itself. The site exposes the participation of the user in this construction; it shows how individual acts of viewing and "typing" or clicking create race just as surely as do large institutions such as schools, medical establishments, and the law. Of course, individual acts are inflected by these institutions; when this is acknowledged they come less to seem like personal "choices" and more like part of a complex or dy-namic by which race occurs and is instantiated in everyday acts of seeing.

Perhaps the most salient example of an institution which regulates racial visual codes and taxonomies has yet gone unmentioned, and that is anthropology. This field's long association with racial typing is referenced in Robert Lee's *Orientals* in his chapter on "The Cold War Origins of the Model Minority Myth." In it, he writes that after Pearl Harbor, "for the first time, being able to tell one Asian group apart from another seemed important to white Americans. Two weeks after the Japanese attack on

Pearl Harbor brought the United States into the War, *Life* magazine ran a two-page pictorial entitled 'How to Tell Japs from Chinese'" (1999: 147). The article provided pictures of representative Japanese and Chinese faces along with commentary that interpreted the visual images in terms of their difference from each other. Some of these markers are described as follows: Chinese are described as having a "parchment yellow complexion, more frequent epicanthic fold, higher bridge, never has rosy cheeks, lighter facial bones, longer narrower face and scant beard," while the Japanese face "betrays aboriginal antecedents, has an earthy yellow complexion, less frequent epicanthic fold, flatter nose, sometimes rosy cheeks, heavy beard, broader shorter face and massive cheek and jawbone" (147). In so doing, "*Life* reassured its audience that cultural difference could also be identified visually" (148), in short, that the "truth" about race, particularly with regard to "Orientals," lies within the systematic and scientific study of the face.[8] This visual culture of racial typing endorsed by anthropological method and convention persisted in the presentation of the images themselves: for "to lend an air of precision, scientific objectivity, and authority to the photos and the accompanying text, *Life*'s editors festooned the pictures with handwritten captions and arrows simulating anthropological field notes" (148).

Alllooksame remediates this older anthropological discourse of phenotypic categorization.[9] In addition, the site's net effect of destabilizing notions of Asian identity based on visual essentialism works to expose the user to her own participation in creating these categories. However, the key difference between this site and the *Life* images lies in its audience and its intention. While the *Life* images are designed to educate a white audience that had never considered or cared about the visual differences between Chinese and Japanese people, the alllooksame.com ones are at least as much for Asian and Asian American users who care very much about the differences, and may need a reverse kind of education. That is to say, while whites could not tell the difference and did not care, many Asian Americans believe that they can. A young Asian American woman in Nam's collection *Yell-Oh Girls!* asserts that, "contrary to what *haole* America thinks, we don't all look alike, and we can tell a Japanese from a Chinese from a Korean from a Filipina from an Indian" (2001: 173). Thus, the site achieves both an Asian American identity as a cultural formation and the kind of "subjectless" identity advocated by Chuh, for it is "Asian/American" interactive new media content produced by and for Asian Americans, yet time it questions that identity by fostering debate and conflict around questions of race and ethnicity. Ultimately, as Suetmatsu writes, "alllooksame is not a statement. It's a question." New media such as the Internet enables this question to remain an open one in ways that older non-interactive media, both textual and visual, do not.

As net critic Geert Lovink writes in *Dark Fiber: Tracking Critical Internet Culture*, "over the last few decades media theory has drawn heavily from literary criticism. Perhaps it is time to reverse the intellectual exchange" (2002: 32). Lovink's call for a "radical upgrade of literary criticism" acknowledges that there are aspects of visual culture on-line that cannot be adequately thought through using literary models. As previously noted, media are multifarious, and multimedia are perhaps even more so. If we shift our focus away from the discourse of *literary* postcolonial theory, we can better perceive the possibilities that the *visual* culture of the Internet can have for challenging notions of racial and cultural essence and identity. There is no doubt that images can be just as complicitous with the colonial project as words; they are no more innocent than novels, advertisements, manifestos, or medical taxonomies of racial difference. And in fact, the most interesting new work on race and postcoloniality in recent years has been in the field of visual culture. Sander Gilman, Anne McClintock, Nicholas Mirzoeff, and Ella Shohat have all produced fascinating work on the ways in which the visual cultures of empire produce racial hegemonies.[10] However, websites such as Dyske Suematsu's alllooksame.com effectively employ interactivity and the spectacle of race on-line in ways that offer distinctive forms of resistance to racial and visual categories. The type of self-critiquing interactivity it offers challenges vision itself as a way of understanding race, culture, and the body on- and off-line.

NOTES

Many thanks to my poweruser sister, Judy Nakamura, and to the editors of this collection, in particular LeiLani Nishime, who made excellent suggestions regarding revisions and was very understanding about deadlines. I also wish to thank my writing group at UW Madison: Victor Bascara, Leslie Bow, Shilpa Davé, Grace Hong, and Michael Peterson, for their generous readings and brilliant comments. Audiences at the 2002 Media and Cultural Studies colloquium series in the Communication Arts Department at Madison, the 2002 Visual Culture Colloquium at Madison, the 2003 Art and Archaeology Graduate Symposium at

Cornell University, and the 2002 American Studies Association conference all contributed valuable comments and support as well. Many thanks to Dyske Suematsu for generous permission to reproduce images from his website.

1. A different form of this essay appeared in the *Iowa Journal of Cultural Studies*, Issue 2, Fall 2002.

2. This is not to claim that readers cannot "interact" with older media such as literature. However, this interaction is largely invisible and does not change the form of the media object itself. In this, it differs from what happens on interactive websites, in which the user changes the appearance of different screens by her actions via a keyboard or mouse.

3. The Chiapas website at http://chiapas.indymedia.org/ is a good example of this.

4. On August 24, 2001, "Oaken Din" wrote, "I am a Chinese guy living in the Los Angeles area. I see Chinese ppl all the time. I'll see Koreans and Japanese ppl here and there when I am out and about in the LA area. There are a lot of Vietnamese, Indonesian, Mongolian, etc. that I bump into. When it comes to telling them apart, I seem to get it right for the most part between Chinese, Korean, and Japanese. But I scored miserably on your test. I got a four. That tells me how much I know. I suck and am forever changed. Thnx for the eye opener."

5. Original spelling, grammar, and formatting are reproduced from the original post as faithfully as possible.

6. Suematsu claims that the test has been taken over 200,000 times since August 2001, and most of the people who posted to the "discussion" section self-identified as Asian.

7. In an article entitled "Testing Out My A-Dar," Harry Mok remarks that when he first started the test, he thought "this was going to be easy. No problem, I'm Chinese. I can spot Chinese people a mile away. I have the Asian sixth sense, an A-dar." After remarking that he failed miserably, he includes Suematsu's comment that "A lot of time just to be polite or politically correct, people go to a difficult long way to find out (what ethnicity or race you are)," Suematsu said. "It's almost like a whether-you're-gay-or-straight kind of thing."

8. See Palumbo-Liu's (1999) discussion of the face as a privileged signifier of Asian identity on pages 87–88, in which he writes that the Asian "face is elaborated as the site of racial negotiations and the transformation of racial identity," and that "it is this 'face,' then, not (only) in its phenotypology but (also) in animation, that demarcates essential differences between groups."

9. See the film *Europa Europa* for a comic critique of this theme of phenotypic racial identification in terms of German visual cultures of identity regarding Jews.

10. See Anne McClintock's seminal *Imperial Leather* (1995), Nick Mirzoeff's *Visual Culture Reader* (1998), which has a section entitled "Race and Identity in Colonial and Postcolonial Culture," and Sander Gilman's *Difference and Pathology: Stereotypes of Sexuality, Race, and Madness* (1985), in particular his chapter on the

Hottentot Venus. It is important to note that though Mirzoeff's collection also has a section entitled "Virtuality: Virtual Bodies and Virtual Spaces," the book lacks any analyses of actual websites or specific examples from the Internet.

WORKS CITED

Ang, Ien. *On Not Speaking Chinese: Living between Asia and the West.* London: Routledge, 2001.

Chuh, Kandice. *Imagine Otherwise: On Asian American Critique.* Durham: Duke University Press, 2003.

Gilman, Sander. *Difference and Pathology: Stereotypes of Sexuality, Race, and Madness.* Ithaca: Cornell University Press, 1985.

Howard, Philip E., Lee Rainie, and Steve Jones. "Days and Nights on the Internet: The Impact of a Diffusing Technology." *American Behavioral Scientist,* Vol. 45, Summer 2001 special issue.

Lee, Robert. *Orientals: Asian Americans in Popular Culture.* Philadelphia: Temple University Press, 1999.

Lovink, Geert. *Dark Fiber: Tracking Critical Internet Culture.* Boston: MIT Press, 2002.

McClintock, Anne. *Imperial Leather: Race, Gender, and Sexuality in the Colonial Context.* New York: Routledge, 1995.

Mirzoeff, Nicholas. (ed.) *The Visual Culture Reader.* London: Routledge, 1998.

Mok, Harry. "Testing Out My A-Dar: Trying to Pick Out Who Is What." Online, http://www.inthefray.com/200203/imagine/same12/same12.html.

Nakamura, Lisa. *Cybertypes: Race, Ethnicity, and Identity on the Internet.* New York: Routledge, 2002.

Nam, Vickie. *Yell-Oh Girls! Emerging Voices Explore Culture, Identity, and Growing Up Asian American.* New York: HarperCollins, 2001.

Nelson, Alondra, et al. (eds.) *Technicolor: Race, Technology, and Everyday Life.* New York: NYU Press, 2001.

Palumbo-Liu, David. *Asian/American: Historical Crossings of a Racial Frontier.* Palo Alto: Stanford University Press, 1999.

Spooner, Tom. "Asian-Americans and the Internet: The Young and the Connected." Pew Internet and American Life Project, December 12, 2001, online, http://www.pewinternet.org.

Chapter 14

Guilty Pleasures
Keanu Reeves, Superman, and Racial Outing

LeiLani Nishime

I was discussing with a friend the relative merits of *The Matrix* and the *Matrix Reloaded* the other day, and I mentioned that the second movie featured many more people of color. My friend responded, "But the savior is still some white guy." I countered with the argument that Reeves is hapa not white.[1] Pleased by my friend's surprised response, I couldn't resist reeling off the names of other hapa celebrities like Dean Cain or The Rock or Rob Schneider or the Tilly sisters (Meg and Jennifer) who recently outed themselves as half-Chinese. By the time I'm done I've added on suspected Asians like Tom Hanks who have yet to disclose. Thus, even though I'm frustrated at the failure of others to recognize these actors as part Asian, I experience, at the same time, no small amount of pleasure in revealing their racial background, and judging from the discussions flying around Asian American and mixed race celebrity chat rooms, I'm not alone.

While the practice of spotting or "outing" mixed-race celebrities may be widespread, it remains a rarely discussed guilty pleasure. Part of the difficulty in addressing the phenomenon lies in its ambiguities. There is an uncomfortable thrill in sitting in a movie theater aware that, unbeknownst to the rest of the audience, a hapa plays the film's heroic messiah. That feeling only intensifies when I get the chance to lean over to the person sitting besides me let him or her in on this exclusive knowledge. Yet what part of that experience inspires guilt and what part brings pleasure? The rush of "claiming" the hapa star is tempered by the politically incorrect glee in being the one to expose his or her racial background. It is this competing tension between claiming and exploiting, celebration and sadism, that is the subject of this essay.

Whether the feeling is politically progressive or regressive remains an open question. While the political expediency versus privacy debate still surrounds the practice of gay outing, celebrity racial outing, particularly in contemporary American culture, is largely unexplored.[2] Queer studies, while struggling with a distinct history and culture, offers a window into a central question of what is at stake and what is gained through discovering and revealing the heritage of mixed-race celebrities. It also may help to account for the gleefully transgressive pleasure of knowing their "true" racial identity. At the same time, the material differences between what is at stake in revealing queer identity and multiracial identity can also help to illuminate the distinct role of outing for multiracial people.

This essay takes Keanu Reeves as iconic figure both as the most visible, or conversely the most invisible, hapa star, since he is undoubtedly the most famous and least acknowledged. He is also surrounded by rumors of homosexuality and thus marks an important intersection between race and sexuality. The lessons learned from Reeves's celebrity can then be applied to the more specific questions of how the process of passing and outing plays out in the cultural realm. Using the television show *Smallville* as a case study, we can see how the interplay between the guilt and pleasure of racial outing can form and inform our reading of even the most familiar of stories.

Queer Theory and Multiraciality

It is no accident that I chose the term "outing" to discuss mixed-race celebrities and Keanu Reeves in particular. Reeves has been trailed by rumors that he is gay since he first came to fame. His placement at the axis between the discourses of race and sexuality make him a critical figure when thinking through the politics and pleasures of racial passing and outing. The book *Gay Fandom and Crossover Stardom* (2001) by Michael DeAngelis devotes an entire chapter to Keanu Reeves. DeAngelis begins his discussion of Reeves by recounting a chatroom debate over whether or not it would hurt Reeves's image to have him play Andrew Cunanon (Cunanon was the half-Filipino serial killer who went on a spree, killing several gay men, including Gianni Versace, in the mid-1990s). The debate centered on Reeves's standing in the gay community, but never mentioned race. The obvious racial connection between the two men was obscured by the focus on sexuality, a blind spot that was replicated by the media surrounding the murders.

In discussing Andrew Cunanon, Teresa Williams-León (2001) argues that, despite his surname, Cunanon's "phenotypical ambiguity and openly gay sexuality marked him as White." Evidence of gay sexuality seems to erase racial markings, an absence that is read as white. Dana Takagi, in her influential article "Maiden Voyage" argues, "In other words, many of us experience the worlds of Asian America and gay America as separate places—emotionally, physically, intellectually" (2000: 356). Race and sexuality seem to cancel each other out in both the popular imagination and the zero-sum world of identity politics. African American critics such as Audre Lorde (1984) and, more recently, Kobena Mercer (1994) have long argued that the gay movement blindly ignores racial issues, while race-based civil rights groups either avoid the issues or deny the existence of gay people of color. Mercer points to a colonizing impulse by white activists in the cultural arena who want to claim the politics of civil rights while marginalizing its originators. Takagi traces the disjuncture between Asian American and queer studies to both homophobia within the Asian American community and the distinct issues and histories of gay liberation and Asian American civil rights.

However, by reading race and sexuality together, the logic of sexual closeting and outing can help us better read racialized passing and outing. Furthermore, an understanding of racial passing as an analog for sexuality can help undermine racial essentialism. For instance, Takagi warns us that "gay" is not interchangeable with "Asian." While they might not be interchangeable, I would argue that they do have crucial points of intersection that can and should be productively explored. Although her broader point that each group has different histories is crucial, she also claims, "First is the relative invisibility of sexual identity compared with racial identity . . . there is a quality of volunteerism in being gay/lesbian that is usually not possible as an Asian American . . . homosexuality is more clearly seen as *constructed* than is racial identity" (emphasis in original, 356). The distinction Takagi makes hinges on the ability of gays and lesbians to remain closeted, thus emphasizing the performativity of sexual identities; while, according to Takagi, racial Others are not able to control how others might read them.

Mixed-race Asian Americans, on the other hand, set up a crucial counterpoint to Takagi. Multiraciality blurs her distinction between gay and

Asian identities by demonstrating how even supposedly involuntary differences like race can be as voluntary (or, perhaps more accurately, as involuntary given the coercion inherent in existing social structures) and constructed as sexuality. Yoking together theories of race and sexuality enables us to more clearly articulate the ways in which race comes into being through its performance. However, the different histories of race and sexuality must also be acknowledged to grasp the distinctions that continue to be drawn between the visibility of race and the invisibility of sexuality. In other words, we often set visible racial differences in opposition to sexual identities. The first is conceived as a natural or biological fact while the latter is believed to be acted out and socially produced. However, both are constructs and the perceived differences point to the ways in which the two identities are produced within separate social contexts.

Race by Association

Just as queer studies has illustrated the ways in which homosexuality has been used to buttress the social norm of heterosexuality, multiraciality casts its shadow on hegemonic notions of race. Investigating mixed-race identity forces one to question all racial categorization. At it most basic level, multiraciality questions the location of race. For many, race is skin deep, and, as such, race resides at the level of the visible, but the figure of the mixed-race celebrity negates the easy equation of race with skin color. The simplest explanation for why Reeves, for example, is not recognized as hapa is that he does not "look Asian."

While that explanation may appeal to a certain commonsense notion of race, it obscures the ways in which our ability to see race is anything but given or natural. Indeed, one of the most powerful holds race has over us is the way it seems to show itself on our faces and skin, an irrefutable and irreducible evidence of difference. Whenever I tell my students that race is a myth they always return to the seemingly self-evident fact that race must exist since we can see it. Yet, as the history of racial mixing can show, our ability to see, a practice believed to be unmediated and prior to culture, cannot be separated from perception. Common wisdom about miscegenation is that we are currently creating a "postethnic" state. In this utopic, raceless future we will form some undifferentiated whole. However, the three-hundred-year history of black-white mixing in America would appear to debunk this theory. The practice of the one-drop rule created a visually heterogeneous group of people simply defined as "black." As a result, we have developed a broader and broader visual definition of black, and our ability to see blackness is well developed. Saying someone "looks black" can encompass features as different as Vanessa Williams and Venus Williams.

Asians have had less clearly demarcated racial boundaries than other racial groups, both juridically and socially. See, for instance, early lawsuits questioning the definitions of "white" and "Caucasian" brought by Asians seeking to circumvent restrictive laws.[3] As a result, we have a more limited vocabulary for seeing Asians, and of course, if one has no race, one is white in America's racial logic. This, added to the general paucity of images of Asians, often makes it more difficult for us to read for racially mixed Asians.

Seeing race is a matter of understanding which visual cues matter and which ones we can ignore. My son Kenzo might be a good example. For those used to seeing Asians and hapa children he looks like my husband, but my husband's relatives can only see the Asian in his face and thus he cannot look like his father since he cannot "look white." On the opposite end of the spectrum, we might look at the more common phenomenon of all Asians "looking alike." If one can only see the features marked as Asian, then one is blinded to specific differences between Asians. Fetishized features such as eye shape or hair texture dominate the field of vision, and those that do not fit codified racial signifiers disappear. When fans or critics dismiss the labeling of Reeves as a mixed-race star by remarking that "no one knows" that Reeves is Asian, it begs the question of who can count as "someone." This is not to say that "blood will tell." Race does not somehow lurk in genetic code, ready to betray itself at the least provocation. Rather race only appears when we go looking for it. Although it seems to have an existential existence that we "discover," it only exists in that moment of discovery.

If race does not have an existential reality, then it follows that race only becomes evident in difference, difference to and difference from some agreed upon norm. Here I would like to draw from theoretical discussions of passing, specifically Judith Butler's reading of Nella Larson's *Passing*. Butler argues that one of the female protagonists, Clare, who passes as white does so, in part, by refusing to ever introduce blackness into conversation. Even a whisper of blackness would cast suspicion on the hegemonic presumption of whiteness. She argues, "if she associates with blacks, she becomes black, where the sign of blackness is contracted, as it were, through proximity, where 'race' itself is figured as a contagion transmissible through proximity" (1993: 171).

The race by association argument certainly does play out in the bizarrely ahistorical, deterritorialized space of *Scorpion King* (2003), for example. The lack of specificity tends to undermine what might be viewed as a breakthrough hapa film with its two hapa romantic leads. Instead, their ethnicity is obscured to match the vaguely Egyptian setting taking place in some timeless, ancient past. It might also explain how Kristin Kreuk manages to appear simultaneously as the Chinese Canadian Laurel Yeung on the Canadian TV show *Edgemont* and as all-American and all-Caucasian Lana Lang on the WB's *Smallville.*

Viewing race and sexuality together help illuminate the ways in which race and multiraciality are constructed by introducing the acknowledged role of volunteerism from queer studies into the supposedly involuntary space of visual racial knowledge. By looking at the popular television show *Smallville* as an exemplary instance of the intersection of race and sexuality, I will return to the political and emotional stakes of outing. First positing the resistant viewer as a participant in spectatorship-as-outing, the contradictory impulses of involved in outing will be explored and exposed.

Say It Ain't So: Queer and Raced Readings of Superman in Smallville

As a kind of case study example, I would like to take a look at the teen fantasy drama *Smallville.* By simultaneously reading for sexuality and race in a series oddly bereft of both, the television show cracks open to enable the knowing viewer to participate in a new and exclusive narrative. In reading for race, I have returned, once again, to queer theory, and most specifically to Alexander Doty's book *Making Things Perfectly Queer.* Doty seeks out queerness in mass culture, arguing, "Unless the text is about queers, it seems to me the queerness of most mass culture texts is less an essential, waiting-to-be-discovered property than the result of acts of production or reception" (1993: xi). Thus, I would like to emphasize the reception of *Smallville* by the fan who may gain pleasure in his or her extratextual and intertextual knowledge.

The top-rated show on the youth-oriented WB, *Smallville* is a contemporary retelling of Superman, the teen years. Set in the archetypal mid-

Western small town, *Smallville* tells the story of Clark Kent (Tom Welling), a high school freshman in the show's first season, who is just beginning to learn about his superpowers. The soapy, and slightly campy, series includes Clark's future nemesis, Lex Luthor (Michael Rosenbaum), and a pre–Lois Lane love interest, Lana Lang (Kristin Kreuk). The series relies heavily on intertextuality and often refers to the audience's knowledge of Superman lore. For example, in an episode in the second season we learn that Clark is afraid of heights, but must get from one skyscraper to the next, so he leaps. The show gives a knowing wink to the audience who knows that Superman can fly, even though Clark does not, while also referring to the famous phrase "able to leap buildings in a single bound."

For this knowing viewer the sexual rather than racial subtext seems more evident and certainly more interesting to its fans. The pilot episode of the show introduces Clark's two main romantic interests. Lana is the overt object of Clark's affections, but the other, and more intriguing, source of sexual tension for the show is the relationship of Clark to Lex Luthor. Although we know that one day Lex will be Clark's archenemy, we first meet him when Clark saves his life. From then on, the two form a strong, although narratively inexplicable, bond. Despite the fact that Clark does not trust Lex and Lex suspects that Clark is lying to him about his true identity, they cannot seem to stay away from each other. While the homoerotics of their longing glances and obsessive interest in each other is unacknowledged on the show, their relationship preoccupies many of the show's fans. The show recap that appears on the website Television without Pity features a "Gayest Look of the Episode" for every show it reviews.

By the end of season two, the writers of the show had created an episode that seems to wink at the "open secret" of Clark and Lex's relationship.[4] The episode entitled "Visitor" sets up an explicit parallel between Clark and Lana and Lex and his fiancée Dr. Helen Bryce (Emanuelle Vagier) and an implicit parallel to the third part of the romantic triangle, Lex and Clark. The episode centers on the two women's struggle to accept the fact that their lovers keep secrets from them. Helen threatens to break off their engagement because, in a fit of Freudian overkill, Lex has a secret room in his mansion that he prohibits her from entering. At the end of the episode, Lex reveals that the secret room is filled with charts and photographs of Clark. The blown up photos of Clark and the documents and artifacts displayed under glass resemble a type of scientific shrine. Ultimately, the secret that Lex tries to keep hidden is his obsession with Clark. While the majority of the show concentrates on whether or not Lana and

Helen can maintain a romantic relationship despite the hidden parts of Clark and Luthor's lives, the show ends with the question of whether Clark and Lex's relationship can stand the same strain. At the same time, it is this secret that attracts Lex to Clark and fuels his continual pursuit. Thus, this particular episode outlines the structure of secrets and revelations that fuel the entire series, and I will argue, the reading relationship of the audience.

In a strange echo of the racial and sexual marking of Reeves, on-line fans who recognize attempts to closet Clark and Lex's attraction to each other fail to explore the basis of Lex's obsession. Lex is haunted by the mystery of Clark's origins. While never stating it outright, he has suggested that he believes that Clark is an alien passing as human, and it is this belief that makes Clark irresistible. The focus on hidden origins recalls similar narratives of racial passing. His alien blood seems to be a barely veiled metaphor for race. Just as a queer reading opens up new interpretive opportunities, the introduction of race can give us new insight into the primary question of origins in the Superman myth.

The story itself can be read as a commentary on racial visibility and invisibility, power and disempowerment. The wholesome, and very white-bread, Clark family adopts Clark Kent, cast as a high school heartthrob. Despite his growing power, he successfully passes as human but must continually hide his true parentage. As the series progresses, Clark becomes ever more driven by the need to know more about "his own kind." Gary Engle argues that Superman is the ultimate immigrant and that his dual identity works through issues of assimilation.[5] Ultimately, Engle claims that Clark Kent, as opposed to Superman, "is the epitome of visible invisibility, someone whose extraordinary ordinariness makes him disappear in a crowd. . . . He is the consummate figure of total cultural assimilation, and significantly, he is not real" (1987: 85). In the television series, however, Clark Kent is not merely the disguise for Superman. In fact, Clark is the primary identity and thus the comic's schematic division of Superman and Clark, the "true" and assimilated selves, is called into question.

Significantly, the only person outside his family who knows the truth is Clark's best friend Pete (Sam Jones III), who seems to be the only African American in town. While race is never alluded to by anyone in the show in a sort of white liberal conspiracy of silence, culturally speaking Pete and Clark are both alienated from the mainstream of their high school. So while race as an explicit subject appears to be verboten, it surfaces repeatedly as the unnamed elephant in the room.

The fear that Clark's secret origins may be discovered reoccurs in almost every episode, but his concerns are not limited to the prying eyes of government scientists. His more pressing worry is the impact of his secret on his budding romantic relationship with Lana Lang, played by the biracial Kristin Kreuk. Clark both yearns to and fears telling Lana who his real parents are. In the same episode "Visitor," another boy in town claims to be an alien, and Clark asks Lana if she could accept the boy if he really was not human. When she responds that although she is ashamed to admit it, it would make a difference, Clark is crushed. Later, Clark's best female friend Chloe (Allison Mack) also hears about the boy who claims to be an alien, but reacts in a completely different way from Lana. She is thrilled at the idea and believes it would mean that "something interesting" had finally happened in her sleepy town. Her sentiments certainly fit with a certain multicultural exoticization of difference.

All this leads to the troubling idea that the sexual tension between Clark and Lana (and Clark and Lex) is predicated on his passing, his need to keep his identity hidden. He rejects Chloe as a love interest even though, or maybe because, she would welcome and accept his true identity. Indeed, a large part of the appeal of Clark for Lana, Lex, and the audience is based on Clark's need to hide his identity. He is romanticized by his brooding and mystery which are based on his need to pass. It is important to recognize the improper pleasure of racial subversion. So certainly, part of the pleasure of the show resides in the sadistic erotics of Clark's abjection.[6] While difficult to admit, the social and political necessity of passing also generates a delight in the threat of discovery and the pursuit (but not the attainment) of the truth.

Both the sexual and racially repressed secrets that haunt the show meet in the constantly battered and bruised body of Clark. Like Lana and Lex, the audience is invited to sexually objectify Clark because of, rather than despite, his abjection. Take, for instance, a scene that replays each week in the opening credits for the show. In the pilot episode, Clark is the victim of a prank played on one freshman every year. The seniors choose Clark, beat him, paint a red "S" for Smallville on his chest (in a humiliating reversal of the Superman "S" he will later wear), and hang him up like a scarecrow in the cornfields that surround the town.[7] Using Lana's kryptonite necklace to poison Clark, the seniors leave him barely conscious in the field. Certainly, one could read the scene as a visual biblical reference, but it is difficult to avoid its erotic overtones.[8] In this modern crucifixion, Clark is bare-chested, waxed and oiled up, all the better to cruise his six-pack abs.

Fig. 14.1. The most downloaded image of Tom Welling (as *Smallville*'s Clark Kent) from the website Devoted to Smallville.

The scene also recalls the photographs of Bruce Webber and advertising for Calvin Klein, both of which borrow copiously from gay pornography. For the knowing viewer, the pleasure of this scene is bound up in recognizing gestures toward gay iconography as well as the initial moment of abjection. Its eroticism is rooted in the lack of any overt recognition of its sexual connotations. Only by being hidden is the pleasure of revelation made possible, so the pleasure is implicated in its own suppression. However, while this cycle of suppression and revelation may explain the guilt part of the guilty pleasure it cannot fully explain the pleasure. I would argue that it extends beyond mere sadism. In order to more fully understand racial passing and outing as subversive and, dare I say it, empowering, I would like to return to the figure of Keanu Reeves before offering an alternative reading of racial outing in Smallville.

Outing and the Pleasures of Interpretation

For Asians, like Latinos, names play an important role in the perception of race. As a writer for the website Goldensea/Asian American Supersite asks, "Would Russell Wong be more successful with a different last name?" (2003). The significance of names was made obvious when Keanu Reeves, whose first name is Hawaiian, appeared on the Tonight Show to promote the film *The Replacements* (2000). Jay Leno began his interview by prompting Reeves to recall his early days in Hollywood when Reeves's agent tried to get him to change his name. Reeves says that his agent asked him to try the name K. C. Reeves because, in the words of Reeves himself, "People, when they heard [the name] Keanu Reeves, they didn't know what I was [this last phrase accompanied by Reeves physically gesturing air quotes]. Whatever that means. I'm not touching that." Then Leno replies off-camera, "What is a Keanu?"

The *Tonight Show* interview perfectly exemplifies Reeves's ability to "cross over" from a racially subcultural audience to a mainstream white one. By "not touching that," Reeves can play to and evoke the pleasure of the knowing viewer who understands "what Keanu means" while he studiously avoiding the words Asian or race. For a mainstream audience, the story merely recounts the misdirected enthusiasms of a Hollywood agent and the racial overtones are gently muted in ethnic difference or individual eccentricity. Reeves's appearance on the *Tonight Show* replays the ambiguity that characterizes his public persona. He never denies his ethnicity yet it is continually forgotten and ignored except by the audience that goes looking for race. Thus he is able to make statements calling himself a "middle-class white kid" while interview after interview states that he is European, Chinese, and Hawaiian. The "what you are" is never defined and does not become a key characteristic.

Another noteworthy aspect of the *Tonight Show* discussion is the fact that it would be difficult to imagine a similar conversation about Reeves's ambiguous sexuality. As DeAngelis points out, Reeves never counterattacks with lawsuits like Tom Cruise, yet he is careful never to confirm or deny the rumors. On the other hand, Reeves's racial message is both more overt and more malleable. He is able to make contradictory statements about being both a "white kid" and part Asian with neither claim raising too many hackles in the mainstream. There appears to be a greater freedom of play and a greater acceptance of ambiguity in questions of race.

It is this lack of definition that resurfaces in Asian American message boards and on-line forums such as IIstix. The question of what "qualifies" as Asian provokes a volley of responses and speaks directly to the pleasure evoked by "claiming" half-Asian stars.[9] The on-line discussions often focus on the right to categorize Reeves as Asian American. On the Asian American interactive site, Goldensea, there is even a poll breaking down Asianness into a series of questions. Is he Asian because he "looks Asian"? Or Asian because he self-identifies as Asian? Or simply Asian because he has Asian blood? These questions, like the questions about "looking Asian," illustrate the powerful place of biraciality or representations of hapas in understanding racial identities. They are not the exceptions to the rule, but rather the exceptions that enable us to see the ways in which the rules are entirely contingent. Ultimately, the questions we ask about hapas are the same questions we must ask about "pure" Asians. What do we mean by race? How do we understand and perform race?

What interests me most about the poll is the issue of "claiming" Reeves as Asian. Generally, in claiming an Asian star we are asking him or her to represent Asians or Asian Americans in some way. Chow Yun Fat, for instance, can show mainstream America that Asian men can be macho, powerful, violent, and, most importantly, cool. The question of Reeves "looking Asian" in order to categorize him as Asian American presupposes that we need to make sure that others can read him as Asian and then transfer that reading to other Asian bodies. But the interest in claiming hapa stars does not end with simple tokenism, it seems, since so many of the fan sites focus on people who are not primarily identified as Asian. In fact, interest in the Asian heritage of stars seems to grow in direct proportion to their ability to pass. Perhaps this can account in part for the interest in claiming a star who, like Reeves, calls himself a "middle-class white kid" rather than one like Russell Wong or Tia Carrera, neither of whom passes as white. Certainly, it could be argued that the interest in Reeves is due to his much greater fame. Yet the two issues cannot be separated since Reeves's stardom may depend on his ability to pass as white in the majority of American theaters. Reeves's allure stems in part from his stealth status, and his popularity on Asian American fan sites grows because of, rather than in spite of, his "hidden" heritage.

I would argue that fans, like myself, revel in the very indeterminacy of the celebrity's identity. The kind of "play" of signifiers and signified advocated by Barthes has been largely denied to racially marked "others" who usually act as fixed points against which the endless play of whiteness is enacted. The figure of the multiracial star enables the knowing viewer to join in the play and create a subversive reading of mainstream texts. As Eve Sedgwick asserts in her landmark work *Epistemology of the Closet*, pursing a gay-centered inquiry into Western canonical texts gives her "invaluable forms of critique and dismantlement within the official tradition" (1986: 58). Her analysis showed her "the urgencies and pleasures of reading against the visible grain of any influential text" (55). However, this presents a paradox. While racially or sexually closeted texts may offer their readers the subversive pleasure of finding a hidden or deeply embedded narrative, the readers' interpretive power depends upon that very closeting. The reader gains the power of interpretation but, in exchange, is excluded from mainstream representation or even legibility. And it is to this paradox that the essay now turns.

Back in *Smallville*, pleasure, as always, is not as simple as it seems. Racial and sexual difference are not just a route to abjection. Even while Clark must hide his superpowers, they are also the source of his strength. While race may be repressed in *Smallville*, it provides the key to a more comprehensive reading of the story. Perhaps the most fruitful example is the symbol of kryptonite. At the heart of Superman lore, kryptonite is Superman's Achilles' heel. Kryptonite consists of meteorite fragments from Superman's home planet of Krypton, and when Superman comes close to the glowing green rock he becomes weak and will eventually die. Clearly kryptonite, as a piece of his home planet, represents Clark's alien, read racially Other, origins. In the series *Smallville*, the rock also makes Clark's veins turn black and begin to visibly throb and thus enacts Butler's race by association theory. Whenever the kryptonite unexpectedly appears, as it seems to in almost every episode, it threatens to expose Clark's secret. Like race, kryptonite seems to be everywhere in Smallville although no one seems to understand it, and everyone denies having any.

Smallville also revives another kryptonite missing from the film and television series. The meteor shower which brought the green kryptonite and Superman to earth also introduces red kryptonite to Smallville. The red kryptonite affects Clark, and all the other show's characters, like a psychoactive drug, lowering their inhibitions and promoting risky and antisocial behavior. Tellingly, it is Clark's African American friend Pete who first "doses" him, sending him on a spree of drinking, womanizing, and other high-risk behaviors. The introduction of racial otherness, symbolized by the red and green kryptonite, not only may expose Clark, but it may also infect the entire town. The transformation of Clark plays to the familiar racial trope of the racial Other as criminal and sexually free. Racial Otherness poses a threat to the entire social order by offering a way out of the social norms of the town. Although the episode in which the red kryptonite first appears ends with the expulsion of the rocks and a restoration of the old order, the series' second season finale ends by Clark reclaiming the red kryptonite and riding out of town in order to "find himself." The red kryptonite illustrates the show's ambivalence toward Clark's origins as both necessary and threatening to his identity since it so completely alters his personality while, at the same time, enabling him to live out his deepest fantasies and leading him on his journey of self-discovery.

Most importantly for the purposes of this essay, Kryptonite also plays a key symbolic role for Lana. At the show's outset, Lana, like Clark, is not being raised by her biological parents. She was orphaned by the meteor shower that brought Clark to earth. Unlike Clark, however, she feels secure in her attachment to her parents, and by extension her heritage, symbolized by the green piece of kryptonite she wears around her neck. Yet as the show progresses she loses track of both her necklace and her lineage. The necklace is involved in a series of exchanges through theft, loss, and gift giving and, at the same time, Lana learns that although the man she thought was her father is dead, her biological father is still alive.

The viewer reading for race, much like Doty's queer reader, can't help but snap to attention when the narrative casts doubt on Lana's parentage as the character of Lana Lang's suddenly mysterious origins intersects with the actress Kristin Kreuk's own multiracial descent. Her uncertainty about her parentage echoes the skepticism of the knowing viewer. The iconic picture of Lang's loving and very Aryan parents never seemed to tell the full story. Lana's discovery draws her closer to Clark as they both try to locate their "real" parents. Clark's attempts to understand and master his biological family's legacy is a continual narrative thread throughout the series. Knowledge of Clark's "true" identity functions for the audience in a manner similar to the knowledge of Kreuk's identity to the aware hapa or Asian audience or the recognition of the homoerotics of Clark and Lex's relationship. Mainstream audiences, unlike the hapless citizens of Smallville, know more and can enjoy the familiar movements toward resolution. However, Smallville takes the audience's insider knowledge of Superman lore to a new level and creates a different relationship to the story itself.

Unlike the last series to take up the Superman myth, Lois and Clark (1993–1997), or the film Superman (1978) and its sequels, the audience already knows how this series will end.[10] In *Lois and Clark* the question of whether Lois would discover Clark's identity or, later in the series, whether they would marry drove the narrative. However, in *Smallville* the action, as the official website tells us, takes place during adolescence "between the boy he thought he was and the man he is destined to become." We know that Clark does not end up with Lana and that Lex will eventually turn against him because we know the adult Superman in his many incarnations. Yet this is key to the allure of the show. In all the Superman stories, because the audience is aware that Clark is Superman it has a clearer grasp of unfolding events than the characters in the story—except Superman himself. However, in *Smallville* that superior access to information is taken a step further since we know more than even the hero does.

In "Lois's Locks: Trust and Representation in *Lois and Clark: The New Adventures of Superman*," Rhonda Wilcox argues that Lois is oblivious to Lex's evil plans, but Clark/Superman has superior knowledge and can see through Lex's facade. She concludes, "The audience is thus aligned with the male lead in knowing more about the villainy of the business world than the female lead does, even though she is at the top of her profession" (2000: 97). The audience's perceptual alignment with Superman is upheld, but in *Smallville* that bond is broken. Rather than the familiar pleasure of identification common to teen drama, a certain distance is maintained. Thus the entire structure of the show replicates the more specific pleasures of a closeted reading of the narrative. If the show creates pleasure by playing to the knowing viewer's superior understanding rather than through identification, the better or deeper the understanding the greater the pleasure. The viewer reading for race and sexuality also has a better grasp of the narrative, albeit an alternative narrative, so he or she can see the stories unfolding better than everyone else, and therefore enjoys the show even more.

While this analysis may suggest a certain equivalence in interpretive power offered by a raced or queer reading, the story makes clear that not all oppressions are created equal. The costs of racial and sexual outing are set in contrast particularly when comparing Lex to Lana. Lex's investigation into Clark's secret is morally suspect; the implication being that Lex would use evidence of Clark's superpowers for his own nefarious purposes. Lana, on the other hand, may feel betrayed but poses no immediate threat. Furthermore, Lana, as the facilitator of Clark's buried racial history is consistently played as innocent and morally pure while Lex is far more ambiguous. Add to this the fact, known to all fans of the Superman myth, that Lex will one day be Clark's enemy, and the differences between the two become clear. Lex acts as a corrupting influence who would frame Clark's outing as a dangerous and maybe fatal move, while Lana offers the possibility of an outing that would alter but may not end their relationship. As a real-world corollary, the revelation of a mixed-race heritage might slow down Michael Rosenbaum's career, but a sexual outing would probably severely curtail if not end it if previous celebrity outings are any predictor. The show suggests that the costs to Clark of revealing his secret, of coming out of the closet racially, would not be the same as coming out sexually. Thus the peculiar overtones of sadism, while present for both readings, are less dire for racial outing.

Smallville is a powerful text for both queer and racialized readings. It illustrates the ways in which such reading offers to both empower and disempower the knowing reader. The very same structure that enables one to create new meanings also depends on the phenomenon of passing and denies the viewer the unadulterated pleasures of identification and representation. The Superman story deals directly with secrets as a source of power and disempowerment, since Clark's abilities force him to pass and cut him off from true intimacy. Yet "outing" the text compensates with other, more complex, pleasures. It enables us to push ourselves into the frame and to recognize the spaces for race and sexuality in texts that may overtly exclude or ignore "us."

In reading Lana/Kreuk as multiracial there is the pleasure of knowing she can transgress the strictures of race. She gets to be the American, small-town cheerleader and Asian as well. The ability to be the one who is unmarked has traditionally been the position of power. Much like the brief historical moments when Asians were juridically "unclaimed," the vaguely demarcated boundaries of hapa identity gives her freedom to play other races while still "representin." As a knowing viewer, I can participate in and applaud this play by outing Lana/Kreuk in the comfort of my own living room. So, why do I watch *Smallville*? It's not for the god-awful dialogue or the corporate rock soundtrack. Nor do I take pleasure in identifying with Lana/Kreuk in a type of raw "Asian sisters" conception of identification. Rather, I enjoy the distance I feel from the character who is not even aware of her own closeted status and the sense that I know and understand more about their beloved Lana than all the inhabitants of Smallville. I watch to see Lana Lang getting past the cultural filters that would claim that race (or sexuality) has no place in Smallville.

NOTES

The author would like to thank Kim Hester-Williams, Lisa Nakamura, and the co-editors of this collection for their thoughtful reading of this essay. Portions of this essay were presented at the 2002 Association of Asian American Studies and the 2003 Society for Cinema and Media Studies conferences. I'd like to thank the audiences at those conference panels for their helpful comments.

1. In this article, I use the term "hapa" to refer specifically to racially mixed Asians. The term, which originated in local Hawaiian dialect, is in popular use among mixed-race Asian Americans; see, for example, the group Hapa Issues Forum. However, it is still a controversial term as some Native Hawaiians have accused mainland Asian Americans of cultural appropriation in their use of the term.

2. See Michaelangelo Signorile, *Queer in America* (1993), and Warren Johansson and William A. Percy's *Outing: Shattering the Conspiracy of Silence* (1994).

3. Specific instances include *Takao Ozawa v. U.S.* (1922) and *U.S. v. Thind* (1923). Ozawa, an American of Japanese descent, and Thind, an American of Asian Indian descent, both brought cases before the U.S. Supreme Court arguing that they should be considered white under the law, an important classification since only white persons were allowed to become citizens. While both lost their cases, they are significant because the issue of racial categorization for Asians was still subject to debate. Further discussion of the cases can be found in Don T. Nakanishi and James S. Lai, *Asian American Politics: Law, Participation, and Policy* (2003).

4. In his on-line journal "Terribly Happy" the author of the *Smallville* recaps, Omar, reports that the writers for the show have written to Television without Pity to say that they read and enjoy the show synopses.

5. While Engle gives a compelling argument for Superman's tie to Jewish ethnicity in the comic, I would argue that the mythology of the television show lends itself even more powerfully to the metaphor of race over ethnicity. Superman is not merely an alien; he is another species entirely. Given the long history of understanding the racial Other as less than or other than human, ideas of racial mixing and passing figure strongly in this reading.

6. I am indebted to Kaja Silverman's book *Male Subjectivity at the Margins* (1992) for introducing me to the concept of male masochism. However, her suggestion of the liberatory potential of the male who says "no" to power presupposes a prior access to that phallic power. I would argue that the position of the raced or queer male body exists in different relation to hegemonic power and, thus, must be read in a different political context.

7. Tasha Oren also pointed out to me the ways in which the scene raises the painful specter of Matthew Shepard and the prevalence of high school gay bashing hidden under the guise of a "prank."

8. See articles by Anton Karl Kozlovic (2003) and Sarah R. Kozloff (1981) who analyze the religious overtones of the Superman story.

9. I would like to point out that an entirely different set of questions arise on multiracial forums as opposed to Asian American forums. While Asian American forums deal specifically with whether or not we can "count" Reeves as Asian, the multiracial forums are more interested in claiming Reeves as part of a separate multiracial category. For a discussion of racial categorization and multiracial people, see articles by Cynthia L. Nakashima (2001) and David Parker and Miri Song (2001).

10. It is worth noting that in the series *Lois and Clark* Superman is played by Dean Cain, who consistently shows up on mixed-race lists as part Japanese.

WORKS CITED

Butler, Judith. *Bodies That Matter: On the Discursive Limits of "Sex."* New York: Routledge, 1993.

DeAngelis, Michael. *Gay Fandom and Crossover Stardom: James Dean, Mel Gibson, and Keanu Reeves.* Durham: Duke University Press, 2001.

Doty, Alexander. *Making Things Perfectly Queer.* Minneapolis: University of Minnesota Press, 1993.

Engle, Gary. "What Makes Superman So Darn American?" In *Superman at Fifty! The Persistence of a Legend.* Eds. Dennis Dooley and Gary Engle. New York: CollierBooks, 1987.

Goldensea/Asian American Supersite. [http://goldsea.com]. Retrieved July 1, 2003.

IIstix: Trapped Inside the Asian Mind. [http://www.iistix.com/_tableofcontents/toc.html]. Retrieved July 1, 2003.

Johansson, Warren, and William A. Percy. *Outing: Shattering the Conspiracy of Silence.* New York: Huntington Park Press, 1994.

Kozloff, Sarah R. "Superman as Savior: Christian Allegory in the Superman Movies." *Journal of Popular Film and Television* 9:2 (Summer 1981): 78–82.

Kozlovic, Anton Karl. "The Unholy Biblical Subtexts and Other Religious Elements Built into *Superman: The Movie* (1978) and *Superman II* (1981)." *Journal of Religion and Film* 7:1 (April 2003): 46–62.

Lorde, Audre. *Sister Outsider.* Trumansburg, N.Y.: Crossing Press, 1984.

Mercer, Kobena. *Welcome to the Jungle: New Positions in Black Cultural Studies.* New York: Routledge, 1994.

Nakanishi, Don T., and James S. Lai. *Asian American Politics: Law, Participation, and Policy.* New York: Rowman and Littlefield, 2003.

Nakashima, Cynthia L. "Servants of Culture: The Symbolic Role of Mixed-Race Asians in American Discourse." In *The Sum of Our Parts: Mixed Heritage Asian*

Americans. Eds. Teresa Williams-León and Cynthia L. Nakashima. Philadelphia: Temple University Press, 2001.

Parker, David, and Miri Song. "Introduction." *Rethinking Mixed Race.* Eds. David Parker and Miri Song. London: Pluto Press, 2001.

Scorpion King. Dir. Chuck Russell. Perf. Dwayne Johnson (The Rock) and Kelly Hsu. Universal Studios. 2003.

Sedgwick, Eve Kosofsky. *Epistemology of the Closet.* Berkeley: University of California Press, 1986, rpr. 1990.

Signorile, Michelangelo. *Queer in America: Sex, the Media, and the Closets of Power.* New York: Random House, 1993.

Silverman, Kaja. *Male Subjectivity at the Margins.* New York: Routledge, 1992.

Smallville. [http://www.thewb.com/Shows/Show/0,7353,%7C%7C126,00.html]. Retrieved July 1, 2003.

Takagi, Dana. "Maiden Voyage: Excursion into Sexuality and Identity Politics in Asian America." In *Asian American Studies: A Reader.* Eds. Jean Yu-wen Shen Wu and Min Song. New Brunswick, N.J.: Rutgers University Press, 2000.

Television without Pity. [http://www.televisionwithoutpity.com]. Retrieved July 1, 2003.

Terribly Happy. [http://www.terribly-happy.com]. Retrieved July 1, 2003.

Wilcox, Rhonda V. "Lois's Locks: Trust and Representation in *Lois and Clark: The New Adventures of Superman.*" In *Fantasy Girls: Gender in the New Universe of Science Fiction and Fantasy Television.* Ed. Elyce Rae Helford. Lanham, Md.: Rowman and Littlefield, 2000.

Williams-León, Teresa. "The Convergence of Passing Zones: Multiracial Gays, Lesbians, and Bisexuals of Asian Descent." In *The Sum of Our Parts: Mixed Heritage Asian Americans.* Eds. Teresa Williams-León and Cynthia L. Nakashima. Philadelphia: Temple University Press, 2001.

Chapter 15

Cibo Matto's *Stereotype A*
Articulating Asian American Hip Pop

Jane C. H. Park

In 1996 Yuka Honda and Miho Hatori, of the now defunct independent hip hop/alternative pop band Cibo Matto, appeared on a special food segment of MTV's *House of Style*. The Japanese-born female musicians served as guides on a culinary tour of fashionable ethnic cuisines in New York City. The stint followed the release of their debut album, *Viva! La Woman* by Warner Bros. Records, which contained songs heavily laced with food themes and imagery. A few years later, Hatori and Honda performed on PBS's *Sessions on West 54th* to promote their second album, *Stereotype A*. In response to host John Hyatt's question, "Do you consider New York your spiritual home?" Hatori replied in the affirmative, saying the group's cultural and musical roots lay in the multicultural milieu of downtown New York. Apparent in these two media representations is a distinct shift in the popular perception of Cibo Matto—from the latest Japanese novelty band in 1996 to a serious Japanese American alternative pop group three years later. How and why did this shift take place? And what strategies does the band's short history provide for dealing differently with gender and racial stereotypes in popular culture?

Introduction

This essay looks at how Cibo Matto (hereafter CM) was marketed to appeal to an American alternative pop and hip hop audience. What racial, sexual, and cultural terms did the music press use to frame and sell CM?

How do these terms relate to historical representations of Asian and Asian American women in the United States? Finally, how did the band acknowledge and engage with these representations in its songs? I try to answer these questions by positioning the group within the larger stories of hip hop and women in popular music and by showing how its unique identity as an Asian American female band contributes to these histories. More specifically, I consider the ways in which CM's music and their image as technologically savvy female artists suggest a new way to critique existing racial and gender stereotypes of Asian and Asian American women in the United States.

No extended academic analysis has been done on this particular group, and little scholarship exists on Asian Americans in popular music. My work on CM does not claim to represent the experiences of minority groups in U.S. media or those of contemporary Japanese female pop bands. Rather, it provides a case study of one such band and its members' attempts to negotiate the double legacy of racism and sexism in the American popular music industry. However, before attempting to answer larger questions about the band's social and political significance, it is necessary to provide some background on its conception, development, and reception.

Not Another Shonen Knife

Journalist Yuka Honda and student Miho Hatori met in New York during the early 1990s while playing in an avant-garde punk band called Leitoh Lychee. When the group broke up, the two decided to start their own band and christened it Cibo Matto ("food crazy" in Italian). Their first self-titled CD was released in 1995 through the Japanese independent label, People's Records, and sold twenty thousand copies.[1] Given the publicity of their recording ventures, their connections with Yoko Ono, the Beastie Boys and the Lounge Lizards, and their growing New York fan base, CM was recruited by Warner Bros. Records in 1996.

Viva! La Woman (hereafter *Viva*) was released and appeared on the lists of top ten hip hop albums for 1996 in *Spin* and *Rolling Stone.* In the album Hatori raps fiercely in broken, heavily accented English against Honda's cool sonic patchwork—eclectic, upbeat samples of popular musical kitsch. Critics seized upon the food imagery in the album and the group's ethnic and gender identities to link them with Shonen Knife (hereafter

SK), another alternative Japanese female band, which also sang about food. The comparison works to a point. Both bands use highly metaphoric, often surrealistic language to evoke a mixture of English and Japanese cultural sensibilities and to conflate lyrically tropes of food, sex, and nation. As well the bands demonstrate a similar kind of musical hybridity in their layering of pop, rock, and punk elements into a kind of uncannily familiar sonic pastiche. This pastiche seems to resonate for an American audience due in part to the bands' ambivalent performance styles—not quite "straight" but not outright parody either.

Outside these similarities, however, the bands had little in common. SK's punk-pop sound and DIY approach affiliated them with the west coast punk and grunge music scene, while CM's music and image linked them to the alternative hip hop and electronica scene in New York.[2] SK songs revolve around supergirly, childlike topics like cats, Barbie dolls, and junk food. Their sound is consistent and easily recognizable: the songs are short with minimalist punk chords, tinny guitar, and heavily accented lyrics that carry a chirpy *carpe diem* message. CM's songs, on the other hand, show a broader stylistic range, mixing different cultural genres—from bossa nova, disco-funk, and jazz to rap, R&B, down tempo, and heavy metal.

Furthermore, CM differs from SK in the way its songs express female sexuality, power, and vulnerability. In other words, *how* CM sings about food, aliens, and sex is noticeably different from the way that SK treats the same topics. Whereas SK celebrates jellybean attacks, CM compares the layers of an artichoke heart to that of a woman whose lover "keeps peeling [her] petals one by one." In a song entitled "Theme," the link between food and sex becomes even more explicit in lyrics like, "He stared me up and down as if I was a restaurant menu." When cute coyness is employed, it is deliberately performative and soon shattered by Ono-esque screams or Beastie-like rapping.

Also, unlike SK members, who remain based in Osaka and identify as native Japanese, Honda and Hatori refer to themselves as an "American band run by Asian people."[3] Hatori makes a connection between their ambiguous national and cultural affiliations and the formal syncretism of their music—a connection I elaborate on later. She jokes, "People always expect you to choose sides between digital or analog, old school or new school, even between Chinese or Italian food. Well, we eat everything."[4]

Finally, while SK is friends with feminist-identified bands L7 and Bikini Kill, its members take a nonfeminist stance, preferring to see themselves as musicians before women: "We never thought of ourselves as a female band."[5] CM members, on the other hand, are quick to identify as feminists and to recognize the sexist and racist stereotypes the press sometimes has conferred on them. Take for instance Yuka Honda's musings in a 1999 interview with Heidi Sherman:

> It's hard for people to take us seriously. We are girls, so they ask us who writes our music. We have all these food titles, so people kind of put us in this novelty band category. With the last album [*Viva*] people would ask us, "Do you think you're stereotyped?" But afterward they would ask, "What's your favorite food?" You know, things they would never ask me if I were the drummer of The Roots.[6]

Cutesy J-Pop, with an Edge

As Honda points out, critics often lumped CK with bands like SK and Pizzicato 5 based on the bands' shared national origin, ambiguous "cute" image, and penchant for food and pop culture themes. One example appears in a 1998 article by music critic Neil Strauss in the *New York Times*. "New Sounds from Japan: A Starter's Kit" presents a kind of Western ethnomusicologist's guide to the obscurely hip music scene of a culture that has become synonymous with high-tech gadgetry, video games, and Japanese animation. It lists several new and upcoming Japanese artists, the majority of them male, in various musical categories.[7] Strauss legitimates these artists by likening their inevitable "invasion" of the U.S. popular music scene to the British rock invasion led by the Beatles in the 1960s. The taxonomy of Japanese musicians ends with a category Strauss labels *kawaii,* which contains the only two female bands in his guide: Shonen Knife and Cibo Matto.

The Japanese term *kawaii* translates as "cute" and is used to describe a gendered aesthetic style that melds the image of the underaged, sometimes coyly innocent nymphet with the pleasures of consumer capitalism. Japanese imports in the United States bearing the mark of the *kawaii* style include the Sanrio family of toys, and anime [Japanese cartoon] television programs such as *Sailor Moon* and *Pokemon.* The schoolgirl look so popular in Japan has found its U.S. equivalent in the explicitly sexual versions of the "bubblegum pop" star personae epitomized by young female musicians like Britney Spears and Christina Aguilera.

Rather than unwittingly or willingly falling under this category, Honda and Hatori playfully critique it. They do so by exploring—in their lyrics, music, and performance styles—the complex set of questions about female objectification, subjectivity, and agency raised by this image of infantilized female sexuality. From the start, CM members quite consciously engaged with the widespread stereotype of Asian women generally and Japanese women specifically as cute, naive, and girlish—a stereotype that links the desirable "innocence" of Japanese women to that of the early 1960s all-American girl. Some critics seemed to comprehend their strategy:

> The bare description of Cibo Matto sounds like a gimmick or a put-on: two Japanese women from the Lower East Side of Manhattan, a vocalist (Miho Hatori) and a sound manipulator (Yuka Honda), with an entire album of songs about food, from "White Pepper Ice Cream" to "Beef Jerky." But in Cibo Matto's songs, food encompasses love and sensuality, memory and anticipation.[8]

Others missed it altogether:

> It's just what you'd expect from a novelty act whose name means "food crazy" in Italian and whose every song is about love, cuisine and love of cuisine.[9]

> The group is two Japanese women, Miho Hatori and Yuka Honda, who live in New York and are infatuated with contemporary pop music that uses "sampling"—a technique that treats a song like a tossed salad, lacing the melody with exotic and arresting sound effects. But that's just the start. Cibo Matto also has a major food fixation. The group's name is Italian for "food crazy."[10]

Others seemed to like what CM was doing, but weren't quite sure what to make of it:

> Imagine that Beck and Bjork had a love child in Tokyo, and you might get some idea of this delightful blend of hip-hop, scat-rap, scraps of reggae and experimental ambient noise. . . . These songs are either very deep or very silly, but either way they often come across like a string of Japanese haiku poems tacked together.[11]

Listening to Cibo Matto's global-economic synthesis feels like crashing into some cartoon netherworld where Abba waltzes with Kraftwerk at Studio 54. In other words, it sounds fake—but not in a bad way. . . . Like a spoonful of sorbet, Cibo Matto dazzles the tongue for an instant, then melts.[12]

Lost and Found in Translation

Most likely, the ambivalent framing of CM results from the relative invisibility of Japanese popular music in mainstream America. Japanese female musicians whose work has migrated to the United States include the pop duo, Pink Lady; the "Japanese Madonna," Matsuda Seiko; the lead singer of postmodern pop group Pizzicato 5, Maki Nomiya; and the indie rock trio, Buffalo Daughter. Of this short list, those who have managed to succeed in the United States, Shonen Knife, Pizzicato 5, Buffalo Daughter, and Cibo Matto, tend to attract an alternative audience that emphasizes the groups' distinctly "Japanese" look and sound.[13] The audience base for these bands seems to differ little from the critics in their attraction to the "exotic" element of the bands' representation.

What is significant here is not so much that these bands self-consciously perform Oriental tropes but that critics and fans have been so quick to conflate these performances with the musicians' racial and gender identities. To a large extent, this kind of reception can be seen as the outcome of the "Japanese chic" trend that began in the early 1980s—a new kind of consumer Orientalism which exploded in the late nineties due to the rising popularity of East Asian aesthetic forms in Hong Kong action cinema, Japanese animation, video games, and fashion. While this kind of crossover brings visibility to Japanese and East Asian peoples and cultures in the West, it often tends to mark them as permanently foreign, since their salability depends on their difference from the perceived norm. Alvin Liu, assistant arts editor for the *San Francisco Bay Guardian,* notes this double bind: "Japanese artists who succeed in the United States . . . offer a new spin on old forms, combining once-familiar pop formulas in ways that may not have occurred to an artist in the United States or Europe" (1999). He goes on to mention that the potential danger for groups that do find an audience in the West lies in their almost inevitable exoticization as "novelty acts" by fans and critics.[14]

CM differs from the other Japanese-born groups mentioned in that, with the release of *SA,* they self-identified as Asian American. By doing so, they challenged the traditional idea of Asian Americans as individuals born in the United States who have assimilated culturally and can speak English fluently. They point instead to a new kind of "Asian American" represented by the growing number of transnational immigrants from East Asia who seem able to negotiate and bridge more easily the "Asian" and "American" elements of their identities. They also point to a growing acceptance in the United States, especially among American youth who have been raised on Japanese and Hong Kong popular culture, of East Asian peoples and styles as not so solidly foreign, but rather uncannily familiar. This acceptance—which often rides a dimly discernible line between appropriation and appreciation—appears heavily in hip hop culture: in the lyrics and styles of groups as diverse as the Wu Tang Clan, Common, Dead Prez, the Beastie Boys, and DMX. The established presence of Asian references in hip hop and CM's association with the alternative hip hop scene in downtown New York laid the groundwork for Hatori and Honda to make their musical debut by deconstructing hip hop, the now global language of youth and popular culture, using another, older global language, that of food and consumption.

In *Representing*, Craig Watkins discusses the cross-marketability of hip hop in social and political terms. He defines hip hop as a social movement in that it "enables its participants to imagine themselves as part of a larger community"—both through the creative use of technology in songs, performances, and recordings and the synergistic production and consumption of hip hop "lifestyles."[15] A group like CM provides a way to look at how this political element of hip hop double translates, to Japan in the 1990s and then back to the United States via Japanese American immigrant artists. In "Hip Hop and Racial Desire in Contemporary Japan," Nina Cornyetz asserts that hip hop provides a political use-value for young Japanese fans—but one different from the use-value for hip hop audiences in other places and times. To explain, she turns to sampling, the process of entering analog sound sources (usually loops from older songs, though for more abstract artists, snippets can come from primary sounds such as recorded traffic noise or the din of restaurant conversations) into the sampler, an instrument that records these sources in digital form, allowing them to be edited, manipulated, and sutured into new compositions.[16]

According to Cornyetz, sampling can be linked to the production of Japanese national subjectivity in two ways. First, it echoes cultural and economic strategies that Japan has used to reposition itself in the global order since World War II. In the same way that disenfranchised black and Latino Bronx youth in the 1970s created a new expressive form by rearranging the musical materials around them, Japan used Western economic and cultural models to assert its identity in the postindustrial transnational world order. Second, contemporary Japanese hip hop fans, like most youth, are positioned outside the dominant culture. In Japan, this culture tries to interpellate them as corporate drones ("sararimen") and well-behaved housewives. Through its musical and visual style, hip hop gives these Japanese youth a tool with which to critique the dominant culture and to construct a future wherein they might reclaim subjectivity on their own terms.[17]

As native-born Japanese women who call New York City home, CM members Hatori and Honda occupy a transnational space that cuts across subculture and dominant culture, Japan and America, commercial and old school hip hop. As Hatori sings in "Sunday Part II," they are living in a "second world." It is a position fraught with misunderstanding and prone to misinterpretation as evidenced by the band's reception. Clearly, the lumping together of CM with other Japanese and female bands on the basis of a combined racial, national, and sexual identity fits squarely into Edward Said's definition of orientalism.[18] At the same time, it also recalls similar ghettoizations in contemporary U.S. popular music—in particular, the commercialized reduction of female groups and musicians such as L7, Hole, P. J. Harvey, and Liz Phair under the banner of "Women in Rock,"[19] and the invisibility of female musicians as producers and DJs relative to their vocalist and MC counterparts.

As the Grammy Awards ceremony demonstrates every year, ghettoizations in the music industry continue to exist along the lines of both gender and race. At the same time, the use of new technologies to create and express different musical styles has begun to challenge the racist and sexist assumptions that undergird the marginalization of women, people of color, and musicians who fit both categories. It is to these technologies and their potential for social and political change that I now turn.

Technology, Race, Gender, . . . and Music

In her article, "Just a Girl?" Gayle Wald describes how the music press used the construction of "innocent" femininity to pit SK and CM against their less "girly" Riot Grrl counterparts. Wald's primary argument is that Riot

Grrls strategically reappropriate the site of girlhood to "construct alternative modes of visibility for women in independent rock." In a brief, provocative section at the end, she contrasts the gendered roles assumed in the music scene by Riot Grrl and these Japanese bands:

> In short, such a deliberate performance [by the Riot Grrls] assumes a subject for whom girlishness precludes, or is in conflict with, cultural agency. But what of women whose modes of access to, and mobility within, the public sphere depend on their supposed embodiment of a girlish ideal?[20]

In other words, what of nonwhite, non-American women whose only form of visible subjectivity within the Western context is one that simultaneously infantilizes them and marks them as "other"? The opposition that Wald describes displaces the prefeminist notion of "girl" from the bodies of white women onto those of Japanese women specifically and Asian women generally. The trivialization of Japanese female bands like CM recalls and troubles the discursive segregation of "pop" and "rock" music that began with the arrival of the Beatles and subsequent ousting of the girl groups in the United States. In her essay "(R)evolution Now," Norma Coates gives a concise summary of the relationship between pop and rock that followed this shift:

> In this schema, rock is metonymic with "authenticity" while "pop" is metonymic with "artifice." Sliding even further down the metonymic slope, "authentic" becomes "masculine" while "artificial" becomes "feminine." Rock, therefore, is "masculine," pop is "feminine," and the two are set in a binary relation to each other, with the masculine . . . on top.[21]

Coates's point on gender applies as well to race and nationality in the context of CM's initial reception as exotic Japanese "others" putting a quaint spin on hip hop. In this perception of the group, the stereotype of Japanese specifically and East Asians generally as clever imitators of Western styles connects neatly to the sexist association of female musicians with pop and artifice. CM easily could have succumbed to the rock-pop, authentic-inauthentic binary by producing a second album that clearly went one way: either explicitly commercial bubblegum pop or "serious" alternative rock. Instead, Hatori and Honda followed in the footsteps of friends like Prince Paul, Dan the Automator, and Yoko Ono by producing, in SA, a generically hybrid work that refuses categorization. As in Viva, they do so through an expert manipulation of musical technologies during recordings and performances.

Later in her essay, Coates could be referring to CM when she posits a potential rethinking of the male, authentic rock–female, inauthentic pop binary based on the use of new musical technologies by marginal groups:

> The onset of new musical trends such as techno, digital sampling, and the increased reliance upon studio technologies to enhance and stimulate musical production has provoked a rethinking of the concept of authenticity.[22]

Coates is referring here to attitudes toward and uses of technology that define hip hop and electronica, an umbrella category for genres such as techno, drum-and-bass, house, and down tempo (formerly trip-hop), which rely heavily on technological instruments: samplers, sequencers, and synthesizers. Consider as well the following description of rap as "a complex fusion of orality and postmodern technology" in Tricia Rose's *Black Noise*:[23]

> The arrangement and selection of sounds rap musicians have invented via samples, turntables, tape machines, and sound systems are at once *deconstructive* (in that they actually take apart recorded musical compositions) and *recuperative* (because they recontextualize these elements creating new meanings for cultural sounds that have been relegated to commercial waste bins).[24]

To put it another way, hip hop and electronica use various technologies to deconstruct and reconstruct sound fragments in much the same way that marginal subjects create identities for themselves in a society that refuses to acknowledge them as wholly human. These subjects recontextualize the cultural labels that have been thrust upon them—poor, female, immigrant, black, Latina, queer, Asian—to create powerful new identities whose truth and strength reside in the continued acknowledgment of their painful histories. In this way, the process of reclaiming marginal identity or experience can be likened to the construction, performance, and reception of hip hop and electronic music. Furthermore, the techniques of sampling, rapping, recording, and sequencing can help create a type of layered, polyglot voice that offers an alternative interpretation of authenticity, the big idea underlying and perpetuating the rock-pop binary. Hip hop and electronica—when it is good and it works—consists of questioning this binary and the notion of the "authentic" self and text as fixed, coherent, and comprehensible.

Racialized Cyborg-Girls

This section begins a discussion that attempts to tie many of the ideas presented so far, particularly issues of nation, gender, and technology. As such, it functions as a kind of preliminary theoretical road map for exploring how female artists of color might produce trenchant social critique through stylistic and cultural juxtapositions that stem from a genuine appreciation for difference. The link between music as art-in-process and self as subject-in-process is a major theme in most of CM's songs, which incorporate a conscious, innovative use of digital technologies. The two project an image of cosmopolitan sophistication, reinforced by the Dada quality of their lyrics and the hip, futuristic image they project on their album covers, music videos, and live performances. For instance, the inside cover of *VLW* foregrounds Hatori and Honda in a studio cluttered with recording equipment, skateboards, and computers. This image runs counter to traditional ideas of the female musician as technologically incompetent, fit only to head a band with her voice and sex appeal or to occupy the background as a backup singer or dancer.

In a *New York Times* article on the 1998 Winter Musical Conference in Miami, Evelyn McDonnell notes the absence of female musicians in electronica. After listing artists such as Bjork and Beth Orton, McDonnell points out that they are mostly vocalists who do not fit the image of the male electronica musician—the "science nerd, madly fiddling with a wall of machines"—now a fixture in the popular music scene thanks to folks such as David Byrne, the Chemical Brothers, Moby, and Fatboy Slim. According to McDonnell, female artists such as Pauline Oliveros, Laurie Anderson, and Cibo Matto who do fiddle with walls of machines disprove the stereotype of women as technophobic. However, when the press does acknowledge such artists, it frames them as exceptions to the general rule: "When women run the gizmos, they are considered . . . iconoclastic loners —performance artists. When men do it, they create a genre in their own image."[25]

While the sexy female geek remains marginal in popular music, alternative-minded artists like CM, Le Tigre, DJ Shortee, and others, along with a burgeoning group of younger female electronica musicians,[26] *have* started to create a genre in their own image, albeit one yet to be widely acknowledged. Consider, for example, the following scene: an October 30, 1999, performance on *Sessions at West 54th*. Yuka Honda, wearing wired bunny ears, nonchalantly inserts floppy disks into a computer synthesizer while a pig-tailed Hatori sings soulfully into the microphone. The boys—Timo Ellis, Duma Love, and Sean Lennon—provide backup. The camera focuses on the two Japanese women performing their artistic and commercial negotiations with "kawaii," jumping up and down, punk-pogo style, shooting quick smiles at each other across the stage.[27] This scene heralds the arrival of what I call the active racialized cyborg-girl, a subject that speaks through, with, and as a new kind of human-machine.

Donna Haraway defined the cyborg in 1991 as an entity simultaneously organic and inorganic, human and machine. In the "Cyborg Manifesto," she uses the trope of the cyborg primarily to critique and trouble heteronormative notions of gender and sexuality, and in *Modest_Witness* (1997) she attempts to do the same with race and ethnicity. CM members perform Haraway's concept of the gender-transgressive cyborg, but put a different spin on it as diasporic Japanese female artists. They do so first, by *defying musical categorization,* revealing the inherent instability of genre categories in popular music and second, by *using technology as image and instrument* to critique historical stereotypes of Asian women in the United States.

Yoko, the Pioneer

The lineage of the racialized cyborg-girl can be traced back to Yoko Ono, the Japanese American musician, poet and performance artist whom Beatles fans still vilify as the "dragon lady" who stole John Lennon away from his British musical brethren. As an incomprehensible Dragon Lady who refused to play the Lotus Blossom, Ono received brutal treatment from the media in the 1960s and 1970s. As she put it in an interview with Amei Wallach, "I think the image of the Asian woman up until me was Madam Butterfly. . . . I was touching a sacred cow, but I also didn't seem to be that vulnerable woman who is going to commit suicide. I was coming right at your face." This rebellious attitude earned Ono labels like "John Rennon's Excrusive Gloupie" from *Esquire* magazine in 1961. After years of condemnation from Beatles fans, Ono is finally being acknowledged as an artist in her own right with her role in the band IMA, which she founded with her son Sean Ono Lennon, and art exhibitions such as "Yes Yoko Ono" at the Whitney Museum in fall 2000.[28]

Lennon and Ono first met at her one-woman show in London's Indica Gallery in 1966 when she was an up-and-coming New York avant-garde artist associated with the Fluxus art movement. Fluxus members John Cage, Nam June Paik, Walter De Maria, Richard Maxfield, Terry Riley, and others were interested in dissolving the barriers between media forms. Their work led eventually to the creation of what is now known as performance art. After marrying Lennon, Ono continued her experiments in sound, video, and image by collaborating with him on B-sides and albums such as *Double Fantasy* and *Yoko Ono/Plastic Ono Band.* She was also a vocal activist in the women's movement and the antiwar movement, and she and Lennon performed their political views with controversial events such as bed-ins, bagism, "happenings," and the scandalous *Two Virgins* album cover, which featured the newlyweds nude.[29] As a cofounder of Fluxus, a collaborator with Lennon, and an undervalued artist who, like Andy Warhol, turned her celebrity into art, Ono paved the way for many contemporary Asian American female artists, including Cibo Matto.

Like Ono, Honda and Hatori posit a new kind of gendered racial identity for Asian Americans. At the same time, like Ono, they remain stuck in a web of old stereotypes that continue to be reproduced in slightly different forms. They engaged with these stereotypes by openly acknowledging and playing with them in their second album.

Playing (with) Stereotypes

Critical reception for *SA* mostly reflected the shift in the band's narrative and formal focus. In this album, the group tried to shake off its image as a food-obsessed novelty band. Honda and Hatori ousted former producers, Mitchell Froom and Tchad Blake, to produce the songs themselves, with the help of several musical friends, including Timo Ellis, Sean Lennon (whom Honda was dating at the time), Marc Ribot, Medeski, Martin & Wood, Soul Coughing, and Buffalo Daughter, another Japanese American female band.[30] Unlike *Viva* the songs in *SA* seldom refer to food and tend to veer toward self-consciously crafted art pop rather than staying within a more recognizably hip hop aesthetic. In the first week of its release, the album shot up to the top of the College Music Journal (CMJ) Chart, the official monitor of alternative radio. A few reviewers continued to take

CM less seriously than their male counterparts. The comment below, for example, attributes CM's elevation to "proper band" status to the addition of two new male members, Sean Lennon and Timo Ellis:

> The 2-year-old Cibo Matto scrambles cocktail music, jazz, funk, hip-hop, punk. . . . They were cute and precious early; midway they were joined by "guests, friends and semi-permanent members, like family," bassist Sean Lennon (famous lineage, plays in IMA) and drummer Russell Simons [*sic*] (John Spencer Blues Explosion/IMA). The sound became more ferocious, and they emerged from the "novelty" shroud.[31]

> The most obvious change, though (between VLW and CM) is that they actually sound like a proper band now, thanks to the presence of Sean Lennon and Timo Ellis.[32]

However, most critics at this point seemed to "get" the band's use of complex cultural juxtapositions and their "knowing wink" at an audience that also presumably "got" the message. Note the use of the adjective "faux" in the comment below, which indicates that the reviewer knows the group is performing a staged form of innocence for a smart, appreciative audience.

> They (Hatori and Honda) were giggly faux-naifs, especially onstage. Fans with New York predilections enjoyed picking up all the allusions, letting the concept carry the group when the music grew thin.[33]

Sonic Fusion Cuisine: Tying It Together

According to Honda, the primary concept behind *Stereotype A* was the work of locating and constructing the self (or selves) in sound rather than in image. Like taste, sound has been relegated to a subordinate position vis-à-vis sight in Western epistemology. The privileging of sight is most evident in the rationalist equation of visibility sometimes with power (the assumption that making visible the histories of marginalized groups automatically grants those groups an equal "voice" in dominant discourse) and at other times with powerlessness (Mulvey's still relevant concept of the male gaze objectifying the "to-be-looked-at" female body in Hollywood cinema).

CM explores the radical possibilities of sound both as art and communication by drawing from and articulating various types of music in new ways. Hip hop, electronica, pop, punk, metal, disco, and noise are just a few of the musical styles showcased in their songs. CM produces a kind of sonic fusion cuisine in both albums. While the fusion element is most apparent in the culinary references in *Viva! La Woman*, the same fascination with throwing together different, sometimes wildly disparate sound fragments—like ingredients in an impromptu recipe—is also evident in *Stereotype A*. Honda talks about the food imagery in *VLW* as universal metaphors: "Food is a great metaphor, because everybody eats. Everybody knows the feeling when you're hungry for five hours and you have some kind of junk food and it tastes so amazing. It's a common experience." And Hatori adds that food and the experience of eating can provide a universal narrative language: "When I wrote the songs on the album, my vocabulary was limited, and using food is the easiest way to tell a story."[34] In both albums, Hatori and Honda try to create an affective language based on eclectic sonic ambience—a language that elicits a particular visceral and emotional response that cannot be contained or adequately described through words and images alone. *Viva* uses food allusions to create this language (stressing the sense of taste and smell), while *SA* uses allusions to popular musical styles (stressing sound).

CM members contend that like taste, sound is one way of breaking down racial and sexual stereotypes, which historically denigrate others' phenotypical traits such as skin color, facial features, and secondary sex characteristics rather than listening to what the others have to say. Honda suggests that people focus less on sight and more on "communication" to locate themselves in relation to others within their social and cultural environments.

> Stereo is . . . what tells you where you are located. Dolphins can see what is happening with their sense of hearing. . . . We have to learn to listen for ourselves. . . . and not just believe everything we're told.[35]

And in "Birthday Cake" Hatori deconstructs feminine cuteness by using it to close a flippantly violent history of the 1960s:

> You were born in the 60's
> You made war with the Vietnamese
> We loved LSD
> We died easily
> Can't we just say c'est la vie?

Extra sugar extra salt
Extra oil and MSG
SHUT UP AND EAT
TOO BAD NO BON APPETIT
You know my love is sweet

Like Ono, CM publicly identify as political activists in interviews. Their friends include members of feminist bands such as Le Tigre and Buffalo Daughter as well as musicians like Mike D of the Beastie Boys who are well known for their activism in the environmental and Free Tibet movements. In the summer of 1999 CM demonstrated its support for political causes by performing at Lilith Fair and the Tibetan Freedom Concert. And in the fall of 2001 the band participated in benefit concerts in New York for the New York Women's Foundation, the New York Association of New Americans, and the American Red Cross Disaster Relief Fund.[36] Regardless of the publicity motive behind such appearances, the band's overt association with such causes bespeaks a political consciousness.

However, Honda and Hatori's political views are most effective when they are performed, subtly and metaphorically, in their songs. Like Honda's creative sampling, which makes up so much of CM's unique sound, Hatori's lyrics create a new kind of identity and home for the transnational subject. Home is a virtual, aurally created space that exists between the first and third worlds as a pastiche of different sounds and languages. In some sense, it exists as *memory,* which music is able to evoke more immediately than any other medium. And it is this version of home as memory and process that one encounters in the song, "Sci Fi Wasabi." Of all the songs on the new album, "Sci Fi Wasabi" best falls under the genre of hip hop for which CM is known. As such, it acts as a kind of bridge between the quirky hip hop "food band" of 1996 and the more seriously kitschy, musically diverse image of CM in 1999.

In "Sci Fi Wasabi," CM appropriates various trappings of rap and mixes them with Japanese cultural signifiers and slang. For example, the song opens with a homonym and *double entendre*: "What's up B," followed by what sounds like a repetition but isn't—"wasabi." The expression "what's up B" is a fairly standard one in hip hop culture with "B" standing for break-boy. "Wasabi" is the hot green mustard mixed with soy sauce used for dipping sushi and sashimi, two distinctly Japanese foods that acquired popularity and cultural cachet in the United States in the 1980s. It alludes here to CM's past association with the food motif even as

308 JANE C. H. PARK

it collapses cultural differences through a simple speech act. The song then races the listener through the streets of downtown New York, which are defamiliarized and rendered virtual through technical, pop-futuristic references: "start buttons," Obi Wan Kenobi, earning "points" as in a video game. The beat mimics sonic speed as Miho rushes on her bike to a destination and a goal. However the goal becomes more and more insignificant as she absorbs the pulsing rhythm of her surroundings.

The final image, of the singer metaphorically flying up to the sky, precludes narrative closure. Miho does not find the key because that was never really the point anyway. If the "key" that Miho has been looking for is "identity," by the end of the song it has become clear that identity cannot be reified, "found," or even "made." Instead, like so many of the other songs in the album, "Sci Fi Wasabi" suggests that identity is a never-ending process undergone over and over again in different emotional, physical, and spiritual states.

Since *Stereotype A,* Honda and Hatori have worked together and separately on various projects including *Butter 08* (Grand Royal, 1996) with Russell Simins and Jamey Staub, and *Handsome Boy Modeling School* (Tommy Boy, 1999) with Prince Paul and Dan the Automator. At present the band is on "indefinite hiatus." In 2002 Hatori assumed the role of "Noodle," the nineteen-year-old Japanese female member of the animated band, Gorillaz, whose industry in-joke debut album went multiplatinum and snagged an Emmy nomination. Currently Hatori is performing bossa nova with Beck's former guitarist Smokey Hormel as part of the duo, Smokey & Miho.[37] Honda broke up with Lennon and released her first solo record, *Memories Are My Only Witness* in spring 2002 on John Zorn's label Tzadik. Described as "moody" and "cinematic," Honda's recent work focuses more on sonic texture and experimentation and less on the dance beats and melodic choruses that characterized CM's style.[38]

Conclusion

By contextualizing Cibo Matto in the arenas of hip hop, women in electronic music, and Asian American representational history, I have tried to show how stereotypes of Asian women in the United States are being performed and negotiated in one small corner of popular music. In response to racial, sexual, and generic stereotyping, Cibo Matto has turned to politically nuanced lyrics, eclectic melodies and sampling techniques, and a technologically astute girly image that defies any monolithic gender or racial identity. Honda and Hatori together and now separately critique the racist and sexist labels conferred upon Asian American women with humor and style—aesthetic strategies that have yet to be adequately theorized as the strong political weapons they can be.

NOTES

1. Carrie Bell, "Warner Bros. Positions Cibo Matto to Break Its 'Stereotype.'" *Billboard*, 1 May 1999, Expanded Academic Database, 28 January 2003.

2. Nirvana and Red Kross were prominent players in the scene. Both groups were also avid fans and friends of SK.

3. J. D. Considine, "Band Builds Lyrical Bridge between Japan and the U.S.," *Los Angeles Times*, 11 August 1999, Calendar, Part F, 4.

4. The official Cibo Matto website: www.wbr.cibomatto.com.

5. Ibid.

6. *Nylon*, fall 1999, 214–215.

7. Neil Strauss, "New Sounds from Japan: A Starter's Kit," *New York Times*, 12 July 1998, home ed.: C9.

8. Jon Pareles, "Cibo Matto: *Viva! La Woman*," *New York Times*, 28 January 1996, 24.

9. Glenn Kardy, "Cibo Matto's Musical Feeding Frenzy," *Daily Yomiyuri*, 1 August 1996, 10.

10. Steven Rosen, "If It Sounds Like Tossed Salad, It Might Be Cibo Matto," *Denver Post*, 17 May 1996, GT-16.

11. Steve Davy, "A Crazy Feast of Food-Centricity," *South China Morning Post*, 17 May 1996, 5.

12. Jeff Gordimer, "Japanese Kitsch—Fake but Groovy," *Fortune*, 21 June 1999, 139(12): 56.

13. See Jeff Yang, Dina Gan, and Terry Hong, *Eastern Standard Time: A Guide to Asian Influence on American Culture*, New York: Houghton Mifflin, 1997, and Mark Schilling, *The Encyclopedia of Japanese Pop Culture*, New York: Weatherhill, 1997.

14. Alvin Liu, "Tired U.S. Pop Looks East," *Asahi Evening News*, 25 March 1999, home ed.: C9+.

15. Ibid.

16. Shout out to my girl Tara Rodgers, editor of electronica webzine Pinknoises, for providing me with this concise definition. E-mail correspondence, 13 July 2000.

17. The historical situation in Japan is more ambiguous and complex than that

of other Asian countries, since it has also played both colonized (by the West) and colonizer (of the East).

18. See Edward Said, *Orientalism,* New York: Vintage Books, 1979, 12.

19. See *Rolling Stone,* 13 November 1997, cover story.

20. Gayle Wald, "Just a Girl? Rock Music, Feminism, and the Cultural Construction of Female Youth," *Signs,* spring 1998, 23:599.

21. Norma Coates, "(R)evolution Now," in Sheila Whiteley, ed., *Sexing the Groove: Popular Music and Gender,* New York: Routledge, 1997, 52.

22. Ibid., 53.

23. Tricia Rose, *Black Noise: Rap Music and Black Culture in Contemporary America,* Hanover, NH: Wesleyan University Press, 1994, 85.

24. Ibid., 65, emphasis added.

25. Evelyn McDonnell, "Why Aren't More Geeks with the Gizmo Girls?" *New York Times,* 12 April 1998, 2.

26. See www.pinknoises.com.

27. Wald, 604–605.

28. Amei Wallach, "The Widow Peaks: Yoko Ono Gets Her Own Moment in a New Avant-Garde," *New York Times Magazine,* 24 September 2000, 58–61.

29. Arion Berger, "Yoko Ono," in *Trouble Girls: Women in Rock,* ed. Barbara O'Dair, New York: Random House, 1997, 246.

30. Bell.

31. Jim Sullivan, "Gourmet Music," *Boston Globe,* 2 May 1996, city ed.: Calendar.

32. Andy Gill, "Pop: Food for Thought; Cibo Matto's First Album Was an Enigmatic Hors d'Oeuvre. Now the Japanese Duo Has Served Up a Sumptuous Main Course," *Independent,* 9 July 1999, features: 15.

33. Jon Pareles, "Novelty Act? Not If Things Go Their Way," *New York Times,* 15 June 1999, late ed.: E9.

34. Elysa Gardner, "Cibo Matto's Food for Thought," *Los Angeles Times,* 5 May 1996, Sunday home ed.: Calendar, 61.

35. The official Cibo Matto website: www.cibomatto.com.

36. Ibid.

37. Joan Anderman, "Brazilian Sound Gives New Life to Smokey, Miho," *Boston Globe,* 15 November 2002, 3d ed.: C12+.

38. Cory Vielma, "Yuka Honda: *Memories Are My Only Witness* (Tzadik)," *SF Weekly,* 17 April 2002, Lexis Nexis, 28 January 2003.

WORKS CITED

Anderman, Joan. "Brazilian Sound Gives New Life to Smokey, Miho." *Boston Globe,* 15 November 2002, 3d ed.: C12+.

Bell, Carrie. "Warner Bros. Positions Cibo Matto to Break Its 'Stereotype.'" *Billboard*, 1 May 1999. Expanded Academic Database. 28 January 2003.

Berger, Arion. "Yoko Ono." In *Trouble Girls: Women in Rock,* ed. Barbara O'Dair (New York: Random House, 1997).

Cibo Matto. *Stereotype A* (Warner Bros. Records, 1999).

———. *Viva! La Woman* (Warner Bros. Records, 1996).

Coates, Norma. "(R)evolution Now? Rock and the Political Potential of Gender." In *Sexing the Groove: Popular Music and Gender,* ed. Sheila Whiteley (London: Routledge, 1997), 50–64.

Considine, J. D. "Band Builds Lyrical Bridge between Japan and the U.S." *Los Angeles Times*, 11 August 1999, home ed.: F4.

Cornyetz, Nina. "Fetishized Blackness: Hip Hop and Racial Desire in Contemporary Japan." *Social Text* 41 (winter 1994).

Davy, Steve. "A Crazy Feast of Food-Centricity." *South China Morning Post*, 17 May 1996: 5.

Dower, John. *War without Mercy: Race and Power in the Pacific War* (New York: Pantheon Books, 1986).

Felder, Rachel. *Manic Pop Thrill* (Hopewell, NJ: Ecco Press, 1993).

Gaar, Gillian. *She's a Rebel: The History of Women in Rock & Roll* (Seattle: Seal Press, 1992).

Garner, Elysa. "Cibo Matto's Food for Thought." *Los Angeles Times*, 5 May 1999, home ed.: 61.

Gill, Andy. "Pop: Food for Thought; Cibo Matto's First Album Was an Enigmatic Hors d'Oeuvre. Now the Japanese Duo Has Served Up a Sumptuous Main Course." *Independent*, 9 July 1999, home ed.: F15.

Gordimer, Jeff. "Japanese Kitsch—Fake but Groovy." *Fortune*, 25 June 1999, 139(12): 56.

Haraway, Donna. "A Cyborg Manifesto." In *Simians, Cyborgs, and Women: The Reinvention of Nature* (New York: Routledge, 1991).

———. *Modest_Witness@Second_Millennium.FemaleMan©_Meets_OncoMouse^{TM}: Feminism and Technoscience* (New York: Routledge, 1997).

Kang, Connie K. "Sunday Report: At a Crossroads; Rising Numbers Bring Greater Influence—and Sometimes Greater Problems—for the State's Asian Americans." *Los Angeles Times*, 12 July 1998, home ed.: A1+.

Kardy, Glenn. "Cibo Matto's Musical Feeding Frenzy." *Daily Yomiyuri*, 1 August 1996, 10.

Kondo, Dorinne. *About Face: Performing Race in Fashion and Theater* (New York: Routledge, 1997).

Lee, Robert. *Orientals: Asian Americans in Popular Culture* (Philadelphia: Temple University Press, 1999).

Lipsitz, George. *The Possessive Investment in Whiteness* (Philadelphia: Temple University Press, 1998).

Liu, Alvin. "Tired U.S. Pop Looks East." *Asahi Evening News,* 25 March 1999, home ed.: C9+.

McDonnell, Evelyn. "Why Aren't More Geeks with the Gizmo Girls?" *New York Times,* 12 April 1998, 2.

Pareles, John. "Cibo Matto: *Viva! La Woman.*" *New York Times,* 28 January 1996, 24.

———. "Novelty Act? Not If Things Go Their Way." *New York Times,* 15 June 1999, E9.

Rose, Tricia. *Black Noise: Rap Music and Black Culture in Contemporary America* (Hanover, NH: Wesleyan University Press, 1994).

Rosen, Steven. "If It Sounds Like Tossed Salad, It Might Be Cibo Matto." *Denver Post,* 17 May 1996, G7–16.

Said, Edward. *Orientalism* (New York: Vintage Books, 1979).

Schilling, Mark. *The Encyclopedia of Japanese Pop Culture* (New York: Weatherhill, 1997).

Strauss, Neil. "New Sounds from Japan: A Starter's Kit." *New York Times,* 12 July 1998, home ed.: C9.

Sullivan, Jim. "Gourmet Music." *Boston Globe.* 2 May 1996, city ed.: C29.

Tajima, Renee. "Lotus Blossoms Don't Bleed." In *Making Waves,* ed. Asian Women United of California (Boston: Beacon Press, 1989).

Vielma, Cory. "Yuka Honda: *Memories Are My Only Witness* (Tzadik)," *SF Weekly,* 17 April 2002, Lexis Nexis, 28 January 2003.

Wald, Gayle. "Just a Girl? Rock Music, Feminism, and the Cultural Construction of Female Youth." *Signs* 23 (Spring 1998).

Wallach, Amei. "The Widow Peaks: Yoko Ono Gets Her Own Moment in a New Avant-Garde." *New York Times Magazine,* 24 September 2999, 58–61.

Whiteley, Sheila, ed. *Sexing the Groove: Popular Music and Gender* (New York: Routledge, 1997).

Yang, Jeff, Dina Gan, and Terry Hong. *Eastern Standard Time: A Guide to Asian Influence on American Culture* (New York: Houghton Mifflin, 1997), 263.

Chapter 16

Apu's Brown Voice
Cultural Inflection and South Asian Accents

Shilpa Davé

> I cannot deny my roots and I cannot keep up this cha-
> rade. I only did it because I love this land, where I have
> the freedom to say, and to think, and to charge whatever
> I want!   —Apu, in "Much Apu about Nothing,"
> airdate May 5, 1996

In this scene from *The Simpsons* episode "Much Apu about Nothing," Apu vents his frustration about falsely posturing in both dress and accent as someone who is culturally and stereotypically represented as American. Driven to obtain an illegal ID card because of the imminent passage of Springfield's Proposition 24 to deport illegal immigrants, Apu dons the garb and behavior that he thinks are typical of a patriotic, legal American, namely, a cowboy hat, N.Y. Mets shirt, and an awkward John Wayne drawl.[1] Apu clearly speaks to the actions of immigrants who feel culturally pressured to assimilate, to act and speak and buy or sell "American" without being able to express their own native origins in order to not stand out. For ethnic Americans expressions of individuality (an American virtue) are often intertwined with a subjectivity that is racialized, be it through religion, food, or dress or speech patterns. Apu attempts to express his American cultural citizenship, which is a permanent part of the popular imagination of a specific nation or culture, in lieu of possessing actual political citizenship of equal rights under the law.[2]

This essay begins with a discussion of the presence and performance of South Asian voices and accents in American culture. Specifically I want to

Fig. 16.1. Apu from *The Simpsons.*

introduce my theory of "brown voice." The term "brown voice" identifies a specific racializing trait among South Asians which simultaneously connotes foreignness and class and cultural privilege. This aspect of South Asian racial identity demonstrates the historical ambiguity of South Asian ethnic and racial classification. On the one hand, South Asian racial identity bears the traces of British colonialism, under which Indians were to be "civilized" and thus turned almost but not quite white. On the other hand,

South Asians have an ambiguous racial identity in the United States, as demonstrated by the 1923 *U.S. vs. Bhagat Singh Thind* case in which the U.S. Supreme Court claimed that despite the fact that science classified "Hindoos" as Caucasian, the "common man" saw them as colored.[3] Given this history of ambiguous and amorphous racial classifications around South Asians, the character of Apu is particularly interesting. Voiced by a white actor in "brown voice," Apu is the only recurrent South Asian representation on television today, and is now a beloved popular icon.

My intent and emphasis on brown voice will help to chronicle how a specific South Asian ethnic citizenship evolves through American popular culture. Hence I ask, "what is the relation between privilege and accent and popular culture?" Ultimately I assert that the practice of *brown voice* is a form of cultural inflection: a variation on cultural citizenship that reinforces a static position for South Asians regardless of their status or occupation in the United States. South Asians are represented as one undifferentiated group who are saddled with one accent and one voice. This image frames South Asians as an acceptable and privileged ethnic group (in comparison to other minority and immigrant groups) that in current times also has considerable political and economic consequences. This static and fixed position, signaled by a singular and stable "voice," develops through the particular historical representation of difference in the mass media combined with prior and current relations of South Asians with British and U.S. culture. In contemporary times this static position is illustrated by what may arguably be the most recognizable Indian accent to American audiences: that of Apu Nahasapeemapetilon on the long-running animated series *The Simpsons*.

As seen above in the episode "Much Apu about Nothing," Apu's cultural appropriation of American icons goes to an extreme and thereby emphasizes how different he is with respect to the other citizens of Springfield. Apu's flawed attempt to impersonate an American with a celebrity accent attaches him to an American cultural history and hence (in his mind) to an American cultural citizenship. But to the audience (including me) this is a humorous scene because we know Apu is not culturally American. In fact when we see Apu onscreen we expect him to speak English with an accent, namely, what we have been taught to think of as an "Indian accent." This satire of ethnic assimilation illustrates how racial and ethnic identities operate beyond the visual and are influenced by the reception of accented speech. It also illustrates the notion of "the charade" of taking up another's cultural behavior and in particular of possessing and/or performing a cultural accent. I am less interested in the phenomenon of cultural masquerade than in the meaning generated by this practice in relation to South Asians in the United States. The character of Apu offers an ideal case study to portray how South Asians are situated and understood in the popular American imagination. Apu, a fictional construction, helps us to revise theories of racial performance and thereby examine American racial hierarchies and formations of Asian American communities in popular culture.

This analysis links Asian American notions of accent to the prevailing theories of minstrelsy and racial and ethnic performance not only on the small and silver screens but also in the largely understudied realm of animated cartoons.[4] Previous studies of minstrelsy and ethnic performance by Eric Lott, Michael Rogin, Robert Lee, and Dorinne Kondo emphasize the visual aspect of performance in relation to individual and racial formation but also discuss the language of race, though not necessarily the performance of accent.[5] By focusing on the concept of voice we can move the discussion of racial subjectivity beyond the visual aspects of racial recognition and expose alternative cultural factors that influence racial perceptions and in particular racialized immigrants.

In feminist and queer studies, theorists such as Kaja Silverman have explored the power dynamics of masculine and feminine voices but have not examined national and ethnic accents in relation to the articulation of power.[6] Sociolinguists such as Rosina Lippi-Green have chronicled how language and accent stereotyping influence social identity formation and how these stereotypes are reinforced by educational institutions and media outlets. However, I am interested in studying the cultural value of accents in relationship to the concept of cultural citizenship. Specifically I ask how does the endorsement of a South Asian accent on television sanction a limited vision of the South Asian presence in the United States and how does that vision reinforce a static American cultural ethnic citizenship?

Practicing Brown Voice

The South Asian voice and in particular the Indian English accent reflects the historically amorphous and ambiguous physical position that South Asians have occupied in American racial hierarchies. To this day many South Asians self-identify by nationality or state affiliation in India. Debates around the racial status of Indians in the United States have been ongoing since the early 1900s. It was only in the 1980 Census that the geographical location of the South Asian continent was added under the racial category Asian American, thereby providing South Asians a viable box to check. Yet even today, South Asians and Asian Americans often hesitate to attend or include each other in Asian American or South Asian community, social, or political gatherings. The title of a collection on South Asian American identity, *A Part, Yet Apart,* explains how South Asians are included in Asian American Studies and yet divided by historical and even physical differences.[7] The distinctive South Asian accent reflects this position and, as I will argue, puts South Asians in the position of being a privileged minority among model minorities because of these physical and historical differences.

The performance of this accent, which I term "brown voice," is the act of speaking in the Indian English accent associated with South Asian nationals and immigrants. Anyone can perform the accent, but its cultural meaning changes depending upon the actor. For example, a South Asian speaking brown voice sounds very different from a white actor playing a South Asian. To be clear, brown voice is a performance in both senses of the word: not only does someone speak but someone also has to receive and recognize the implications or at least the intent of the accent which marks someone as South Asian. Brown voice is just as much about how we "hear" and understand Indian accents as it is about the person doing the talking. It represents the vocalization of the model minority. The performance of brown voice comes out as an inflected version of English but specifically not as words out of order. It is an accessible dose of foreignness rather than an irritating form of speaking that resembles American English.[8] Apu speaks in brown voice in *The Simpsons,* a rote and consistent accent that is foreign but understandable.

Unlike other forms of Asian English often seen as broken English, Indian English has a unique phonetic signature in which meaning is indicated by which syllables are stressed in particular words.[9] John Honey, in *Does Accent Matter? The Pygmalion Factor,* describes reactions to accents as "distractions" rather than unintelligibility—the distraction from what you are saying to how you are saying it creates an interesting effect when it comes to Indian English. Honey reasons that "the greatest source of unintelligibility in the Indian English accent is its pattern of word stress—that is deciding which syllable in a word gets the emphasis" (106). Unlike Australians, New Zealanders, or South Africans, Indians tend to stress different syllables (one researcher estimated that one in five of all words are stressed differently in Indian English).[10]

Word stress is a promising approach to the study of cultural communication because it does not ridicule the intelligence or aptitude of the speaker, but rather converges on the process by which expression of intelligibility is registered by prioritizing meaning. It does not ask, "Why can't you speak my language?" but "Why are you speaking it that way?" so that the basic structure is correct but the interpretation of what is important in communication is variable. With brown voice, the cultural perception of the accent is associated not only with a model minority Asian immigrant group but specifically with a privileged minority—Indians who are understood to speak a more culturally receptive accented English. In other words, now that the language has been learned the most difficult barrier to be overcome is the reception and communication of meaning of your speech and to achieve cultural fluency.

Brown voice, then, can be understood as the cultural performative practice of manipulating meaning and creating a cultural difference. Although perceived and received as a "foreign accent" in American culture Indian English is in fact a native form of speech in India where the two national languages are English and Hindi. Many middle-class Indians are educated in English-speaking schools (also known as English-medium schools) where all subjects are taught in English. However there are a multitude of accent variations. So although it would be more appropriate to think of Indian English as an inflected version of English that more closely resembles British English or Black English, American culture perceives South Asians talking with the accent of a non-native speaker.

In contemporary culture, South Asians and South Asian culture (bindis, henna, mehndi, clothing, and fabrics) are some of the current fashionable consumer commodities. Indians are hip and to imitate their accents (in theater, film, or just for fun in both ethnic and white communities) is not considered a sign of bad education or breeding but just the opposite—Indian accents imply a model minority and in multicultural politics this is the type of minority the United States wants to promote because they fit the image of entrepreneurs, computer engineers, and successful immigrants in general. The constant performance of brown voice therefore establishes one sound and one image for South Asians in the cultural imagination and hence freezes the perception of the group in a static definition. Thus although South Asians occupy the privileged position of being recognized as successful foreigners, this position does not allow the perception of South Asians to expand and thereby prevents South Asians from establishing any kind of presence other than as outsiders in American communities. If the image of South Asians is continually that of immigrant foreigners then how can South Asians ever be seen as movers and shakers let alone stakeholders in American life—as cultural citizens?

In terms of racial theory, brown voice is instructive in thinking about how race is separated from the visual and instead voice becomes another marker of cultural subjectivity. Perceiving race beyond the body helps us to identify and question racial constructions of identity that remain buried under the term Asian American or in a binary black-white paradigm by placing voice at the center of our analysis.

The Sounds of Difference in Radio and Animation

Mediated performance of race and ethnicity were devised and created in radio and set the standards for later forms of mass media such as television. In essence, voice was crucial to the articulation of difference in radio. Racialized performances of voice first occurred on a national level on the radio. As Michele Hilmes points out in her intuitive study in the long-neglected field of radio, *Radio Voices: American Broadcasting, 1922–1952,* not only is the history of radio the precursor to narrative forms in television but it is also directly linked to the formation of American national identity. The growth of radio stations and the public practice of listening to the radio emerged during the national debates over naturalization and immigration laws in the 1920s. Hilmes maintains that the linguistic unity fostered by national American radio influenced the perception and judgment value of voices that deviated from what was considered the national norm. During the same time, the national radio of Great Britain (BBC) was actively creating a national voice that spoke with a manufactured (no one spoke quite like this) upper-class Oxford English accent even though most of the population spoke with an entirely different phonetic deviation.[11] To the British, accent had already become more important than appearance as a class indicator, as seen in George Bernard Shaw's stage drama *Pygmalion.* In the United States, however, racial and ethnic characteristics were broadcast to all residents through the use of radio drama.

In the early days of radio serial programs, writers borrowed from the vaudeville traditions of racial dialect and characterizations and consciously re-created these accents to construct and indicate race in a nonvisual medium. The common narrative device through which difference (and in particular "blackness") was expressed was the theme of "cultural incompetence." Hilmes writes: "One signification of cultural incompetence involves language use and 'funny accents,' a device milked by 'Dutch' acts, Irish acts, Jewish caricatures, and the state Italian since the dawn of vaudeville. Other 'ethnic' traits involved the common situation of the immigrant: 'humorous' native customs that clashed with American norms" (89), including plays on language pronunciation and cultural misunderstanding. Hilmes argues that although radio had the technology and opportunity to create a "race-less" society, instead it solidified the racial hierarchies of the 1920s and 1930s through the continued production of accents and in the case of black drama (the popular show *Amos 'n' Andy*, for example), the continued practice of blackface minstrelsy in which whites voiced black characters.[12]

As Michael Rogin discusses in his reading of the film, *The Jazz Singer* (1927), the story of Al Jolson performing blackface complicates Jewish and black cultural constructions but also reiterates the notion of American exceptionalism or the establishment of hierarchical relations of race and ethnicity within American identity and American citizenship. The theory of brown voice combines accents and hierarchies together with Asian American Studies and therefore intervenes in the black-white paradigm set up in both studies of whiteness and critical race theory. Instead brown voice redirects attention to the way the expression of national language exposes hierarchies of identity both within and without racial groups.

In an animated series, the fact that the bodies are physically drawn and therefore not real brings the voice (as in radio) to the forefront. Most animation, unlike radio and film, is predicated on the notion of fantasy and make-believe.[13] Early animated shorts of Felix the Cat and Mickey Mouse emphasize the simultaneously humorous and fictional nature of the medium. Although the process of animation from conception to production is grounded in the visual, when coupled with the dynamics of voice animation it disconnects race from the body. In the case of animation the analysis of race transitions from the physical performance to the vocal performance. That the impact and importance of voice actors has long been recognized by the television industry is indicated by the fact that the cast of *The Simpsons* has won two Emmy Awards for best voiceovers for a series. The award implies not only industry as well as audience knowledge of who plays what voices but also recognizes the proficiency and importance of voice in the creation of character.

Speaking with brown voice is more than a ventriloquist performance because with ventriloquism the manipulation of the puppet or the dummy is a visual as well as an aural joke that the audience understands and has accepted. This does not happen in animation because we cannot see the living body (as opposed to the fabricated animated representation) from which the voice emerges except in shows where this has become the gimmick. In *The Simpsons,* for example, celebrities often do heavily hyped guest voice-overs that overshadow the character illustrations. As an animated series, *The Simpsons* rearranges reality and allows the audience an even greater distance from the characters than do live action situation comedies. Characteristics that emphasize this freedom from reality include a controlled environment such as the unchanging town of Springfield, a frozen time in which characters do not age, and the two-dimensional visual nature of animation. Because of the audience's suspension of disbelief, animated series can often tackle issues and situations that would be unbelievable or inappropriate on live action sitcoms.[14] Events ranging from alien takeovers to political satires to social commentaries are now common fare for shows such as *The Simpsons, Beavis and Butt-head,* and *King of the Hill.*

Unlike blackface, the manufactured voice also allows racial and ethnic accents to proliferate because unlike physical acts of discrimination, vocal mimicry is meant to be humorous and is not seen as insulting or demeaning. Peter Sellers's offensive portrayal of Indian Hrundi Bakshi in *The Party* (1968) would not go unchallenged today because of the very visual impact of racist stereotyping in the film. The practice of brown voice avoids most of the problems of racial stereotyping because it is not physical.[15] Animation foregrounds the sound and resonance of voice but not the person whose voice it is. The voice is disembodied from the speaker and attached to something else (animals, fictional people, trees).

With the advent of *The Simpsons,* however, guest voices and celebrity voices became the vogue. As cultural consumers not only do we recognize voices but in *The Simpsons* the producers and creators want us to recognize them and even pair up the celebrity with an animated body that looks like the individual. Feature animated films have latched on to this practice and promoted films on the basis of whose voice is starring as a particular character.[16] But the actors depicting the main characters of the show do not want to be recognized for a single voice but instead pride themselves on the number of different voices they can do. Whereas celebrity voices are linked to the singularity of the actor's physical image, the main characters are freed by the multiplicity of voices which can perform any accent, any gender, or any age. It is this anonymity that allows Hank Azaria to voice the character of Apu because although most of America (and the world) knows about the character Apu, they cannot identify Azaria as the man that voices him. If a celebrity like Paul McCartney or Tom Cruise performed brown voice the reaction of the public and Asian American groups would be very different and could generate the same furor that fueled the *Miss Saigon* protests in New York City in 1992.[17]

To perform an accent is to be technically superior at your craft (Meryl Streep and Nicole Kidman, among others, are considered masters of the accent). However, the performance of brown voice should foster a recognition and acknowledgment that there are particular racial histories and hierarchies that allow certain accents to be read as funny and others to be vilified. Eric Garrison from *The Simpson Archive* writes, "Apu started out in concept as a simple convenience clerk. According to show writer Mike Reiss though, when Hank Azaria (the voice of Apu) started to voice act the script, Azaria couldn't help but give Apu an Indian accent." "We couldn't help it," says Reiss, "Once Apu was given an Indian accent, Apu Nahasapeemapetilon was born." What comes first, the accent or the character? In this case the accent defined Apu and created not only a humorous speaker but a culturally popular and significant South Asian American representation on American television.

The Voice of Apu: White Face, Brown Voice

The Simpsons is the longest-running situation comedy in American television history and is broadcast in syndication to more than sixty countries around the world, including Japan, India, and the United Kingdom, where it is even more of a phenomenon than in the United States.[18] Apu Nahasapeemapetilon, the proprietor of the Springfield Kwik-E-Mart, represents not only the most recognizable South Asian character on television, but he is also one of the *only* South Asian characters on television.

Over thirteen years Apu has appeared in a variety of episodes. His first extended appearances took place during the first season of the series on Fox in 1990. Throughout the series we learn that Apu is a Hindu ("Homer the Heretic") and a vegetarian ("Lisa the Vegetarian"). He emigrated from India to the United States to pursue his doctorate in computer science at Springfield Heights Institute of Technology (also known by its initials).

While he was a computer science Ph.D. student he began working in the Kwik-E-Mart and eight years later eventually bought and ran the store ("Much Apu about Nothing"). Later he gets married ("The Two Mrs. Nahasapeemapetilon"), romances his wife ("I'm with Cupid"), and has eight children ("Eight Misbehaving"). He acts (both literally and figuratively) as a vehicle to introduce current views and debates about minorities in the United States.

As a result of the fame and singularity of his character, Apu emerges as a highly politicized representation of a Hindu from India who fulfills the "model minority" stereotype of success through tolerance and hard work. Apu presents a complex mix of the multiple and often contradictory positions of ethnic and racial immigrants with regard to American political and social culture. For example, in the show Apu is depicted as a foundational member of the Springfield USA community where his "Indianness" does not factor into his roles in the community. For all practical purposes, he is merely a citizen of Springfield until creator Matt Groening chooses to frame an episode specifically around his character. In these cases, his foreignness and "Indianness" are highlighted in relation to issues of immigration, citizenship, arranged marriage and its consequences, and spirituality.[19]

In 2003, Nancy Basile, a correspondent on the website for animated tv.com (www.animatedtv.about.com/cs/lists/tp/sicharacters.html) listed Apu as number six on her top ten Simpsons characters after the Simpson family members and Mr. Burns. Basile writes, "Apu seems to always have a quip ready at the counter of his Kwik-E-Mart. He cleverly gouges Springfield citizens with his prices. His patient explanations of Hinduism to Homer tickle me silly. Finally, he's got a killer singing voice in "Streetcar Named Desire."[20] Her affection for the character showcases his versatility and, importantly, his patience in teaching Homer. Part of Apu's appeal, in reading her description, is his role as a cultural spokesperson. However, in the Indian American community debates vacillate between whether Apu's popularity and presence in the show is a sign of Indians making it in the United States or whether Apu's success reinforces Indian immigrant stereotypes and limits all future Indian characters to Apu-like roles.[21] In the film *The Guru* (2003), the main character and his friends (all Indian immigrants) bemoan the fact that the only famous Indian in America, Apu, is a cartoon.

The character of Apu developed by creator Matt Groening and his writing team went from being a greedy storekeeper obsessed with crime, to a cultural and spiritual spokesperson for India, to a naturalized citizen and family man.[22] Hank Azaria, the son of Greek immigrants, has been the voice of over a hundred different characters on *The Simpsons,* including Moe Szyslak (the owner of Moe's bar) and Police Chief Wiggum, but his most famous character is Apu Nahasapeemapetilon. For over thirteen years he has been the voice and character of Apu and hence the de facto voice of all South Asians on television.[23] Because of the popularity and longevity of his character, Azaria has been instrumental (whether he claims this position or not) in standardizing for television culture who Indian immigrants are and what they sound like because there are no other types of characters. As Joe Rhodes reports in *TV Guide,* "It was Groening who suggested that Apu be Indian, though 'we were worried he might be considered an offensive stereotype,' writer Al Jean says. 'But then we did the first read-through, and Hank said, 'Hello, Mr. Homer' with his accent, and it got such a huge laugh, we knew it had to stay.' The writers made Apu a Pakistani of great dignity and industry."[24] So the writers did think about the consequences of brown voice but the impression of a good joke trumped any concerns they might have had about the stereotype.[25]

In a published interview in the weekly *India Abroad* (with a high subscription to Indian Americans), while Azaria admitted he did not have any training for his Indian accent he said he learned his accent "from listening. In Los Angeles, going to 7-11s, hearing Indian and Pakistani clerks" (Ali).[26] Interestingly, as Al Jean's quotation shows, even the writers have difficulty identifying Apu's roots and like Azaria cannot distinguish between India (a democracy that has a largely Hindu population) and Pakistan (a military-based government that is primarily Muslim), nor are they aware of the tensions that currently and historically have defined the two nations. This lack of understanding on the part of the writers signals how South Asians are lumped into one group regardless of significant linguistic, religious, political, and cultural histories. This representation influences many other characterizations of South Asian Americans and hence the popular conception of South Asians in general.

To be clear, the figure of Apu can be read through dual though not necessarily competing registers. The first is through a close examination of the character of Apu. From this point of view, Groening is able to present a diverse and liberal exchange of ideas about various issues involving government, big business, social issues, and art and politics. Indeed, it might be argued that Groening presents a progressive vision where Apu is an in-

Fig. 16.2. Actor Hank Azaria, the voice of Apu.

tegral part of the Springfield community and his ethnicity and cultural background do not determine his activities in Springfield. Groening describes Apu by saying, "I think he really loves his job and the power that it gives him to frustrate other people" (Garrison). Apu is also shown as a foundational member of the community where his Indianness does not define all his roles in the community. Similarly, Indian American director M. Night Shyamalan often introduces a secondary character played by an Indian or minority character (usually himself) in his films who by their very presence visually confirm the diverse world we live in by showing brown people who are doctors, art consumers, potential drug dealers, and engaged couples without marking them as "foreign" or "strange." He highlights the presence of South Asians without stereotyping what they are by accent or race or religion but rather by locating South Asians as an everyday part of American cultural geography.

However, Apu bears closer scrutiny because of his voice. As I have shown, Apu's voice holds great power and influence over how South Asian cultural identity is seen in the United States. In a speech delivered to the American Society of Newspaper Editors in 1991, Matt Groening pointed out that the subtext of his show is that "[t]he people in power don't always have your best interests in mind."[27] Media portrayals of South Asians on television shows such as *Seinfeld* (the character Babu) and *The Simpsons* have ignored or deemphasized racial categorizations of South Asians and instead, in comedic formats, have focused on how cultural categorizations of religion and marriage emphasize the foreign nature of South Asians.[28] To have a brown voice is to be heard and read as foreign but also to register a highly specialized educational, class, and historical status that is seldom associated with other Asian American immigrant groups and is fairly specific to individuals from the Indian subcontinent.

How Do Indians Speak English?
Mimicry and the Model Minority

Brown voice is particularly useful in reevaluating postcolonial theories of native-colonizer relations by rethinking and reevaluating Homi Bhabha's theory of mimicry. Brown voice is mimicry in reverse but not its opposite. In fact the two concepts are connected because brown voice, like mimicry, depends on the notion of an authentic native figure by which to gauge one's identity. However, while mimicry exposes the cracks of the British enterprise to reform the natives, brown voice operates in a slightly different manner. Instead of exposing the performer to ridicule, it gives the performer of brown voice control over how he or she is going to be received and hence culturally constructed. Brown voice elides difference into one manageable form of difference. This practice resembles the homogenization of ethnic and racial differences by American multiculturalism under the label of diversity or the description of America as a "melting pot." As such, the sanctioning of brown voice performance is an endorsement of conservative social policy with regard to race.

Like mimicry, brown voice exposes the flaws of being cast as a privileged or model minority. For Hank Azaria, his vocal performance of brown voice becomes a rearrangement of sounds and syllables, a sound that is consumed and can be sold to a television audience as foreign. When I saw the accent emerging from Azaria's mouth in an episode of "The

Actor's Studio" on the Bravo Network I found the experience jarring because the physical image did not match the voice. Instead Azaria's verbal and facial expressions were not humorous. The utilization of brown voice in this case highlighted how someone else, namely, a white actor, was staging Indian cultural fluency and the glass ceiling of what Indians could achieve in terms of cultural citizenship. South Asians are not evolving in roles on American television beyond the role of Apu, but more importantly this allows us to think about ethnicity beyond the visual.

But to go further, the implementation of brown voice also seeks to divorce accent from race and thereby remove any hint of racial overtones from voice. In other words, the performance of brown voice participates in the simplification of racial identities. As a result, the accented voice becomes a consumer product that can be traded without regard to cultural, ethnic, and racial history. Simultaneously, the practice of brown voice ensures that although Indians are striving for cultural citizenship, the nature of the accent will always be read as foreign and the racial hierarchies of the United States will remain intact.

As previously noted, the documented status of South Asians has gravitated between their racial categorization as "Caucasian" and their political inclusion in the Asian American community. To complicate this further, many South Asians reject racial categorization and refer to themselves as Indian or Pakistani or Sri Lankan.[29] Building on racial, caste, and class hierarchies under the British Raj, Indians have allied themselves with white Americans and fought for their title as Caucasians. Susan Koshy in "Morphing Race into Ethnicity" discusses how Asian Americans have reconfigured the language and categorization of "white" in the law in their zeal to achieve equality with whites in American culture. As detailed by Vijay Prasad and others, South Asians have used the myth of their Aryan origins to support a fundamental Indian nationalist position, to ally themselves with whiteness, and to draw on their former position as the most lucrative colony in the British Empire—the jewel in the crown.[30]

In 1835 Lord Thomas Babington Macaulay, the governor general of India, instituted an educational policy that he believed would transform the natives into perfect British citizens. His "Minute on Education" proclaimed that Indian natives educated in English and taught an English curriculum would become "a class who may be interpreters between us and the millions whom we govern; a class of persons, Indians in blood and color, but English in taste, in opinions, in morals, and in intellect."[31] The English could thus reproduce themselves in the empire through the education of a select number of natives. The resulting "class of inter-preters" would serve as a bridge between them and the masses of India—Indian intellectuals created without any sexual overtones or hints of mis-cegenation between the English and the natives. The creation would be the hybrid of the best in Indian and British culture.[32] This educated class could also represent India in the Western world.

The creation of a new class of English Indians was another way for the British empire to construct a tangible other and simultaneously reinforce British identity. However, in his now classic 1984 essay, "On Mimicry and Man: The Ambivalence of Colonial Discourse," Homi Bhabha points out the subversive potential of creating an imitation Englishman who may speak English but who may not necessarily agree with the philosophy of imperialism. British colonial mimicry is about the native adopting the habits and mannerisms of the colonizer or in this case the Indian becom-ing the perfect British citizen. But as Bhabha argues, mimicry also exposes the flaws in the British imperial project because the Indian can never truly be a British citizen. If he or she were, the empire could not maintain the hierarchies on which it was built. Mimicry, Bhabha explains, employs both "resemblance and menace."[33] The resemblance of mimicry is comforting because of its familiarity. Its menace, on the other hand, exposes the con-tradictions of trying to reproduce the native in the colonial's image be-cause that very image is unstable and susceptible to misinterpretation. The recognition that the colonial project may be flawed undermines the entire act of mimicry and the solid comforting image of British superiority. Thus full transformation is prevented and the native is only a potential project who is always trying but never succeeding.

In Asian American studies, fluency in English has particular resonance. In Hawai'i the interplay between pidgin and Standard English is directly related to citizenship.[34] The ability to speak standard English is associated with class and upward mobility through better schools to better jobs. As in the case of brown voice, local speech does not destabilize the legacy of colonialism but rather it highlights the effects of that history. In Hawai'i the class system emphasizes the primacy of speech over racial and ethnic position. In other words, the way you speak determines the way you are treated and the community to which you belong even before you are visu-ally recognized. The development of an educated class in the context of the American empire is about access to the privileges of whiteness, which is associated with enunciated English but not necessarily accentless Eng-lish.

Although Indian independence was achieved over fifty years ago, the image of Indians in the world is that of the highly educated English-speaking immigrant. Often people's general perception that Indians speak English intelligibly (though not without an accent) amplifies the notion that all Indians are educated. This image has grown to include working-class and service-industry wage earners such as taxi drivers, convenience store owners, and motel owners. When people encounter South Asian immigrants in these venues they assume that all South Asians are highly educated and perhaps they were once engineers or computer specialists or doctors but have experienced occupational downgrading. South Asian subjectivity is framed by national origin as well as religious and cultural practices that distinguish their immigration status and history in the United States. In other words, South Asian immigrants have been highly individualized as a group by their cultural behavior that separates them physically and psychologically from the term and group identity of Asian American even though their racial classification (since 1980) has been Asian American. Consequently many Indians have difficulty identifying themselves as an Asian American minority and prefer to foreground their status as "Indians," which is more closely affiliated with the privileges of "whiteness."

Rosina Lippi-Green asserts that "Accent serves as the first point of gate-keeping. . . . Accent becomes a litmus test for exclusion, an excuse to turn away, to refuse to recognize the other" (64). Accent discrimination is not a novel experience in the United States. But it is rarely expressed in discussions of racial hierarchies except to indicate difference or foreignness. In a well-known study of undergraduate students' comprehension of lecture material, students listened to a lecture recorded by the same speaking voice (a native speaker of English from Ohio) and half were shown the slide of a white woman while the other half were shown the slide of an Asian woman. Students who saw the photo of the Asian woman recorded lower comprehension scores and were more likely to register the presence of a foreign accent in their responses to the lecture.[35] In this case the physical appearance of the supposed teacher heavily influenced the understanding of the material by students even when there was no accent. This study clearly illustrates that accent reception is subjective. It also matches representations of Asians in the popular media, which usually portray only one type of "Asian" accent even though the difference between a Beijing accent and a Hong Kong accent is as variable as a Chicago and a New England accent. In popular culture Asians are shown speaking "broken

English" that is a cause of frustration and anger or ridicule among those listening to them. Indian English, on the other hand, usually does not invoke the same feelings.

In terms of American immigration and assimilation politics, we can argue that accented English in any form makes us reflect on who and what can represent a true American or occupy the space of a "cultural citizen." The concept of brown voice brings with it the full force of colonial legacy. Over 150 years of interaction with British English have influenced how Indians and Indian Americans respond to and utilize English in daily life.[36] However, since Indian independence (in spite of the flurry of British Raj dramas in the 1980s) the notion of brown voice has also reflected educational expertise, particularly in the areas of medicine and computer and software technology. We need only scan the headlines of the business and economics or technology sections of the newspaper to see the influence of Indians and South Asian immigrants on the global and national economies.

Ultimately, the theory of brown voice causes us to rethink how we see and hear racial identity beyond the visual and how we process the cultural meaning of accents. The effect of the accent among South Asians has been rendered acceptable through the character of Apu who has made it familiar and loved and also funny. But the performance of brown voice connotes class privilege, the kind of poshness associated with education that we hear from Salman Rushdie or Merchant Ivory, or from Miss India and Miss Universe beauty pageant contestants. Brown voice accentuates the ambiguous nature of South Asian racial and cultural identity in the United States because regardless of their status or occupation in the United States, South Asians are heard (and seen) with only one accent and one voice that presents South Asians in one form: the character of Apu.

To break out of brown voice through accent variation or in other ways is to defy the expectations of the audience and to allow other accents to emerge out of brown bodies. It redesigns our experiences of racial and national identity. In the late 1990s and the early years of the twenty-first century, a diversity of Indian accents have been featured in independent, national, and international films. These films have served to revoice Indians around the world and signal some movement in the fixed positions of South Asians. A number of new films—from the international Bollywood hit *Kabhi Khushi Kabhie Gham* (2002), to the independent British hit *Bend It Like Beckham* (2002), to Mira Nair's hit *Monsoon Wedding* (2002), and M. Night Shyamalan's top-grossing *Sixth Sense* (1999)—all these films and their Indian or Indian American directors interrogate and play with the accents and voices that emerge from brown bodies. In these films one hears London City girl slang, middle-class Indian English, working-class Indian English, as well as American English and Canadian English. In *The Sixth Sense,* M. Night Shyamalan has a cameo of a physician but we hear his distinctly "American" voice before we see his brown face. The film is about interacting and seeing/hearing dead people. In this scene it is a dis-embodied voice (that you pay no mind to) until the camera suddenly flashes on the brown doctor's face. The visual shock of seeing a brown face without an accent (as well as the director) is then transferred to the drama of the scene. It is a brilliant directorial move especially since this is the first time we hear/see a nonwhite person speak in the film.

These interventions by Indian and Indian American directors in the film industry move beyond the physical and more significantly vocal re-straints of racial hierarchies and help to challenge and expand the privi-leged positions of South Asians in popular culture.

NOTES

I want to thank LeiLani Nishime and Tasha Oren for their invaluable comments and suggestions regarding this essay. I also want to thank Victor Basquera, Leslie Bow, Grace Hong, Lisa Nakamura, and Michael Peterson at UW-Madison for their helpful hints and support and encouragement of this project.

1. Although the episode is Matt Groening's satire about the politics of Califor-nia's Proposition 109, it is also about the competing notions of citizenship and the social contracts of citizenship that bind the community together. According to Animatedtv.com this is also Groening's third-favorite episode in his list of top ten.

2. See Shilpa Davé, "Community Beauty": Transnational Embodiments and Cultural Citizenship in "Miss India Georgia," *Lit: Literature Interpretation Theory* 12:3 (2001): 335–358.

3. For more information on the various classifications of Asian Indians, in-cluding the 1923 *U.S. vs. Thind* case, see Ron Takaki, *Strangers from a Different Shore* (Boston: Little, Brown, 1998), and Sucheng Chan, *Asian Americans: An Inter-pretative History* (Boston: Twayne, 1991).

4. Eric Lott, in *Love and Theft: Blackface Minstrelsy and the American Working Class* (New York: Oxford UP, 1993), argues that the performance of blackface is not only an acknowledgment of the notion of racial or black culture but that the act of performing illuminates what it is to live with "whiteness." The popular forum of minstrelsy allows Lott to insightfully explore racial norms and attitudes in the

nineteenth century as expressed in daily life, and use these insights to study the consequences of racial cross-dressing and playacting. Michael Rogin, in *Blackface, White Noise: Jewish Immigrants in the Hollywood Melting Pot* (Berkeley: U of California P, 1996), expands on the performance of blackface as a racial commentary by exploring how ethnicity and race are portrayed on the silver screen. Carol A. Stabile and Mark Harrison, eds., *Prime Time Animation: Television Animation and American Culture* (New York: Routledge, 2003), features historical and critical analysis of televised animated shows in relation to American cultural life, but does not address the racial politics of performance.

5. In particular Lee, Lott, and Rogin discuss situations in which the performers sing in a particular accent or, as with Al Jolson, where he hides his religion and ethnicity under the paint of race in *The Jazz Singer*. Michelle Hilmes discusses the voice and accents in her study on radio drama. But there has been virtually no work on the voices behind the animated scripts that have been generated since the 1930s.

6. See Kaja Silverman, *The Acoustic Mirror* (Bloomington: Indiana UP, 1988). I want to thank David Eng for pointing out the significance of queer theory to this work.

7. See Lavina Shankar and Rajini Srikanth, eds., *A Part, Yet Apart: South Asians in Asian America* (Philadelphia: Temple UP, 1998).

8. In the British speech exercise book *Drop Your Foreign Accent* (1932), the author declares in his preface:

> Your most distinguished speaker, wonderful though his fluency may be, correct his grammar and admirable his choice of works, is the awkward man as long as he has not dropped his foreign accent. . . . He irritates. There is a distinct element of courtesy in the foreigner's correct pronunciation—the thought: I have deemed it worth my while to grapple with the difficulties of your language, till I have overcome them. This pleases as much as slovenly pronunciation displeases. It is an open letter of recommendation, like a clear handwriting, a neat dress or a handsome face. (7)

In other words, good pronunciation reflects respect for the dominant culture and if you pronounce the words correctly you too can become a good citizen. The author's "irritation" arises from the fact that he is advocating a unified and homogeneous nationalism, and the presence of different races and social classes is contrary to that ideal.

9. Broken English is an interesting phrase—to break English is to shake up the notion of a unified national identity, an identity not rooted in the experience of immigration but in the way in which we express ourselves culturally—the American accent.

10. Significantly, these are "mostly 'content' words which carry most of the meaning of the sentence rather than 'connecting' words which are often less cru-

cial" (107). Some examples are: deVELop versus DEVlop, neCESSary versus NEC-essary, PREpare versus prePARE, or CAssette vs. caSSETTE.

11. See "Moreover: Broadcasting to the Nation," *Economist,* London, March 27, 1999, 86.

12. The 1930s radio program *Amos 'n' Andy* was one of the first radio dramas to feature black characters (voiced by white men) and also the most popular one of its time.

13. See Stabile and Harrison, *Prime Time Animation.*

14. As Wendy Hilton-Morrow and David McMahan note in their essay, "The Flintstones to Futurama: Networks and Prime Time Animation," in *Prime Time Animation: Television Animation and American Culture,* the first prime-time ani-mated drama to deliver social commentary and satire was *The Flintstones* which first aired on ABC in 1961. It went off the air in 1966 and reappeared in syndication on Saturday mornings in the 1970s.

15. The most notable exception, as my colleague Lisa Nakamura pointed out to me, is Jar Jar Binks from the latest *Star Wars* films. Not only did his accent irritate, but it inflamed talk about racial representations and computer graphic characters. There are websites which allow one to download the latest films from which fans have eliminated the character Jar Jar.

16. See, for example, the 2003 ads for the animated feature *Sinbad* that heavily promoted Brad Pitt as the voice of Sinbad and Academy-award-winning Cather-ine Zeta-Jones and Michelle Pfeiffer as his costars.

17. In 1992 Asian American groups protested the New York production casting of Jonathan Pryce, a white British man, as the Eurasian engineer in the Broadway musical *Miss Saigon.* Although he had played the part in London, Asian American groups were appalled by his yellowface makeup. But their main objection was that no Asian Americans were allowed to audition for the part. After the initial run on Broadway, subsequent shows cast Asian or Asian American actors as the engineer.

18. Anita Ramdharry, "Ay Carumba: *The Simpsons*: A Transnational Text," mas-ter's thesis, University of North Dakota, 2001.

19. As my colleagues Grace Hong and Victor Bascara have observed to me, Apu is a part of Homer's bowling team rather than a member of "The Stereotypes" team in the episode "Pin Pals."

20. See animatedtv.about.com/cs/lists/tp/sicharacters.html.

21. See Amit Rai, "The World according to Apu: A Look at Network Televi-sion's Only Regular South Asian Character," in *India Currents,* March 31, 1994, vol. 7, no. 12, 7. Rai notes that Apu is depicted as a greedy storekeeper. This portrayal dates back to colonial narratives that feature the greedy native who can be bribed but ultimately is killed by his greed. We see variations on this theme in films rang-ing from the Indiana Jones films to *The Mummy.*

22. Robert Lee, *Orientals: Asian American Popular Culture* (Philadelphia: Temple

UP, 2000), asserts that Asians fall into two categories: the alien and/or the foreigner. The alien is considered an ever-present pollutant whereas the foreigner is seen as a sojourner or traveler who will eventually go away. Both labels imply a distance from the community. Lee contends that "Orientals" have been produced by popular culture to fit these categories. Although Apu is a part of the Springfield community, his alienness is magnified when the show focuses on him.

23. In the first season George Takei is the guest voice of Akira, a waiter at a Japanese sushi restaurant, and Sab Shimono does the voice-over of the master chef. So Asian Americans are brought in to do voice-overs but not characters.

24. Joe Rhodes, "Flash! 24 Simpsons Stars Reveal Themselves," *TV Guide*, October 21, 2000, 27.

25. However, the success of TV sitcoms does depend on adherence to a particular genre narrative that includes resolution of a problem in thirty minutes, which undermines Groening's efforts to keep pushing the limit with his show. Groening's efforts with Apu have had mixed results. When Apu is featured in an episode the show focuses on his cultural behavior, which is often funny at the expense of Indian religion and culture. In an article written on the widely popular website *The Simpson Archive*, Eric Garrison reflects on the cultural messages of the show: "Already, the show had a few stereotypes, or portraits of the modern American family. The first few seasons of 'The Simpsons' pointed fun at many American issues and provided their own ethical solutions to many moral dilemmas. In the seasons to come, more characters would enter the show, and the show itself would grow from a small cast, to a cast of hundreds. One of the main issues that some of the public would begin to hold against the show was stereotyping." The influence of the show and its impact on American culture have been widely discussed on the respected listserve alt.tv.simpsons.

26. S. Ali, "Will the Real Apu Please Stand Up?" *India Abroad*, vol. 33, no. 10, December 7, 2001, M5.

27. This quotation is excerpted from Paul Cantor, "The Simpsons' America," in the *Wilson Quarterly* 25, no. 3 (Summer 2001): 33, and from an article in *Political Theory* (December 1999). Political scientist Paul Cantor convincingly applies this statement to the show's tendency to lampoon both the political right and left and portray the lack of trust of those in power, especially those who are not local community members.

28. One of the earliest cartoon depictions of a recurring Indian character was Hadji (voiced by Michael Bravo), the sidekick of adventure boy-sleuth Jonny Quest in *The Adventures of Jonny Quest*. I vividly remember watching this show in syndication in the 1970s and being very pleased to see an Indian boy on television. Some of the episodes were set in India so I also saw some Indian girls. It was also initially aired as a prime-time animated series on ABC. Produced in 1964 by Hanna-Barbera Studios, Hadji was the turban-clad boy who had "magic" or mystical powers that usually went wrong and made the situation

worse for the boys. A 1990s update presents Hadji as the now adopted son of Dr. Quest (and so Jonny's brother) who is particularly adept at science and computer work.

More recently, MTV's animated series *Clone High* (2002) has featured a teenage Gandhi (a computer nerd in this incarnation). This series has drawn some criticism from Indians around the world for the way it depicts a teenage clone of Gandhi. Other characters include Cleopatra, Genghis Khan, John F. Kennedy, Jr., Joan of Arc, and Abraham Lincoln. I find the show a fascinating and humorous study of how historical figures linked to important cultural movements react to the social world of American high school.

29. See Susan Koshy's excellent article on the class narrative of South Asian exceptionalism, "Morphing Race into Ethnicity," *boundary* 2 (Spring 2001): 153–194.

30. See Vijay Prasad, "Of a Girmit Consciousness," in *The Karma of Brown Folk* (Minneapolis: U of Minnesota P, 2000).

31. T. Macaulay, "Minute on Education," in *Sources of Indian Tradition*, vol. 2, ed. William Theodore de Bary (New York: Columbia UP, 1958), 49.

32. In his groundbreaking work, *Orientalism*, Edward Said enumerates the many ways in which Europe has constructed a tangible other, the East, in order to reinforce its own identity as a masterful civilized power. In essence, colonies such as India were conceptualized as "a locale requiring Western attention, reconstruction, even redemption. The Orient existed as a place isolated from the mainstream of European progress in the sciences, arts, and commerce." Edward Said, *Orientalism* (New York: Vintage, 1978), 206.

33. Homi K. Bhabha, "Of Mimicry and Man: The Ambivalence of Colonial Discourse," chapter 4 in *The Location of Culture* (London: Routledge, 1994), 86.

34. See Morris Young, "Whose Paradise? Hawai'i, Desire, and the Global-Local Tensions of Popular Culture," this volume.

35. D. L. Rubin's 1992 study of the effects of accent and ethnicity on interactions between undergraduates and non-native teaching assistants is cited in Rosina Lippi-Green, *English with an Accent: Language, Ideology, and Discrimination* (London: Routledge, 1997), 127.

36. The amalgamation of Hindi and English, Hinglish, is common in Bollywood films as well as in Indian immigrant communities.

BIBLIOGRAPHY

Ali, S. "Will the Real Apu Please Stand Up?" *India Abroad.* Vol. 33, No. 10, December 7, 2001, M5.

Basile, Nancy. "Top Ten Simpsons Characters." www.animatedtv.com, 2003.

Bhabha, Homi K. "Of Mimicry and Man: The Ambivalence of Colonial Discourse." Chapter 4 in *The Location of Culture*. London: Routledge, 1994.

Cantor, Paul. "The Simpsons' America." *Wilson Quarterly* 25, no. 3 (Summer 2001): 33..

Garrison, Eric. "A Reflection of Society and a Message on Family." *The Simpson Archive* (www.snpp.com/other/papers/eg.paper.html).

Groening, Matt. *The Simpsons: A Complete Guide to Our Favorite Family.* New York: Harper Perennial, 1997.

Hilmes, Michele. *Radio Voices: American Broadcasting, 1922–1952.* Minneapolis: U of Minnesota P, 1997.

Honey, John. *Does Accent Matter? The Pygmalion Factor.* London: Faber and Faber, 1989.

Lee, Robert. *Orientals: Asian Americans in Popular Culture.* Philadelphia: Temple UP, 2000.

Lippi-Green Rosina. *English with an Accent: Language, Ideology, and Discrimination.* New York: Routledge, 1997.

Macaulay, Thomas. "Minute on Education." In *Sources of Indian Tradition.* Vol. 2. Ed. William Theodore de Bary. New York: Columbia UP, 1958, 49.

"Much Apu about Nothing." *The Simpsons.* Broadcast on FOX on May 5, 1996.

Rai, Amit. "The World according to Apu: A Look at Network Television's Only Regular South Asian Character." *India Currents,* March 31, 1994, vol. 7, no. 12.

Rhodes, Joe. "Flash! 24 Simpsons Stars Reveal Themselves." *TV Guide,* October 21, 2000.

Rogin, Michael. *Blackface, White Noise: Jewish Immigrants in the Hollywood Melting Pot.* Berkeley: U of California P, 1996.

Stabile, Carol A., and Mark Harrison, eds. *Prime Time Animation: Television Animation and American Culture.* New York: Routledge, 2003.

Chapter 17

Secret Asian Man

Angry Asians and the Politics of Cultural Visibility

Tasha G. Oren

At a festival postscreening discussion of Justin Lin's *Better Luck Tomorrow*, an enthusiastic Roger Ebert praised the work, hailing it as a generational breakthrough: a film mostly populated by Asian American actors that isn't "about" Asian Americanness. Public prodding revealed the difficulty of such an argument as Justin Lin uncomfortably straddled the line between being an Asian American director of an Asian American production and being an up-and-coming young director with an MTV and Paramount distribution deal and a film poised to perform that most American of transformations: from an independent labor of love to a mainstream success.

To a largely white, Midwestern audience, Lin and Ebert attempted to distance the film from a particular Asian American reading in the face of cringingly simpleton questions about "bad" representations of Asians and the film's "message" to either white or Asian America. The film, which depicts overachieving highschoolers' quest for the golden ring of academic distinction and their descent into petty crime and finally murder, had already achieved much-coveted buzz in the festival circuit and been dubbed "explosive" and "disturbing." In light of Lin's first-hand encounter with the burdens of representation, I kept my observation—that its depiction of characters both chafing against and bound to the constriction of obligation spoke so elegantly to a facet of Asian American experience—to myself.

For Lin and his fans, the politics of race played out on two fronts simultaneously. First, in the three-dimensionality of the characters and the text's ability to acknowledge identity politics without placing it in the film's narrative center. Second, in the film's industrial context as a player in the mainstream entertainment economy. To his critics, however—many of them Asian American—a different racial politics was at stake; a particular vision of the importance of representation and the great cost of doing it "wrong."

The film's description as "controversial" and the widely reported confrontation between Lin and a livid audience member at Sundance who accused the director of creating negative representations of Asian Americans reveal the complexities of such a cultural intervention. The scrutiny *Better Luck Tomorrow* received was here revealed as rooted in past cultural grievances and fueled by anger. As much as Lin's film represents a fresh and exciting moment for Asian American popular culture by virtue of its entry into a mainstream consumer space,[1] the strong responses the film has garnered speak to the weight of historical erasure and distortion, and the difficulties inherent in the project of extricating Asian American representations from the context of their cultural history.[2] Regardless of Lin's achievement, there is no escaping cultural memory.

Since all texts (indeed all shared symbols) contain within them layers of history, cultural change requires not only the forging of fresh symbols but also a reckoning with old ones. This essay seeks to explore how such reckonings are dealt with in new cultural texts. More importantly, it argues for the importance of such moments in the volatile terrain of negotiation that is American popular culture.

The Uses of Grievance

The past few years have offered potent and often contradictory moments for Asian Americans both politically and culturally. Amidst new triumphs of breakthrough political advancements, particular incidents—such as the Wen Ho Lee case or Rep. Howard Coble's public proclamation about both the benevolence and necessity of the interment of Japanese Americans during World War II—provoked deep cultural anger as it reawakened old wounds in Asian American communities.

Anger, as we know, is the most potent fuel for activism—especially for minority activism in the United States, where public expressions of grievance are activism's most common public face and often its cultural voice. Moreover, much of the most visible public expression of grievance for Asian Americans recently has been over cultural signification: media representations and the pernicious repetition of stereotypes. In the recent past, protests over the film *Year of the Dragon* or the casting of *Miss Saigon* brought such moments of cultural anger into mainstream visibility. Currently, dismay over Halloween costumes such as Urban Outfitters "Chinaman" mask, the widely marketed "Kung Fool" costume, and most recently, the Abercrombie and Fitch T-shirt designs have given rise to more expressions of rage and grievance—and their public expression.

In light of the place of anger in cultural politics, I set out to explore the relationship between anger, politics, and popular culture as a way into thinking about the process of cultural and political change. I began by asking: what do Asian Americans mean in popular mainstream culture? To whom? And how do these meanings construct and delimit politics? I conclude by suggesting that the association between anger and cultural visibility illuminates the Abercrombie and Fitch T-shirt controversy, as well as provides new ways of thinking about Asian American presence in media texts.

Despite the anger certain representations evoked within the Asian American community,[3] in the popular, mainstream imagination, expressions of Asian American anger are rare, and rarer still are representations of Asian American racial grievance in popular media texts.

In *The Melancholy of Race,* Anne AnLin Cheng defines racial grief as the combination of rage and shame, and focuses her analysis on the possibility of transformation from grief to grievance, "from suffering an injury to speaking out against that injury." In that transformation, she notes, is the cultural turn from being subjected to grief to being a subject who speaks that grievance.[4] What, she asks, "can political agency mean for someone operating in a symbolic, cultural economy that has already pre-assigned them as a deficit?"

The long cultural history of representational distortion and erasures in popular cultural texts has been the subject of Asian American scholarship for several decades now.[5] Aside from critiques of representation, scholars have explored the intersection of politics and culture through an examination of Asian American history.[6] Many of the origins of Asian American literature are themselves sourced in anger over cultural erasures and misrepresentation (think here of Frank Chin's work or the in-your-face titles of the groundbreaking *Aiiieeeee!* collection or *Charlie Chan Is Dead,* books that articulated cultural anger and exclusion as their animating force). More recent work has turned to Asian American theater, writing, film, and other media forms as alternative spaces for cultural representation (work by Peter Feng, Laura Hyun Yi Kang, Karen Shimakawa, Dorinne Kondo, and Jun Xing, among others) with some scholars focusing specifically on Asian American cultural spheres as places to counter the grief of racial abjection. My own concern here differs from these scholars' focus on alternatives to mainstream culture, and is more specific than most critical attentions to representations of Asian Americans in mainstream texts. I am, instead, interested in the expressions of racial anger and grief in popular mainstream culture and their connections to political action. In short, I am after the symbolic process where grievances are addressed through a recognition of racial grief. Analysis of such expressions within popular culture, I suggest, can illustrate the particular challenges for Asian American cultural presence that strives beyond the blind-alley dichotomy of "positive and negative representations." I offer a consideration of audience identification within the economy of mainstream culture as a way out of this unproductive mode of thinking in an attempt to show how cultural work, in the form of racial grievance, can be harnessed to push the borders of popular meaning making.

In what follows, I will consider moments in which such anger (the expression of racial grievance) is performed in mainstream texts, beginning with popular films and then what I see as "bridging texts": Asian American cultural production that gives voice to such grievances *within* mainstream cultural texts. As my extended example, I use the work of Tak Toyoshima and his nationally distributed comic, *Secret Asian Man.*

As a central question, then, I take up the cultural expression of racial anger (both in and about cultural practices from representations in films to caricatures on T-shirts) as an instructive lens through which to view—and build—the active presence of Asian Americans within popular culture.

Angry Asians and the Challenges of Visibility

Expressions of anger in popular texts are interesting not only because of their narrative weight and cinematic value but also because the right to express one's grievances explicitly is a privilege. The melancholy of racialized people, as Cheng demonstrates in her analysis of African American and Asian American literary texts, is often sourced in their visual erasure

—the refusal or casual inability of white mainstream culture to see, to pay attention. Thus so many mainstream texts catch the racialized figure only in the periphery of their collective eye, seeing merely an outline devoid of subjectivity and the dignity of particularity. In this sense, I am interested in representations of anger not only as Asian American responses to past grievances, but also as in and of themselves a process of coming into visibility.

Finding expressions of Asian American racial grievance in popular texts reveals its own striking deficit. Such a lack is brought into relief when compared to the commonplace representation of African American racial grievance, so common in fact that it is often played for laughs in popular action films and comedies—as in the trope of the "oversensitive" black man.[7]

Tropes and formulaic textual constructions are among the building blocks for popular mainstream culture. They are "built in" to the industries' modes of production, our genre-based expectations, and the demographically minded patterns of marketing and consumption. Formulaic repetitions and clichés, then, are not mere testaments to a lack of an imagination; they are there because they are presumed to tap into a cultural imaginary (that amorphous collection of images, frames of reference, textual knowledge, and collective experience that together make up the closest thing to a shared symbolic alphabet through which we make meaning out of culture). As I will argue, popular perceptions of racial sensitivities are an important factor in shaping patterns within popular media products. While many scholars have emphasized the pernicious and often blatantly racist representations in mainstream media, I want to highlight a somewhat modest but commonplace operational disregard—what I call the "oops" factor (or, more accurately, "Oops, I did it again"). Much of the anger directed toward producers of mass consumable popular culture is at heart about cultural blindness and insensitivity that repeats and replicates itself with new textual iterations. In my search for articulations of Asian American racial anger and grievance in such texts, what I am in fact after are moments that rupture formulaic disregard and offer new ways of articulating Asian American experience and its popular understandings.

Typically, Asian American racial exclusion and discrimination is alluded to only in historically specific narratives that bracket off such experiences in a now-repaired past. Even among such media texts, representation rarely equals subjectivity. In the two most famous (and popular) examples, the internment of Japanese Americans in the films *Come See the Paradise* and *Snow Falling on Cedars* (both adaptations of novels)[8] is not so much experienced as *witnessed* by the narratives' white male protagonists, mirroring what a cautious film industry imagines to be its "general" audience.[9]

The task of finding contemporary media narratives is further complicated by a global entertainment complex on the one hand and the global dynamic of transnational labor mobility on the other—as well as the reality that first-generation Asian immigrants now outnumber American-born Asian Americans, creating a cultural category in which diasporic, global, and national cultural elements are all but inextricable.[10] To this extent, finding any Asian Americans (angry or content) in mainstream texts is already a challenge, as contemporary Hollywood duplicates its own conditions of production by concocting endless narratives where capable Asian foreigners arrive to ably assist local (American) police officers or distressed-but-plucky heroines, spectacularly dispatching the bad guys in a flurry of jabs, kicks, and broken English punch lines. These perpetual foreigners (usually Chow-Yun Fat, Jet Li, or Jackie Chan) then disappear to their home countries, free of local ties or the faintest tinge of sexual entanglements. While I am loath to argue for a kind a definitional barrier to definitively separate the Asian American from the Asian, I do want to stress that even in our current globalizing age, politics, policies, and rights are defined almost exclusively under the logic of the nation-state and so, to the extent that popular culture articulates politics, national affiliation does matter.

One of the few examples of such a direct demand for visibility is from Joel Shumacher's 1993 film *Falling Down*. This example is particularly interesting since the film is so insistently about racial antagonism, rage, and hysterical violence—marked by a disturbing ambivalence toward the main character, an angry white man (Michael Douglas) pushed to the brink. As he wanders through a sweaty, multihued, third-world-like Los Angeles embarking on a series of escalating rampages, his first victim, an immigrant Korean grocer, arrives at the police station to lodge a complaint. When a veteran officer and hero (Robert Duvall) off-handedly asks an Asian American officer to translate the man's agitated Korean, the officer (Steve Park) replies evenly: "This man is Korean. I, since you've never bothered to notice, am Japanese." Such an articulation of difference—while a minor beat in this charged narrative—is striking because it is so rare while addressing such a common grievance.

As Herman Gray has argued, mainstream meanings are not made through individual texts but rather across and through the relationships among various texts (both fiction and nonfiction). Similarly, John Fiske's formulation of media culture as a relay station that airs and amplifies social issues by injecting them into popular media storytelling helps us think through the importance of popular representations without falling into the tired and ultimately peripheral question of "positive" or "negative" representations. The example of *Falling Down* is particularly instructive here in its role as the consummate popular record of the uses of racial anger for political gain—so deftly employed in the trope of the "angry white man" that backlashed its way into popular and ultimately governmental politics.[11]

In James Foley's *The Corruptor* (1999), racial grievance is related more directly to media representation, as a Chinese American cop acknowledges that common trope of racial difference in action films, the dick joke. Here, two Chinese American cops (Andrew Pang and Chow-Yun Fat, in his only role as an Asian American) taunt a young white cop (Mark Wahlberg) who has chosen to work in the Chinatown district by suggesting he has a "a bad case of Yellow-Fever." When the three get drunk at a local bar, the officer expands on his theory: "It's dick size," he pronounces, undeterred by the laughter, "White people believe all Asians got little dicks. You think that when an Asian chick sees your pecker, she's gonna think it's Mount St. Helen's. It's true! And then you look at the tiny hands on most Asian chicks, and think your weenie is going to look like a sewer pipe in her fist."

"He's discovered my secret," giggles Wahlberg to the rising laughter around the table. "Well, the joke's on you," Pang retorts, "because this Chinaman is hung like a fucking . . ." When a fellow officer erupts with laughter, shouting "gnat," the cop becomes agitated, yelling, "You want to see? You want to see?" Jumping up, he begins undoing his pants, as his drinking buddies, quickly sobering, protest for him to "put that thing away."

Sexuality is understandably a central filter for stereotypical representation, as many scholars have noted, following Edward Said's field-defining exploration of the orientalist impulse. But masculinity—even in its purely physical expression of power, speed, and size—functions as a complex signifier that, as Susan Jeffords has argued, speaks to contemporary definitions of nation and citizenship.[12] As Jeffords argues, cultural articulations of national identity and politics are often bound up in representations of masculinity as their fixation over lost and regained control consistently stage interrogations of race, masculinity, and difference.[13] Here sexuality is not central to the signification process, rather, it stands in for the issues and grievances of the social, national, and cultural body. Thus, it is hardly surprising that most expressions of racial grievance in popular texts find their voice in male bodies.[14]

Among the slim offerings of Asian American subjectivity in popular films, *Dragon: The Bruce Lee Story* (Rob Cohen, 1993) is a rarity indeed. While anger in particular has not been the lens through which critics have approached it, the narrative has attracted much scholarly attention for its focus on Asian American racial and cultural exclusion. Many considerations of the narrative have pointed out the problematic staging of a pivotal scene where Asian American media stereotypes are expressly interrogated. In this much-examined moment, Bruce Lee (Jason Scott Lee) and his white future wife Linda (Lauren Holly) are watching *Breakfast at Tiffany's,* one of Linda's favorite films. When a buck-toothed, kimono-clad Mickey Rooney emerges as the ornery upstairs neighbor, Mr. Yunioshi, Linda, along with the rest of the theater audience, roars with laughter until she catches a glimpse of her date, who solemnly sits beside her, choking back rage. Linda's laughter dies abruptly; she looks at the screen again with newly acquired consciousness and says, "Let's get out of here."[15] In its emphasis on the white observer, the scene replays the familiar structure in mainstream narratives of racial abjection, where white empathy is injected as an audience surrogate, making racial injury legible. Unlike the yellow-faced Rooney, whose ridiculous complaining make up the film's comic relief, Lee does not protest; he quietly swallows rage and toughs it out. As the scene's construction suggests, it is Lee's controlled inaction (and Linda's agency) that make his grief sympathetic.

To get angry, of course, is in bad form; it is to make a spectacle of oneself and demand attention—often a last-ditch effort, a lashing out. Thus, the expression of anger in popular texts is simultaneously an act of agency and loss: loss of temper, composure, and self-control. Or, as popular parlance would have it, one simply "loses it." When Bruce Lee finally "loses it" and articulates racial rage directly, he is both terrifying and hysterical.

After losing the lead in *Kung-fu*—a television show he helped develop —to David Carradine, Lee leaves the United States and finds fame as a martial arts star in Hong Kong. When his wife arrives with their children to persuade Bruce to return, he explodes: "I'm somebody here, I'm special!" he yells. "Back there I'm just a gook, just another wet-back, Charlie-Chan-low-pay-gook-dishwasher in a stinking tacky restaurant." As

Linda watches, terrified, Lee turns, violently swiping a nearby dresser and sending its contents crashing to the ground. When he turns to face her again, his body contorts to become the iconic servile Chinaman; he slopes forward, his face twisted into a bucktoothed mask, his hands twitching before him as he assumes a mocking heavily accented voice: "Sure, sure mister white man, pleeesee, no ticky, no shirty, order one from column A and one from column B. Me happy to work on the railroads, me happy to dig the mines for you." Lee turns his destructive rage on a nearby door, punching through it as he screams, "Mr. White Man!"

Freud's original definition of hysteria as repressed trauma—a traumatic memory whose conscious repression causes a symptomatic physical eruption—is certainly evocative here. David Eng's reading of various protagonists of Asian American literature as male hysterics further reminds us of the long feminist tradition of regarding the social meaning of hysteria as a discourse of protest and a product of complaint against the social order. It is, then, worth noting the relationship between power and anger in *Dragon,* and the differences between these two scenes. Lee's frustrated outburst only occurs at the near-end of the film, when he has achieved unparalleled success as a film star and idol in Asia. While the latter scene is certainly constructed to communicate profound unease (again, our identification point remains with Linda throughout) it occurs—in this cinematic universe—as a near-end point in Lee's life trajectory: he has achieved stardom just as he tires of bumping up against the racist ceiling of the American media industry, and gains fame and power as he loses his wide-eyed, dogged optimism that cultural history and a racist past could be easily transcended. It is only here, in a spectacular unleashing of racialized grievance, that Lee turns to a Chinese American past, conjuring the very chain of cultural images that has claimed him.

The expression of anger in popular film, as the examples above suggest, is a complicated bargain. Its articulation suggests both privilege and a last resort, a luxury and the explosion of bottled-up frustration. Yet, in the common mythologies of American popular storytelling, it is also therapeutic: a beneficial catharsis. Consider the metaphorical case of repressed anger that spills beyond the edges of the screen, in the publicity materials for a recent (and unlikely) summer action release, Ang Lee's *The Hulk.* Much of the advance publicity for the film focused on Lee's unusual involvement in the creation of his CGI green monster. Lee, whose diverse films share only a fascination with emotional repression, not only directed the film but served as a physical model for the monster's facial expressions and movements. As one entertainment reporter observed, "the soft spoken Asian man" would "become the Hulk. . . . His slightly hunched body crouches menacingly; his tired face contorts with rage. He lowers his shoulders and lumbers a step. He trashes. It makes for a strange spectacle, as if there's something awful inside that's bucking wildly to be released."[16]

This final example may be fanciful, but it is also suggestive. For the film's narrative reliance on the director, "profoundly uncomfortable with revealing his own emotions," letting out "his inner hulk" is itself thoroughly imbued with the trope of Asian repression. And so, Lee's encounter with the therapeutics of trashing reads as strangely triumphant: "It's difficult for me to throw a fit," Lee tells an interviewer, likening the Hulk to Jackie Chan in Arnold Schwarzenegger's body. "Really, only I knew how he should act. . . . It felt fucking great."

Exoticize My Fist: Racial Grievance as Pop Culture

For Slavoj Zizek, hysteria is a failure of interpellation; a refusal (or inability) to submit.[17] As a quick review of popular films can attest, such refusals by Asian Americans are few and far between, which bears out Lisa Lowe's assertion that popular films often use a multicultural aesthetic as a fiction of racial reconciliation. As Lowe argues, it is local cultural productions that emerge from particular communities that disrupt and reveal such fictions of reconciliation. And nowhere do such disruptive narratives of refusal thrive more consistently and successfully than on-line.

In numerous sites ranging from popular e-zines to blogs and parody pages Asian American cultural activists, artists, and fans critique and challenge common representations. In websites like *Angry Asian Guy, Big Bad Chinese Mama, AsiaZine, Exoticize My Fist,* and many others, young Asian Americans use raw anger, parody, and media criticism to voice racial grievance, expose and mock stereotypes, and create new cultural expressions. The popularity of such sites is instructive as it suggests the degree to which racial anger—so absent from the mainstream representational palette or collective political imagination—resonates so thoroughly as a mode of engagement. Due both to their particular address and limited exposure, many such sites make up alternatives, rather than correctives, to mainstream popular culture. However, texts like these can also function as "in between" locations that address cultural and representational rage not only to knowing Asian American audiences but to a mainstream pop culture audience. These audiences understand such interventions not as insular grievances from a misrepresented and underrepresented minority but as popular cultural texts whose appeal reaches well beyond particular identity politics. Located between the corporate mainstream of Hollywood narratives and mostly narrow targeting of Asian American–specific e-zines is Tak Toyoshima's print and on-line comic strip *Secret Asian Man* (SAM).

I consider Toyoshima's work a "bridging text" since it has consistently managed to maintain a dual identity. While the strip is featured in several Asian American publications—such as the on-line magazine *Asian American Village* and print publications such as *Asian Week*—the majority of its readers are not Asian Americans, and the independent strip maintains a broad appeal in urban markets and college campuses. Toyoshima's work— the only syndicated comic strip to date to feature an Asian American protagonist—not only bridges the gap but directly speaks to it in sharp, often satirical weekly installments that began in the Boston-based magazine *Shovel* (succeeded by *The Weekly Dig*) and are currently carried by an evergrowing number of websites and alternative newspapers nationwide. The strips often address Asian American presence in popular culture—with media images in film and television a recurring preoccupation (see figures 17.1 and 17.2).

Tak Toyoshima, who is also the author of the comic book *The Couch*, had worked on the popular strip *The Tick* before creating SAM. As he told me, *Secret Asian Man* is his most personal strip and began as a reflection of his own frustration with Asian American absence from the medium:

It definitely started as a little more bitter, a little more on the angry side, more on the frustration side. . . . Having experience in the comics world in general, I knew I wanted a reaction, I didn't want something that people will just look at, say "oh, that's nice" and turn the page. I wanted it to stick . . . do something they probably haven't heard and will remember, at least.

He speculated that the reason his strip has found such a wide readership was that the audience he first envisioned was unfamiliar with an Asian American perspective:

At that time, I wanted to be in that back roads, Tennessee newspaper— where they don't get that stuff. I felt there it would have the most effect. . . .

I wanted to put something out there that some people maybe never even thought of. Maybe that's why the audience is so varied.

Toyoshima's strips run the gamut from personal history (a current series chronicles his own biography from childhood to his marriage) to controver-

Fig. 17.1. "Asians on TV," by Tak Toyoshima.

Fig. 17.2. Secret Asian Man, "Never Gets the Girl," by Tak Toyoshima.

Fig. 17.3. Secret Asian Man, "Where Are You (really) From?" by Tak Toyoshima.

sial commentary on national politics (a strip that ridiculed the dominance of Christian religious discourse in official and media responses to 9/11 caused a flurry of threats and advertiser pullouts). Other themes include Asian American history (Tak has published several strips that celebrate little-known Asian Americans or reference past victimization like the Japanese American internment) and current issues (one strip had Wen Ho Lee on an FBI-chaperoned family visit, trussed-up like Hannibal Lechter in *Silence of the Lambs*).

While some strips offer a multicultural perspective as normative (see Figure 17.3), others suggest the more problematic dimensions in the mainstreaming of multicultural identities (see Figures 17.4 and 17.5). These images often provoke readers "in unexpected ways," Toyoshima observed. "I get equal amounts of hate mail and fan mail; I've gotten hate mail from Asian American organizations—after using the word 'chink' in a strip, I was threatened with physical violence."[18]

As with my own interest in notions of racial grief and racial sensitivity, SAM is less concerned with the "real" of racial or ethnic identity (a common and thorny question in discussions of strategies of representation) than with its cultural perception and value. In thinking about SAM as a particular articulation of Asian American identity, the strip's focus emerges as insistently individuated. Unlike many arguments about Asian American representation, it does not strive to "correct" impressions by

Fig. 17.4. "Ethnic Claiming," by Tak Toyoshima.

Fig. 17.5. "Selling Asian Heritage," by Tak Toyoshima.

insisting on a variety and diversity of images within the Asian American community. Instead, it uses the character of SAM as a kind of comic archetype to highlight such perceptions and stage them as at once personal and iconic. In this sense it both "speaks to" and speaks in the parlance of pop culture (see figure 17.6). Yet, as many of the strips suggest, cultural visibility and mainstream perceptions have a real impact on the field of political action. For Toyoshima, the absence of the Asian American perspective in political discourse is a common theme (see figure 17.7), as is the frequently strained relationship between the Asian American and African American communities (see figure 17.8). Here, SAM often highlights the role of perceived sensitivity and the acknowledgement of grievance as important cultural markers. As the strip in figure 17.9 suggests, presence in the sphere of popular culture is a discreet political battleground with hierarchies of importance that carry their own representational politics.

Fig. 17.6. Secret Asian Man, "Who're You Calling Little?" by Tak Toyoshima.

Fig. 17.7. "Asians and the Affirmative Action Debate," by Tak Toyoshima.

Fig. 17.8. "Sure Shaq, We Can All Take a Joke," by Tak Toyoshima.

Fig. 17.9. "At the Movies," by Tak Toyoshima.

Why So Sensitive? The Oops Factor, the Wedge, and the Productive Politics of Public Grievance

In asking about the critical awareness Toyoshima raises for a potential viewer, I am not arguing that cultural texts participate in the formation of individual identities, nor even that they shape social attitudes toward particular groups. Rather, I am interested in the degree to which popular representations communicate a complex social hierarchy of "what counts." As this strip obliquely points out, mainstream representations of African Americans in media demonstrate a general (if superficial) awareness of the demands for racial inclusion. Obviously, such progressive moves do not speak to the elimination of racism as much as they communicate a social sensitivity to racism's presence.

It is this perception of sensitivity that I want to stress here, primarily since, as recent controversies indicate, popular representations (from media to T-shirts and Halloween costumes) repeatedly miscalculate the "sensitivities" of Asian Americans and the ability of images to give offense. The reason for such disregard cannot be limited to Asian Americans' lack of consumer visibility—in fact, as Abercrombie and Fitch repeatedly contended, their T-shirts were designed precisely for the young, hip, West Coast Asian American market. Further, it is precisely the dearth of cultural representation of Asian American racial anger that is itself part of the same cultural imaginary that allows A&F to envisage that its pastiche racist iconography will prompt not grief and grievance but pleasure and purchase—oops! Asian Americans' lack of an association with racial anger in the cultural imagination, then, facilitates their understanding as an economically viable consumer demographic at play in a field of cultural signification free of past grievance—in short, as honorary whites.

Writing about the "benign neglect" that has seen the common omission of Asian Americans from the popular imaginary, David Palumbo-Liu suggests that such "negatively articulated equivalence with whites" stems from the assumption that Asian Americans are not "minorities," since that designation is largely constructed as a category of economic disadvantage. "Therefore," he writes, "the sensitivities of the American political economy are excused from laboring to 'include' Asian Americans—we have already made it 'inside.'"[19]

A similar kind of "negatively articulated equivalence" appeared to operate for Justin Lin when he met with MTV executives. As Lin observed, the demographic pie chart that accounted for their ethnic-specific target audience segments had no "Asian wedge." As Lin was told by the executive who would promote his film, Asian Americans did not require their own wedge because in their consumer and taste habits, they resembled whites and so were assumed viewers, folded "within" the white wedge—oops.[20]

However, as one SAM strip suggests, angry responses to such moments of disregard and miscalculation can sway the scales of cultural weight (see figure 17.10). If asking questions of popular culture means gaining an insight into the workings of cultural politics, what is to be gained here? The answer lies in the connection between the workings of pop culture as a social frame of reference—undergirded as it is by economics of profit—to the question of minority representations and their presence in mainstream culture within the logic of capitalism. In fact, as spokesmen for the big business of mainstream culture like to pronounce, entertainment is democratic, with the dollar as its voting currency. One could, of course, launch into this debate and present myriad ways in which such an argument is both wrong-headed and self-serving, but we can also jump headlong into such a construction and ask: how, within the logic of this popular representational economy, can Asian America be a well-served constituency?

Producers and artists like Tak Toyoshima or Justin Lin (as only two examples) help reposition the problems of representation precisely by their refusal to engage with the problem of authenticity (who are Asian Americans?). Instead, they address Asian American presence within mainstream culture (where are Asian Americans?!). As Cheng helps us see it, mourning over past erasures is an important part of the work of culture, but such expressions of grievance must be taken up in public. In this sense, to talk about culture is always, necessarily, to talk about politics.

Thinking Asian, Feeling White: On Audience Address and the Challenge Ahead

In his study of audiences' emotional engagement with fictional characters on the screen, Murray Smith contends that what is generally referred to as "identification" actually consists of two separate processes and discreet cinematic affects, which he terms "levels of engagement":

> The first of these, what I will call *alignment,* concerns the way a film gives us access to the actions, thoughts, and feelings of characters. The second, *alle-*

Fig. 17.10. "A Public Service Message," by Tak Toyoshima.

giance, concerns the way a film attempts to marshal our sympathies for or against the various characters in the world of the fiction.[21]

We can think of Smith's model as differentiating between characters' subjectivity (the subjectivity-granting mechanisms that the film bestows on selected characters rather than others) and the apparatus that encourages us—through the narrative and cinematic codes—to find such subjectivities personally relevant to our "I" beyond the fictional world. Moreover, Smith's model may be applied to the very Hollywood logic that has delegated Asian Americans to the role of often-sympathetic peripherals. Recall my earlier examples of *Come See the Paradise* and *Snow Falling on Cedars* to see how general moral *alignment* with the long-suffering Asian Americans is maintained, while *allegiance* is strictly reserved for the white male through whom the audience experiences the narrative. To put it bluntly, we are urged to *understand* the Asian American (surely, one cannot fault the white filmmakers in either case for refusing to acknowledge historical wrongs) but to *feel* white. Let me propose an important parallel here: Abercrombie and Fitch's miscalculation appears to rest on the same Hollywood assumption of racial ventriloquism: that young, hip Asian Americans were aligned with the funny logic of such outmoded stereotypes while their allegiance lay deeply outside such grievance and its painful resuscitation, well ensconced in the mainstream—nestled in the (honorary) white wedge.

Fig. 17.11. "Sshhhh! It's *Starting,*" by Tak Toyoshima.

Returning to Justin Lin's bouts with self-representation, his reluctance to call his film Asian American is understandable. The trap for Asian American cultural production that aims for a mainstream audience is to successfully differentiate (narrative) *perspective* from (audience) *address.* This task is more challenging than it seems since fictional narratives in mainstream media have long functioned through two parallel tracks, with a blind adherence to an astonishingly narrow model of audience identification: a race-blind narrative (the "just so happens to be" conceit) and the race-specific narrative in which full comprehension of the hero's racial category figures prominently in the film's narrative address and its ability to produce audience investment and identification. In such a narrow formulation, it is no wonder that Lin and others prefer the former.

But the power and appeal of *Better Luck Tomorrow* and *Secret Asian Man* to mainstream audiences is neither in the transcendence of their particularities (the secret handshake of racial experience) nor the humanist "universal" of "race blind" (or "practically white") narratives. Instead, their cultural work is in reconfiguring Asian American experience into the common vocabulary of mainstream entertainment fiction and its history.

The mainstream expressions of racial grievance, of anger, of a refusal to "suck it up" are at once metaphoric and actual interceptions. In their textual presence and performance they can short-circuit old "oops" formulas by insisting on the specificity of experience. Through the reverberating and amplifying capabilities of popular culture, a little anger goes a long way.

NOTES

1. On billboards, magazine ads, and trailers, the film is marketed as a teen coming-of-age story with no reference to its Asian American cast. This, in itself, is a first.

2. Similar displeasure was often expressed toward comedienne Margaret Cho whose material turns equally on raunchy sexual humor, fun with Asian American stereotypes, and tales of culture clashes with her Korean immigrant parents.

3. While the loud outcry over the T-shirts brought increased attention to Abercrombie and Fitch, it also persuaded them to pull the offending T-shirts from their shelves.

4. Anne AnLin Cheng, *The Melancholy of Race,* New York: Oxford University Press, 2000.

5. Among the most influential are Robert Lee's *Orientals,* Eugene Franklin Wong's *On Visual Media Racism,* Darrell Y. Hamamoto's *Monitored Peril,* Gina Marchetti's *Romance and the "Yellow Peril,"* and Richard Fung's *Looking for My Penis).*

6. Among these are Lisa Lowe's *Immigrant Acts: On Asian American Cultural Politics,* Durham: Duke University Press, 1997, David Palumbo-Liu's *Asian/American: Historical Crossings of a Racial Frontier,* Stanford: Stanford University Press, 1999, and Gary Okihiro's *Margins and Mainstreams: Asians in American History and Culture,* Seattle: University of Washington Press, 1994.

7. Such representations are common in action films like the *Lethal Weapon* series or in the biting web-comic-turned-film *Undercover Brother.*

8. Note here that *Come See the Paradise* is a loose adaptation that was much contested by its authors.

9. Laura Hyun-Yi Kang offers an extensive narrative analysis of *Year of the Dragon, Come See the Paradise,* and the PBS production of *Thousand Pieces of Gold* as such problematic texts in "The Desiring of Asian Female Bodies: Interracial Romance and Cinematic Subjection," in *Screening Asian Americans,* ed. Peter X. Feng, New Brunswick: Rutgers University Press, 2002.

10. The international smash hit *Crouching Tiger, Hidden Dragon* illustrates the difficulties of such definitions as the multinational production was referred to in various mainstream publications as a Hollywood film, a transnational production, and a foreign or Honk Kong film (and by extension director Ang Lee was described in the American press as American, Asian American, and Taiwanese).

11. I am indebted to David Eng for his suggestion that the angry white man phenomenon can be understood not only as backlash in popular politics but also as embodied in the politics of George Bush (both father and son).

12. Susan Jeffords, *Hard Bodies: Hollywood Masculinity and the Reagan Era,* New Brunswick: Rutgers University Press, 1994.

13. Nowhere is this parallel more visible than in the popular action film—a genre so thoroughly invested in the law and the successful containment of disorder.

14. My examples in this essay focus on the Asian American male not to privilege him or to argue for his particular abjection in the media landscape, but as examples of emotional outbursts prominent in narratives that articulate racialized anger. As many scholars working in the fields of feminist, queer, race, and ethnic studies have already shown, each set of representations is caught up in a network of intersecting issues and significations that are shared in some instances and divergent in others.

I am interested in emotional performance particularly because it is so narrowly inscribed within the palette of mainstream American media fictions (inscriptions that are, for the most part, gendered and sexed, but also class- and race-based). As such, formula narratives rely on emotional content and performance (emotionally motivated physical violence) for their power and effect. Further, masculinity as a representational presence is most often analyzed in the structure of dichotomies (gendered, sexualized, or racialized—class rarely figures in U.S. scholarly analysis) in which the white, straight male is read as an ideological straining that labors to put the woman, the queer, and the racial or ethnic other in their place. My interests here diverge somewhat as I am not interested in reading the Asian American *in relation* to a white or black counterpart, but in examining anger as a particularly complex representational note that has real utility in "real-life" politics.

15. Meaghan Morris offers an extensive shot-by-shot analysis of the shift in perspective in this scene in her essay, "Learning from Bruce Lee: Pedagogy and Political Correctness in Martial Arts Cinema," in *Keyframes: Popular Cinema and Cultural Studies,* eds. Matthew Tinkcom and Amy Villarejo, London: Routledge, 2001.

16. I am indebted to Shilpa Davé for pointing out this connection and its coverage.

17. Slavoj Zizek, *The Sublime Object of Ideology,* New York: Verso, 1989. See a discussion in *Racial Castration: Managing Masculinity in Asian America,* Durham: Duke University Press, 2001.

18. Readers' letters often become a source of ongoing discussions, where readers debate, dismiss, or praise other published responses, granting the strips a discursive life of their own. As it brings various readers into dialogue, Toyoshima's work provides a public and dynamic illustration of how multiple points of view

and varied cultural experiences often serve as lenses through which readers consume and make meaning of popular culture.

19. David Palumbo-Liu, *Asian/American: Historical Crossings of Racial Frontiers*, Stanford: Stanford University Press, 1999, 4.

20. This anecdote was reported to me by Tak Toyoshima after a conversation with Lin. It has since been publicized on several Asian American websites about the film.

21. Murray Smith, *Engaging Characters: Fiction, Emotion and the Cinema*, New York: Oxford University Press, 1995.

About the Contributors

Victor Bascara is Assistant Professor of English and Asian American Studies at the University of Wisconsin–Madison. He is currently working on a book entitled *Unburdening Empire: Asian American Cultural Politics and the Emergence of United States Imperialism.*

Hye Seung Chung is Postdoctoral Fellow in the Department of Asian Languages and Cultures at the University of Michigan. Her dissertation investigates the politics of cross-ethnic performance and masquerade circulating around the film and television images of Korean American actor Philip Ahn.

Shilpa Davé is Assistant Professor of American Studies at Brandeis University. She is currently working on a book entitled *Privileged Minorities: South Asian Ethnic Citizenship and American Popular Culture,* which explores political and cultural citizenship in contemporary South Asian American literature and popular culture.

Jigna Desai is Assistant Professor in the Department of Women's Studies at the University of Minnesota. She is the author of *Beyond Bollywood: The Cultural Politics of South Asian Diasporic Film.*

Vicente M. Diaz is Assistant Professor of Asia Pacific American Studies in the American Culture Program at the University of Michigan–Ann Arbor. His research includes work on Pacific history and Micronesian studies.

Rebecca Chiyoko King-O'Riain is a lecturer in the Department of Sociology at the National University of Ireland, Maynooth. She is completing a manuscript on the changing demographics of the Japanese American community in California and Hawaii through a case study of community beauty pageants.

Robert G. Lee is Associate Professor of American Civilizations at Brown University. He is the author of *Orientals: Asian Americans in Popular Culture,* a study of nineteenth- and twentieth-century popular representations of Asians in the United States.

Sunaina Maira is Associate Professor of Asian American Studies at the University of California–Davis. She is the author of *Desis in the House: Indian American Youth Culture in New York* and coeditor of *Contours of the Heart: South Asians Map North America* and of the forthcoming collection *Youthscapes: Popular Culture, National Ideologies, Global Markets.*

Anita Mannur is a Freeman Foundation Postdoctoral Fellow in Asian and Asian American Studies at Wesleyan University. She is the coeditor with Jana Evans Braziel of *Theorizing Diaspora: A Reader.*

Lisa Nakamura is Assistant Professor of English at the University of Wisconsin–Madison, where she teaches in the Communication Arts Department. She is the author of *Cybertypes: Race, Ethnicity, and Identity on the Internet* and the coeditor of *Race in Cyberspace.*

LeiLani Nishime is Associate Professor of American Multicultural Studies at Sonoma State University. She is currently working on a book examining the representations of interracial and Asian American relations in mainstream Hollywood film.

Amy Abugo Ongiri is Assistant Professor of English at the University of Florida. Her current work, entitled *Spectacular Blackness: The Cultural Articulations of the Black Power Movement and the Search to Define a Black Aesthetic,* addresses the cultural and political articulations of the Black Power movement.

Tasha G. Oren is Assistant Professor of Film and Media Studies at the University of Wisconsin–Milwaukee. She is the author of *Demon in the Box:*

Jews, Arabs, Politics and Culture in the Making of Israeli Television and coeditor of *Global Currents: Media and Technology Now.*

Jane C. H. Park is Assistant Professor in the Honors College and Film and Video Studies at the University of Oklahoma. Her areas of interest include film and media studies, ethnic studies, Asian American studies, and gender studies. She is currently writing a book on "oriental" imagery in U.S. science fiction films.

Hiram Perez is Assistant Professor in the Department of English at Montclair State University. He is working on a book in which he argues that race is a secret. As he completes this project, he continues to struggle to write about the relationship between shame and racial embodiment while plotting a course through his own shamefulness. Together with Dr. Caroline Streeter (UCLA) he is editing a collection of essays on celebrity and minority cultures.

Christine So is Assistant Professor in the Department of English at Georgetown University. She is currently completing a book on the consumption of Asian American culture in the era of global capitalism.

Kieu Link Caroline Valerde is Assistant Professor of Asian Studies at the University of California at Davis. She is currently researching the Vietnamese diaspora and gender theory as a Southeast Asian Studies Fellow at the Australian National University and is completing a manuscript on Vietnamese American community–Vietnam transnational linkages.

Morris Young is Associate Professor of English and Director of Graduate Studies at Miami University in Oxford, Ohio. He is the author of *Minor Re/Visions: Asian American Literacy Narratives as a Rhetoric of Citizenship.*

Index

Asian American literary studies, 184
Asian American literature, and hysteria, 345
Asian American popular culture: and fashion, 20; and film, 3. *See also* popular culture
Asian American representation: and Cibo Matto, 308–309; and film, 337–338; and popular culture, 350–351
Asian American studies, 1–2, 264; definition of, 3–4; and English language, 328; and queer studies, 275
Asian American subjectivity, and film, 344
Asian American Village (online), 347
Asian American women: and United States representation, 293. *See also* Asian women
Asian Americans, 150; and activism, 338–340; and American whites, 353–354; and assimilation, 158; and citizenship, 129; and cultural politics, 120; features of, 277; in film, 163; and fusion cuisine, 73–75; and gay community, 275; in higher education, 214; and history, 123; and Hollywood, 154–155, 355; and identity, 173; and labor, 133n26; and masculinity, 174; and media representation, 338–340; and political economy, 119; and queer identity, 118; and racial anger, 341–342, 346–353, 353–354; Keanu Reeves, 283–284; and repression, 346; and South Asian Americans, 328; and South Asians, 327; and spectatorship, 170; and white Americans, 355
Asian culture: and martial arts, 249; image of, in America, xii–xiii
Asian English, 317
Asian iconography: and consumerism, 20–21; and trance music, 27; and trance parties, 26
Asian immigrants: and America, xii, xiv, 235; and Hollywood, 283, 342
Asian popular culture: and black American culture, 251; and language, 250
Asian Week, 347
Asian women: in U.S., 308; and U.S. military, 240. *See also* Asian American women; women
Asians: and Guam, 101; and slavery, 157
AsiaZine (website), and racial anger, 346
assimilation, 157, 174, 208; and accent, 78; and Asian Americans, 77, 85, 158; and cultural preservation, 216; and ethnicity, 86; and fusion, 84; and identity, 298, 315–316; and imperialism, 328; and Japanese American pageants, 218; and Japanese Americans, 206–207, 214–215; and labor, 129; and language, 166; and Ming Tsai, 82; and multiculturalism, 89; and Nisei Week, 217; and race, 86; and Superman, 280; and *The Simpsons,* 313; and U.S. immigration, 330
Aunt Jemima, 106
Australia: and Bollywood films, 55; and Chinese memoirs, 140; and Chinese women's memoirs, 137; and Vietnamese refugees, 51n. 2
Australian English, 317
authenticity, 13; and Asian American representation, 354; and Asian racial construction, 8; and *The Byrds of Paradise,* 189; and Chinese history, 147; and Chinese women's narrative memoir, 141; and culture, 218; and electronica, 301–302; and fusion cuisine, 87–88; and gender, 68; and globalization,

5; and Hawaii, 198; and hip hop, 301–302; and Japanese Americans, 214; and multiracialism, 216, 217; and Orientalism, 20–21; and patriarchy, 112n. 9; and race, 218; and rock music, 300; and South Asian Americans, 62; and subculture, 16; and tourism, 194; and voice, 326; and women, 138; and youth subculture, 17
authoritarianism, and consumerism, 41
Autobiography of an Ex-Colored Man (Johnson), 241n. 6
Axis powers, 165
Azaria, Hank: and accent, 326–327; and Apu, 322; and *The Simpsons,* 324

Back to Bataan (film), 163, 165. *See also* Ahn, Philip
Bakshi, Ralph, and *Coonskin,* 249
Bali, Indonesia, and *Ming's Quest* (TV), 78
Barbera, Joseph, 260
BBC (national radio of Britain), and accent, 319
Basille, Nancy, on Apu, 323
Beastie Boys, 293, 298
Beatles, the, 34, 295, 299, 303
Beavis and Butthead (TV), 321; and popular culture, 118
Beck, 296
Behind the Rising Sun (film), 163. *See also* Ahn, Philip
Bend It Like Beckham (film) 58, 59; and South Asian accent, 330. *See also* Chadha, Gurinder
Benton, James Grant: and Hawaiian Creole English, 200–201n. 14; and *Twelf Nite o Wateva,* 193
Berry, Halle, 225
Betrayal from the East (film), 165. *See also* Ahn, Philip
Better Luck Tomorrow (film), and Asian American representation, 337–338; identity politics in, 337–338; and popular culture, 356
B-Flat, 48–49, 50–51
Bgoc, Tuan, 33
Bhabha, Homi, and mimicry, 326, 328
Big Aiiieeeee!, The (Chin et al, eds.), 2, 339. *See also* Chin, Frank
Big Bad Chinese Mama (website), 346
Bikini Kill, 294
Bitter Tea of General Yen, The (film), 154
Bjork, 296, 302
black American culture: and Asian popular culture, 251; and kung fu films, 255; and martial arts film, 252; and nationalism, 257. *See also* culture
black Americans: and assimilation, 86; and citizenship, 236; and features of, 277; and media, 353; and nationalism, 226; and spectacle of body and violence, 257; and spectatorship, 252; and television, 260n. 1
Black Belt Jones (film), 250
black cultural nationalism, in *Black Creation,* 257; in *Black World,* 257; in *Jet* and *Ebony,* 257
black identity, 230, 253, 254–255; and commodification, 232; and consumption, 232; and democracy, 241n. 3. *See also* identity
black nationalism, 232

183–184, 187; and Indian film, 69; and music, 40; and popular culture, 341; and South Asian American culture, 63; and Western culture, 143

coolies. *See* labor

Coonskin (film), 249

Coppola, Francis Ford, 259n. 1

Cornyetz, Nina, on "Hip Hop and Racial Desire in Contemportaty Japan," 298–299

Corruptor, The (film), and racial grievance, 343

cosmopolitanism, 18, 79, 143, 256; and Cibo Matto, 302; and cuisine, 76; in India, 61; and national identity, 27–28; and nationalism, 23–24; and Orientalism, 20–21; and Padma Lakshimi, 82. *See also* citizenship

Couch, The (film), 347. *See also* Toyoshima, Tak

Crabbe, Larry "Buster," in *Red Barry,* 163

Crenshaw, Kimberlé, and critical race scholarship, 235

creolization, and politics, 105

critical race theory, 223; and queer theory, 119–120

Crosby, Bing, in *Anything Goes,* 163

Crothers, Scatman, 249

Crouching Tiger, Hidden Dragon, 57; international status of, 357n. 10

Cruise, Tom, 322

Cuanon, Andrew, and race and sexuality, 274–275

Cuba: and father image, 110; and Spanish American War, 107

cultural citizenship: and accent, 316; and South Asian accent, 317; and South Asians in United States, 315, 319, 327

cultural criticism, 223

cultural globalization, 13; and travel, 14–15. *See also* globalization

cultural history, and economy, 4. *See also* history

cultural identity: and Cibo Matto, 307–308; cultural isolation, 1; and language, 294; South Asian, 330

cultural production, 205, 219; Asian American, 2, 3, 356; and *The Byrds of Paradise,* 190; and communism, 48; and Doi Moi, 40–41; and film, 62; and global markets, 27; and globalization, 5; and Hawaii, 184, 197–198; and hybridity, 33; and identity, 38–39; and language, 185; and multiculturalism, 346; and Orientalism, 22; and popular culture, 6; and Vietnamese American music, 37–38; and women, 204. *See also* racial production

Cultural Revolution, 137, 142, 144

culture: and American citizenship, 320; and American identity, 207, 320; American mainstream, 1, 192, 208-209, 315; and Apu, 323; and authenticity, 218; and beauty, 210; British, 315; and Chamorros, 105; Chinese, 121–122; and citizenship, 152; and clothing, 150; and consumerism, 321; and cuisine, 76; East and West, 76–78; global, 144; Japanese, 307; and language, 185; and legitimacy, 195; and literature, 193; and martial arts film, 259; and memory, 338; and nation, 131; preservation of, 216; and race, 240–241; and spectatorship, 173;

and stereotypes, 323, 324; and West, 189–190. *See also* Asian American popular culture; local culture; subculture; Vietnamese culture; youth culture

Dan the Automator, 300

dance, and youth culture, 17–18

Dangerous to Know (film), 162. *See also* Wong, Anna May

Daughter of Shanghai (film), 154, 155–159, 166, 169, 175; and Anna May Wong, 162; and gaze of recognition, 173; and publicity, 166; review of, in *M. G. Herald,* 168

Daughter of the Dragon (film), 160. *See also* Wong, Anna May

DDLJ (film), 59

De Maria, Walter, 304

Dead Prez, 298

DeAngelis, Michael, 283; and *Gay Fandom and Crossover Stardom,* 274

Deejay Kalyx, and electronic music, 16

Degeneres, Ellen, 119

Demilitarized Zone, 172

Democracy: American, 235; and black identity, 241n. 3; and China, 145; and India, 324; and minority representation, 228; and multiculturalism, 226; and race, 231. *See also* American democracy, and race

Desmond, Jane, and the Spanish American War, 110

Diamond, Heidi, 77

diaspora, 5, 60; Asian, 88; Chinese, 140, 144, 147; and Chinese women, 137; and culture, 56; and hybridity, 63; and nation, 36–27; South Asian, 62; Vietnamese, 34, 36; and Vietnamese music, 42–43, 46–47. *See also* South Asian diaspora; immigration

Diawara, Manthia, and black spectatorship studies, 172

Dietrich, Marlene, in *Blonde Venus,* 170

Dilwale Dulhaniya Le Jayenge (film), and nonresident Indians, 60

Dirty Laundry: A History of Heroes (Fung), 121

disenfranchisement: and music, 299; and race, 223

DJ Shortee, 302

DMX, 298

Does Accent Matter? The Pygmalion Factor (Honey), 317

Doherty, Thomas, on Philip Ahn and ethnicity, 165

Doi Moi, and cultural production, 40–41

Dolemite (film), 258

Dolemite II: The Human Tornado (film), 129, 258

domesticity, 128, 129; and Asian labor in the U.S., 120–121; and class, 132n. 4; and gay identity, 131; and gender, 106; and race, 106; conventional and queer, 126–127. *See also* queer domesticity

Dominguez, Virginia, and Spanish American War, 110

Doomed to Die (film), 161

Dornenburg, Andrew, 75

Doty, Alexander: and *Making Things Perfectly Queer,* 278; and queer theory, 286